Everyman, I will go with thee,
and be thy guide

William Shakespeare

OTHELLO

Edited by
JOHN F. ANDREWS

Foreword by
JAMES EARL JONES

EVERYMAN
J. M. DENT · LONDON
CHARLES E. TUTTLE
VERMONT

J. M. Dent
Orion Publishing Group
Orion House
5 Upper St Martin's Lane
London WC2H 9EA
and
Charles E. Tuttle Co.
28 South Main Street, Rutland
Vermont 05701, USA

Photoset by Deltatype Ltd, Ellesmere Port, Cheshire
Printed in Great Britain by
The Guernsey Press Co. Ltd, Guernsey, C.I.

British Library Cataloguing-in-Publication-Data is available
upon request

ISBN 0 460 87517 5

CONTENTS

NOTE ON THE AUTHOR AND EDITOR

WILLIAM SHAKESPEARE is held to have been born on St George's day, 23 April 1564. The eldest son of a prosperous glove-maker in Stratford-upon-Avon, he was probably educated at the town's grammar school.

Tradition holds that between 1585 and 1592, Shakespeare first became a schoolteacher and then set off for London. By 1594 he was a leading member of the Lord Chamberlain's Men, helping to direct their business affairs, as well as being a playwright and actor. In 1598 he became a part-owner of the company, which was the most distinguished of its age. However, he maintained his contacts with Stratford, and his family appears to have remained there.

From about 1610 he seems to have grown increasingly involved in the town's affairs, suggesting a withdrawal from London. He died on 23 April 1616, in his 53rd year, and was buried at Holy Trinity two days later.

JOHN F. ANDREWS has recently completed a 19-volume edition, *The Guild Shakespeare*, for the Doubleday Book and Music Clubs. He is also the editor of a 3-volume reference set, *William Shakespeare: His World, His Work, His Influence*, and the former editor (1974–85) of the journal *Shakespeare Quarterly*. From 1974 to 1984, he was director of Academic Programs at the Folger Shakespeare Library in Washington and Chairman of the Folger Institute.

CHRONOLOGY OF SHAKESPEARE'S LIFE

Year*	Age	Life
1564		Shakespeare baptized 26 April at Stratford-upon-Avon
1582	18	Marries Anne Hathaway
1583	19	Daughter, Susanna, born
1585	21	Twin son and daughter, Hamnet and Judith, born
1590–1	26	*The Two Gentlemen of Verona* & *The Taming of the Shrew*
1591	27	*2 & 3 Henry VI*
1592	28	*Titus Andronicus* & *1 Henry VI*
1592–3		*Richard III*
1593	29	*Venus and Adonis* published
1594	30	*The Comedy of Errors. The Rape of Lucrece* published
1594–5		*Love's Labour's Lost*
1595	31	*A Midsummer Night's Dream, Romeo and Juliet,* & *Richard II.* An established member of Lord Chamberlain's Men
1596	32	*King John.* Hamnet dies
1596–7		*The Merchant of Venice* & *1 Henry IV*

* It is rarely possible to be certain about the dates at which plays of this period were written. For Shakespeare's plays, this chronology follows the dates preferred by Stanley Wells and Gary Taylor, the editors of The Oxford Shakespeare. Publication dates are given for poetry and books.

CHRONOLOGY OF HIS TIMES

Year	Literary Context	Historical Events
1565–7	Golding, Ovid's *Metamorphoses*, tr.	Elizabeth I reigning
1574	*A Mirror for Magistrates* (3rd ed.)	
1576	London's first playhouse built	
1578	John Lyly, *Euphues*	
1579	North, Plutarch's *Lives*, tr.	
	Spenser, *Shepherd's Calender*	
1587	Marlowe, *I Tamburlaine*	Mary Queen of Scots executed
1588	Holinshed's *Chronicles* (2nd ed.)	Defeat of Spanish Armada
1589	Kyd, *Spanish Tragedy*	Civil war in France
	Marlowe, *Jew of Malta*	
1590	Spenser, *Faerie Queene*, Bks I–III	
1591	Sidney, *Astrophel and Stella*	Proclamation against Jesuits
1592	Marlowe, *Dr Faustus* & *Edward II*	Scottish witchcraft trials
		Plague closes theatres from June
1593	Marlowe killed	
1594	Nashe, *Unfortunate Traveller*	Theatres reopen in summer
1594–6		Extreme food shortages
1595	Sidney, *An Apologie for Poetry*	Riots in London
1596		Calais captured by Spanish
		Cadiz expedition

Year	Age	Life
1597	33	Buys New Place in Stratford
		The Lord Chamberlain's Men's lease to play at the Theatre expires; until 1599 they play mainly at the Curtain
1597–8		*The Merry Wives of Windsor* & *2 Henry IV*
1598	34	*Much Ado About Nothing*
1598–9		*Henry V*
1599	35	*Julius Caesar*. One of syndicate responsible for building the Globe in Southwark, where the Lord Chamberlain's Men now play
1599–1600		*As You Like It*
1600–1		*Hamlet*
1601	37	*Twelfth Night*. His father is buried in Stratford
1602	38	*Troilus and Cressida*. Invests £320 in land near Stratford*
1603	39	*Measure for Measure*. The Lord Chamberlain's Men become the King's Men. They play at court more than all the other companies combined
1603–4		*Othello*
c.1604	40	Shakespeare sues Philip Rogers of Stratford for debt
1604–5		*All's Well That Ends Well*
1605	41	*Timon of Athens*. Invests £440 in Stratford tithes
1605–6		*King Lear*
1606	42	*Macbeth* & *Antony and Cleopatra*
1607	43	*Pericles*. Susanna marries the physician John Hall in Stratford
1608	44	*Coriolanus*. The King's Men lease Blackfriars, an indoor theatre. His only grandchild is born. His mother dies
1609	45	*The Winter's Tale*. 'Sonnets' and 'A Lover's Complaint' published
1610	46	*Cymbeline*
1611	47	*The Tempest*
1613	49	*Henry VIII*. Buys house in London for £140
1613–14		*The Two Noble Kinsmen*
1616	52	Judith marries Thomas Quiney, a vintner, in Stratford. On 23 April Shakespeare dies; is buried two days later
1623		Publication of the First Folio. His widow dies in August

* A schoolmaster would earn around £20 a year at this time.

Year	Literary Context	Historical Events
1597	Bacon, *Essays*	
1598	Marlowe and Chapman, *Hero and Leander* Jonson, *Every Man in his Humour*	Rebellion in Ireland
1599	Children's companies begin playing Thomas Dekker's *Shoemaker's Holiday*	Essex fails in Ireland
1601	'War of the Theatres' Jonson, *Poetaster*	Essex rebels and is executed
1602		Tyrone defeated in Ireland
1603	Florio, Montaigne's *Essays*, tr.	Elizabeth I dies, James I accedes Raleigh found guilty of treason
1604	Marston, *The Malcontent*	Peace with Spain
1605	Bacon, *Advancement of Learning*	Gunpowder plot
1606	Jonson, *Volpone*	
1607	Tourneur, *The Revenger's Tragedy*, published	Virginia colonized Enclosure riots
1609		Oath of allegiance Truce in Netherlands
1610	Jonson, *Alchemist*	
1611	Authorised Version of the Bible Donne, *Anatomy of the World*	
1612	Webster, *White Devil*	Prince Henry dies
1613	Webster, *Duchess of Malfi*	Princess Elizabeth marries
1614	Jonson, *Bartholomew Fair*	
1616	Folio edition of Jonson's plays	

Biographical note, chronology and plot summary compiled by John Lee, University of Newcastle, 1995.

FOREWORD TO *Othello*

Othello is usually thought of as a play about jealousy. But it's not that simple. Unlike Leontes in *The Winter's Tale*, Othello never reaches the point where you could describe him as obsessed with jealousy. Confused, yes; jealous, no. He has one conception of Desdemona: his portrait of the wonderful, lovely lady he married. Then Iago holds up to him the picture of another creature: a deceiving wanton. There's no way that Othello can put these two images together in a single woman. So he goes mad. His confusion drives him insane.

This doesn't mean that Othello is a simpleton, a buffoon. He's sometimes played that way, but it's a terrible mistake to do so. What we must always remember is that *Othello* is the tragedy of a great man. He's of royal descent, and he is a noble exemplar of the culture that built the magnificent Alhambra in Granada.

The Moors were a proud, highly educated people, with a tradition of learning and intellectual achievement that placed them ahead of many European societies. They were anything but savages or barbarians, and their strength is conveyed through the commanding presence of the General we meet in the opening acts of the play.

Much of the grandeur we observe in Othello is a reflection of the marvels he has witnessed and the extraordinary adventures he has endured. His travels have carried him to every corner of the known world. A comparable hero today would have tales to tell about his expeditions to the Moon, to Mars and Venus. With his trusted ensign Iago, Othello has visited the most exotic settings imaginable. He has gained rich insights and benefited from special revelations; he has an understanding of cosmic forces. In the process he has acquired unbounded confidence in his own abilities. And he has learned to put complete trust in the brother-in-arms who has shared so many of his experiences.

But now he's attempting to break into the most exclusive circle of the super-subtle Venetians. He rightly feels that he deserves the best, and without a moment's hesitation he simply draws on his personal charisma to woo and win the love of the most desirable woman in this most sophisticated of European capitals. It's a bold move, but he carries it off with the same aplomb he's always brought to his martial exploits.

Along the way, unfortunately, without realizing it, he has grievously offended the man on whom he has come to depend for assistance and counsel.

So long as he remains in the field as a soldier, Othello's role in Venetian affairs is clearly and securely defined. But once he alters that role by eloping with the daughter of a prominent Senator, the Moor subjects himself to a new set of challenges. For all his majesty as a warrior, Othello is regarded as an outsider by at least some members of the society he seeks to join through marriage to Desdemona. He is thus in no position to ignore the observations and advice of a guide he accepts as an insider.

Iago knows his Venice very acutely. He's a man of keen intelligence and proven ability, but he doesn't have the status or the family connections of a Cassio. As a result, he gets passed over for the promotion that would give him the recognition he believes himself to merit.

That turns him into a bitter cynic. He's not a petty man, and his is not a petty tragedy. But as he broods upon the way he's been mistreated, he plots the kind of retaliation that only a mind made petty by disillusionment would undertake.

The key to Iago's success as an avenger is the degree to which he manages to combine the personalities of two different people. To those he manipulates upon the stage, he must come across at all times as a truly good man. Meanwhile to the audience he must be evil personified.

An actor portraying Iago must be careful not to overplay the calculation that goes into his character. Iago is always thinking, always plotting. But he doesn't have everything planned out from the beginning. At first he has only a vague notion of how he'll achieve his purposes. He gets more inventive as he discovers, often to his own surprise, how trusting and believing everyone else is.

What the actor playing Iago must bear in mind is that the ensign's actions are motivated by real pain. He's not being a villain just for the fun of it. He's a man who has been deeply wounded – so much so that he's become a borderline schizophrenic – and he's striking back in a rage that allows him to seem quite calm even as he stokes the white-hot flames that seethe within his breast.

Iago's wife Aemilia is sometimes blamed for her role in the tragedy. But even she is for a long time taken in by her husband. And once she finds herself in a compromising situation, she initially acts in accordance with the teaching that a wife has no right to disobey her husband. Like Iago, she is trapped in a social role, and it is only at the end of the play that she rebels and speaks out against the mate she'd vowed to cherish as her lord and master.

Desdemona doesn't always hold her own in a production of *Othello*. She can be played as a weak innocent. It's very important, however, for her purity to be communicated as a kind of strength, because in many ways Desdemona (whose name means 'disdemon', or the negation of the demonic) is the real centre of the drama. What she represents are what modern audiences tend to think of as archaic moral values, but she and the virtue she stands for are what the men in the play are fighting over. Desdemona and her spiritual qualities are what *Othello* is all about. If her presence is not as intensely felt as that of Othello and Iago, then, a performance of Shakespeare's tragedy is severely diminished.

The most successful renderings of *Othello* in my experience have been directed by women. They've had powerfully realized Desdemonas. And I think they've also drawn out more of the emotional range and depth – including the agony – of the play's male characters.

I've been asked if I'd like to direct the play. Probably not. But I hope to keep doing the role of Othello until I'm satisfied that I've gotten it right.

JAMES EARL JONES

JAMES EARL JONES and the New York Shakespeare Festival were launched simultaneously and in alliance nearly four decades ago. For Joseph Papp and the Festival, Jones played his first of seven 'Othellos' in 1964, one year after he made his film debut in Stanley Kubrick's *Dr Strangelove*. Jones was nominated for a best actor Oscar for *The Great White Hope,* for which he'd won a Tony on stage. He will be long remembered for his film part as the voice of Darth Vader in the *Star Wars* trilogy, and for his roles in *Field of Dreams* and *The Hunt for Red October.*

Othello is usually defined as a domestic tragedy. In its exposure of the fragility of those ties that bind a man and woman in marriage, it can be as heart-rending as *Romeo and Juliet*. In its exploration of the agonies of doubt, it can be as gripping and every bit as terrifying as *Macbeth*. In its interrogation of the inadequacies of earthly justice, meanwhile, it can be as disturbing, and in its own terms as theologically and philosophically unsettling, as *King Lear*.

Because *Othello* anatomizes the follies occasioned by jealousy, there is something to be gained from setting it beside a comedy like *The Merry Wives of Windsor* or a romance such as *The Winter's Tale*. In many respects, however, it seems closer to *Hamlet*. Like the Prince of Denmark, its protagonist begins as a man of 'Free and Open Nature' (I.iii.406). He endeavours to act nobly. He places a premium on the maintenance of his 'Good Name' (III.iii.152). And even more than the melancholy Dane, he proves susceptible to those who know how to play upon the zeal with which he safeguards his treasured honour. As a consequence, the action of this tormented drama has many affinities with history's most celebrated revenge tragedy.

To the degree that Iago, the malefactor who undermines Othello, is impelled by something more specific than what Samuel Taylor Coleridge labelled 'motiveless malignity', what drives him is a determination to prove the General 'an Ass' (II.i.324) for selecting the more refined but supposedly less experienced Michael Cassio as his Lieutenant. Iago's contempt is directed primarily at the commander who has passed over the more senior candidate for an important position. But it also extends to the rival who has won the post that Iago himself coveted. And not only does Iago resent what he regards as an undeserved promotion for Cassio; he also harbours suspicions that Othello and his new deputy have both 'leap'd into' his 'Seat' and enjoyed the intimacies of his wife Aemilia. In response to these presumed insults, Iago vows to be 'even'd' with the two of them (II.i. 310–14).

The 'Poison' (III.iii.315) Iago uses to advance his purpose is administered in successive doses. First he takes advantage of Cassio's weakness for alcohol to cast him out of favour with his superior. Then he persuades the cashiered Lieutenant to solicit the Moor's own 'General' (II.iii.325) in the expectation that Desdemona will plead with her new husband for Cassio's reinstatement. Through these and other schemes Iago places himself in a position to do what he can to turn Desdemona's 'Virtue into Pitch, / And out of her own Goodness make the Net / That shall en-mash them all' (II.iii.372–74).

Iago now proceeds to a series of 'Proofs' (III.iii.314) that will lend plausibility to his insinuation that the Moor should 'look to' his wife. Reminding Othello that he remains an alien in the 'super-subtle' Venetian society he has sought to enter surreptitiously (I.iii.361), Iago gradually unravels the self-confidence of the 'all in all sufficient' Moor (IV.i.269) until he is able to twist a man 'of Royal Siege' (I.ii.22) into a recidivist barbarian who thinks himself the laughing-stock of a vaunting 'Roman' (IV.i.120). It is humiliating enough for the mighty warrior to believe that his own assistant has cuckolded him; what makes his plight even more unbearable is Iago's assertion that Cassio now scorns the 'foolish Woman' he has seduced as if she were no more to be prized than a common whore (IV.i.179–81).

Once Othello becomes persuaded that Desdemona is indeed guilty of infidelity, his untutored reaction is to exclaim, 'But yet the Pity of it, Iago: oh Iago, the Pity of it, Iago.' Recognizing the danger that his prey might be moved to mercy rather than malice, Iago alertly steps in to divert the Moor's sympathy with a remark that is guaranteed to rekindle wrath. 'If you are so fond over her Iniquity,' he says, 'give her Patent to offend, for if it touch not you, it comes near no body' (IV.i.201–5). Here as elsewhere, Iago's method is to make Othello focus not on Desdemona but on his own sense of injured merit. By stressing that the Moor's 'Honour' is part and parcel of Desdemona's, Iago eventually spurs him to a 'rash and most unfortunate' act that proves his undoing (V.ii.276).

It is a sign of Othello's worthiness that to the end he retains the magnanimity that initially made him vulnerable to Iago's cunning. For all his machinations, Iago is never able to reduce the Moor entirely to a blunt instrument of his tormentor's vengeance. Before Othello can bring himself to execute Desdemona he must first delude himself into believing that he is a minister of divine justice. And even in that role his innate generosity constrains him to offer his wife a moment to prepare her soul for Heaven. When Desdemona refuses to confess to a crime that would have been inconceivable to her, her husband becomes furious again. But one of the things that makes what he does pathetic rather than culpably malicious is the fact that he continues to express devotion to his bride even as he forces himself to snuff out her life. In that as well as in a more cynical sense that accords with Iago's strategy, Othello becomes 'an honourable Murderer' (V.ii.288). No matter how we judge the Moor's final speech and 'bloody Period', then, we have to concur with Cassio's assessment that the hero was 'great of Heart' (V.ii.351–55).

The earliest recorded performance of the play was in November 1604, when Shakespeare's company – by then no longer known as the Lord Chamberlain's Men but as His Majesty's Servants – presented *Othello* at court to their new patron, King James I. In all likelihood the play had been written some time before its production at Whitehall (as early as 1603, perhaps), and by the end of 1604 it was probably an established feature of the Globe repertory. It first appeared in print six years after Shakespeare's death, in a 1622 Quarto that seems to have owed something to an authorial draft of the script, and it reappeared in a fuller and smoother text a year later in the 1623 memorial volume we refer to today as the First Folio.

The principal source for *Othello* was a novella from the *Hecatommithi* ('One Hundred Tales') of Giraldi Cinthio. Cinthio's collection was first published in Venice in 1565, and Shakespeare probably read it in the original Italian. It is conceivable that he also consulted a 1584 French version by Gabriel Chappuys, but if so he appears to have derived little from that retelling that was not present in Cinthio's rendering of the story. Our best evidence, then, is that the operatic tragedy we know as *Othello* sprang from a crude narrative about an overreaching Moor who brought his troubles upon himself by marrying a woman of different race, religion, and mode of life, and who was eventually duped into beating his innocent wife to death with a sandbag.

In Cinthio's story 'il Moro' is a pagan rather than a Christian. And the character who corresponds to Iago is motivated by jealousy over Desdemona (and the hatred engendered by her rejection of his attentions), rather than by anger over any slight by her husband. Shakespeare ennobled the title character in a number of ways. He gave Iago a much more active role as stage manager of Othello's downfall. And he made several alterations in the personality of the Moor's Lady to transfigure her into the 'divine Desdemona' (II.i.73) of the concluding scenes. As a result he metamorphosed the 'sordid story of a garrison intrigue'* into what many regard as the most touching episode in the annals of world drama.

John F. Andrews

* This phrase is from Helen Gardner's British Academy Lecture for 1955; see her comments in the 'Perspectives on *Othello*' section below. For other observations about Shakespeare's adaptation of the material he found in Cinthio, consult the excerpts from Thomas Rymer (1692), Lewis Theobald (1733), Charlotte Lennox (1753–54), G. R. Hibbard (1968), and Susan Snyder (1972) in the 'Perspectives' section.

THE TEXT OF THE EVERYMAN SHAKESPEARE

Background

THE EARLY PRINTINGS OF SHAKESPEARE'S WORKS

Many of us enjoy our first encounter with Shakespeare when we're introduced to *Julius Caesar* or *Macbeth* at school. It may therefore surprise us that neither of these tragedies could ever have been read, let alone studied, by most of the playwright's contemporaries. They began as scripts for performance and, along with seventeen other titles that never saw print during Shakespeare's lifetime, they made their inaugural appearance as 'literary' works seven years after his death, in the 1623 collection we know today as the First Folio.

The Folio contained thirty-six titles in all. Of these, half had been issued previously in the small paperbacks we now refer to as quartos.* Like several of the plays first published in the Folio, the most trustworthy of the quarto printings appear to have been set either from Shakespeare's own manuscripts or from faithful copies of them. It's not impossible that the poet himself prepared some of these works for the press, and it's intriguing to imagine him reviewing proof-pages as the words he'd written for actors to speak and embody were being transposed into the type that readers would filter through their eyes, minds, and imaginations. But, alas, there's no indisputable evidence that Shakespeare had any direct involvement with the publication of these early editions of his plays.

What about the scripts that achieved print for the first time in the Folio? Had the dramatist taken any steps to give the permanency of book form to those texts? We don't know. All we

---

* Quartos derived their name from the four-leaf units of which these small books were comprised: large sheets of paper that had been folded twice after printing to yield four leaves, or eight pages. Folios, volumes with twice the page-size of quartos, were put together from two-leaf units: sheets that had been folded once after printing to yield four pages.

can say is that when he fell fatally ill in 1616, Shakespeare was denied any opportunities he might otherwise have taken to ensure that his 'insubstantial Pageants' survived the mortal who was now slipping into the 'dark Backward and Abysm of Time'.

Fortunately, two of the playwright's colleagues felt an obligation, as they put it, 'to procure his Orphans Guardians'. Sometime after his death John Heminge (or Heminges) and Henry Condell made arrangements to preserve Shakespeare's theatrical compositions in a manner that would keep them vibrant for all time. They dedicated their endeavour to two noblemen who had helped see England's foremost acting company through some of its most trying vicissitudes. They solicited several poetic tributes for the volume, among them a now-famous eulogy by fellow writer Ben Jonson. They commissioned an engraved portrait of Shakespeare to adorn the frontispiece. And they did their utmost to display the author's dramatic works in a style that would both dignify them and make them accessible to 'the great Variety of Readers'.

As they readied Shakespeare's plays for the compositors who would set them into stately Folio columns, Heminge and Condell (or editors designated to carry out their wishes) revised and augmented many of the entrances, exits, and other stage directions in the manuscripts. They divided most of the works into acts and scenes.* For a number of plays they appended 'Names of the Actors', or casts of characters. Meanwhile they made every effort to guarantee that the Folio printers had reliable copy-texts for each of the titles: authoritative manuscripts for the plays that had not been published previously, and good quarto printings (annotated in some instances to insert staging details, mark script changes, and add supplementary material) for the ones that had been issued prior to the Folio. For several titles they supplied texts that were substantively different from, if not always demonstrably superior to, the quarto versions that preceded them.

Like even the most accurate of printings that preceded it, the Folio collection was flawed by minor blemishes. But it more than fulfilled the purpose of its generous-minded compilers: 'to keep

---

* The early quartos, reflecting the unbroken sequence that probably typified Elizabethan and Jacobean performances of the plays, had been printed without the structural demarcations usual in Renaissance editions of classical drama.

the memory of so worthy a Friend and Fellow alive as was our Shakespeare'. In the process it provided a publishing model that remains instructive today.

MODERN EDITIONS OF THE PLAYS AND POEMS

When we compare the First Folio and its predecessors with the usual modern edition of Shakespeare's works, we're more apt to be impressed by the differences than by the similarities. Today's texts of Renaissance drama are normally produced in conformity with twentieth-century standards of punctuation and usage; as a consequence they look more neat, clean, and, to our eyes, 'right' than do the original printings. Thanks to an editorial tradition that extends back to the early eighteenth century and beyond, most of the rough spots in the early printings of Shakespeare have long been smoothed away. Textual scholars have ferreted out redundancies and eradicated inconsistencies. They've mended what they've perceived to be errors and oversights in the playscripts, and they've systematically attended to what they've construed as misreadings by the copyists and compositors who transmitted these playscripts to posterity. They've added '[Within]' brackets and other theatrical notations. They've revised stage directions they've judged incomplete or inadequate in the initial printings. They've regularized disparities in the speech headings. They've gone back to the playwright's sources and reinstated the proper forms for many of the character and place names which a presumably hasty or inattentive author got 'wrong' as he conferred identities on his dramatis personae and stage locales. They've replaced obsolete words like *bankrout* with their modern heirs (in this case *bankrupt*). And in a multitude of other ways they've accommodated Shakespeare to the tastes, interests, and expectations of latter-day readers.

The results, on the whole, have been splendid. But interpreting the artistic designs of a complex writer is always problematical, and the task is especially challenging when that writer happens to have been a poet who felt unconstrained by many of the 'rules' that more conventional dramatists respected. The undertaking becomes further complicated when new rules, and new criteria of linguistic and social correctness, are imposed by subsequent generations of artists and critics.

To some degree in his own era, but even more in the neoclassical period (1660–1800) that came in its wake, Shakespeare's most ardent admirers thought it necessary to apologize for what Ben Jonson hinted at in his allusion to the 'small Latin, and less Greek' of an untutored prodigy. To be sure, the 'sweet Swan of Avon' sustained his popularity; in fact his reputation rose so steadily that by the end of the eighteenth century he'd eclipsed Jonson and his other peers and become the object of near-universal Bardolatry. But in the theatre most of his plays were being adapted in ways that were deemed advisable to tame their supposed wildness and bring them into conformity with the decorum of a society that took pride in its refinement. As one might expect, some of the attitudes that induced theatre proprietors to metamorphose an unpolished poet from the provinces into something closer to an urbane man of letters also influenced Shakespeare's editors. Persuaded that the dramatist's works were marred by crudities that needed expunging, they applied their ministrations to the canon with painstaking diligence.

Twentieth-century editors have moved away from many of the presuppositions that guided a succession of earlier improvers. But a glance at the textual apparatus accompanying virtually any modern publication of the plays and poems will show that emendations and editorial procedures deriving from such fore-bears as the sets published by Nicholas Rowe (1709), Alexander Pope (1723–5, 1728), Lewis Theobald (1733, 1740, 1757), Thomas Hanmer (1743–5, 1770–1), Samuel Johnson (1765), Edward Capell (1768), George Steevens (1773), and Edmond Malone (1790) retain a strong hold on today's renderings of the playwright's works. The consequence is a 'Shakespeare' who offers the tidiness we've come to expect in our libraries of treasured authors, but not necessarily the playwright a reader of the Second Quarto of *Romeo and Juliet* in 1599 would still be able to recognize as a contemporary.

OLD LIGHT ON THE TOPIC

Over the last two decades we've learned from art curators that paintings by Old Masters such as Michelangelo and Rembrandt look a lot brighter when centuries of grime are removed from their surfaces – when hues that had become dulled with soot and other extraneous matter are allowed to radiate again with something approximating their pristine luminosity. We've learned from conductors like Christopher Hogwood that there are aesthetic rewards to be gained from a return to the scorings and instruments with which Renaissance and Baroque musical compositions were first presented. We've learned from twentieth-century experiments in the performance of Shakespeare's plays that an open, multi-level stage, analogous to that on which the scripts were originally enacted, does more justice to their dramaturgical techniques than does a proscenium auditorium devised for works that came later in the development of Western theatre. We've learned from archaeological excavations in London's Bankside area that the foundations of playhouses such as the Rose and the Globe look rather different from what many historians had expected. And we're now learning from a close scrutiny of Shakespeare's texts that they too look different, and function differently, when we accept them for what they are and resist the impulse to 'normalize' features that strike us initially as quirky, unkempt, or unsophisticated.

The Aims that Guide the Everyman Text

Like other modern editions of the dramatist's plays and poems, The Everyman Shakespeare owes an incalculable debt to the scholarship that has led to so many excellent renderings of the author's works. But in an attempt to draw fresh inspiration from the spirit that animated those remarkable achievements at the outset, the Everyman edition departs in a number of respects from the usual post-Folio approach to the presentation of Shakespeare's texts.

RESTORING SOME OF THE NUANCES OF
RENAISSANCE PUNCTUATION

In its punctuation, Everyman attempts to give equal emphasis to sound and sense. In places where Renaissance practice calls for heavier punctuation than we'd normally employ – to mark the caesural pause in the middle of a line of verse, for instance – Everyman sometimes retains commas that other modern editions omit. Meanwhile, in places where current practice usually calls for the inclusion of commas – after vocatives and interjections such as 'O' and 'alas', say, or before 'Madam' or 'Sir' in phrases such as 'Ay Madam' or 'Yes Sir' – Everyman follows the original printings and omits them.

Occasionally the absence of a comma has a significant bearing on what an expression means, or can mean. At one point in *Othello*, for example, Iago tells the Moor 'marry Patience' (IV.i.90). Inserting a comma after 'marry', as most of today's editions do, limits Iago's utterance to one that says 'Come now, have patience.' Leaving the clause as it stands in the Folio, the way the Everyman text does, permits Iago's words to have the additional, agonizingly ironic sense 'Be wed to Patience'.

The early texts generally deploy exclamation points quite sparingly, and the Everyman text follows suit. Everyman also follows the early editions, more often than not, when they use question marks in places that seem unusual by current standards: at the ends of what we'd normally treat as exclamations, for example, or at the ends of interrogative clauses in sentences that we'd ordinarily denote as questions in their entirety.

The early texts make no orthographic distinction between simple plurals and either singular or plural possessives, and there are times when the context doesn't indicate whether a word spelled *Sisters*, say, should be rendered *Sisters*, *Sisters'*, or *Sister's* in today's usage. In such situations the Everyman edition prints the word in the form modern usage prescribes for plurals.

REVIVING SOME OF THE FLEXIBILITY OF RENAISSANCE SPELLING

Spelling had not become standardized by Shakespeare's time, and that meant that many words could take a variety of forms. Like James Joyce and some of the other innovative prose and verse stylists of our own century, Shakespeare revelled in the freedom a largely unanchored language provided, and with that in mind Everyman retains original spelling forms (or adaptations of those forms that preserve their key distinctions from modern spellings) whenever there is any reason to suspect that they might have a bearing on how a word was intended to be pronounced or on what it meant, or could have meant, in the playwright's day. When there is any likelihood that multiple forms of the same word could be significant, moreover, the Everyman text mirrors the diversity to be found in the original printings.

In many cases this practice affects the personalities of Shakespeare's characters. One of the heroine's most familiar questions in *Romeo and Juliet* is 'What's in a Name?' For two and a half centuries readers – and as a consequence actors, directors, theatre audiences, and commentators – have been led to believe that Juliet was addressing this query to a Romeo named 'Montague'. In fact 'Montague' *was* the name Shakespeare found in his principal source for the play. For reasons that will become apparent to anyone who examines the tragedy in detail, however, the playwright changed his protagonist's surname to 'Mountague', a word that plays on both 'mount' and 'ague' (fever).* Setting aside an editorial practice that began with Lewis Theobald in the middle of the eighteenth century, Everyman resurrects the name the dramatist himself gave Juliet's lover.

Readers of *The Merchant of Venice* in the Everyman set will be amused to learn that the character modern editions usually identify as 'Lancelot' is in reality 'Launcelet', a name that calls attention to the clown's lusty 'little lance'. Like Costard in *Love's Labour's Lost*, another stage bumpkin who was probably played by the actor Will Kemp, Launcelet is an upright 'Member of the Commonwealth'; we eventually learn that he's left a pliant wench 'with Child'.

Readers of *Hamlet* will find that 'Fortinbras' (as the name of the Prince's Norwegian opposite is rendered in the First Folio and in most modern editions) appears in the earlier, authoritative 1604 Second Quarto of the play as 'Fortinbrasse'. In the opening scene of that text a surname that meant 'strong in arms' in French is introduced to the accompaniment of puns on *brazen*, in the phrase

---

* For anyone who doubts that Shakespeare's alteration of Romeo's family name was part of a conscious artistic plan, it may be worth noting that 'Capulet', like 'Capilet' in *Twelfth Night* and *All's Well That Ends Well*, means 'small horse'.

'brazon Cannon', and on *metal,* in the phrase 'unimprooued mettle'. In the same play readers of the Everyman text will encounter 'Ostricke', the ostrich-like courtier who invites the Prince of Denmark to participate in the fateful fencing match that draws *Hamlet* to a close. Only in its final entrance direction for the obsequious fop does the Second Quarto call this character 'Osrick', the name he bears in all the Folio text's references to him and in most modern editions of Shakespeare's most popular tragedy.

Readers of the Everyman *Macbeth* will discover that the fabled 'Weird Sisters' appear only as the 'weyward' or 'weyard' Sisters. Shakespeare and his contemporaries knew that in his *Chronicles of England, Scotland, and Ireland* Raphael Holinshed had used the term 'weird sisters' to describe the witches who accost Macbeth and Banquo on the heath; but no doubt because he wished to play on *wayward,* the playwright changed their name to *weyward.* Like Samuel Johnson, who thought punning vulgar and lamented Shakespeare's proclivity to seduction by this 'fatal Cleopatra', Lewis Theobald saw no reason to retain the playwright's weyward spelling of the witches' name. He thus restored the 'correct' form from Holinshed, and editors ever since have generally done likewise.

In many instances Renaissance English had a single spelling for what we now define as two separate words. For example, *humane* combines the senses of 'human' and 'humane' in modern English. In the First Folio printing of *Macbeth* the protagonist's wife expresses a concern that her husband is 'too full o'th' Milke of humane kindnesse'. As she phrases it, *humane kindnesse* can mean several things, among them 'humankind-ness', 'human kindness', and 'humane kindness'. It is thus a reminder that to be true to his or her own 'kind' a human being must be 'kind' in the sense we now attach to 'humane'. To disregard this logic, as the protagonist and his wife will soon prove, is to disregard a principle as basic to the cosmos as the laws of gravity.

In a way that parallels *humane, bad* could mean either 'bad' or 'bade', *borne* either 'born' or 'borne', *ere* either 'ere' (before) or 'e'er' (ever), *least* either 'least' or 'lest', *lye* either 'lie' or 'lye', *nere* either 'ne'er' or 'near' (though the usual spellings for the latter were *neare* or *neere*), *powre* either 'pour' or 'power', *then* either 'than' or 'then', and *tide* either 'tide' or 'tied'.

There were a number of word-forms that functioned in Renaissance English as interchangeable doublets. *Travail* could mean 'travel', for example, and *travel* could mean 'travail'. By the same token, *deer* could mean *dear* and vice versa, *dew* could mean *due*, *hart* could mean *heart*, and (as we've already noted) *mettle* could mean *metal*.

A particularly interesting instance of the equivocal or double meanings some word-forms had in Shakespeare's time is *loose*, which can often become either 'loose' or 'lose' when we render it in modern English. In *The Comedy of Errors* when Antipholus of Syracuse compares himself to 'a Drop / Of Water that in the Ocean seeks another Drop' and then says he will 'loose' himself in quest of his long-lost twin, he means both (a) that he will release himself into a vast unknown, and (b) that he will lose his own identity, if necessary, to be reunited with the brother for whom he searches. On the other hand, in *Hamlet* when Polonius says he'll 'loose' his daughter to the Prince, he little suspects that by so doing he will also lose his daughter.

In some cases the playwright employs word-forms that can be translated into words we wouldn't think of as related today: *sowre*, for instance, which can mean 'sour', 'sower', or 'sore', depending on the context. In other cases he uses forms that do have modern counterparts, but not counterparts with the same potential for multiple connotation. For example, *onely* usually means 'only' in the modern sense; but occasionally Shakespeare gives it a figurative, adverbial twist that would require a nonce word such as 'one-ly' to replicate in current English.

In a few cases Shakespeare employs word-forms that have only seeming equivalents in modern usage. For example, *abhominable*, which meant 'inhuman' (derived, however incorrectly, from *ab*, 'away from', and *homine*, 'man') to the poet and his contemporaries, is not the same word as our *abominable* (ill-omened, abhorrent). In his advice to the visiting players Hamlet complains about incompetent actors who imitate 'Humanity so abhominably' as to make the characters they depict seem unrecognizable as men. Modern readers who don't realize the distinction between

Shakespeare's word and our own, and who see *abominable* on the page before them, don't register the full import of the Prince's satire.

Modern English treats as single words a number of word-forms that were normally spelled as two words in Shakespeare's time. What we render as *myself*, for example, and use primarily as a reflexive or intensifying pronoun, is almost invariably spelled *my self* in Shakespeare's works; so also with *her self*, *thy self*, *your self*, and *it self* (where *it* functions as *its* does today). Often there is no discernible difference between Shakespeare's usage and our own. At other times there is, however, as we are reminded when we come across a phrase such as 'our innocent self' in *Macbeth* and think how strained it would sound in modern parlance, or as we observe when we note how naturally the self is objectified in the balanced clauses of the Balcony Scene in *Romeo and Juliet*:

> Romeo, doffe thy name,
> And for thy name, which is no part of thee,
> Take all my selfe.

Yet another difference between Renaissance orthography and our own can be exemplified with words such as *today*, *tonight*, and *tomorrow*, which (unlike *yesterday*) were treated as two words in Shakespeare's time. In *Macbeth* when the Folio prints 'Duncan comes here to Night', the unattached *to* can function either as a preposition (with *Night* as its object, or in this case the king's destination) or as the first part of an infinitive (with *Night* operating figuratively as a verb). Consider the ambiguity a Renaissance reader would have detected in the original publication of one of the most celebrated soliloquies in all of Shakespeare:

> To morrow, and to morrow, and to morrow,
> Creeps in this petty pace from day to day,
> To the last Syllable of Recorded time:
> And all our yesterdayes, have lighted Fooles
> The way to dusty death.

Here, by implication, the route 'to morrow' is identical with 'the way to dusty death', a relationship we miss if we don't know that for Macbeth, and for the audiences who first heard these lines spoken, *to morrow* was not a single word but a potentially equivocal two-word phrase.

RECAPTURING THE ABILITY TO HEAR WITH OUR EYES

When we fail to recall that Shakespeare's scripts were designed initially to provide words for people to hear in the theatre, we sometimes overlook a fact that is fundamental to the artistic structure of a work like *Macbeth*: that the messages a sequence of sounds convey through the ear are, if anything, even more significant than the messages a sequence of letters, punctuation marks, and white spaces on a printed page transmit through the eye. A telling illustration of this point, and of the potential for ambiguous or multiple implication in any Shakespearean script, may be found in the dethronement scene of *Richard II*. When Henry Bullingbrook asks the King if he is ready to resign his crown, Richard replies 'I, no no I; for I must nothing be.' Here the punctuation in the 1608 Fourth Quarto (the earliest text to print this richly complex passage) permits each *I* to signify either 'ay' or 'I' (*I* being the usual spelling for 'ay' in Shakespeare's time). Understanding *I* to mean 'I' permits additional play on *no*, which can be heard (at least in its first occurrence) as 'know'. Meanwhile the second and third soundings of *I*, if not the first, can also be heard as 'eye'. In the context in which this line occurs, that sense echoes a thematically pertinent passage from Matthew 18:9: 'if thine eye offend thee, pluck it out'.

But these are not all the implications *I* can have here. It can also represent the Roman numeral for '1', which will soon be reduced, as Richard notes, to 'nothing' (0), along with the speaker's title, his worldly possessions, his manhood, and eventually his life. In Shakespeare's time, to become 'nothing' was, *inter alia*, to be emasculated, to be made a 'weaker vessel' (1 Peter 3:7) with 'no thing'. As the Fool in *King Lear* reminds another monarch who has abdicated his throne, a man in want of an 'I' is impotent, 'an O without a Figure' (I.iv.207). In addition to its other dimensions, then, Richard's reply is a statement that can be formulated mathematically, and in symbols that anticipate the binary system behind today's computer technology: '1, 0, 0, 1, for 1 must 0 be.'

Modern editions usually render Richard's line 'Ay, no; no, ay;

for I must nothing be.' Presenting the line in that fashion makes good sense of what Richard is saying. But as we've seen, it doesn't make total sense of it, and it doesn't call attention to Richard's paradoxes in the same way that hearing or seeing three undifferentiated *I*'s is likely to have done for Shakespeare's contemporaries. Their culture was more attuned than ours is to the oral and aural dimensions of language, and if we want to appreciate the special qualities of their dramatic art we need to train ourselves to 'hear' the word-forms we see on the page. We must learn to recognize that for many of what we tend to think of as fixed linkages between sound and meaning (the vowel 'I', say, and the word 'eye'), there were alternative linkages (such as the vowel 'I' and the words 'I' and 'Ay') that could be just as pertinent to what the playwright was communicating through the ears of his theatre patrons at a given moment. As the word *audience* itself may help us to remember, people in Shakespeare's time normally spoke of 'hearing' rather than 'seeing' a play.

In its text of *Richard II*, the Everyman edition reproduces the title character's line as it appears in the early printings of the tragedy. Ideally the orthographic oddity of the repeated *I*'s will encourage today's readers to ponder Richard's utterance, and the play it epitomizes, as a characteristically Shakespearean enigma.

OTHER ASPECTS OF THE EVERYMAN TEXT

Now for a few words about other features of the Everyman text.

One of the first things readers will notice about this edition is its bountiful use of capitalized words. In this practice as in others, the Everyman exemplar is the First Folio, and especially the works in the Folio sections billed as 'Histories' and 'Tragedies'.* Everyman makes no attempt to adhere to the Folio printings with literal exactitude. In some instances the Folio capitalizes words that the

---

* The quarto printings employ far fewer capital letters than does the Folio. Capitalization seems to have been regarded as a means of recognizing the status ascribed to certain words (*Noble*, for example, is almost always capitalized), titles (not only King, Queen, Duke, and Duchess, but Sir and Madam), genres (tragedies were regarded as more 'serious' than comedies in more than one sense), and forms of publication (quartos, being associated with ephemera such as 'plays', were not thought to be as 'grave' as the folios that bestowed immortality on 'works', writings that, in the words of Ben Jonson's eulogy to Shakespeare, were 'not of an age, but for all time').

Everyman text of the same passage lowercases; in other instances Everyman capitalizes words not uppercased in the Folio. The objective is merely to suggest something of the flavour, and what appears to have been the rationale, of Renaissance capitalization, in the hope that today's audiences will be made continually aware that the works they're contemplating derive from an earlier epoch.

Readers will also notice that instead of cluttering the text with stage directions such as '[Aside]' or '[To Rosse]', the Everyman text employs unobtrusive dashes to indicate shifts in mode of address. In an effort to keep the page relatively clear of words not supplied by the original printings, Everyman also exercises restraint in its addition of editor-generated stage directions. Where the dialogue makes it obvious that a significant action occurs, the Everyman text inserts a square-bracketed phrase such as '[Fleance escapes]'. Where what the dialogue implies is subject to differing interpretations, however, the Everyman text provides a facing-page note to discuss the most plausible inferences.

Like other modern editions, the Everyman text combines into 'shared' verse lines (lines divided among two or more speakers) many of the part-lines to be found in the early publications of the plays. One exception to the usual modern procedure is that Everyman indents some lines that are not components of shared verses. At times, for example, the opening line of a scene stops short of the metrical norm, a pentameter (five-foot) or hexameter (six-foot) line comprised predominantly of iambic units (unstressed syllables followed by stressed ones). In such cases Everyman uses indentation as a reminder that scenes can begin as well as end in mid-line (an extension of the ancient convention that an epic commences *in media res*, 'in the midst of the action'). Everyman also uses indentation to reflect what appear to be pauses in the dialogue, either to allow other activity to transpire (as happens in *Macbeth*, II.iii.87, when a brief line 'What's the Business?' follows a Folio stage direction that reads *'Bell rings. Enter Lady'*) or to permit a character to hesitate for a moment of reflection (as happens a few seconds later in the same scene when Macduff responds to a demand to 'Speak, speak' with the reply 'O gentle Lady, / 'Tis not for you to hear what I can speak').

Readers of the Everyman edition will note that many word-forms are printed with apostrophes to indicate contractions (*to't* for 'to it', for example, or *o'th'* for 'of the') or syllabic elisions (*look'd* for 'looked', for instance, or *nev'r* or *ne'er* for 'never'). In many cases these departures from ordinary spelling occur in verse contexts that call for the deletion of syllables which if voiced would result in minor violations of the metrical norm. Thus in *Twelfth Night*, II.iv.107, *loved* is syncopated to *lov'd* in Viola's statement 'My Father had a Daughter lov'd a Man'. On the other hand, in *A Midsummer Night's Dream*, II.i.26, *loved* is treated as a fully voiced two-syllable word in 'But she, perforce, withholds the loved Boy'. In situations such as these Everyman almost invariably retains the word-forms to be found in the early printings that have been adopted as control texts. At times this policy results in lines whose metre can be construed in different ways by different interpreters. In *A Midsummer Night's Dream*, III.ii.292, to cite one line for illustrative purposes, it could be argued that the first *Personage* should be syncopated to *Pers'nage* when Hermia says, 'And with her Personage, her tall Personage'. By the same token it could be maintained that words such as *even*, *Heaven*, and *whether* should be syncopated in pronunciation when, as is usual, they occur in positions that would normally demand a sound with the metrical value of a single syllable. The frequency with which syllabic elisions crop up in the original editions of Shakespeare's works would seem to suggest that the playwright and his colleagues placed a premium on metrical regularity. At the same time, the frequent absence of syncopated or contracted word-forms in settings where the metre would lead us to expect them (*I am* is only rarely rendered as *I'm*, for example, though it continually appears in positions that invite compression to one syllable) could be viewed as evidence that Shakespeare was anything but rigid in such matters, and may even have consciously opted for the subtle variations that derive from occasional unstressed syllabic additions to an otherwise steady march of iambic feet. Given the metrical ambiguity of the early texts, it is difficult if not impossible to determine how 'smooth' the verse-speaking was intended to be in the theatres for which Shakespeare wrote his scripts. Rather than impose a fixed order that might be incompatible with the poet's own aesthetic principles, then, the Everyman text merely preserves the metrical inconsistencies to be observed in the Quarto and Folio printings of Shakespeare's plays and poems.

Everyman also retains many of the other anomalies in the early texts. Among other things, this practice affects the way characters are depicted. In *A Midsummer Night's Dream*, for example, the ruler of Athens is usually identified in speech headings and stage directions as 'Theseus', but sometimes he is referred to by his title as 'Duke'. In the same play Oberon's merry sprite goes by two different names: 'Puck' and 'Robin Goodfellow'.

Readers of the Everyman edition will sometimes discover that characters they've known, or known about, for years don't appear in the original printings. When they open the pages of the Everyman *Macbeth*, for example, they'll learn that Shakespeare's audiences were unaware of any woman with the title 'Lady Macbeth'. In the only authoritative text we have of the Scottish tragedy, the protagonist's spouse goes by such names as 'Macbeth's Lady', 'Macbeth's Wife', or simply 'Lady', but at no time is she listed or mentioned as 'Lady Macbeth'. The same is true of the character usually designated 'Lady Capulet' in modern editions of *Romeo and Juliet*. 'Capulet's Wife' makes appearances as 'Mother', 'Old Lady', 'Lady', or simply 'Wife'; but she's never termed 'Lady Capulet', and her husband never treats her with the dignity such a title would connote.

Rather than 'correct' the grammar in Shakespeare's works to eliminate what modern usage would categorize as solecisms (as when Mercutio says 'my Wits faints' in *Romeo and Juliet*), the Everyman text leaves it intact. Among other things, this principle applies to instances in which archaic forms preserve idioms that differ slightly from related modern expressions (as in the clause 'you are too blame', where 'too' frequently functions as an adverb and 'blame' is used, not as a verb, but as an adjective roughly equivalent to 'blameworthy').

Finally, and most importantly, the Everyman edition leaves unchanged any reading in the original text that is not manifestly erroneous. Unlike other modern renderings of Shakespeare's works, Everyman substitutes emendations only when obvious problems can be dealt with by obvious solutions.

The Everyman Text of Othello

Like several of Shakespeare's other plays (among them *Hamlet, King Lear,* and *Romeo and Juliet*), *Othello* comes down to us in multiple forms.

The earliest publication of the tragedy was a 1622 quarto that seems to have been set largely, if not entirely, from an edited exemplar of the author's 'foul papers'.* It has been suggested that at least some of what became the First Quarto *Othello* was filtered through the acting company's book-keeper (the man who prepared, maintained, and when necessary updated a prompt copy of each drama for use in the theatre), and that what look like errors of faulty memory may have resulted either from this transcriber's proclivity to rely too heavily upon his recollection of the dialogue with which he was so familiar, or from his tendency to try storing too much material in his head as he produced a presentable rendering of Shakespeare's unpolished holograph. It has also been hypothesized that the *Othello* which appeared in Q1 was a version of the work that had been cut in places, perhaps in response to such contingencies as the troupe's temporary dependence upon a leading boy actor who couldn't carry a tune and whose presence in the cast would thus have compelled Shakespeare and his colleagues to excise the 'Willow' song from Act IV, scene iii of any performances in which this youth played Desdemona.

Notwithstanding its minor defects, the 1622 publication has much to commend it. One important modern editor, M. R. Ridley (who completed an *Othello* in 1958 for The Arden Shakespeare), has made the First Quarto his principal authority for the play's text. And most of the twentieth-century scholars who have taken

---

* A draft of the script which antedated any refinements that would have occurred as it was adapted and rehearsed for performance. Unlike the works that had been published in Shakespeare's lifetime, Q1 *Othello* was partly divided into acts and scenes. There are reasons to doubt that the quarto's primitive structural demarcations were authorial, however, and a collation of the 1622 version of the play with the one that emerged a year later will show that whoever prepared the Q1 text for its typesetters did so with less sophistication than the editors of the 1623 Folio brought to most of the works they supplied with act and scene divisions.

another tack and based their editions primarily upon the 1623 First Folio printing have nevertheless opted for Q1 readings in a fifth of the instances in which the Folio and Quarto differ.

The Folio *Othello* appears to derive from a later version of the drama. It contains approximately 160 lines or part-lines that had not been included in the 1622 quarto. Whether inadvertently or deliberately, it omits a handful of short speeches and speaker designations, a score of pertinent stage directions, and more than three dozen incidental words and phrases that had been present in Q1. In compliance with a 1606 act prohibiting profanity in the theatre, it also deletes or substitutes milder expletives for some fifty of the oaths that had added spice to the earlier script. Meanwhile it introduces more than a thousand other substantive variations from the First Quarto.

How the 1623 *Othello* was compiled remains an unresolved question. A few interpreters attribute the Folio text's peculiarities to scribes or compositors, with some critics assigning the bulk of F1's divergences from Q1 to editorial high-handedness or incompetence and others ascribing them either to intelligent, responsible emendation or to the difficulties that even seasoned and conscientious journeymen would have encountered if they were forced to contend with an extensively revised and partially indecipherable playscript. But even those scholars who adduce credible evidence of scribal or compositorial interference in the transmission of the Folio *Othello* are hard pressed to account for many features of the 1623 text that seem to evince a dramatist's rethinking of certain features in his original design. The dominant view today, therefore, is that the majority of F1's departures from the Q1 *Othello* are the consequence of artistic decisions by the author.

Just when those artistic decisions would have been made, however, and how extensive they were, is subject to debate. Would Shakespeare's own revisions have included the removal of most of the oaths to be found in the script that eventually made its way into print in the 1622 quarto? And if so, would a mature poet have preferred the linguistic mildness of the revised *Othello* to the more vigorous form that many of the play's exchanges had taken before he and his colleagues were subjected to a new imposition of theatrical censorship? As usual, we have no way of knowing the answers to such questions. And here as elsewhere it is difficult if not impossible to settle on a principle of discrimination that will permit us to make confident judgements about which Folio variants from the Quarto to adopt as authorial – or in any event as acceptable to a writer who would rather have left his original text undisturbed – and which ones to reject as deriving from non-authorial sources.

Like most twentieth-century editions, the Everyman *Othello* is anchored on the Folio printing, the rendering of the drama that appears, in most respects at least, to incorporate the playwright's maturer vision. In a way that sets it apart from other modern texts, however, Everyman draws upon the 1622 quarto only when necessary to fill lacunae in the Folio script, to reinstate oaths that seem thematically integral, if not indispensable, to the contexts from which they have been expunged in the Folio printing, and to emend any Folio passages that are so manifestly inferior to their Quarto counterparts as to be exegetically problematic or indefensible.*

In the passages that follow, Everyman supplements the Folio text with the indicated material from the First Quarto.

I.i.	1	Tush
	4	'Sblood
	14	And in Conclusion,
	31	God
	81	*Brabantio at a Window.*
	84	Zounds,
	106	Zounds,
	115	now
	159	*in his Night-gown*
I.ii.	28	*Officers and*
	87	I
I.iii.	105	DUKE
	139	and
	199	into your Favour
	246	did

---

* If the Everyman text draws only sparingly from Q1 (1622), it also derives little or nothing from the later seventeenth-century quartos of *Othello* – Q2 (a 1630 printing that draws on both Q1 and F1), Q3 (1655), Q4 (1681), Q5 (1687), and Q6 (1695) – and from the folios of 1632 (F2), 1663–4 (F3), and 1685 (F4).

	356–57	She must have Change, she must:
	361	a
	346–86	RODERIGO . . . chang'd.
II.i.	82	And bring all Cyprus comfort
	88	me
	92	the
	200	*They kiss.*
II.ii.	13	Heaven
II.iii.	113	God
	140	*Exit Roderigo.*
	147	*within* Help, help.
	148	Zouns
	161	Sir
	164	hold
	166	Zouns
	170	hold
	255	now
	266	Sir
	296	God,
	345	here
III.i.	6	call'd
	33	Do, good my Friend.
	52–53	to . . . Front
III.iii.	145	then
	158	By Heaven,
	180	well
	243	hold
	381	Sir
	411	and
	440	*He kneels.* Placed at line 439 in Q1.
	441	perhaps
	453	*Iago kneels.*
III.iv.	38	yet
	80	Heaven
	83	Sir
IV.i.	37	'Zouns
	54	No, forbear:
	106	now
	112	a
	166	Faith
	173	*Exit Cassio.*
	219	*A Trumpet.*
	252	an

IV.ii.	31	But not the Words
	45	Why
	79	Impudent Strumpet
	164	And he does chide with you.
	166	you
	180	Faith
IV.iii.	19	in them
	22	thee
V.i.	43	*with a Light*
	72	O
	99	out
	118	Fough,
V.ii.	0	*with a Light*
	36	so
	53	Yes
	83	DESDEMONA ... LORD.
	121	*She dies.*
	137	Nay,
	191	*Othello falls on the Bed.*
	229	*The ... Wife.*
	230	*Exit Iago.*
	234	here
	237	*Exeunt [Exit in Q1] ... Gratiano.*
	245	*She dies.*
	350	*He stabs himself.*
	353	*He dies.*

In a few passages Everyman adopts First Quarto readings in preference to those in the First Folio printing of *Othello*. In the following list the first entry, in boldface, is the accepted Q1 reading, and the second entry, in regular type, is the rejected reading from the Folio.

I.i.	154	**Pains** apines
I.iii.	106	**overt** over
	114	**Sagittary,** Sagittary.
	121	**till** tell
	139	**Heads** head
	141	**other** others
	142	**Anthropaphagi** Anthropaphague
	143	**Do grow** Grew
	206	**preserv'd** presern'd

	392	**a Snipe** Supe
	395	**H'as [Ha's]** She ha's
	401	**Knavery** knavery —
		see. see —
II.i.	33	**prays** pray
	34	**foul** fowl
	216	***Exeunt*** *Exit*
	285	**you. Provoke** you, provoke
	299	**for wife** for wift
II.iii.	15	**Desdemona,** Desdemona:
	79	**Englishman** Englishmen
	91	**too** to
	98	**'Fore God,** Why
	160	**God's will** Alas
	163	**Bell?** bell.
	170	**hold, hold** hold,
	200	**Danger;** danger,
	202	**me,** me.
	244	**forget;** forget,
	355	**were't** were
	374	**How . . . Roderigo?** Placed before '*Enter Roderigo*' in F1.
	391	**By th' Mass** In troth
III.i.	22	**hear** hear me,
	27	**General's Wife** General
III.iii.	103	**By Heaven** Alas
	136	**But some** Wherein
	144	**oft** of
	414	**sigh'd** sigh
		kiss'd kiss
	415	**Cried** Cry
	444	**feels** keeps
III.iv.	55	**faith** indeed
	77	**seem't.** seem't?
	92	**Zouns** Away
	159	***Exeunt Desdemona and Aemilia.*** *Exit.*
IV.i.	132	**beckons** becomes
	146	***Enter Bianca.*** Placed after line 147 in F1.
	283	**denote** deonte
IV.ii.	28	**nay** May
	164	**other.** other
	240	**Fortune:** fortune,

V.i.	98	**Man.** man?
V.ii.	87	**Pain** pain?
	276	***Enter . . . Chair.*** *Enter Lodovico, Cassio, Montano, and Iago, with Officers.*
	287	**thee?** thee.
	291	**Death?** death.
	304	**another;** another,
	356	**Sea,** sea:

In a handful of instances Everyman emends the Folio text by drawing upon a source other than the First Quarto. In the list that follows, the first entry, in boldface, is the reading adopted by the Everyman edition; unless otherwise specified, the second entry is the reading to be found in the First Folio.

I.iii.	14	**Rhodes:** Rhodes,
	45	**him;** him,
	56	**and** snd
	216	**Words:** words,
	221	**leagu'd** league
	314	**Guinea** Ginny Q1 Gynney F1
	383	**to** too
II.ii	110	**of Doors** adores Q1 of doore F1
III.iii.	190	**keep't** keep Q1 kept F1
	460	**to't** too't
IV.i.	234	**Paper.** paper: Q1 paper, F1
IV.ii.	117	**Drink** drink Q1 drink: F1
	152	**them,** them:
IV.iii.	32	**here.** here,
V.ii.	87	**Pain.** pain – Q1 pain? F1

In many instances the Everyman *Othello* retains Folio readings in ways that distinguish it from other modern editions of the play. In the following list the first entry, in boldface, is the F1 reading adopted by the Everyman text, and the second entry, in regular type, is the reading to be found in some if not most of today's other editions. Where the usual twentieth-century reading derives from Q1, the second entry so specifies.

I.i.
    1 **me,** me;
   12 **bumbast** bombast
   21 **devision** division (so also in IV.i.235)
          Battaile battle (so also in I.iii.86, 128)
   22 **Spinster. Unless** spinster – unless
          Theorique: theoric,
   23 **tongued** toged (Q1)
   28 **other's** other (Q1)
   35 **Letter,** letter
   47 **naught** nought (so also in I.i.162; compare II.i.89)
   65 **fall** full (Q1)
   71 **chances** changes
   72 **loose** lose (compare I.iii.209, II.iii.216, 275,
          III.iii.311, 372, III.iv.23, 67)
   83 **Why? Wherefore** Why, wherefore
   84 **rob'd** robb'd (compare I.iii.206)
   98 **Knavery** bravery (Q1)
  101 **Spirits** spirit (Q1)
          their them (Q1)
  103 **What** What,
  112 **Germaines** germens
  122 **odd Even** odd-even
  124 **Gundelier** gondolier
  125 **Moor:** Moor –
  128 **me,** me
  146 **producted** produc'd (Q1)
  152 **Fadom** fathom
  156 **Flag,** flag
  163 **Oh** O (so also in I.i.165, 168, 175; I.ii.62; I.iii.58,
          309; II.i.44, 82, 91, 114, 119, 145, 163, 186, 202,
          208; II.iii.35, 71, 88, 264, 287, 296, 315; III.i.8;
          III.iii.5, 161, 165, 262, 297, 337, 340, 364, 367,
          386, 411, 440; III.iv.35, 167, 171; IV.i.19, 72, 76,
          139, 144, 188, 194, 198, 202, 207, 261; IV.ii.64,
          65, 71, 86, 138, 142, 228; IV.iii.2, 5; V.i.30, 39, 52,
          56, 59, 71, 72, 78, 79, 91, 93, 99, 116; V.ii.17, 74,
          89, 97, 101, 102, 105, 117, 118, 119, 121, 126,
          131, 145, 156, 162, 179, 191, 193, 218, 226, 231,
          248, 258, 266, 275, 285, 312, 355, 363)
  177 **her,** her

I.ii.
    4 **sometime** sometimes (Q1)
   14 **or** and (Q1)
   21 **promulgate** provulgate (Q1)
   34 **Duke's** Duke (Q1)
   37 **haste,** haste –

50 **to night** tonight (compare I.iii.50, 276, 379; II.i.220,
   276; II.iii.1, 7, 31, 37, 48, 52, 57, 238, 378;
   III.iii.55, 56, 58, 427; IV.i.163, 186, 265; IV.ii.101,
   238; IV.iii.28; V.i.112; V.ii.26, 80, 81)
63 **enchaunted** enchanted
68 **Dearlings** darlings (Q1)
72 **delight?** delight!
84 **Whether** *either* Where (Q1) *or* Whither
88 **gratious** gracious
91 **him.** him?
92 **Counsel** council (so also in I.ii.93)
94 **spight** spite

I.iii.   1 **this** these (Q1)
           19 **Gaze, when** gaze. When
           20 **Turk;** Turk,
           25 **in. If** in – if
           35 **injointed** enjointed
           36 **I** Ay (so also in II.iii.262; IV.ii.62, 64, 204, 237;
              V.ii.24, 27, 35, 53, 184, 231, 292)
           54 **perticular** particular (Q1)
           64 **ere** e'er (so also in IV.ii.149, V.ii.193)
           69 **Grace,** grace.
           83 **now,** now
          103 **powreful** powerful (compare II.i.78, II.iii.368,
              IV.iii.88, V.ii.155, 211)
          109 SENATOR I SENATOR (Q1; so also in I.iii.276, 289)
          118 **onely** only (so also in I.iii.167
          120 **Auncient** ancient (so also in II.i.66)
          128 **Fortune** fortunes (Q1)
          129 **past** pass'd (so also in I.iii.165)
          131 **bad** bade (so also in I.iii.162, II.i.155, IV.i.83,
              IV.iii.20)
          137 **Traveller's** travel's (Q1)
          138 **Antars** antres (Q1)
              Desarts deserts
          140 **speak.** speak –
              Process, process –
          145 **hence:** thence, (Q1)
          153 **instinctively** intentively (Q1)
          157 **Kisses** sighs (Q1)
          173 **speak?** speak. (Q1)
          177 **Mistress,** Mistress.
          182 **Duty,** duty;
          184 **shew'd** show'd (compare II.i.100, II.iii.304, 364;
              III.iii.105, 113, 189, 198; III.iv.96; IV.ii.218, 246;
              V.iii.196, 231)

187 **be with you bu'y** (Q1)
  have ha' (Q1)
196 **them 'em**
206 **Rob'd** robb'd (compare I.i.84)
217 **pierc'd** pierced (Q1)
  Ears ear (compare I.iii.402)
222 **more Sovereign** sovereign (Q1)
229 **Coach** couch (cooch Q1)
239 **Why at her Father's?** If you please, / Be't at her father's.
240 **Nor would I there recide.** Nor I: I would not there reside.
261 **Heat, the** heat (the
262 **my defunct** me defunct)
266 **When** For (Q1)
268 **Instrument** instruments (Q1)
274 **Hast** haste
277 OTHELLO **With all my Heart.** Most editions insert two part-lines from Q1 before this line: DESDEMONA Tonight, my Lord? / DUKE This night.
281 **Ancient,** ancient;
282 **Trust:** trust.
319 **Fig, fig!**
323 **Time** *either* thyme *or* tine
328 **Brain** beam (balance Q1)
333 **or** our (Q1)
342 **steed** stead
353 **as Bitter as** as accrb as the (Q1)
355 **Errors** error (Q1)
402 **Ears** ear (compare I.iii.217)

II.i.　　3 **Maine** mane *or* main (compare II.i.23, 39)
　　9 **Mortics,** mortice?
　 25 **in:** in,
　 26 **Veronessa,** Veronessa;
　 34 **Heavens** Heaven (Q1)
　 39 **blew** blue
　 42 **Arrivancy** arrivance (Q1)
　 43 **you, the** to the (Q1)
　　 the warlike this warlike *or* this worthy (Q1)
　 53 GENTLEMAN [MESSENGER]
　 56 GENTLEMAN [2] GENTLEMAN (so also in II.i.59, 95)
　 65 **tyre** tire
　　 Ingeniuer ingener
　　 ENTER GENTLEMAN ENTER [SECOND] GENTLEMAN

89 **ought** aught (so also in II.iii.203, III.iii.99, 101, V.ii.337)

93 **But hark, a Sail.** This sentence is usually placed after line 94.

95 **this** their (Q1)

100 **Curtesy** courtesy (Q1; so also in II.i.266, II.iii.33)

105 **leave** list (Q1)

112 **Divels** devils (compare II.i.230; III.iii.289, 302, 303, 317, 363; III.iii.467; III.iv.43, 129; IV.i.6, 8, 46, 151, 244, 248; IV.i.6, 8, 46, 151, 244, 248; IV.ii.34; V.ii.127, 129, 214, 280, 295)

127 **Freeze** frieze

134 **fit** hit (Q1)

160 **Wights** wight (Q1)

166 **Counsailor** counsellor (compare III.iii.108, IV.ii.92)

172 **give** gyve

178 **and** an (Q1)
Curtsy courtesy (Q1; compare II.i.100)

180 **Cluster** clyster (clister Q1)

190 **Olympus** Olympus –

217 **thither** hither (Q1)

232 **a Game** again (Q1)

233 **Appetite.** appetite,

250 **of Occasion** out of occasions (Q1)
he's has (Q1)

252 **it self. A** itself, a

255 **after.** after; (Q1)

272 **Mutabilities** mutualities (Q1)

285 **happely** happily (haply Q1; compare IV.ii.42)

287 **Mutiny. Whose** mutiny, whose

291 **them. And** them, and

311 **Seat. The** seat, the

314 **Wife.** wife;

321 **right** rank

322 **Night-cape** nightcap (Q1)

II.ii.   5 **Addition** addiction (mind Q1)

II.iii.   27 **Stope** stoup

52 **carous'd.** carous'd

64 **Heaven** God (Q1)

74 **Heaven** God (Q1)

77 **Germaine** German

96 **And** Then (Q1)

102 **Heav'n's** God's (Q1)

132 **his Prologue** the prologue (Q1)

145 **Island,** island:
146 **well:** well,
148 **Zouns** 'Zounds
164 **Fie, fie** God's will
173 **Turks?** Turks,
174 **Ottamites.** Ottamites?
182 **thee?** thee. (Q1)
188 **Odds.** odds; (Q1)
195 **Noted. And** noted, and (Q1)
197 **thus,** thus
198 **Opinion,** opinion
210 **If I once stir** Zouns, if I stir (Q1)
224 **This** Thus (Q1)
234 **Least** Lest (Q1; so also in IV.i.211, IV.ii.33)
236 **then** the (Q1)
243 **report,** report.
263 **Heaven** God (Q1)
275 **Looser** loser (Q1)
278 **, then** than (so also in IV.ii.174)
279 **Brains?** brains!
299 **Beasts.** beasts!
300 **Why? But** Why, but (Q1)
308 **hartily** heartily (Q1)
317 **Ingredient** ingredience (Q1)
322 **Drunk?** drunk!
324 **I** I'll (Q1)
328 **Devotement** denotement
340 **protest** protest,
    and, and
348 **Villain?** villain, (Q1)
349 **Advise** advice (Q1)
356 **Sin:** sin, (Q1)
374 **en-mash** enmesh (Q1)
382 **Patience?** patience!
387 **hath** hast (Q1)

III.i.   5 MUSICIAN [1] MUSICIAN (so also in III.i.7, 9, 15, 19)
           29 **Quillets,** quillets.

III.ii.   3 **Works,** works;

III.iii.   25 **Boord** board
           38 **your** you (Q1)
           50 **Ay sooth** Yes, faith (Q1)
           68 **on?** on.
              What? What,
              Cassio? Cassio,

69   **woing** wooing (Q1)
71   **Part, to** part? To
72   **Trust me** By'r lady (Q1)
80   **Waight** weight
86   **strait** straight (Q1)
92   **he** you (Q1)
99   **Indeed?** Indeed!
108 **Counsaile** counsel (Q1; compare II.i.166, IV.ii.92)
109 **Of** In (Q1)
     Indeed? Indeed!
110 **contract,** contract
125 **Certaine** Certain
127 **this?** this.
132 **that:** that
     free free to (Q1)
133 **False?** false,
146 **conceits** conjects (Q1)
166 **soundly** strongly (Q1)
167 **Poor,** Poor
     Content, content
170 **Heaven** God (Q1)
172 **Jealousy;** jealousy?
175 **Is to** Is once to (Q1)
177 **exufflicate** exsufflicate
     blow'd blown (Q1)
178 **Jealious** jealous (compare III.iii.193, 313; III.iv.29,
     30, 93, 149, 151–53, 176; V.ii.339)
197 **Heaven** God (Q1)
206 **too** to (compare III.iii.276, III.iv.92)
211 **Trust me,** I'faith (Q1)
212 **your** my (Q1)
217 **which** as (Q1)
253 **Quantities** qualities (Q1)
     learn'd learned (Q1)
255 **Iesses** jesses
264 **Appetites?** appetites!
267 **to** of (Q1)
272 **False, false, O** then (Q1)
     mock'd mocks
279 **Why** Faith (Q1)
282 *Exit.* This stage direction is normally delayed until
     after line 283, where it usually reads '*Exit [with
     Othello].*'
298 **Handkerchief.** handkerchief? (Q1)
302 **No: but** No, faith, (Q1)
334 **this?** this. (Q1)

352 **borne** born (so also in III.iv.31, 154; IV.ii.67)
367 **My** Her (Q2)
385 **Super-vision** supervisor (Q1)
389 **boulster** bolster
418 **'Tis IAGO** 'Tis (Q1)
419 **IAGO And** And (Q1)
424 **Wive's** wife's (so also in III.iii.427)
429 **it was** that was (Q1)
465 **a-part** apart (Q1)

III.iv.
  2 **lyes** lies (compare III.iv.6, 9, 13)
 14 **out?** out,
 27 **Cruzadoes** crusadoes (Q1)
 72 **sow'd** sew'd
 75 **Indeed,** I'faith (Q1)
 77 **Heaven** God (Q1)
 86 **mis-gives** misgives
 89 **OTHELLO ... Time.** Most editions insert two half-lines from Q1: 'DESDEMONA I pray talk me of Cassio. / OTHELLO The handkercher.'
 91 **In sooth** I'faith (Q1)
106 **Intirely** Entirely
147 **indited** indicted
157 **here about** hereabout
161 **is't** is it (Q1)
162 **Indeed,** I'faith (Q1)
164 **What?** What,
168 **prest** press'd
172 **Friend,** friend;
178 **in good troth** by my faith
179 **Chamber,** chamber.
189 **Night?** night. (Q1)

IV.i.
 31 **Why,** Faith (Q1)
 47 **works,** work (Q1)
 48 **chast** chaste (so also in IV.i.74)
 49 **ho?** ho!
    Lord? Lord!
 80 **resulting** unsuiting (Q1)
 90 **marry** marry,
 98 **Cloath** clothes (Q1)
104 **conserve** conster (Q1)
110 **Dow'r** power (Q1)
    speed? speed! (speed. Q1)
113 **indeed** i'faith (Q1)
120 **ye** you (Q1)

121 **marry** marry her (Q1)
Customer; customer?
124 **they laugh** laugh (Q1)
125 **Why** Faith (Q1)
goes that you goes you shall (Q1)
137 **and falls** and, by this hand, falls (Q1)
140 **Iesture** gesture
163 **If** 'An (Q1; so also in IV.i.164)
169 **Yes,** Faith (Q1)
174 **Iago.** Iago? (Q1)
182 **Woman?** woman!
199 **Condition?** condition! (condition. Q1)
206 **me?** me!
208 **Officer?** officer!
242 **Trust me** By my troth (Q1)
274 **breath** breathe (Q1)
280 **his** this (Q1)

IV.ii.
14 **requit** requite (Q1)
43 **and moving** unmoving (Q1)
55 **there** there,
58 **thence,** thence!
59 **Cestern** cistern
62 **I here** Ay, here
64 **Oh I,** O, ay,
97 **Madam?** madam. (Q1)
123 **And** all (Q1)
137 **Heavens** Heaven (Q1)
152 **them,** or them in (Q2; not in Q1)
158 **'Whore',** 'whore'.
167 **Meat,** meat.
172 **dafts** daff'st (doffst Q1)
173 **Devise** device
176 **it.** it;
180 **and** for
193 **Nay** By this hand (Q1)
200 **Solicitation.** solicitation;
204 **I:** Ay, (compare I.iii.36)
230 **Accident.** accident;
233 **removing** removing of (Q1)
236 **do.** do?
250 **wast.** waste

IV.iii.
12 **bid** bade (bad Q1; compare I.iii.131)
Father, faith
22 **shrowd** shroud
24 **Barbary,** Barbary;

	25	**love:** love,
	26	**Willow, Willow;**
	39	**singing** sighing (Q2)
	40	**Sycamour** sycamore
	47	**high** hie (compare V.i.34)
	68	**In** Good (Q1)
	69	**In** By my (Q1)
	70	**done** done't (done it Q1)
	74	**why** 'Ud's pity (Q1)
	91	**despight** despite
	95	**Sowre** sour
	98	**is:** and is. And
	104	**Heaven** God
V.i.	1	**Bark** bulk (Q1)
	22	**But** Be't
		heard hear
	32	**Wrong, wrong!**
	33	**Deer** dear (Q1)
	34	**highs** hies (Q1; compare IV.iii.47)
	35	**For** Forth (Q1)
	37	**ho?** ho! (ho, Q1)
	43	**come:** come? (come, Q1)
	47	**Do** Did (Q1)
	60	**inhumane** inhuman
	62	**Town?** town!
	67	**is't** is it (Q1)
	69	**Gentlemen,** gentlemen!
	85	**Roderigo?** Roderigo!
		Yes, 'tis O Heaven, (Q1)
	88	**Gratiano?** Gratiano! (Gratiano, Q1)
	93	**said,** said:
	100	**Gentlemen** Gentlewoman (Q1)
	102	**if** an' (Q1)
	106	**What is** What's (Q1)
	108	**Roderigo,** Roderigo
V.ii.	5	**Alablaster** alabaster
	10	**thy Light** thine (Q1)
	22	**Tears:** tears.
	32	**by:** by.
	33	**Heavens** Heaven
		fore-fend, forfend!
	39	**rowle** roll
	44	**nether-** nether
	50	**Soul:** soul!
	58	**O Heaven** Then Lord (Q1)

65　makes makest (Q1)
78　Strumpet: strumpet!
81　if an'
84　Lord? Lord!
　　ho? ho!
　　Lord? Lord!
88　ho? ho!
　　Lord? Lord!
94　No, No.
96　Wife: wife!
99　Moon; moon,
104　What's . . . now? This question is usually placed after
　　'Enter Aemilia.'
110　Venetian, Venetian
114　murder'd murdered (Q1)
115　Alas! O Lord (Q1)
123　hear heard (Q1)
125　Hell, hell:
127　Folly: folly, (Q1)
138　World, world
150　Day: day!
　　Heart, heart.
152　worst: worst!
159　help: help!
194　Uncle, uncle;
198　him: him,
200　Turn: turn,
211　Heaven God (Q1)
　　Powres God (Q1)
212　Come, Zouns (Q1)
217　Woman. woman? (Q1)
222　steal't steal it (Q1)
235　without, without;
243　Moor, Moor;
272　Sight: sight!
286　cursed damned (Q1)
296　Body. body? (Q1)
310　Interim nick (Q1)
315　it but it (Q1)
316　Purpose, purpose
341　Judean Indian (Q1)
364　aboord aboard

OTHELLO

NAMES OF THE ACTORS

DUKE OF VENICE
BRABANTIO, a Senator; Father to Desdemona
Other SENATORS

GRATIANO, Brother to Brabantio ⎱ Two Noble
LODOVICO, Kinsman to Brabantio ⎰ Venetians

DESDEMONA, Daughter to Brabantio; Wife to Othello
OTHELLO, the Moor

CASSIO, an honourable Lieutenant
IAGO, an Ancient (Ensign); a Villain
AEMILIA, Wife to Iago
RODERIGO, a gull'd Gentleman
MONTANO, Governor of Cyprus
GENTLEMEN of Cyprus
SAILORS
BIANCA, a Courtesan
CLOWN

OFFICERS
MESSENGER
HERALD
MUSICIANS
ATTENDANTS

I.1   The opening scene takes place at night on a street in Venice.

1   **Tush** a mild expletive. Like many of the play's oaths, it appears in the 1622 Quarto text but is omitted from the 1623 Folio version of *Othello*, which was evidently prepared in accordance with a 1606 statute prohibiting the use of profanity. Like most modern editions, the Everyman Shakespeare restores many of the oaths expurgated from the Folio text.
    never tell me don't speak to me any further about it.

2   **had my Purse** had access to my money. Roderigo has been paying Iago as an agent to help him woo the daughter of a wealthy Venetian. A *Purse* was a pouch tied with 'Strings' (line 3).

3   **shouldst . . . this** should be aware of what we've been discussing. Apparently Roderigo has just learned that the woman whose love he has sought is now in the arms of another suitor. In due course we will learn that Roderigo's successful rival has eloped with Desdemona, the child of a Senator named Brabantio.

4   **'Sblood** by God's blood (a reference to the Crucifixion).
    hear me listen to what I'm trying to tell you.

5   **abhor** shun; retreat in revulsion or horror from.

6   **him** We soon discover that Iago and Roderigo are speaking of Othello, a General who has promoted an officer other than Iago to serve as his Lieutenant.

7   **Great . . . City** statesmen of weighty influence.

9   **Off-capp'd to him** removed their caps respectfully as they came to him on Iago's behalf. The Quarto prints 'Oft-capt', with the suggestion that Iago's advocates approached the General on numerous occasions. A *Suit* is an entreaty or request, a petition.

10   **Price** value, merits.
    worse a Place lower a rank.

11   **as . . . Purposes** with the haughtiness of one who feels he can afford to disregard the opinions and appeals of important dignitaries.

12   **Evades . . . Circumstance** puts them off with overblown military jargon. *Bumbast* (bombast) is cotton stuffing to pad a quilt or garment.

ACT I

Scene 1

Enter Iago and Roderigo.

RODERIGO Tush, never tell me, I take it much
    unkindly
  That thou, Iago, who hast had my Purse
  As if the Strings were thine, shouldst know of
    this.
IAGO 'Sblood, but you'll not hear me. If ever I
  Did dream of such a matter, abhor me.
RODERIGO   Thou toldst   5
  Me thou didst hold him in thy Hate.
IAGO   Despise
  Me if I do not. Three Great Ones of the City,
  In personal Suit to make me his Lieutenant,
  Off-capp'd to him: and by the Faith of Man
  I know my Price, I am worth no worse a Place.   10
  But he, as loving his own Pride and Purposes,
  Evades them, with a bumbast Circumstance,
  Horribly stuff'd with Epithets of War,
  And in Conclusion non-suits my Mediators.
  For 'Certes,' says he, 'I have already chose   15
  My Officer.' And what was he?

---

13 **Epithets of War** military jargon.

14 **non-suits** puts out of suit (literally, makes suit-less or naked);
    refuses. Compare line 8.

15 **Certes** certainly, in truth ('Forsooth', line 17).

17   **Arithmatician**   arithmetical theoretician, a man with no
      practical expertise ('Practice', line 25) other than his
      manipulation of numbers.

19   **A Fellow ... Wife**   Iago probably means that Cassio is more
      like a peace-loving housewife at her spinning wheel (line 22)
      than a manly soldier in the field. In Shakespeare's principal
      source for *Othello*, the character corresponding to Cassio is
      married.

21   **devision of a Battaile**   devising (deploying) of a battalion for
      battle.

22   **bookish Theorique**   theory derived solely from reading.

23   **Wherein ... propose**   in which the prattling Senators can
      discourse. Most editions follow the Quarto here and print
      toged (wearing togas).

25   **Practice**   experience. But *Practice* can also refer to cunning or
      manipulation. See I.iii.100–2.

26   **had th' Election**   was singled out for the position. *Election* can
      function as a theological term for salvation (selection as one
      of God's chosen vessels); compare Cassio's comments in
      II.iii.102–13, and see the related treatment of the concept in
      The Merchant of Venice, II.ix.3.

27   **Rhodes, Cyprus**   Mediterranean islands that the Venetians had
      fought to win and defend from the Muslim Turks.

28   **Christen'd**   Christian; under the aegis of baptised magistrates,
      and thus part of the European realm referred to as
      'Christendom'.

29   **Be-lee'd**   becalmed (by having another ship cut off its supply of
      wind), with slackened sails.

30   **Counter-caster**   accountant (casting, or calculating, sums by
      means of metal counters); another term for 'Debitor and
      Creditor' (line 29).

31   **God ... Mark**   God defend us [by blessing those who employ
      the sign or mark of the Cross to ward off evil].

32   **Auncient**   ancient, ensign (standard-bearer) or aide-de-camp.
      Moorship plays sardonically on 'Worship', an honorific for a
      social superior. In this play the distinction between the Moors
      (Arab invaders of Spain and North Africa) and the Negroid
      peoples of Africa is largely obliterated.

Forsooth, a great Arithmatician,
One Michael Cassio, a Florentine,
A Fellow almost damn'd in a fair Wife,
That never set a Squadron in the Field,   20
Nor the devision of a Battaile knows
More than a Spinster. Unless the bookish
   Theorique:
Wherein the tongued Consuls can propose
As masterly as he. Mere Prattle, without
Practice, is all his Soldiership. But he,   25
Sir, had th' Election; and I, of whom his Eyes
Had seen the Proof at Rhodes, at Cyprus, and
On other's grounds, Christen'd and Heathen,
   must be
Be-lee'd and calm'd by Debitor and Creditor.
This Counter-caster, he, in good time, must his   30
Lieutenant be, and I, God bless the Mark,
His Moorship's Auncient.
RODERIGO   By Heaven, I rather would have been
   his Hangman.
IAGO   Why, there's no Remedy. 'Tis the Curse of
   Service;
Preferment goes by Letter, and Affection,   35
And not by old Gradation, where each Second
Stood Heir to th' First. Now Sir, be judge your
   self
Whether I in any just Term am affin'd
To love the Moor?

35–36 **Preferment ... Gradation** advancement (promotion) is
        determined by influence and favouritism rather than by
        traditional procedures based on seniority.

38   **just Term** respect based on justice.
       affin'd both (a) bound, attached, and (b) related. Iago goes on
        (lines 55–57) to describe an affinity with the Moor. *Affin'd*
        derives from the Latin *finis*, end, and it can thus carry
        'destined' as one of its implications.

40   **follow him**   Roderigo means 'be loyal to him'. Iago will give the phrase two different meanings: (a) pretend to serve him, and (b) follow his example by doing what he would do in my situation.

41   **serve . . . him**   get even by turning the tables on him.

44   **Knee-crooking**   curtsying. Compare *Hamlet*, III.ii.63–69, where the Prince derides 'candied' flatterers who 'crook the pregnant Hinges of the Knee / Where Thrift may follow Fawning.' Here *Knave* means (a) servant, rather than (b) villain.

45   **doting . . . Bondage**   foolishly enamoured of his subservient position.

47   **naught but Provender**   nothing more than the food required to keep him functioning like an obedient beast of burden.
            cashier'd   discharged. Iago puns on the name and expertise of the 'Arithmatician' Othello has selected; by choosing Cassio, the General has cast off Iago's own 'Service' as if it were of no more 'Price' than a worn-out 'Counter'.

48   **Whip me**   whip [for me]. Iago uses a colloquial formula known to grammarians as an 'ethic dative' or 'ethical dative'.

49   **trimm'd . . . Duty**   attired in all the appearance and expressions of dutiful obeisance.

52   **lin'd their Coats**   prospered, by stuffing their apparel with wealth. Compare lines 11–14. *Throwing* (line 51), casting, anticipates lines 71–72.

53   **Do themselves Homage**   treat themselves, rather than their supposed 'Masters' (line 42), with due respect.
            Soul   spirit; the assertion of a real man's 'peculiar End' (line 59), his personal interest and ambition.

61–62 **The . . . extern**   the inborn (genuine) motives and shapes of my will in my outward behaviour. *Complement* means 'compliant manners', both (a) those that accord with decorum, and (b) those that flatter others.

64   **Daws**   jackdaws, small crow-like birds, also known as choughs. Antonio alludes to their prating stupidity in *The Tempest*, II.i.247–48, when he says 'I myself could make / A Chough of as deep Chat.'

RODERIGO   I would not follow him then.

IAGO   O Sir, content you.   40
   I follow him to serve my Turn upon him.
   We cannot all be Masters, nor all Masters
   Cannot be truly follow'd. You shall mark
   Many a duteous and Knee-crooking Knave
   That, doting on his own obsequious Bondage,   45
   Wears out his Time, much like his Master's Ass,
   For naught but Provender, and when he'd old
     cashier'd.
   Whip me such Honest Knaves. Others there are
   Who, trimm'd in Forms, and Visages of Duty,
   Keep yet their Hearts attending on themselves,   50
   And, throwing but Shows of Service on their
     Lords,
   Do well thrive by them; and when they have lin'd
     their Coats
   Do themselves Homage. These Fellows have some
     Soul,
   And such a one do I profess my self.
   For, Sir, it is as sure as you are Roderigo,   55
   Were I the Moor, I would not be Iago:
   In following him, I follow but my self.
   Heaven is my Judge, not I for Love and Duty,
   But seeming so, for my peculiar End:
   For when my outward Action doth demonstrate   60
   The native Act and Figure of my Heart
   In Complement extern, 'tis not long after
   But I will wear my Heart upon my Sleeve
   For Daws to peck at; I am not what I am.

65 **fall** Roderigo probably means 'full', the word to be found in the Quarto. But *fall* (which, like *foll*, may have been a dialectal pronunciation of *full*) suggests that Othello's 'Fortune' may be setting him up for a fall.

Thick-lips a slur on Othello's negroid features.

owe possess. But Roderigo's phrasing is a reminder that those who appear to own a 'Fortune' often 'owe' it as well, since it can be taken away just as easily as it has been acquired. Compare *Macbeth*, I.iv.10–11.

66 **carry't thus** pull it off this way. Roderigo's expression can also function in a literal sense, with the implication that Othello is toting a 'Fortune' like the men described earlier as either lining their coats (line 52) or serving as beasts of burden (line 46). Meanwhile Roderigo's racial innuendo evokes the image of an African warrior with a ready spear.

67 **make after him** either (a) pursue Othello, or (b) rouse the father of Othello's bride.

68 **Incense** enflame. Iago's verb anticipates lines 75–76.

69 **though . . . dwell** even though he now occupies a lush paradisal setting.

70 **plague . . . Flies** irritate him with an infestation similar to that visited on Pharaoh and the Egyptians; see Exodus 8:20–24. Compare III.iii.175–78, IV.ii.64–65.

71 **chances of Vexation** random disturbances.

72 **As . . . Colour** as may diminish some of its lustre, attractiveness. Iago is probably hinting at two genital senses: (a) male 'blood' (arousal), and (b) female 'collar'. Here as elsewhere, *loose* can mean both (a) lose, and (b) loose, release, relinquish.

74 **timorous Accent** terrified and terrifying tone, 'terrible Summons' (line 81).

75 **by . . . Negligence** at night when someone has been negligent. Iago implies that Desdemona's father has been insufficiently watchful, with the result that Othello has penetrated his defences and started a fire in the 'Troy' under Brabantio's supervision.

79 **Bags** moneybags. Compare lines 1–3.

81 **Reason** basis. *Reason* could be pronounced in a way that echoed *raising*, and that sense will soon prove pertinent; see the note to line 151.

RODERIGO   What a fall Fortune does the Thick-
    lips owe   65
  If he can carry't thus?
IAGO   Call up her Father.
  Rouse him, make after him, poison his Delight,
  Proclaim him in the Streets. Incense her
    Kinsmen,
  And though he in a fertile Climate dwell,
  Plague him with Flies: though that his Joy be
    Joy,   70
  Yet throw such chances of Vexation on't
  As it may loose some Colour.
RODERIGO   Here is her Father's House, I'll call
    aloud.
IAGO   Do, with like timorous Accent, and dire Yell,
  As when, by Night and Negligence, the Fire   75
  Is spied in populous Cities.
RODERIGO   — What ho: Brabantio, Signior Brabantio,
    ho.
IAGO   Awake: what ho, Brabantio. Thieves, Thieves.
  Look to your House, your Daughter, and your
    Bags,
  Thieves, Thieves.   80

            Brabantio at a Window.

BRABANTIO   What is the Reason of this terrible
    Summons?
  What is the matter there?
RODERIGO   Signior, is all
  Your Family within?
IAGO   Are your Doors lock'd?
BRABANTIO   Why? Wherefore ask you this?

84 **'Zounds** [by] God's wounds (an oath referring to the Crucifixion of Christ).
rob'd both (a) robed (in your nightshirt), and (b) robb'd. Like the Folio, the Quarto spells this word with one *b*. Compare line 103, where both texts print *robbing*.

85 **your . . . burst** your citadel has been breached. *Gown* probably refers to Brabantio's dressing gown, but it plays on *rob'd* (line 84) to hint at his senatorial robe.

87 **black Ram** Iago compares Othello to the kind of beast who would be most likely to rape a 'white Ewe' (line 88).
tupping both (a) topping, covering, and (b) ramming. *Very* means 'truly', 'precisely'.

88 **Ewe** female sheep. Iago is punning on *you*, continuing the notion that Brabantio's daughter, his pure 'Heart', is 'half [his] Soul' (lines 85–86). Compare *The Tempest*, IV.i.3, where Prospero refers to Miranda as 'a third of mine own Life'.
snorting snoring. Iago's phrasing hints at the snorting of a farm animal, such as a bull or a ram.

89 **Devil** Since the Devil was frequently depicted as black, Iago implies that the 'Ram' who has stolen Brabantio's daughter is Evil incarnate. Lines 86–90 allude to two of Zeus's erotic exploits, (a) his taking the form of a bull to woo Europa, and (b) Io's being transformed into a heifer after Hera, Zeus's wife, found out about her husband's desire for this unfortunate maiden.

92 **what are you?** what is your identity?

94 **charg'd** commanded.
haunt hover.

97 **distemp'ring Draughts** intoxicating beverages. To be 'distempered' was to have one's temper (self-governance) subverted or thrown off balance by an unruly will or by an excess of one of the humours, the four elements (substances) that were thought to comprise all matter.

98 **Knavery** villainous trickery. Most editions adopt the Quarto's *bravery*, defiance.

99 **start** startle, disturb.

100 **be sure** rest assured.

101 **My . . . Place** my aroused passions and my influential position.

104 **Grange** solitary farmhouse in an unprotected rural setting. Compare lines 66–68, 74–80.

IAGO   'Zounds, Sir, y'are rob'd,
  For shame put on your Gown; your Heart is burst,   85
  You have lost half your Soul. Even now, now,
  Very now, an old black Ram is tupping your
  White Ewe. Arise, arise, awake the snorting
  Citizens with the Bell, or else the Devil
  Will make a Grandsire of you. Arise, I say.   90
BRABANTIO   What, have you lost your Wits?
RODERIGO   Most reverend Signior,
  Do you know my Voice?
BRABANTIO   Not I: what are you?
RODERIGO   My name is Roderigo.
BRABANTIO   The worser Welcome.
  I have charg'd thee not to haunt about my Doors.
  In honest Plainness thou hast heard me say,   95
  My Daughter is not for thee. And now in Madness,
  Being full of Supper and distemp'ring Draughts,
  Upon malicious Knavery, dost thou come
  To start my Quiet.
RODERIGO   Sir, Sir, Sir.
BRABANTIO   But thou must needs be sure,   100
  My Spirits and my Place have in their Power
  To make this bitter to thee.
RODERIGO   Patience, good Sir.
BRABANTIO   What tell'st thou me of Robbing? This
    is Venice:
  My House is not a Grange.
RODERIGO   Most grave Brabantio,
  In simple and pure Soul, I come to you.   105
IAGO   'Zounds, Sir, you are one of those that will

---

105   **simple**   innocent, guileless.

106   **'Zounds**   by God's wounds. Like the oath in line 84, this word
      appears only in the Quarto text.

107   **if . . . you** even if the Devil himself entreated you to do so.

110   **Barbary** a spirited breed from Arabia, often referred to simply as a 'barb'. Compare IV.iii.24–31. *Cover'd* (line 109) echoes line 87 and anticipates III.iii.386.
      Nephews grandsons (from the Latin *nepotes*).

111   **neigh** answer (defy you with 'nay') in the language of horses ('Coursers'). See the second note to line 88.

112   **Gennets for Germaines** small Spanish horses (jennets) for cousins (germans), blood relatives.

113   **profane** irreverent, filthy-talking.

115–   **making . . . Backs** Iago alludes profanely to the biblical
16   teaching that a husband and wife are 'one flesh' (Genesis 2:24, Ephesians 5:31).

117   **Thou . . . Senator** Brabantio's *Thou* is the familiarity of address that conveys contempt. Iago's respectful *You* in reply is a polite warning to the old man that his dignity as a 'Senator' is being threatened, not by a suitor he distrusts but by an officer to whom he has given both hospitality and unlimited access to his daughter.

118   **This . . . answer** you'll be held accountable for this.

120   **Pleasure** will, preference.
      wise knowing, well-advised.
      Consent Like *Pleasure*, this word hints at the activity described in lines 115–16 and echoes *cunnus*, the Latin term for the female genitalia. In the next line *partly* continues the innuendo. See *All's Well That Ends Well*, II.v.65–67, for similar wordplay on *part*; and see II.ii of the same play for an indication of the suggestiveness of phrases such as 'answer any thing' (line 119).

122   **odd Even** Roderigo probably means 'midnight', when the two extremities of Day (at odds with Night) are equidistant from the most 'dull' (dark and quiet) part of the night. Compare II.iii.126–28.

124   **of common Hire** available to all comers. Compare *Hamlet*, I.ii.72–74, for a related use of *common*.
      Gundelier gondolier (the pole-man of a Venetian gondola).

126   **and your Allowance** and something you have permitted. *Knave* (servingman) echoes lines 44, 98.

127   **saucy** audacious, insolent.

not serve God, if the Devil bid you. Because we
come to do you Service, and you think we are
Ruffians, you'll have your Daughter cover'd
with a Barbary Horse, you'll have your Nephews   110
neigh to you, you'll have Coursers for Cousins,
and Gennets for Germaines.

BRABANTIO   What profane Wretch art thou?

IAGO   I am one, Sir, that comes to tell you, your
Daughter and the Moor are now making the Beast   115
with two Backs.

BRABANTIO   Thou art a Villain.

IAGO   You are a Senator.

BRABANTIO   This thou shalt answer. I know thee,
    Roderigo.

RODERIGO   Sir, I will answer any thing. But I
    beseech you,
If't be your Pleasure, and most wise Consent   120
(As partly I find it is), that your fair
    Daughter,
At this odd Even and dull Watch o'th' Night,
Transported with no worse nor better Guard,
But with a Knave of common Hire, a Gundelier,
To the gross Clasps of a lascivious Moor: 125
If this be known to you, and your Allowance,
We then have done you bold and saucy Wrongs.
But if you know not this, my Manners tell me,
We have your wrong Rebuke. Do not believe
That from the Sense of all Civility   130
I thus would play and trifle with your
    Reverence.

128– **my . . . Rebuke**   my sense of etiquette tells me, you have
29   wronged us with an undeserved reprimand.

130 **from . . . Civility**   in defiance of all the decorum of polite
    society.

132 **Leave** permission to leave your custody.

133 **hath . . . Revolt** has committed a shocking act of rebellion [defying both your authority and society's norms of proper behaviour]. Here as in line 125 *gross* means both (a) enormous, and (b) coarse, foul.

134 **Wit** intelligence, sensitivity (as in line 91). But see *As You Like It*, IV.i.175–81, for a genital sense.

135 **extravagant** vagabond, unruly; 'wheeling' beyond his prescribed limits like a planet roving out of its proper orbit. Here *Stranger* means 'foreigner', 'alien'.

136 **here and every where** In *Hamlet*, I.v.149, the Prince uses the Latin phrase from which this expression derives; both there and here it suggests a demonic ability to disregard normal boundaries.

136– **Straight . . . self** immediately resolve any doubts you may have
37 about what I am telling you. *Straight* and *satisfy* are both words that suggest the 'saucy Wrongs' (line 127) Othello is being accused of committing.

140 **Strike . . . Tinder** strike a spark with a tinder-box to reignite the household fires.

141 **Taper** candle, torch.
  People servants.

142 **Accident** chance occurrence.

143 **oppresses** overburdens.

145 **meet . . . Place** fitting, nor appropriate to my position.

146 **producted** produced; led forth.

148 **How . . . Check** no matter how this causes him to be chafed (galled) and restrained (checked) with a rebuke. Iago may be playing on *check* in the sense that pertains to chess.

149 **with Safety cast him** rid itself of him (like an expendable knight or pawn on the chessboard) without putting its own security at risk.

150 **loud** urgent, clamorous.

Your Daughter (if you have not given her Leave,
I say again) hath made a gross Revolt,
Tying her Duty, Beauty, Wit, and Fortunes
In an extravagant and wheeling Stranger,   135
Of here and every where. Straight satisfy
Your self. If she be in her Chamber, or
Your House, let loose on me the Justice of
The State for thus deluding you.
BRABANTIO — Strike on the Tinder, ho.   140
Give me a Taper; call up all my People.
This Accident is not unlike my Dream,
Belief of it oppresses me already.
Light, I say, Light.   *Exit.*
IAGO   — Farewell: for I must leave you.
It seems not meet, nor wholesome to my Place   145
To be producted, as if I stay I shall,
Against the Moor. For I do know the State,
How ever this may gall him with some Check, *can't get rid of him*
Cannot with Safety cast him: for he's embark'd *Iago can't side against him*
With such loud Reason to the Cyprus Wars,   150
Which even now stands in Act, that for their
   Souls

---

151 **Which ... Act** on which 'the State' (Senate) is even now
      deliberating. The expression *stands in Act* can apply with
      equal force to 'the Cyprus Wars' that are already in
      preparation, if not in progress. Iago's phrasing can also refer
      to the 'Act' in which, he implies, the Moor 'now stands' in *his*
      'gross Revolt'. Here as in line 81, *Reason* hints at *raising*;
      compare 'Excitements of my Reason and my Blood' in
      Hamlet, IV.iv.55, and see *The Merchant of Venice*,
      III.v.76–81.

152   **Fadom**   fathom (a six-foot measure of depth). Iago refers to Othello's weight in Venetian military affairs (as measured by the depth of the water a ship of his bulk would displace).

155   **Life**   livelihood, occupational security.

156   **show . . . Love**   appear to be his faithful ensign (see the note to line 32) and carry his banner aloft.

157   **That**   so that.

158   **Sagittary**   the name of an inn. The name derives from the zodiacal sign in which Sagittarius the Archer is depicted shooting his bow. Sagittarius was a Centaur (a beast with the body of a horse and the head and torso of a man), a creature proverbially associated with unbridled lust. Sagittarius' expertise with an arrow is not unrelated to the kind of 'raised Search' that Iago believes to be under way at the Sagittary. In *The Comedy of Errors*, I.ii.9, a comparable inn is named the Centaur.
    raised Search   the search party you are able to arouse.

S.D.   **Night-gown**   dressing gown. See the notes to lines 84, 85.

161   **what's . . . Time**   what remains of my now wretched lifespan. *Bitterness* (line 162) echoes lines 101–2.

164   **Who . . . Father?**   In view of all the griefs that fatherhood entails, who would willingly take on such a burden?

166   **Past Thought**   beyond my capacity to conceive of it.
    moe   more. *Raise* (line 167) echoes lines 81, 150 (see the note to line 151), and 158.

169   **Treason . . . Blood**   both (a) unruliness of the passions, and (b) treachery at the hands of one's own offspring. Compare *The Merchant of Venice*, III.i.37–44.

170–   **Fathers . . . act**   From now on, fathers, put no faith in what
71   your daughters' manner would lead you to believe is on their minds. As the actor playing Brabantio speaks this line, he is probably meant to look towards the theatre audience.

171   **Charms**   magical spells.

172–   **the . . . abus'd**   the mentality and behaviour proper to youthful
73   innocence may be deceived and misused.

Another of his Fadom they have none
To lead their Business. In which regard,
Though I do hate him as I do Hell Pains,
Yet for Necessity of present Life   155
I must show out a Flag, and Sign of Love,
Which is indeed but Sign. That you shall
    surely find him,   *all fake*
Lead to the Sagittary the raised Search:
And there will I be with him. So farewell.   *Exit.*

Enter Brabantio in his Night-gown,
with Servants and Torches.

BRABANTIO   It is too true an Evil. Gone she is,   160
And what's to come of my despised Time
Is naught but Bitterness. Now, Roderigo,
Where didst thou see her? — Oh unhappy Girl.   *apostrophe*
— With the Moor, say'st thou? Who would be
    a Father?
How didst thou know 'twas she? Oh she
    deceives me   165
Past Thought. What said she to you? — Get moe
    Tapers:
Raise all my Kindred. — Are they married, think
    you?
RODERIGO   Truly I think they are.
BRABANTIO   Oh Heaven, how got
She out? Oh Treason of the Blood.
— Fathers, from hence trust not your Daughters'
    Minds   170
By what you see them act. — Is there not Charms,   *Magic*
By which the Property of Youth and Maidhood
May be abus'd? Have you not read, Roderigo,
Of some such thing?
RODERIGO   Yes Sir: I have indeed.

175 **Oh . . . her** Brabantio's attitude towards Roderigo has changed dramatically; an unwelcome intruder has now become a prospective son-in-law. Here, as frequently elsewhere (see lines 163–64, 168–69), the Folio spelling suggests a moan or groan that is more intense than the vocative *O* to be found in contexts where simple direct address is indicated; see V.i.30–31, where the Folio employs both *Oh* and *O*. Unlike most of today's editions, Everyman normally reproduces the *O/oh* forms to be found in the printing adopted as copy-text for each passage.

176 **Some . . . another** Some of you go in one direction, others in another.

178 **discover** both (a) find, and (b) dis-cover (see the note to line 110), disclose.

178– **I think . . . me** I think I can lead you to him if you are willing
79   to assemble a party of armed men and accompany me there. *Guard* recalls line 123.

182 **of might** of sufficient strength [to subdue this villain]. Most editions follow the Quarto and print *of night* here.

183 **I will . . . Pains** I will show you that I can properly reciprocate your efforts on my behalf. *Pains* echoes line 154.

I.ii   This scene takes place at the Sagittary.

1   **trade** transactions.

2   **very stuff** the essential substance. Compare the use of *very* in I.i.87.

3   **contriv'd** deliberate or premeditated.

4   **to . . . service** to meet my needs, serve my turn. Compare I.i.41, 48–52, 57, 107–12.

5   **yerk'd** struck (here meaning 'jabbed' or 'stabbed'); jerked.

6   **prated** clamoured uncontrollably. Compare I.i.24–25.

7   **scurvy** vile (literally, scabby), contemptuous.
    provoking defiant (calling for a response from any man who would preserve his honour).

8   **Godliness** grace, religious duty.

9   **I did . . . him** I could barely resist retaliating; it was hard for me to leave him unharmed. The words *hard* and *forbear* carry hints of the kinds of bearing up that Othello and Desdemona stand accused of. See the notes to I.i.66, 87, 115–16, 136–37, 151, 152, 166.

BRABANTIO   – Call up my Brother. – Oh would you
   had had her.   175
  – Some one way, some another. – Do you know
Where we may apprehend her, and the Moor?
RODERIGO   I think I can discover him, if you please
To get good Guard, and go along with me.
BRABANTIO   Pray you lead on. At every House I'll
   call   180
(I may command at most) 'Get Weapons, ho,
And raise some special Officers of might.'
On, good Roderigo, I will deserve your Pains.   *Exeunt.*

                        ↖reward

Scene 2

Enter Othello, Iago, Attendants, with Torches.

IAGO   Though in the trade of War I have slain Men,
Yet do I hold it very stuff o'th' Conscience
To do no contriv'd Murder: I lack Iniquity
Sometime to do me service. Nine or ten times
I had thought t' have yerk'd him here under the
   Ribs.   5
OTHELLO   'Tis better as it is.
IAGO   Nay, but he prated,
And spoke such scurvy and provoking Terms
Against your Honour, that with the little
   Godliness
I have, I did full hard forbear him. But
I pray you, Sir, are you fast married?   10
Be assur'd of this, that the Magnifico

---

10   **fast**   (a) indissolubly (not merely engaged), with wordplay on
      (b) quickly. Iago may be asking whether Othello's marriage
      has already been consummated.

11   **Magnifico**   powerful Venetian noble.

12–14 **and . . . Duke's**   and has at his command a powerful voice, to all intents and purposes the same two-vote authority the Duke himself enjoys. See I.iii.214–15 for an ironic echo of 'a Voice . . . as double as the Duke's'.

14 **divorce you**   see that your union is severed.

15 **Restraint or Grievance**   restriction or penalty (based on a 'Grievance', a formal complaint in a court of justice), short of having your marriage annulled (line 14).

16 **enforce it on**   assure that it is enforced.
Cable   latitude, scope. We would now say 'give him rope'.

17 **his Spight**   whatever his malice leads him to.

18 **the Signory**   the governing oligarchy of Venice (the Duke and the Senate).

19 **out-tongue**   speak more forcibly than. Compare I.i.23, 150.
know   be disclosed.

21 **promulgate**   make public (from *provulgate*, the word in the Quarto text).

22 **Royal Siege**   royalty (literally, regal seats or thrones). Compare *Measure for Measure*, IV.ii.103, and for a different meaning, 'stool' in the excremental sense, see *The Tempest*, II.ii.115.
Demerits   Othello means 'merits'; but demerits could also mean 'offences', and that sense is compatible with what Iago has said in I.i.147–53.

23 **speak, unbonneted**   proclaim themselves without bonneting (removing their caps) to anyone as a sign of deference. Compare I.i.9.

26 **unhoused**   unconfined, free-ranging. See I.i.135–36.

27 **Circumscription**   encircling constraints; confinement.

28 **Sea's worth**   Othello is probably thinking of the 'sunken Wrack and sum-less Treasuries' (*Henry V*, I.ii.165) to be found on the bottom of the ocean.

29 **raised**   roused. See the second note to I.i.166.

31 **Parts**   qualities and merits. See the third note to I.i.120.

33 **Janus**   the two-faced God of Doorways; his temple was open only in wartime. It is, of course, appropriate that a character who has said 'I am not what I am' (I.i.64, a sacrilegious echo of Exodus 3:14, where the God of Moses says 'I am that I am') should swear in the name of the equivocating god Janus.

Is much belov'd, and hath in his Effect
A Voice potential as double as
The Duke's. He will divorce you. Or put upon
You what Restraint or Grievance the Law, with
   all   15
His Might to enforce it on, will give him
   Cable.
OTHELLO   Let him do his Spight; my Services   *he is very powerful;*
Which I have done the Signory   *did a lot for the*
Shall out-tongue his Complaints. 'Tis yet to   *city*
   know
(Which, when I know that Boasting is an Honour, I   20
Shall promulgate) I fetch my Life and Being   *- background is royalty*
From Men of Royal Siege. And my Demerits
May speak, unbonneted, to as proud a Fortune
As this that I have reach'd. For know, Iago,
But that I love the gentle Desdemona,   25
I would not my unhoused free Condition
Put into Circumscription, and Confine,
For the Sea's worth. But look, what Lights come
   yond?

    Enter Cassio, with Officers and Torches.

IAGO   Those are the raised Father, and his Friends.
You were best go in.
OTHELLO   Not I: I must be found.   30
My Parts, my Title, and my perfect Soul
Shall manifest me rightly. Is it they?
IAGO   By Janus, I think no.   *Allusion (Mythological)*
OTHELLO   The Servants of
The Duke's? And my Lieutenant? – The goodness of
The Night upon you, Friends, what is the News?   35
CASSIO   The Duke does greet you, General, and he

37 **Requires** needs, desires.
haste, post-haste 'Instant' (line 38).

39 **as . . . divine** so far as I can determine.

40 **a . . . Heat** a matter of great urgency. Cassio's phrasing
provides an inadvertent reminder of another 'Business of some
Heat' that will soon be called to the Duke's attention.

41 **sequent** successive.

43 **rais'd and met** awakened and brought together. Compare line
29.

44 **hotly call'd for** Cassio means 'urgently sought after'. But what
Iago has disclosed in the previous scene charges this phrase
with an additional implication that Cassio little suspects.

46 **several Quests** separate search parties. Like 'Lodging' and
'search you out' (lines 45, 47), this phrase is suggestive in the
present context. *Lodging* anticipates III.iv.7–13.

49 **what . . . here?** what brings him here? *Makes* echoes I.i.67,
114–16.

50 **to night** tonight. But here as elsewhere the Renaissance
rendering of this expression permits additional
interpretations.
Carract Iago refers to a carrack (a large trading ship of the sort
deployed by the Spanish and Portuguese to transport
treasures). But the word Iago uses was also a variant of both
carat (a measure referring to the purity of gold or to the
weight of a precious gem) and *character* (an engraved letter or
symbol). Iago's verb, *boarded*, implicitly compares Othello to
both a pirate and a successful seducer.

51 **lawful Prize** booty the state will allow him to retain.
made a made man, in two senses: (a) rich for life (as in *A
Midsummer Night's Dream*, IV.ii.18), and (b) fixed up
sexually (in the sense of *made* that remains current today).
Iago's phrasing plays on line 49.

53 **Marry** truly, indeed. This expression derived from an oath
referring to the Virgin Mary. Here, and frequently elsewhere,
Shakespeare employs it in a context relevant to the more usual
modern sense of *marry*.
Have with you I'll accompany you.

56 **He . . . Intent** he means you ill. Iago's phrasing keeps us
mindful that, from Brabantio's perspective, Othello 'comes to
bad intent', both as a formerly welcome guest in the Senator's
household and as the seducer who has apparently just taken
his daughter's maidenhead.

Requires your haste, post-haste Appearance,
    even on
The Instant.
OTHELLO   What is the matter, think you?
CASSIO   Something
From Cyprus, as I may divine:
It is a Business of some Heat. The Galleys   40
Have sent a dozen sequent Messengers
This very Night, at one another's Heels:
And many of the Consuls, rais'd and met,
Are at the Duke's already. You have been hotly
    call'd for,
When, being not at your Lodging to be found,   45
The Senate hath sent about three several Quests,
To search you out.
OTHELLO   'Tis well I am found by you:
I will but spend a Word here in the House,
And go with you.   [*Exit.*]
CASSIO   Auncient, what makes he here?
IAGO Faith, he to night hath boarded a Land
    Carract: I metaphor (pirate taking over a vessel)   50
If it prove lawful Prize, he's made for ever.
CASSIO   I do not understand.
IAGO   He's married.
CASSIO   To who?
IAGO   Marry, to —   pun

                [*Enter Othello.*]

                — Come, Captain, will you go?
OTHELLO   Have with you.
CASSIO   Here comes another Troop to seek for you.

Enter Brabantio, Roderigo, with Officers and Torches.

IAGO   It is Brabantio: General, be advis'd,   55
    He comes to bad Intent.

58 **I am for you** I'll take you on. Iago is pretending to be
particularly at odds with Roderigo, since he has just told
Othello that Roderigo was the one who aroused Brabantio.

59 **Keep up** put back in their scabbards. Othello's cool command
suggests that he was not speaking idly when he said that his
'Parts', 'Title' and 'perfect Soul' would 'manifest [him] rightly'
(lines 31–32). *Keep up* echoes the suggestive imagery of lines
9, 10, 29, 40–47, 56.

60 **Years** the reverence due to aged dignity. Othello's phrasing
alludes to the literal meaning of *Senator* (elder); meanwhile it
implicitly emphasizes that Brabantio's 'Years' have not been
sufficient to command respect from the 'Thief' who has
persuaded Desdemona to marry him without her father's
permission.

62 **stow'd** hidden away, like pirated cargo.

63 **enchaunted her** used magical powers to overpower her free
will.

64 **For . . . Sense** for I'll appeal to everything that accords with
common sense [in asking you]. The phrase *things of Sense*
carries unintended genital implications.

66 **tender** young, innocent, malleable, and vulnerable, like the
'tender plant' described in Isaiah 53:2.

67 **opposite to** opposed to, uninterested in.

68 **wealthy . . . Nation** Brabantio's description of the Venetian
youth whom Desdemona has 'shunn'd' suggests a delicate
refinement in stark contrast with the 'foul' coarseness he
associates with Othello. The Folio's *Dearlings* is a more
'tender' word than the Quarto's *darlings*, of which it is a
variant.

69 **t' . . . Mock** to make herself the scorn of everyone in her
civilized society.

70 **Run . . . Guardage** escape from her protective guardian.
Guardage echoes I.i.179. Meanwhile *sooty*, coal black,
conveys the idea that Othello's 'Bosom' is not only dark but
'foul' (line 62, anticipating line 73), both dirty and wicked.

71 **to . . . delight** something to be feared rather than attracted to
and delighted in. *Delight* recalls I.i.67.

OTHELLO   — Holla, stand there.

RODERIGO   — Signior, it is the Moor.

BRABANTIO   — Down with him, Thief.

IAGO   You, Roderigo? Come Sir, I am for you.

OTHELLO   Keep up your bright Swords, for the Dew
   will rust them.
— Good Signior, you shall more command with
   Years   60
Than with your Weapons.

BRABANTIO   Oh, thou foul Thief, where hast thou
   stow'd my Daughter?
Damn'd as thou art, thou hast enchaunted her,
For I'll refer me to all things of Sense,
If she in Chains of Magic were not bound,   65
Whether a Maid so tender, fair, and happy,
So opposite to Marriage that she shunn'd
The wealthy curled Dearlings of our Nation,
Would ever have, t' incur a general Mock,
Run from her Guardage to the sooty Bosom   70
Of such a thing as thou: to fear, not to
   delight?
Judge me the World, if 'tis not gross in Sense
That thou hast practis'd on her with foul
   Charms,

72–73 **Judge ... Charms** let the world decide if it is not obvious that
      you have tricked her with evil spells. Here the primary
      meaning of *gross* is 'manifest', but the word could also mean
      'foul'; compare I.i.125, 133. One might have expected
      Brabantio to accuse Othello of a breach of custom, if not of
      law (for even courting a gentleman's daughter without his
      consent); instead the old man's accusations are limited to
      Othello's presumed means of beguilement. *Sense* echoes line
      64.

74   **Abus'd**   both (a) deceived, and (b) misused. Compare line 78.
      Minerals   drugs extracted from non-organic matter.

75   **weakens Motion**   subdues free agency (narcotizes) and
      emotion.
      disputed on   subjected to investigation by those with expertise
      in such matters.

76   **probable . . . thinking**   provable, indeed so obvious that you
      can touch it. Compare line 72.

77   **attach**   arrest, 'apprehend'.

79   **Arts inhibited**   prohibited skills.
      out of warrant   unwarranted; illegal, forbidden.

82   **of my inclining**   who support me. *Inclining* can refer to the kind
      of virile disposition that portends a 'direct Session' (line 86);
      compare *Macbeth*, IV.iii.74–76, and *Measure for Measure*,
      III.i.414–15.

84   **Whether**   where (the word in the Quarto), whither.

85–87 **till . . . answer**   until, under the usual legal procedures and in
      accord with the court calandar, you are brought to trial. For
      senses of *Fit* and *answer* that are pertinent to Brabantio's
      grievance against Othello, see the bawdy exchanges between
      the Countess and the Clown (Lavatch) in *All's Well That
      Ends Well*, II.ii.

88   **satisfi'd**   responded to. With unruffled aplomb, Othello informs
      Brabantio that he is subject to a high calling.

93   **Counsel**   consultation with members of his ruling council. See
      the note to I.i.120.

95   **an idle Cause**   an inconsequential case. *Cause* and *case* both
      derive from the Latin word *causa*.

97   **as . . . own**   as if it had happened to them.

98   **may . . . free**   are permitted to go unimpeded and unpunished.

99   **Bond-slaves . . . be**   we will cease to be a civilized European
      society. Brabantio is so obsessed with Othello's skin colour,
      and the stereotypes he associates with it, that he is unable to
      focus on what would be at issue if the man who has eloped
      with his daughter were not a Moor.

Abus'd her delicate Youth with Drugs or
   Minerals

[handwritten: Serious charges (Black Magic)]

That weakens Motion. I'll have't disputed on,   75
'Tis probable and palpable to thinking;
I therefore apprehend and do attach thee,
For an Abuser of the World, a Practiser
Of Arts inhibited, and out of warrant.
  – Lay hold upon him, if he do resist   80
Subdue him at his Peril.

OTHELLO   Hold your Hands,
Both you of my inclining and the rest.
Were it my Cue to fight, I should have known it
Without a <u>Prompter</u>. – Whether will you that I go
To answer this your Charge?

[handwritten: Theatrical Metaphor]

BRABANTIO   To Prison, till   85
Fit time of Law and course of direct Session
Call thee to answer.

OTHELLO   What if I do obey?
How may the Duke be therewith satisfi'd,
Whose Messengers are here about my side,
Upon some present Business of the State,   90
To bring me to him.

OFFICER   'Tis true, most worthy Signior,
The Duke's in Counsel, and your Noble Self
I am sure is sent for.

BRABANTIO   How? The Duke in Counsel?
In this time of the Night? Bring him away;
Mine's not an idle Cause. The Duke himself,   95
Or any of my Brothers of the State,
Cannot but feel this Wrong as 'twere their own:
For if such Actions may have Passage free,
Bond-slaves and Pagans shall our Statesmen be. *Exeunt*.

I.iii This scene takes us to the Council chamber where the Duke and his advisers are deliberating over the Turkish threat to Venetian security.

1 **Composition** coherence, consistency.
this News this new collection of reports.

2 **Credit** credibility.
disproportioned lacking in agreement.

5 **jump** coincide, agree.
a just Accompt an exact account (count or number).

6–7 **As ... Difference** since in those instances where reports are based on estimates it is to be expected that there will be variances. *Aim* means 'rough calculation'. *Cases* echoes I.ii.95.

9 **Nay ... Judgement** No, you're right: the information we have is good enough for us to rely upon as a basis for sound adjudication of the evidence.

10–12 **I ... Sense** I do not draw assurance from the small discrepancies in the reports so much as I derive fear from the central point in which they concur [that the Turks are heading for Cyprus].

14 **The ... Rhodes** [now] the fleet the Turks have prepared is headed [instead] for Rhodes. *Makes* recalls I.ii.49.

17 **How ... Change?** How do you construe this change of direction?

18 **By ... Reason** by any test that accords with rational analysis. *Reason* echoes I.i.150–51.
a Pageant a [mere] display, a decoy.

19 **To ... Gaze** to distract our attention with a deception.

20 **Importancy** importance, strategic significance.

23 **So ... it** and he may with an easier 'debate' (a less risky 'Question' or battle) carry off an attack on it than on Rhodes. Compare the phrasing in I.i.65–66.

Scene 3

Enter Duke, Senators, and Officers.

DUKE   There's no Composition in this News
That gives them Credit.
1 SENATOR   Indeed, they are disproportioned:
My Letters say a hundred and seven Galleys.
DUKE   And mine a hundred forty.
2 SENATOR   And mine two hundred.
But though they jump not on a just Accompt,   5
(As in these Cases where the Aim reports,
'Tis oft with Difference), yet do they all
   confirm
A Turkish Fleet, and bearing up to Cyprus.
DUKE   Nay, it is possible enough to Judgement:
I do not so secure me in the Error   10
But the main Article I do approve
In fearful Sense.
SAILOR *within*   What ho, what ho, what ho.

Enter Sailor.

OFFICER   A Messenger from the Galleys.
DUKE   Now? What's the Business?
SAILOR   The Turkish Preparation makes for Rhodes:
So was I bid report here to the State,   15
By Signior Angelo.   *Exit.*
DUKE   – How say you by this Change?
1 SENATOR   This cannot be
By no assay of Reason. 'Tis a Pageant
To keep us in false Gaze, when we consider
Th' Importancy of Cyprus to the Turk;   20
And let our selves again but understand
That as it more concerns the Turk than Rhodes,
So may he with more facile Question bear it,

24-26 **For ... in**   because it is not in such a condition of defensive
readiness, but is lacking in the military capabilities that shield
Rhodes.

27   **unskilful**   incompetent as a strategist.

28   **leave ... first**   delay taking advantage of an opportunity to
attack a relatively vulnerable target, especially when it is the
objective of primary significance to him.

29-30 **Neglecting ... profitless**   passing over a chance to win an easy
victory, and one that would benefit him, in order to arouse a
dangerous adversary and wage a battle that wouldn't gain
him anything of consequence even if he should unexpectedly
win it.

31   **in all Confidence**   we can be sure.

33   **Ottamites**   Turks. Their territory became known as the
Ottoman Empire. The phrase *Reverend and Gracious* refers to
the Duke and the Senators rather than to the 'Ottamites'.
Compare *Hamlet*, III.i.40, where *gracious* is usually construed
as an honorific for the King.

35   **injointed ... Fleet**   joined with a fleet that departed later. The
Messenger's verb prepares the way for Brabantio's accusation
that Othello has 'injointed' with Desdemona. Compare I.ii.43.

36   **I**   both (a) I, and (b) Ay.

37-38 **re-stem ... Course**   steer back in the opposite direction.

38   **bearing ... Appearance**   conducting their affairs openly and
with no further camouflage. The Messenger's report confirms
the soundness of the judgement the Duke and the First
Senator have brought to bear upon the situation. Unlike the
Senator introduced in the first scene, they come across as
calm, collected, and objective, even when confronted with a
national crisis that forces them into council in the middle of
the night. The Messenger's phrasing is a reminder that
Othello will soon be bearing *his* 'Purposes' with 'frank
Appearance' towards the assembled Senate. *Bearing* echoes
line 23.

40   **Servitor**   subordinate, servant [in charge of Cyprus].

41-42 **With ... him**   with unqualified devotion informs you thus and
hopes that you will take his word for the peril Cyprus is in.
The phrase *free Duty* echoes *frank Appearance* (line 38).

45   **post ... dispatch**   proceed as expeditiously as you can.
Compare I.ii.36-38.

For that it stands not in such Warlike Brace
But altogether lacks th' Abilities   25
That Rhodes is dress'd in. If we make Thought
   of this,
We must not think the Turk is so unskilful
To leave that latest which concerns him first,
Neglecting an Attempt of Ease and Gain
To wake and wage a Danger profitless.   30
DUKE   Nay, in all Confidence he's not for Rhodes.
OFFICER   Here is more News.

Enter a Messenger.

MESSENGER   The Ottamites, Reverend and Gracious,
   Steering with due Course toward the Isle of
    Rhodes,
   Have there injointed them with an after Fleet.   35
I SENATOR   I, so I thought: how many, as you
   guess?
MESSENGER   Of thirty Sail: and now they do
   re-stem
   Their backward Course, bearing with frank
    Appearance
   Their Purposes toward Cyprus. Signior Montano,
   Your trusty and most valiant Servitor,   40
   With his free Duty recommends you thus
   And prays you to believe him.   [*Exit Messenger.*]
DUKE   'Tis certain then
   For Cyprus: Marcus Luccios, is not he
   In Town?
I SENATOR   He's now in Florence.
DUKE   Write from us
   To him; post post-haste, dispatch.   45
I SENATOR   Here comes Brabantio, and the valiant
   Moor.

Enter Brabantio, Othello, Cassio, Iago,
Roderigo, and Officers.

47   **straight** immediately. The Duke's adverb reinforces the suggestiveness of lines 24–26, 35; compare I.i.136–37, and see the note to I.ii.59.

49   **I . . . you** In view of the First Senator's announcement in line 46, the Duke's failure to greet the eminent Brabantio before he addresses Othello is an indication of everyone's preoccupation with the emergency at hand. The man of the hour receives the Duke's initial attention.

50   **We . . . to night** This statement could be construed as a mild rebuke: 'Why were you not to be found when we needed you?' It confirms the Officer's earlier comment that Brabantio has been 'sent for' (I.ii.93). And it calls attention to the fact that the Duke has just said nothing to 'Valiant Othello' about the 'three several Quests' (I.ii.46) that have been dispatched to seek *him* out. Despite his powerful 'Place' (line 52) in the Venetian hierarchy, Brabantio is being treated as if he were a person of little importance.

52   **ought** aught, anything. *Place* recalls I.i.10, 101–2; *Business* echoes I.ii.40, 89–90.

53–54 **nor . . . me** nor is it the matter that concerns Venice that seizes my attention. Brabantio's inability to see beyond his 'particular Grief' makes him appear unstatesmanlike and even a bit unpatriotic – anything but a grave Senator. *Rais'd* recalls I.ii.43.

55   **flood-gate and o'erbearing** Both adjectives evoke images of an overwhelming current of floodwater. But *o'erbearing* also hints at the 'Nature' of the supposed offence. Compare lines 23, 37–39.

60   **Mountebanks** quacks and charlatans. The overwrought Brabantio throws out another unprovable charge. Again the word he uses is unintentionally suggestive: *Mountebank* calls to mind the 'Barbary Horse' that Iago has charged with mounting Brabantio's daughter to make 'the Beast with two Backs' (I.i.110, 115–16). *Abus'd* recalls I.ii.73–74.

61   **prepost'rously** against nature (literally, with the normal positions reversed), a concept implicit in the notion of being 'cover'd' by a horse (see I.i.109–10) instead of riding it.

63   **Sans . . . not** without witchcraft would not be possible.

64   **Proceeding** The Duke's phrasing is an apt projection of the kind of crime Othello stands accused of. Here *ere* can mean both (a) before, and (b) e'er (ever). *Foul* echoes I.ii.62–75.

DUKE   Valiant Othello, we must straight employ
   you
  Against the general Enemy Ottoman.
  – I did not see you: welcome, gentle Signior,
  We lack'd your Counsel, and your Help to night.   50
BRABANTIO   So did I yours. Good your Grace, pardon
  me.
  Neither my Place nor ought I heard of Business
  Hath rais'd me from my Bed; nor doth the
   general Care
  Take hold on me. For my perticular Grief
  Is of so flood-gate and o'erbearing Nature   55
  That it engluts and swallows other Sorrows,
  And it is still it self.
DUKE   Why? What's the matter?
BRABANTIO   My Daughter, oh my Daughter!
SENATOR   Dead?
BRABANTIO   Ay, to me.
  She is abus'd, stol'n from me, and corrupted
  By Spells and Medicines bought of Mountebanks;   60
  For Nature so prepost'rously to err,
  Being not deficient, blind, or lame of Sense,
  Sans Witchcraft could not.
DUKE   Who ere he be that in this foul Proceeding
  Hath thus beguil'd your Daughter of her self,   65
  And you of her, the bloody Book of Law
  You shall your self read in the bitter Letter
  After your own Sense; yea, though our proper
   Son

---

65   **beguil'd . . . self**   deceived Desdemona into doing something
        incompatible with her true character.

67–68 **You . . . Sense**   you shall yourself read out, sentencing this
        offender to the severest penalty allowed by the law's strictest
        provisions. *Bitter* recalls I.i.162; *Sense* echoes lines 10–12, 62.

68–69 **though . . . Action**   even if my own son were the subject of your charge. Again the phrasing fits the context. See the note to I.i.151.

71   **Your . . . Affairs**   your special commission owing to the state's crisis.

73   **in . . . part**   on your own behalf. See the note to I.i.120.

77   **I . . . Daughter**   Othello implicitly admits to 'Offending' (line 79) a Senator he refers to unceremoniously as 'this Old Man'. See the notes to I.i.117, I.ii.56, 60.

79   **Head and Front**   utmost 'Extent' (line 80); compare line 64.

80   **Rude**   unpolished, rustic. Like Mark Antony, Othello depicts himself as 'a plain, blunt Man' (*Julius Caesar*, III.ii.215). But what he will proceed to do is tell 'a round unvarnish'd Tale' (line 89) that is anything but artless in the 'Magic' (line 91) of its effect. He will thus claim as 'lawful Prize' (I.ii.51) a daughter he has 'ta'en away' in what Brabantio rightly feels to be a 'Rude' (uncivilized) manner.

82   **Pith**   substance, strength.

83   **nine Moons wasted**   Othello probably means 'nine months ago'. But his phrasing also suggests that his 'Arms' are now nine-twelfths expended – that he is entering the final phase of his lifetime.

83–84 **us'd . . . Field**   been accustomed to doing their most valuable work on the field of battle. *Action* echoes lines 68–69.

86   **Broils and Battaile**   wars and army battalions.

87   **grace my Cause**   help my case (adorn it more appealingly).

Stood in your Action.

BRABANTIO   Humbly I thank your Grace,
Here is the Man; this Moor, whom now it seems   70
Your special Mandate for the State Affairs
Hath hither brought.

ALL   We are very sorry for't.

DUKE — What in your own part can you say to this?

BRABANTIO   Nothing, but this is so.

OTHELLO   Most potent, grave, and reverend Signiors,   75
My very noble and approv'd good Masters,
That I have ta'en away this Old Man's Daughter,
It is most true; true I have married her;
The very Head and Front of my Offending
Hath this Extent, no more. Rude am I in my
    Speech,   80
And little bless'd with the soft Phrase of Peace;
For since these Arms of mine had seven years'
    Pith,
Till now, some nine Moons wasted, they have
    us'd
Their dearest Action in the tented Field;
And little of this great World can I speak   85
More than pertains to feats of Broils and
    Battaile;
And therefore little shall I grace my Cause
In speaking for my self. Yet, by your gratious
    Patience,
I will a round unvarnish'd Tale deliver
Of my whole course of Love: what Drugs, what
    Charms,   90
What Conjuration, and what mighty Magic

---

88   **gratious**   gracious. The Folio spelling retains the link with the
        Latin *gratia*, most familiar from the prayer commencing *Ave
        Maria, gratia plena*, 'Hail, Mary, full of grace'. See the note to
        II.i.85.

89   **round**   open, direct, plain.

91   **Conjuration**   invoking of demonic spirits.

92   **withal**   with. *Proceeding* echoes line 64.

94   **her Motion**   any 'bold' (uninhibited) emotion or impulse she might feel. *Motion* recalls I.ii.73–75.

95   **in spight of**   despite; in defiance of. Lines 95–97 echo I.ii.62–71.

96   **Country**   the nation from which she hailed. Without realizing it, Brabantio alludes to the female 'Nature' that led Desdemona to 'fall in Love' with Othello; see the note to I.i.120, and compare the Prince's bawdy reference to 'Country Matters' in *Hamlet*, III.ii.122.

98   **imperfect**   deficient, 'maim'd'.

99   **confess**   believe, profess.

100–2 **must . . . be**   Brabantio means that a sound judgement will conclude that there must be other (demonic) explanations for such aberrant behaviour. *Practices* (tricks or cunning stratagems) recalls I.i.24–25, I.ii.73.

102   **vouch**   avouch, attest.

103   **powreful**   both (a) pourful (as in *Macbeth*, I.iii.96–98, I.v.28), and (b) powerful (as in *Macbeth*, IV.i.18).

104   **Dram**   an eighth of an ounce in apothecaries' weight.
      conjur'd . . . Effect   invoked (literally, sworn together) for this purpose. Like *cunning* (line 101), *conjur'd* echoes the Latin word for the presumed object of Othello's 'Practices'. See the note to I.i.120, and compare lines 90–93. *Effect* recalls I.ii.11–14.

107   **thin Habits**   superficial appearances. Here *Habits* means 'garments'. Compare the imagery in I.i.11–14, 48–53, 60–64, 109–10, 155–57, I.ii.25–28, I.iii.18–26.
      poor Likelihoods   implausible analogies; improbable explanations.

108   **modern Seeming**   commonplace, popular comparisons (conjectures). *Seeming* echoes I.i.58–59.
      prefer   present [as charges].

110   **forced Courses**   coercive measures.

(For such Proceeding I am charg'd withal)
I won his Daughter.

BRABANTIO   A Maiden never bold,
  Of Spirit so still, and quiet, that her Motion
  Blush'd at her self; and she, in spight of
    Nature,   95
  Of Years, of Country, Credit, every thing,
  To fall in love with what she fear'd to look
    on;
  It is a Judgement maim'd, and most imperfect,
  That will confess Perfection so could err
  Against all Rules of Nature, and must be driven   100
  To find out Practices of cunning Hell
  Why this should be. I therefore vouch again
  That with some Mixtures powreful o'er the
    Blood,
  Or with some Dram (conjur'd to this Effect)
  He wrought upon her.

DUKE   To vouch this is no Proof   105
  Without more wider and more overt Test
  Than these thin Habits, and poor Likelihoods
  Of modern Seeming, do prefer against him.

SENATOR   — But Othello, speak:
  Did you by indirect and forced Courses   110
  Subdue and poison this young Maid's Affections?
  Or came it by Request, and such fair Question
  As Soul to Soul affordeth?

112– **Or . . . affordeth?**   Or did you win her love by asking for it in
13   the course of such unforced dialogue as one person permits
      another in ordinary conversation? The tone of the Senator's
      question implies that Othello will be given the benefit of the
      doubt. Brabantio's far-fetched accusations have done nothing
      to 'grace' his own 'Cause' (line 87); instead they have made
      him seem so bigoted, irrational, and overbearing as to suggest
      that Othello obtained Desdemona's hand in the only way that
      would have been possible under the circumstances.

118 **onely** only, solely. The Elizabethan spelling is a reminder that this word derives from *one*.

120 **the Place** the inn where she may be found. *Place* recalls line 52.

122 **Blood** both (a) nature, passions (as in I.i.169), and (b) 'Breeding' (line 238), ancestry (see I.ii.21–22).

127 **Still** continually, always. So also in line 145. Othello's description of Brabantio's hospitality suggests that Othello is aware that he betrayed a kind host's trust. See the note to line 77.

128 **Battailes** both (a) battles, and (b) armies.

129 **have past** both (a) have in my past, and (b) have passed (experienced and surpassed).

131 **bad** bade. So also in line 162, and in II.i.155, IV.i.83, IV.iii.20.

132 **disastrous Chances** ill-starred happenings. *Chances* echoes I.i.71–72.

133 **moving Accidents** wrenching occurrences, stirring events. Compare line 94.

134 **i'th' . . . Breach** in life-threatening situations where openings had been forced in fortifications or battle-lines.

136 **Redemption** ransom. This word is a subtle reminder that Othello is not the pagan Brabantio has depicted in I.ii.99. Compare II.iii.355.

137 **Portance** comportment; bearing, behaviour. *Portance* echoes line 20; compare lines 23, 38–39, 54–56.

138 **Antars** antres; caves.
Desarts idle barren deserts or wildernesses. Othello's description of his adventures echoes a passage in Hebrews 11:32–40, where the pre-Christian heroes of the faith are described as having 'wandered in deserts, and in mountains, and in dens and caves of the earth' to obtain 'a good report'.

140 **Hint** (a) opportunity (from a verb, *hent*, meaning 'to seize or grasp'), (b) hint (cue), and (c) purpose.
Process way of proceeding.

142 **Anthropophagi** Greek for 'man-eaters'.

OTHELLO   I do beseech you,
  Send for the Lady to the Sagittary,
  And let her speak of me before her Father;   115
  If you do find me foul in her Report,
  The Trust, the Office, I do hold of you
  Not onely take away, but let your Sentence
  Even fall upon my Life.
DUKE   Fetch Desdemona hither.
OTHELLO — Auncient, conduct them: you best know
  the Place.   [*Exit Iago, with others.*]   120
  — And till she come, as truly as to Heaven,
  I do confess the Vices of my Blood;
  So justly to your grave Ears I'll present
  How I did thrive in this fair Lady's Love,
  And she in mine.
DUKE   Say it, Othello.   125
OTHELLO Her Father lov'd me, oft invited me,
  Still question'd me the Story of my Life,
  From Year to Year: the Battailes, Sieges,
    Fortune
  That I have past.
  I ran it through, even from my Boyish Days   130
  To th' very Moment that he bad me tell it,
  Wherein I spoke of most disastrous Chances:
  Of moving Accidents by Flood and Field,
  Of Hair-breadth Scapes i'th' imminent deadly
    Breach,
  Of being taken by the insolent Foe   135
  And sold to Slavery; of my Redemption thence,
  And Portance in my Traveller's History;
  Wherein of Antars vast, and Desarts idle,
  Rough Quarries, Rocks, and Hills whose Heads
    touch Heaven,
  It was my Hint to speak. Such was my Process,   140
  And of the Cannibals that each other eat,
  The Anthropophagi, and Men whose Heads
  Do grow beneath their Shoulders. These things
    to hear

146   **dispatch**   handle, deal with. Compare line 45.

149   **a pliant Hour**   an hour when she seemed likely to be compliant to my desire to tell her 'all my Pilgrimage' (line 151).

151   **dilate**   expand upon (see the note to line 265); relate in full detail. The word *Pilgrimage* is another echo of Hebrews 11; in verses 13–16 the author of that New Testament epistle says that those who 'died in faith' during previous eras were 'strangers and pilgrims on the earth' who sought 'a better country, that is, an heavenly'.

152   **Whereof**   of which.
        by Parcels   in bits and pieces.

153   **instinctively**   in such a way as to penetrate her consciousness thoroughly [so that she felt my sufferings as if they were her own]. Most editions adopt the Quarto's *intentively*.

154   **beguile her of**   steal from her. Compare lines 65 and 208.

157   **Kisses**   Most editions opt for the Quarto's *sighs*.

158   **passing strange**   surpassingly extraordinary. *Strange* often carries suggestions of the numinous (that which is so far beyond ordinary experience as to inspire awe). Desdemona's response, then, is not altogether different from what might have been expected if Othello had indeed used 'Witchcraft' (line 167) to impress her.

165   **past**   passed; overcome, surmounted (with a strong hint of the sense of *passing* in line 158). Compare line 129.

167   **onely**   only, solely. Here as elsewhere the spelling in the original texts suggests play on *one* (see the note to line 118), in this instance with a reminder of Othello's assertive 'one-liness'.

168   **witness it**   bear witness to it (with a tinge of the New Testament use of *witness* to describe a profession of faith).

171–   **Take . . . Hands**   The Duke acknowledges that Brabantio has
73   been wronged. But he goes on to say that the best way to deal with 'broken Weapons' is to recognize that even a 'mangled' implement is better than none at all.

Would Desdemona seriously incline;
But still the House Affairs would draw her
   hence: 145
Which ever as she could with haste dispatch,
She'd come again, and with a greedy Ear
Devour up my Discourse. Which I observing,
Took once a pliant Hour, and found good Means
To draw from her a Prayer of earnest Heart   150
That I would all my Pilgrimage dilate,
Whereof by Parcels she had something heard,
But not instinctively: I did consent,
And often did beguile her of her Tears
When I did speak of some distressful Stroke   155
That my Youth suffer'd. My Story being done,
She gave me for my Pains a World of Kisses:
She swore in faith 'twas strange, 'twas passing
   strange,
'Twas pitiful, 'twas wondrous pitiful.
She wish'd she had not heard it, yet she wish'd   160
That Heaven had made her such a Man. She
   thank'd me,
And bad me, if I had a Friend that lov'd her,
I should teach him how to tell my Story,
And that would woo her. Upon this Hint I spake:
She lov'd me for the Dangers I had past,   165
And I lov'd her that she did pity them.
This onely is the Witchcraft I have us'd.
Here comes the Lady: let her witness it.

      Enter Desdemona, Iago, Attendants.

DUKE   I think this Tale would win my Daughter
   too.
   – Good Brabantio,   170
Take up this mangled Matter at the best:
Men do their broken Weapons rather use
Than their bare Hands.
BRABANTIO   I pray you hear her speak?
If she confess that she was half the Wooer,

175 **bad** unjust, unmerited.

176 **Light** alight, fall.

177– **Do . . . Obedience?** Once again, Shakespeare has Brabantio
78 focus on a tangential issue. Instead of asking Desdemona
what her duty to her father *was*, he asks her whether she *now*
owes more obedience to her husband or to her father. *Confess*
echoes line 99.

181 **learn** teach. *Bound* (line 180) recalls I.ii.64–65.

182 **respect** love and obey. Behind Desdemona's remarks an
Elizabethan audience would have heard Exodus 20:12,
'Honour thy father and thy mother', a duty that would
normally have imposed on a child the necessity of obtaining
parental consent before marriage.

183 **hitherto** prior to now [nothing but].

185 **preferring you before** placing you ahead of. Desdemona
alludes to the wedding ceremony and to Genesis 2:24,
'Therefore shall a man leave his father and his mother, and
cleave unto his wife.' See the note to I.i.115–16. *Prefer* recalls
line 108.

186 **challenge** assert, claim.

189 **get it** beget it from my own flesh.

195– **For . . . them** for your elopement would make me turn tyrant
96 and hobble any other daughters I had. *Clogs* were heavy
blocks of wood; compare *All's Well That Ends Well*, II.v.59.

197 **like your self** in the way you would if you were more
father-like (like your true self) now.
lay a Sentence lay down (like a bricklayer) a statement of
principle (from the Latin *sententia*, maxim). The Duke
pointedly avoids the kind of sentence (punishment) that
Brabantio had earlier demanded.

198 **Grise** degree, step.

201 **By . . . depended** by accepting the worst that has happened,
despite the hopes we depended on to prevent it. *Past* (lines
200, 202) echoes lines 129, 165.

202 **Mischief** both (a) misfortune, and (b) harm, grievance.

203 **next** most immediate; quickest.

205 **Patience . . . makes** a patient bearing of Fortune's 'Injury' turns
that injury into a way of mocking Fortune [by showing her
that she has no real power to hurt us after all].

Destruction on my Head if my bad Blame   175
Light on the Man. — Come hither, gentle
  Mistress,
Do you perceive in all this Noble Company
Where most you owe Obedience?

DESDEMONA   My noble Father,
  I do perceive here a divided Duty.
  To you I am bound for Life and Education: 180
  My Life and Education both do learn me
  How to respect you. You are the Lord of Duty,
  I am hitherto your Daughter. But here's my
    Husband;
  And so much Duty as my Mother shew'd
  To you, preferring you before her Father,   185
  So much I challenge that I may profess
  Due to the Moor my Lord.

BRABANTIO   God be with you; I have done.
  — Please it your Grace, on to the State
    Affairs;
  I had rather to adopt a Child than get It.
  — Come hither, Moor;   190
  I here do give thee that with all my Heart
  Which, but thou hast already, with all my Heart
  I would keep from thee. — For your sake, Jewel,
  I am glad at Soul I have no other Child,
  For thy Escape would teach me Tyranny   195
  To hang Clogs on them. — I have done, my Lord.

DUKE   Let me speak like your self, and lay a
    Sentence,
  Which as a Grise, or Step, may help these Lovers
  Into your Favour.
  When Remedies are past, the Griefs are ended   200
  By seeing the Worst, which late on Hopes
    depended.
  To mourn a Mischief that is past and gone
  Is the next way to draw new Mischief on.
  What cannot be preserv'd, when Fortune takes,
  Patience her Injury a Mock'ry makes.   205

206 **The Rob'd** both (a) the person who has been robbed (suffered 'Mischief'), and (b) the person who nevertheless remains attired in a robe. Compare I.i.84, and see the note to line 107.

207 **He . . . Grief** [Whereas] the person who wastes away in unavailing grief ends up robbing himself. *Bootless* (to no avail) puns on *boot-less* (robbed of footwear).

209 **loose** both (a) let go, and (b) lose. Compare I.i.72.

210– **He . . . hears** the person who has no further burdens to carry
11 away than the relief that he has been acquitted has no difficulty accepting the moral. Brabantio is probably playing on two senses of *Sentence*: (a) sententious moralizing (see the note to line 197), and (b) sentences for crimes committed (with the implication that Othello is the man who should now be hearing the Duke pronounce a sentence rather than drawing 'Comfort' from the *sententiae* directed at Brabantio). See I.i.147–49. *Bears* echoes *bare* (line 173); compare lines 23, 38–39, 54–56. *Nothing* recalls line 74, and here as in III.iii.71–74 it hints at a genital sense, deriving from the notion that a woman either has 'no thing' or 'an O-thing'.

214– **These . . . Equivocal** These kinds of abstract generalizations,
15 whether they tell us how to respond to sweet fortune or to bitter, can be used to support any moral one chooses to apply at a given moment (as Brabantio has shown in lines 208–9). *Equivocal* (literally, speaking with two equal voices) recalls I.i.122 and I.ii.11–14.

222– **allowed Sufficiency** recognized ability. The phrase is a
23 reminder that Othello has been 'allowed' his 'Sufficiency'. See the note to III.iv.88, and compare IV.i.268–69.

223 **Opinion** both (a) [your] reputation, and (b) public confidence [in you].

224 **Mistress of Effects** determiner of decisions. *Effects* echoes line 104.
safer Voice securer (more confident) vote. Compare I.ii.11–14, and see the note to lines 214–15.

225 **slubber** slobber; smear over, sully.

226 **Gloss** sheen. *Gloss* often refers to an attractiveness that is specious, and here the word keeps us aware that under different circumstances the Duke might have been less disposed to gloss over the means Othello employed to obtain his 'new Fortunes'.

The Rob'd that smiles steals something from
   the Thief;
He robs himself that spends a bootless Grief.
BRABANTIO   So let the Turk of Cyprus us beguile,
We loose it not so long as we can smile:
He bears the Sentence well that nothing bears   210
But the free Comfort which from thence he
   hears;
But he bears both the Sentence and the Sorrow
That to pay Grief must of poor Patience
   borrow.
These Sentences, to Sugar or to Gall,
Being strong on both sides, are Equivocal.   215
But Words are Words, I never yet did hear
That the bruised Heart was pierced through the
   Ears.
I humbly beseech you proceed to th' Affairs of
   State.
DUKE   The Turk with a most mighty Preparation
makes for Cyprus. – Othello, the Fortitude of   220
the place is best known to you. And though we
have there a Substitute of most allowed
Sufficiency, yet Opinion, a more Sovereign
Mistress of Effects, throws a more safer Voice
on you. You must therefore be content to slubber   225
the Gloss of your new Fortunes with this more
stubborn and boist'rous Expedition.
OTHELLO   The Tyrant Custom, most grave Senators,
Hath made the flinty and steel Coach of War
My thrice-driven Bed of Down. I do agnize   230

---

227   **stubborn . . . Expedition**   harsh, painful emergency mission.

228   **The Tyrant Custom**   the life to which 'stubborn' (rough,
     unyielding) custom has subjected and inured me.

230   **thrice-driven**   much-winnowed (to sort out all but the softest
     down).
     agnize   acknowledge (with a suggestion that Othello feels most
     at home when he can *agonize*, suffer, to some degree).

231–
32 **A . . . Hardness** an innate eagerness to seek out hardship. Othello's phrasing recalls another kind of 'Hardness'. Compare I.ii.9.

234 **State** both (a) majesty, authority, and (b) seat of power (chair of state). Compare lines 15–16, 70–72, 188, and see I.i.137–39, 147–49, I.ii.87–91, 95–97.

235–
38 **fit . . . Breeding** fitting arrangements for my wife: such accommodations and attendance as will accord with her birth and upbringing. *Place* echoes line 120. *Fit* recalls I.ii.85–87.

239 **Why . . . Father's?** This speech is here rendered as it appears in the Folio, with the Duke couching a recommendation in the form of a question. In the Quarto (followed by most modern editions), the Duke says, 'If you please, be't at her father's.'

240 **recide** both (a) return (literally, fall back), and (b) reside.

243 **Unfolding** disclosure of my thoughts.
     prosperous favourable (capable of fostering prosperity in others).

244–
45 **a . . . Simpleness** a grant of favour to assist me in my new life as a woman bereft of paternal shelter.

247 **My . . . Fortunes** the directness and vehement disruptiveness with which I seized my own fortunes. So much for the quiet 'Maiden' Brabantio described in lines 93–97; compare I.i.170–71.

248 **subdu'd** both (a) subjected (as in I.ii.81), and (b) drawn away to (the original Latin sense). Desdemona's words imply that instead of being made more 'pliant' (line 149) and soft, her 'Heart' has acquired some of the 'Quality' (line 249) of Othello's martial discipline, a 'Hardness' (line 232) that makes her 'Valiant' (line 251) enough to 'trumpet' her 'Violence' (line 247) like a 'Captain's Captain' (II.i.74).

249 **Quality** nature, character, profession.

250 **I . . . Mind** I saw Othello's 'face' in the disposition he displayed. Compare lines 259–63.

251 **Parts** both (a) physical and mental attributes, and (b) deeds. Compare I.ii.31–32.

254 **Moth of Peace** both (a) insignificant mote, and (b) idle parasite.

255 **Rites** all of marriage's rights and rituals.

A natural and prompt Alacrity
I find in Hardness, and do undertake
This present Wars against the Ottamites.
Most humbly therefore bending to your State,
I crave fit Disposition for my Wife,   235
Due Reference of Place, and Exhibition,
With such Accommodation and Besort
As levels with her Breeding.

DUKE   Why at her Father's?

BRABANTIO   I will not have it so.

OTHELLO   Nor I.

DESDEMONA   Nor would I there recide,   240
To put my Father in impatient Thoughts
By being in his Eye. Most gracious Duke,
To my Unfolding lend your prosperous Ear,
And let me find a Charter in your Voice
T'assist my Simpleness.

DUKE   What would you, Desdemona?   245

DESDEMONA   That I did love the Moor, to live
   with him,
My downright Violence, and Storm of Fortunes,
May trumpet to the World. My Heart's subdu'd
Even to the very Quality of my Lord.
I saw Othello's Visage in his Mind,   250
And to his Honours and his Valiant Parts
Did I my Soul and Fortunes consecrate;
So that, dear Lords, if I be left behind
A Moth of Peace, and he go to the War,
The Rites for why I love him are bereft me   255
And I a heavy Interim shall support
By his dear Absence. Let me go with him.

OTHELLO   Let her have your Voice.
Vouch with me, Heaven, I therefore beg it not

256- **I . . . Absence** I will be required to bear up under a weighty
57   waiting period with nothing but his absence to assist me. Here
         dear means (a) costly (in the love I'll be deprived of), and (b)
         heartfelt. Voice (line 258) echoes line 224.

261– **the . . . Satisfaction** what remains of the youthful affections
62   (desires) in my largely dried-up sexual appetite.

265   **great Business** weighty affairs of state. But Othello's phrasing
      is also a reminder that his own 'great' (both large and
      enlarged) 'Business' is not completely 'defunct' (withered
      away). *Business* echoes lines 52–53, 269.

267   **seel** sew shut, seal over.

268   **My . . . Instrument** my acute and duty-bound vision and
      powers of military oversight.

269   **Disports** recreational pursuits.

270   **Helm** helmet.

271   **indign** disgraceful (the opposite of *dignified*).

272   **Estimation** esteem; honour, reputation.

274   **th' . . . Hast** the crisis that convened us demands that we
      respond with haste. But the Folio's *hast* can also be construed
      'has't', another reminder that Othello's own 'Affair'
      proclaims that 'he has it' as he and Desdemona 'privately
      determine' (line 273). *Affair* echoes line 218.

276   **to night** tonight. But the ambiguity in the Renaissance spelling
      will prove pertinent in more than one sense. See the note to
      I.ii.50. In the Quarto text (followed here by many modern
      editions) the equivalent of this statement ('You must hence to
      night') concludes the Duke's speech in lines 273–75.
      With . . . Heart Othello's answer portrays him as decisive and
      responsible. In the Quarto version of this moment,
      Desdemona replies to 'You must hence to night' with 'To
      night, my Lord?' and the Duke answers, 'This night.' Only
      then does Othello say, 'With all my heart.' In all likelihood
      the Folio's omission of the exchange between Desdemona and
      the Duke reflects an authorial decision to avoid having
      Desdemona appear too 'bold' (line 93) at this juncture.

279   **our Commission** the papers officially specifying the terms of
      your appointment.

280– **of . . . you** pertaining to the responsibilities you are now to
81   assume. *Quality* echoes line 249; *Respect* recalls line 182.

283   **Conveyance** escort, safekeeping on the journey.

287   **If . . . lack** if it is true that Virtue carries a beauty that gives
      pleasure. Compare I.ii.71.

To please the Palate of my Appetite,   260
Nor to comply with Heat, the young Affects
In my defunct and proper Satisfaction,
But to be free and bounteous to her Mind;
And Heaven defend your good Souls that you
    think
I will your serious and great Business scant   265
When she is with me. No, when light-wing'd Toys
Of feather'd Cupid seel with wanton Dullness
My speculative and offic'd Instrument,
That my Disports corrupt and taint my Business,
Let Housewives made a Skillet of my Helm,   270
And all indign and base Adversities
Make head against my Estimation.
DUKE Be it as you shall privately determine,
Either for her Stay or Going: th' Affair cries
    Hast,
And Speed must answer it.   275
SENATOR You must away to night.
OTHELLO   With all my Heart.
DUKE — At nine i'th' Morning, here we'll meet
    again.
   Othello, leave some Officer behind,
And he shall our Commission bring to you:
And such things else of Quality and Respect   280
As doth import you.
OTHELLO   So please your Grace, my Ancient,
A Man he is of Honesty and Trust:
To his Conveyance I assign my Wife,
With what else needful your good Grace shall
    think
To be sent after me.
DUKE   Let it be so: 285
Good night to every one. — And noble Signior,
If Virtue no delighted Beauty lack,

288 **Fair** (a) light-complexioned, (b) beautiful, and (c) good.
  Black (a) dark-complexioned, (b) ugly, and (c) evil.

290 **Look to her** keep a wary eye upon her. Compare Iago's words
  to Brabantio in I.i.79.

292 **her Faith** both (a) her fidelity to me, and (b) my faith in her.

294 **attend on her** be her personal attendant.

295 **And . . . Advantage** and follow me to Cyprus with them (a) as
  soon as possible, and (b) in the manner most in keeping with
  Desdemona's rank.

297 **wordly Matter** Othello distinguishes between the 'Matter' he
  and his bride will have time for now and what will have to be
  postponed till a later time. Many editions adopt the Quarto's
  worldly, in this passage.
  Direction guidance. Compare II.iii.4, 124–26.

298 **obey the Time** subordinate what we would 'privately
  determine' (line 273) to what our public roles require of us.
  Spend echoes I.ii.48–49.

303 **incontinently** both (a) immediately (as in IV.iii.10), and (b)
  impulsively, without any attempt to contain or restrain my
  distraught passions.

307 **Prescription** both (a) a time-honoured right, and (b) a doctor's
  prescribed treatment.

314 **Guinea Hen** Iago's dismissive term for a loose woman (spelled
  Gynney in the Folio, and *Ginny* in the Quarto).
  change exchange. But another sense, 'transform' (here
  dehumanize), is also conceivable.

317 **fond** both (a) infatuated [with Desdemona], and (b) foolish.

318 **Virtue** 'Power' (line 326). Virtue derives from the Latin *vir*,
  man, and *virtus*, manliness. Compare lines 287–88.

319 **A Fig** both (a) something of no consequence, and (b) 'a fig on
  it', an expletive frequently accompanied by a rude gesture.

321 **Wills** capacities for choice, for self-determination. *Will* is also a
  word for 'desire', and it can refer to the genitalia of either
  'Gender' (line 324).

322 **Nettles** a dry, prickly herb, frequently treated as a symbol of
  lechery (the 'carnal Stings' referred to in line 333).

Your Son-in-law is far more Fair than Black.
SENATOR   Adieu, brave Moor, use Desdemona well.
BRABANTIO   Look to her, Moor, if thou hast Eyes
  to see:
  She has deceiv'd her Father, and may thee.   290
      Exit [with the Duke and the other Senators].
OTHELLO   My Life upon her Faith. – Honest Iago,
  My Desdemona must I leave to thee:
  I prythee let thy Wife attend on her,
  And bring them after in the best Advantage.   295
  – Come, Desdemona, I have but an Hour
  Of Love, of wordly Matter, and Direction
  To spend with thee. We must obey the Time.
      Exit [with Desdemona].
RODERIGO   Iago.
IAGO   What sayst thou, Noble Heart?   300
RODERIGO   What will I do, think'st thou?
IAGO   Why go to Bed and sleep.
RODERIGO   I will incontinently drown my self.
IAGO   If thou dost, I shall never love thee after.
  Why, thou silly Gentleman?   305
RODERIGO   It is Silliness to live, when to live
  is Torment; and then have we a Prescription to
  die, when Death is our Physician.
IAGO   Oh villainous: I have look'd upon the World
  for four times seven Years, and since I could   310
  distinguish betwixt a Benefit and an Injury I
  never found man that knew how to love himself.
  Ere I would say I would drown my self for the
  love of a Guinea Hen, I would change my
  Humanity with a Baboon.   315
RODERIGO   What should I do? I confess it is
  my Shame to be so fond, but it is not in my
  Virtue to amend it.
IAGO   Virtue? A Fig, 'tis in our selves that we
  are thus, or thus. Our Bodies are our Gardens,   320
  to the which our Wills are Gardeners. So that
  if we will plant Nettles, or sow Lettuce, set

322–   **set Hyssop**   plant a moist, fragrant herb associated (like lettuce)
23   with spiritual purification. In Psalm 51:7 David says, 'Purge
        me with hyssop, and I shall be clean; wash me, and I shall be
        whiter than snow.'
       Time   both (a) thyme, a herb that symbolized the value of
        finding the sweetness (spiritual nourishment) in adversity, and
        (b) time [for cultivation, as distinguished from 'idleness', line
        325].

324   **Gender**   type, genus.
       distract it   detract (literally, 'draw away') from its health.

326   **manured with Industry**   cultivated with conscientious labour.
        The literal meaning of *manure* is 'work with one's hands'.

327   **corrigible Authority**   ability to correct, control, or discipline.
        Lines 321–27 allude to such biblical passages as Hosea 8:7
        ('For they have sown the wind, and they shall reap the
        whirlwind') and Galatians 6:7–9 (an elaboration of the
        teaching that 'whatsoever a man soweth, that shall he also
        reap').

328   **Brain**   supervisory agency. Most editions adopt the Quarto's
        balance or emend to *beam*. *Reason* recalls line 18.

329   **poise**   counterbalance (on a pair of scales).

330   **Blood and Baseness**   passions and bestial desires. *Blood* echoes
        I.i.169, I.iii.103, 122.

331   **prepost'rous Conclusions**   perverted ends. Compare line 61.
        Here Iago uses *Conclusions* in its literal sense – comings
        together.

332   **raging Motions**   turbulent drives; overpowering impulses.
        Motions recalls lines 94, 133.

333   **unbitted**   unbridled (a horse not fitted with a bit).

334–   **Sect or Scion**   cutting (section) or graft from a tree of a
35   particular type or class (sect).

339   **blind**   too young to have their eyes open.

340   **knit**   knotted, tied. Compare I.ii.63–65, 99, I.iii.194–96,
        IV.ii.59–60.

341–   **Cables . . . Toughness**   cables of perpetual endurance. Compare
42   I.ii.16.

Hyssop, and weed up Time, supply it with one
Gender of Herbs, or distract it with many,
either to have it sterile with Idleness, or   325
manured with Industry, why the Power and
corrigible Authority of this lies in our Wills.
If the Brain of our Lives had not one Scale
of Reason to poise another of Sensuality, the
Blood and Baseness of our Natures would conduct   330
us to most prepost'rous Conclusions. But we
have Reason to cool our raging Motions, our
carnal Stings, or unbitted Lusts: whereof I
take this, that you call Love, to be a Sect or
Scion.   335

RODERIGO   It cannot be.

IAGO   It is merely a Lust of the Blood, and a
Permission of the Will. Come, be a Man: drown
thy self? Drown Cats, and blind Puppies. I have
profess'd me thy Friend, and I confess me knit   340
to thy Deserving, with Cables of perdurable
Toughness. I could never better steed thee
than now. Put Money in thy Purse; follow thou

---

342   **steed**   stead, help. The spelling in the original texts is a
        reminder that this was a homonym for the word meaning
        'horse'. Iago is 'steeding' Roderigo by (a) spurring on his
        sexual passion while pretending to counsel against lust, and
        (b) steering him the way a rider manipulates a mount.

343   **Put . . . Purse**   husband your financial resources [and bide your
        time patiently until Desdemona is again receptive to the gifts
        you entrust me to use as your go-between to woo her]. *Purse*
        recalls I.i.1–3.

344 **defeat thy Favour** de-feature (alter) your facial appearance.

349 **an answerable Sequestration** a similarly violent serverance as
its sequel. *Answerable* echoes lines 274–75; see the note to
I.ii.85–87.

353 **Locusts** the sweet-juiced fruit of the carob tree.

354 **Coloquintida** colocynth; a purgative, 'bitter apple'. *Bitter*
recalls lines 67–68; it also echoes *unbitted*, line 333.
change both (a) alter in her will (desire, preference), and (b)
exchange [casting off an older lover for a younger one].
Compare lines 314, 350–51, 356, 386.

358 **delicate** voluptuous, exquisite, ingenious, and delight-filled.
Compare I.i.67, I.ii.71, 74, I.iii.286–88.

360 **Sanctimony** a sacred ritual, 'a frail [vulnerable] Vow'.
Compare *The Tempest*, IV.i.13–19.

361 **erring Barbarian** Iago probably means that Othello is straying
from his native religion in adopting Christianity (compare
I.ii.99). But he also implies that the Moor has strayed from his
ordained course by wedding a 'super-subtle Venetian'. Here
subtle means both (a) refined, sophisticated, and (b) crafty.

362 **Wits** cunning stratagems. Like *Will* (see the note to line 321),
Wit can refer both to erotic desire and to the genitalia; see
Romeo and Juliet, I.iii.42. Compare I.i.91 and II.i.130–34.
Hard echoes lines 230–32.

364 **A . . . drowning** a pox on drowining (let drowning die of
syphilis).

365 **hang'd** Iago is referring both to another means of dying and
another means of 'dying' (achieving orgasm); see the note to
III.iii.27. See *Measure for Measure*, II.i.250 and IV.ii.41–56
for similar wordplay on *hanging* as a term for what Iago calls
'compassing [embracing] thy Joy' (line 366). Iago's jest is
inspired by the proverb 'He that is born to be hanged shall
never be drowned.'

366 **Joy** erotic delight. Compare I.i.70–72.

368 **fast to** loyally devoted (fixed) to. *Fast* recalls I.ii.10.

369 **depend . . . Issue** await (literally, hang on) the outcome.

372 **My . . . hearted** my case against him is rooted deep in my
heart. *Cause* recalls line 87. *Reason* (line 373) echoes lines
328–31.

the Wars, defeat thy Favour with an usurp'd
Beard. I say put Money in thy Purse. It cannot   345
be long that Desdemona should continue her Love
to the Moor – put Money in thy Purse – nor he his
to her. It was a violent Commencement in her, and
thou shalt see an answerable Sequestration: put but
Money in thy Purse. These Moors are changeable   350
in their Wills: fill thy Purse with Money.
The Food that to him now is as luscious as
Locusts shall be to him shortly as bitter as
Coloquintida. She must change for Youth: when
she is sated with his Body, she will find the   355
Errors of her Choice. She must have Change, she
must: therefore put Money in thy Purse. If thou
wilt needs damn thy self, do it a more delicate
way than Drowning. Make all the Money thou
canst. If Sanctimony, and a frail Vow, betwixt   360
an erring Barbarian and a super-subtle Venetian,
be not too hard for my Wits, and all the Tribe
of Hell, thou shalt enjoy her: therefore make
Money. A pox of drowning thy self, it is clean
out of the Way. Seek thou rather to be hang'd   365
in compassing thy Joy than to be drown'd and
go without her.

RODERIGO   Wilt thou be fast to my Hopes, if I
depend on the Issue?

IAGO   Thou art sure of me: go make Money. I have   370
told thee often, and I retell thee again, and
again, I hate the Moor. My Cause is hearted;
thine hath no less Reason. Let us be
conjunctive in our Revenge against him. If
thou canst cuckold him, thou dost thy self a   375
Pleasure, me a Sport. There are many Events
in the Womb of Time, which will be delivered.

---

374   **conjunctive**   joined together. See the third note to I.i.120.

378   **Traverse** Forward, march! Compare the metaphors in lines 342–43.

382   **betimes** early. So also in II.iii.342. *Lodging* (line 381) recalls I.ii.45–46.

383   **Go to** begone. *Go to* is usually an expression of disapproval, dismissal, derision, or incredulity.

386   **chang'd** transformed. See the note to line 354. Roderigo's final line (389) echoes Luke 18:18–23, where Jesus tells a rich young ruler to 'sell all that thou hast, and distribute unto the poor, and thou shalt have treasure in heaven; and come, follow me'. Unlike the youth in the Gospels, Roderigo heeds the advice of his 'saviour' and is converted; but he too ends 'very sorrowful'. Lines 384–86 occur only in the Quarto text; line 389 is unique to the Folio.

390   **my Fool my Purse** my foolish dupe my means of support. See the note to I.i.2.

391   **profane** misuse (a perversion of the usual sense: treat sacrilegiously). Compare I.i.113.

392   **Snipe** woodcock, proverbial for the gullibility that leads it into snares. *Sport* (line 393) echoes line 269.

395   **H'as . . . Office** he has performed my conjugal duties. *Office* recalls line 117.

396   **for . . . kind** as a result of nothing more than that kind of suspicion.

397   **Will . . . Surety** will act just as I would if I knew it for certain.

399   **proper** both (a) handsome, and (b) civilized in his manners.

400   **plume . . . Will** deck my will with plumes (feathers). Since Othello has supposedly put Iago's manhood ('Will') down (both physically, as implied in line 395, and by promoting Cassio, rather than Iago, to the lieutenantry), Iago will attempt to reinstate it by putting down both men.

402   **abuse** both (a) deceive, and (b) misuse.

403   **he** Cassio.

404   **Person** [attractive] face and physique.
    a smooth Dispose an affable, courtly manner. *Dispose* recalls line 235.

405   **fram'd** made, designed.

Traverse, go, provide thy Money. We will have
more of this to morrow. Adieu.

RODERIGO   Where shall we meet i'th' Morning?   380

IAGO   At my Lodging.

RODERIGO   I'll be with thee betimes.

IAGO   Go to, farewell. Do you hear, Roderigo?

RODERIGO   What say you?

IAGO   No more of Drowning, do you hear?   385

RODERIGO   I am chang'd.

IAGO   Go to, farewell: put Money enough in your
Purse.

RODERIGO   I'll sell all my Land.   *Exit.*

IAGO   Thus do I ever make my Fool my Purse: 390
For I mine own gain'd Knowledge should profane
If I would Time expend with such a Snipe
But for my Sport, and Profit. I hate the Moor,
And it is thought abroad that 'twixt my Sheets
H'as done my Office. I know not if't be true,   395
But I, for mere Suspicion in that kind,
Will do as if for Surety. He holds me well,
The better shall my Purpose work on him.
Cassio's a proper Man: let me see now,
To get his Place, and to plume up my Will   400
In double Knavery. How? How? Let's see.
After some Time, to abuse Othello's Ears
That he is too familiar with his Wife.
He hath a Person, and a smooth Dispose
To be suspected: fram'd to make Women false.   405
The Moor is of a free and open Nature,
That thinks men honest that but seem to be so,

408   **tenderly**   tamely. Compare I.ii.66.

410   **engend'red**   conceived. Iago depicts his device as a seminal
implantation; he will conpensate for his impotence in the
normal world of affairs by begetting a vengeful monster to be
delivered by the midwives 'Hell and Night'.

And will as tenderly be led by th' Nose
As Asses are.
I have't, it is engend'red: Hell and Night   410
Must bring this monstrous Birth to the World's
   Light.   *Exit.*

II.i   This scene takes place in Cyprus, not far from a jutting headland ('Cape'). Montano is the present governor of the island, soon to be replaced by Othello, whose ship is still at sea at the moment.

2   **high wrought Flood**   heavily worked-up sea. Brabantio has used similar phrasing in I.iii.105.

3   **Heaven**   sky.
       Maine   either (a) main (horizon, whether defined by the sea or the mainland), or (b) mane (comparing the horizon to the line of hair on the neck of a horse or lion). Compare lines 13, 39.

4   **Descry**   discern; see on the horizon.

6   **Battlements**   low walls, with apertures for shooting, atop a fort or castle.

7   **ruffian'd so**   acted so rough. Compare I.i.107–10.

8   **Ribs of Oak**   oak beams in the ship's structure.
       when . . . them   when the liquid mountains (waves) descend on them. Here *melt* means 'dissolve'.

9   **hold the Morties**   remain mortised; keep their joints fastened.
       What . . . this?   What news [of calamities at sea] shall this result in?

10   **Segregation**   dispersal; a variation on what Iago has moments earlier called 'an answerable Sequestration' (I.iii.349).

11   **foaming**   frothy.

12   **chidden Billow**   whipped-up (scolded) or 'enchafed' (line 17) sea.

13   **Maine**   (a) main (ocean), (b) main (might), and (c) mane. Compare line 3.

14   **the burning Bear**   probably Ursa Minor, the Little Bear constellation (the principal feature of which is the Little Dipper, of which Polaris, the fixed Pole or North Star, is a member).

15   **And . . . Pole**   and drown the two stars that guard the North Star and are used by pilots to navigate their ships. Not only is the storm so fierce that the waters are virtually indistinguishable from the sky; it makes any attempt at steering a fleet futile.

16   **like Molestation**   comparable disruption.

18   **embay'd**   securely harboured in a protected bay.

ACT II

Scene 1

Enter Montano, and two Gentlemen.

MONTANO   What from the Cape can you discern
   at Sea?
1 GENTLEMAN   Nothing at all, it is a high
   wrought Flood:
I cannot 'twixt the Heaven and the Maine
Descry a Sail.
MONTANO   Me thinks the Wind hath spoke aloud
   at Land,   5
A fuller Blast ne'er shook our Battlements:
If it hath ruffian'd so upon the Sea,
What Ribs of Oak, when Mountains melt on them,
Can hold the Morties. What shall we hear of
   this?
2 GENTLEMAN   A Segregation of the Turkish Fleet: 10
For do but stand upon the foaming Shore,
The chidden Billow seems to pelt the Clouds,
The Wind-shak'd Surge, with high and monstrous
   Maine,
Seems to cast Water on the burning Bear,
And quench the Guards of th' ever-fixed Pole.   15
I never did like Molestation view
On the enchafed Flood.
MONTANO   If that the Turkish Fleet
Be not enshelter'd, and embay'd, they are
   drown'd:

19 **bear it out** withstand it. Compare I.iii.23, 38, 54–57, 210–11, and see Sonnet 116, lines 11–12.

21 **desperate Tempest** The tempest is called 'desperate' (a) because its ferocity is like that of a fighter whose situation is so hopeless that he feels he has nothing to lose, and (b) because it fills with despair anyone who would seek to endure it (line 19).

22 **Designment** design, expedition.

23 **Wrack** shipwreck.
    Sufferance suffering (casualties).

26 **Veronessa** This word appears to apply to Cassio (despite his being called a Florentine in I.i.18), but it may refer to a ship (a Verinessa, or cutter) whose name derived from the Italian verb *verrinare*, 'to cut through'.

29 **And . . . Cyprus** and is commissioned to assume full powers here in Cyprus.

30 **on't** of it.

32 **Touching** regarding. *Comfort* (line 31) recalls I.iii.210–11 and anticipates lines 81–82, 195–97.

33–34 **parted . . . Tempest** Here is yet another reference to a violent parting (see line 10). The Third Gentleman's phrasing recalls what Desdemona has said to the Duke in I.iii.246–48, and it keeps us mindful of the 'foul and violent Tempest' that severed Brabantio from his daughter, his new son-in-law, and his colleagues in Act I.

39–40 **Even . . . Regard** [gazing out] even to the point where the blue hues of the sea and the sky become indistinguishable to our 'Regard' (vision). Here as elsewhere (see *Hamlet*, V.i.267), *blew* (blue) appears to play on the past tense of *blow* (see lines 2, 5–9, 11–17).

41–42 **For . . . Arrivancy** for every minute we expect more arrivals. Compare *Importancy*, I.iii.20.

43 **Thanks you** thanks to you.

44 **approve** care for, admire. Cassio is probably alluding to the solicitude he observes in those who are out watching for the much-loved Othello's arrival rather than sheltering themselves from 'the Elements' (the stormy air and water). Compare I.iii.11, 76, and see line 49.

It is impossible to bear it out.

Enter a Gentleman.

3 GENTLEMAN   News, Lads: our Wars are done.   20
The desperate Tempest hath so bang'd the Turks
That their Designment halts. A noble Ship
Of Venice hath seen a grievous Wrack and
  Sufferance
On most part of their Fleet.
MONTANO   How? Is this true?
3 GENTLEMAN   The Ship is here put in: 25
A Veronessa, Michael Cassio,
Lieutenant to the warlike Moor, Othello,
Is come on Shore, the Moor himself at Sea,
And is in full Commission here for Cyprus.
MONTANO   I am glad on't: 'tis a worthy Governor.   30
3 GENTLEMAN   But this same Cassio, though he
  speak of Comfort,
Touching the Turkish Loss, yet he looks sadly,
And prays the Moor be safe; for they were
  parted
With foul and violent Tempest.
MONTANO   Pray Heavens he be:
For I have serv'd him, and the Man commands   35
Like a full Soldier. Let's to the Seaside, ho,
As well to see the Vessel that's come in
As to throw out our Eyes for brave Othello,
Even till we make the Maine, and th' Aerial blew,
An indistinct Regard.
GENTLEMAN   Come, let's do so;   40
For every Minute is Expectancy
Of more Arrivancy.

Enter Cassio.

CASSIO   Thanks you, the Valiant of the warlike
  Isle,
That so approve the Moor: oh let the Heavens
Give him Defence against the Elements,   45

47   **well shipp'd**   on a ship that is capable of withstanding such buffeting.

48   **Bark**   sailing vessel.
       stoutly timber'd   constructed of strong 'Ribs of Oak' (line 8).

49   **approv'd Allowance**   proven reputation. Compare line 44 and I.iii.222–23. *Pilot* (line 48) means either (a) helmsman or (b) ship's captain.

50–51 **Therefore . . . Cure**   For that reason my hopes [for his safe arrival], though they have been indulged almost to excess (surfeiting), are yet strong in their unflagging expectation of a 'Cure' (the event that will fulfil and thereby heal them). *Stand* recalls I.iii.24 and II.i.11; *bold* echoes I.iii.93.

53   **The . . . empty**   no one remains indoors now.

55   **My . . . Governor**   In the imaginings my 'Hopes' inspire, he bears the form of Othello.

56   **They . . . Courtesy**   The Gentleman refers to a cannon shot, a maritime 'curtsy', that shows the arriving vessel to be a friendly one.

61   **Most fortunately**   in a way that shows him to be exceedingly blessed.

62   **That . . . Fame**   who so far surpasses any attempt at description, and even the most extravagant of reports, that she can only be thought of as a paragon (a wonder beyond compare).

63   **the . . . Pens**   the flourishes of those 'Pens' (poets) that attempt to proclaim her praises. In heraldry, a *blazon* is either a coat of arms or a detailed description of one.

64–65 **And . . . Ingeniuer**   and in the unique apparel in which Creation has clothed her, [she] does (a) attire the genius of the pen that attempts to adorn her with praise, and (b) tire out (exhaust) the ability of the pen that tries to match her adornments with its own. *Tyre* can also mean 'tear'. Compare *3 Henry VI*, I.i.269–71. It is difficult to determine whether the Folio's *Ingeniuer* is meant to be pronounced 'ingeniver' or 'ingeniuer (engineer)'; in any case it here refers to a poet who invents or devises an artistic work by drawing on his genius (creative intelligence). Most editions emend to *enginer*.

67   **Speed**   both (a) good fortune, and (b) rapidity. This word echoes I.iii.274–75.

For I have lost him on a dangerous Sea.
MONTANO   Is he well shipp'd?
CASSIO   His Bark is stoutly timber'd, and his
    Pilot
Of very expert and approv'd Allowance;
Therefore my Hopes, not surfeited to Death,   50
Stand in bold Cure.
[VOICES] *within*   A Sail, a Sail, a Sail.
CASSIO   What Noise?
GENTLEMAN   The Town is empty; on the Brow
    o' th' Sea
Stand ranks of People, and they cry, 'A Sail.'
CASSIO   My Hopes do shape him for the Governor.   55
GENTLEMAN   They do discharge their Shot of
    Courtesy:
Our Friends at least.
CASSIO   I pray you, Sir, go forth,
And give us truth who 'tis that is arriv'd.
GENTLEMAN   I shall.   *Exit.*
MONTANO   But good Lieutenant, is your General
    wiv'd?   60
CASSIO   Most fortunately: he hath achiev'd a
    Maid
That paragons Description, and wild Fame:
One that excels the Quirks of blazoning Pens,
And in th' essential Vesture of Creation
Does tyre the Ingeniuer.

               Enter Gentleman.

             How now? Who has put in?   65
GENTLEMAN   'Tis one Iago, Auncient to the
    General.
CASSIO   H'as had most favourable and happy Speed:
Tempests themselves, high Seas, and howling
    Winds,

69   **gutter'd**   either (a) jagged, incised with gutters, or (b) 'ensteep'd' (submerged), or both.

        congregated Sands   sand bars (here described as if they were a lurking band of treacherous thieves).

70   **ensteep'd . . . Keel**   steeped (submerged) in water as they lie in wait to snare the innocent and unsuspecting bottom of a ship. *Enclog* echoes I.iii.194–96.

71–72 **As . . . Natures**   as if they noticed, appreciated, and made special exceptions for Beauty, and thus declined to perform in accordance with their usual death-dealing natures. Cassio implies that the 'divine Desdemona' has immortal powers that overcome the 'mortal' dangers the rocks and sand would normally pose.

73   **What**   who (what Lady).

74   **Captain**   Cassio's sense is probably close to that of Sonnet 52, where Shakespeare refers to 'Captain Jewels'. Desdemona is both (a) the chief ornament in Othello's crown, and (b) the goddess he worships.

75   **in the Conduct**   under the escort. See I.iii.278–85.

76–77 **Whose . . . Speed**   who arrives here a week early. *Speed* echoes line 67.

78–82 **And . . . comfort**   Cassio's prayer implies that by swelling Othello's 'Sail' with his 'Breath', 'Great Jove' will empower the Moor to come into 'this Bay with his tall Ship', heat Desdemona with the bellows of 'Love's quick Pants', and thereby enflame the smouldering 'Spirits' of all Cyprus. The word *extincted* recalls Othello's reference to his own 'defunct' heat in I.iii.261–62, and it suggests that if Jove's spirit will give 'renew'd Fire' to the Moor, Othello in turn will kindle the spirits of everyone beneath him. *Great* recalls I.iii.265; *powreful* (powerful) echoes I.iii.103. The Fire imagery of lines 78–82 echoes 'blazoning Pens' (line 63), and it suggests that Othello's own 'Pen' (a word that frequently plays on *penis*, as in *The Merchant of Venice*, V.i.236–37) will perform an act of 'Creation' (line 64) that parallels Jove's own.

85   **Hail . . . Lady**   Cassio's greeting echoes Luke 1:28, where the angel Gabriel greets another virgin with the words 'Hail, thou that art highly favoured, the Lord is with thee: blessed art thou among women.' See the note to I.iii.88.

The gutter'd Rocks, and congregated Sands,
Traitors ensteep'd to enclog the guiltless
    Keel,   70
As having sense of Beauty, do omit
Their mortal Natures, letting go safely by
The divine Desdemona.
MONTANO   What is she?
CASSIO   She that I spake of: our great Captain's
    Captain,
Left in the Conduct of the bold Iago,   75
Whose Footing here anticipates our Thoughts
A Se'ennight's Speed. – Great Jove, Othello
    guard,
And swell his Sail with thine own powreful
    Breath,
That he may bless this Bay with his tall Ship,
Make Love's quick Pants in Desdemona's Arms,   80
Give renew'd Fire to our extincted Spirits,
And bring all Cyprus comfort.

        Enter Desdemona, Iago, Roderigo, and Aemilia.

                              Oh behold,
The Riches of the Ship is come on Shore:
You men of Cyprus, let her have your Knees.
– Hail to thee, Lady: and the Grace of Heaven,   85
Before, behind thee, and on every Hand,
Enwheel thee round.
DESDEMONA   I thank you, valiant Cassio.
What Tidings can you tell me of my Lord?
CASSIO   He is not yet arriv'd, nor know I ought

---

87   **Enwheel thee round**   encircle you [and thereby protect you].
        Cassio's phrasing is unintentionally 'Equivocal' (I.iii.215),
        because *Enwheel* can also mean 'wheel around in a circle'. If
        'our great Captain's Captain' is now at the top of Fortune's
        cycle, she may soon find herself wheeling downwards. See the
        first note to I.i.65.

89   **ought**   anything (literally, nothing).

91 **how . . . Company?** how did you become separated? *Lost* echoes lines 32, 46.

98 **gall your Patience** irritate you. Compare I.iii.204–15.

99 **extend my Manners** carry my greeting (probably a kiss on the lips) to the limit of what courtly 'Breeding' permits. Evidently Cassio has just given Aemilia an open display of 'Curtesy' (line 100). He is probably assuring Iago that what might appear to be an inappropriate familiarity is not to be so interpreted; but he may also be reminding Iago that 'the Lieutenant' is socially superior to 'the Ancient' (II.iii.111–12). *Breeding* echoes I.iii.238; *bold* (line 100) recalls line 51. *Shew* (show) hints at *eschew* (shunning), for which it can function as an aphetic form. *Curtesy* (courtesy) plays on *cur*; compare *The Merchant of Venice*, I.iii.112–30, and *Julius Caesar*, III.i.39–46.

104 **Alas . . . Speech** Desdemona seems to be saying that Aemilia's silence contradicts what Iago has just said about her.

105 **still . . . sleep** every time I am at liberty to get some rest.

108 **chides with Thinking** scolds silently (keeping her thoughts unexpressed but nevertheless revealing her disapproval through her manner). *Chides* echoes line 12.

110 **Pictures . . . Doors** models of decorum in public. Most interpreters assume that Iago means 'painted pictures' (women covered with cosmetics); that is probably at least part of what he is saying. Iago alludes to the proverb 'Women are in church saints, abroad angels, at home devils.'

111 **Bells** either (a) as melodious as bells, or (b) with tongues as clamorous as bell-clappers.

112 **Saints . . . Injuries** sanctimonious when you hurt others or believe yourselves to be mistreated.
    Divels devils. The Folio spelling, here retained, is the most common form of the word in Shakespeare's texts.

113 **Players . . . Huswifery** either (a) mere pretenders in your housekeeping, or (b) playful wantons rather than industrious and faithful housewives.
    Huswives either (a) thrifty housewives when your husbands desire your love, or (b) hussies (whores) when you share your beds with cuckolders (see I.iii.393–405).

115 **Turk** infidel. See the notes to I.i.27, 28.

But that he's well, and will be shortly here.   90
DESDEMONA   Oh but I fear: how lost you Company?
CASSIO   The great Contention of the Sea and Skies
  Parted our Fellowship. But hark, a Sail.
[VOICES] *within*   A Sail, a Sail.
GENTLEMAN   They give this Greeting to the
  Citadel: 95
  This likewise is a Friend.
CASSIO   See for the News.
                              [*Exit Gentleman.*]
  – Good Ancient, you are welcome. – Welcome,
  Mistress.
  – Let it not gall your Patience, good Iago,
  That I extend my Manners. 'Tis my Breeding
  That gives me this bold shew of Curtesy.   100
IAGO   Sir, would she give you so much of her
  Lips
  As of her Tongue she oft bestows on me,
  You would have enough.
DESDEMONA   Alas: she has no Speech.
IAGO   In faith too much:
  I find it still when I have leave to sleep.   105
  Marry, before your Ladyship, I grant,
  She puts her Tongue a little in her Heart,
  And chides with Thinking.
AEMILIA   You have little Cause to say so.
IAGO   Come on, come on: you are Pictures out of
  Doors,   110
  Bells in your Parlours, Wild-cats in your
  Kitchens,
  Saints in your Injuries, Divels being offended,
  Players in your Huswifery, and Huswives in
  Your Beds.
DESDEMONA   Oh, fie upon thee, Slanderer.
IAGO   Nay, it is true, or else I am a Turk: 115
  You rise to play, and go to Bed to work.

117   **write my Praise**   both (a) extol me, and (b) compose my epitaph. Compare lines 60–65, 67–73.

121   **assay**   try. This word echoes I.iii.17–18.

123–
24   **beguile . . . otherwise**   [attempt to] deceive my real self [anxious about Othello's safety] by pretending to be in a holiday mood. Desdemona may speak these lines privately, in soliloquy. 'The thing I am' recalls Iago's 'I am not what I am' (I.i.64); both sentences echo Exodus 3:14. See the note to I.ii.33. *Beguile* recalls I.iii.65, 154, 208.

126–
27   **I . . . Freeze**   I am trying to come up with something; but in truth a well-devised praise is as hard for me to pluck out of my head as it would be for me to remove sticky birdlime from frieze, coarse woollen fabric.

128   **labours**   both (a) works hard, and (b) is in labour. Iago's phrasing recalls what he said in I.iii.376–77, 410–11.

130   **Wit**   Iago probably means both (a) intellectual acuity, mental quickness, and (b) erotic desire (like *Will*, *Wit* frequently carries a genital sense in Shakespeare). Desdemona's response (line 132) suggests that she picks up on the first meaning only. See the notes to I.iii.288, 362.

133–
34   **If . . . fit**   Here Iago's riddle, which puns on *White/Wight* (person) and plays on a copulative sense of *fit*, hints at the marriage of Othello and Desdemona and implies that she may be the 'Black' (lustful) one. See the note to I.ii.85–87. Lines 133–34 parallel what Iago told Roderigo in I.iii.345–64; they also recall I.i.70–72, I.ii.62–71.

137   **Foolish**   Here Iago means 'wanton', inclined to fool around. *Folly* (line 138) also means 'unchastity'.

139   **fond Paradoxes**   foolish heresies (views contrary to orthodox opinion).

145   **Ignorance**   wilful ignoring of any distinction between 'Fair' and 'Foul'. *Heavy* (both dull and oppressive) echoes I.iii.256–57.

AEMILIA   You shall not write my Praise.

IAGO   No, let me not.

DESDEMONA   What wouldst write of me, if thou
  should'st praise me?

IAGO   Oh gentle Lady, do not put me to't,
  For I am nothing if not critical.   120

DESDEMONA   Come on, assay. There's one gone to
  the Harbour?

IAGO   Ay Madam.

DESDEMONA   I am not merry: but I do beguile
  The thing I am by seeming otherwise.
  Come, how wouldst thou praise me?   125

IAGO   I am about it, but indeed my Invention
  Comes from my Pate as Birdlime does from
    Freeze:
  It plucks out Brains and all. But my Muse
    labours,
  And thus she is deliver'd.
        If she be Fair and Wise, Fairness and Wit,   130
        The one's for use, the other useth it.

DESDEMONA   Well prais'd: how if she be Black
  and Witty?

IAGO   *If she be Black, and thereto have a Wit,*
        She'll find a White that shall her Blackness
            fit.

DESDEMONA   Worse, and worse.   135

AEMILIA   How if Fair, and Foolish?

IAGO   *She never yet was Foolish that was Fair:*
        For even her Folly help'd her to an Heir.

DESDEMONA   These are old fond Paradoxes,
  to make Fools laugh i'th' Alehouse. What
  miserable Praise hast thou for her that's Foul   140
  and Foolish?

IAGO   *There's none so Foul and Foolish thereunto*
        But does Foul Pranks which Fair and Wise Ones do.

DESDEMONA   Oh heavy Ignorance: thou praisest   145

74

147–   **One . . . self** One whose merit was so unimpeachable that it
49   justly forced even Malice itself to vouch for her virtue.
        Authority echoes I.iii.326–27.

150   **proud** (a) haughty, unruly, (b) wayward (unfaithful), and (c)
        aroused by lust (see Sonnet 151, lines 7–12).

152   **went never gay** never adorned herself in cosmetics and gaudy
        attire.

153   **Fled . . . may** denied herself what she wanted, even though she
        knew she might have had it. Compare I.iii.93–97.

154–   **She . . . fly** She who, though having an opportunity to get even
55   for an injury, instead accepted her 'Wrong' with patience and
        banished her feelings of ill will. This couplet echoes the
        Duke's sentences in I.iii.200–7. *Bad* (bade) recalls I.iii.131.

157   **To . . . Tail** to engage in an intimate exchange. Here *Cod's
        Head* and *Salmon's Tail* probably refer to the male and female
        genitalia, though the latter could as readily refer to the penis
        (the Latin word for 'tail') of another male, perhaps a man
        other than a woman's husband. *Change* echoes I.iii.354, 386.

158   **think** be tempted (feel normal desire without acting on it).

162   **To . . . Beer** To nurse children (or innocuous spouses) and
        keep track of payments for weak brew. Iago's 'impotent
        Conclusion' – his irreverent and 'liberal' (cynical) reduction of
        all women to either 'Folly' or passive inconsequence – shows
        him to be a 'Scholar' (critic) indeed (lines 120, 163–68).
        Conclusion recalls I.iii.331; *profane* echoes I.iii.390–93.

166   **Counsailor** counsellor. Here the Folio spelling reinforces
        Desdemona's charge that Iago is 'liberal' (bawdy); it suggests
        that he sails upon, partakes in the sale of, sexual favours.
        Compare *Measure for Measure*, I.ii.110–11, where
        Counsellors puns on 'coun-sellers' (with *coun* alluding to
        cunnus, as noted in I.i.120).

167   **speaks home** goes straight to the point.

167–   **you . . . Scholar** you may appreciate him more for his
68   soldier-like bluntness than for the opinions that derive from
        his study of human nature.

169   **said** done. Iago soliloquizes as he watches Cassio and
        Desdemona.

170–   **With . . . Cassio** Iago compares himself to a spider. *Web*
71   anticipates III.iv.69; *Fly* recalls I.i.70; *ensnare* echoes the
        imagery of lines 68–73, 85–87, 126–28, 172–73.

the Worst best. But what Praise couldst thou
bestow on a Deserving Woman indeed? One that
in the authority of her Merit did justly put
on the Vouch of very Malice it self.

IAGO *She that was ever Fair, and never Proud,* 150
Had Tongue at will, and yet was never loud:
Never lack'd Gold, and yet went never gay,
Fled from her Wish, and yet said 'Now I may'.
She that, being anger'd, her Revenge being nigh,
Bad her Wrong stay, and her Displeasure fly, 155
She that in Wisdom never was so Frail
To change the Cod's Head for the Salmon's Tail:
She that could think, and nev'r disclose her Mind,
See Suitors following, and not look behind,
She was a Wight, if ever such Wights were — 160

DESDEMONA To do what?

IAGO *To suckle Fools, and chronicle small Beer.*

DESDEMONA Oh most lame and impotent Conclusion.
Do not learn of him, Aemilia, though he be thy
Husband. — How say you, Cassio, is he not a 165
most profane and liberal Counsailor?

CASSIO He speaks home, Madam; you may relish
him more in the Soldier than in the Scholar.

IAGO — He takes her by the Palm: ay, well said,
whisper. With as little a Web as this will I 170
ensnare as great a Fly as Cassio. Ay, smile
upon her, do: I will give thee in thine own

---

172 **give** requite. Most editions emend *give* to *gyve* (fetter, trap), a
reading consistent with the Quarto's 'catch you in your own
courtesies' at this point in the text. But Iago may be punning
on *give* and *gyve*, with the implication that he will repay
Cassio with a kind of 'Courtship' that answers to what Cassio
has given him (lines 98–100). *Give* echoes lines 95, 100.

174 **Tricks** (a) habits, characteristic expressions, (b) skills, and (c) trifles. *Tricks* can also refer to sexual encounters, especially purchased ones (see *Measure for Measure*, III.i.110–12), and that sense is pertinent to the device Iago will use to 'strip' Cassio.

176 **kiss'd . . . Fingers** a conventional display of courteous respect.

177 **play the Sir** perform the role of a gentle courtier. *Play* echoes line 113.

178 **Curtsy** bowing and scraping. See the notes to lines 56, 99.

180 **Cluster-pipes** clyster syringes (to administer enemas or douches). The coarseness of Iago's image is reinforced by the offstage flatulent sound of the Moor's 'Trumpet' (line 182).

184 **Warrior** comrade in arms (see line 80). Othello's epithet echoes line 74 and anticipates II.iii.324–25.

189 **labouring Bark** hard-working ship. But Othello's other phrases hint at the labour of childbirth and the 'Content' and 'Calms' that come with (a) intercourse, (b) delivery, and (c) excretion (continuing the imagery of line 180). Compare lines 128–29 and I.iii.410–11. *Bark* echoes line 48; *Joy* (line 186) recalls I.iii.366.

190 **Olympus high** as high as Mount Olympus (home of the Gods in the classical pantheon). Compare *Hamlet*, V.i.264–66, 292–95, and *Julius Caesar*, III.i.75, for allusions to Olympus that hint ominously at the downfalls of characters who tempt the Heavens with *hubris* (overweening pride) or *pleonexia* (self-satisfaction).

193 **absolute** pure, complete, perfect. This moment of reunion, resolution, and inner peace – a serenity that follows a pair of tempests (a figurative one in Venice, and another, literal one at sea) – resembles the harmony and at-one-ment to be found at the end of most of Shakespeare's comedies. Tragically, it will prove to be the calm before another storm. *Content* echoes line 185 and recalls I.i.40, I.iii.225–27; *Comfort* echoes lines 31–34.

195 **Succeeds . . . Fate** can follow this in the remaining time that inscrutable Fate has ordained for me.

Courtship. You say true, 'tis so indeed. If
such Tricks as these strip you out of your
Lieutenantry, it had been better you had not   175
kiss'd your three Fingers so oft, which now
again you are most apt to play the Sir in.
Very good: well kiss'd, and excellent Curtsy,
'tis so indeed. Yet again, your Fingers to
your Lips? Would they were Cluster-pipes for   180
your sake.
— The Moor, I know his Trumpet.

CASSIO   'Tis truly so.

DESDEMONA   Let's meet him, and receive him.

CASSIO   Lo, where he comes.

Enter Othello and Attendants.

OTHELLO   O, my fair Warrior.

DESDEMONA   My dear Othello.

OTHELLO   It gives me Wonder great as my Content   185
To see you here before me. Oh my Soul's Joy:
If after every Tempest come such Calms,
May the Winds blow till they have waken'd
   Death;
And let the labouring Bark climb Hills of Seas
Olympus high, and duck again as low   190
As Hell's from Heaven. If it were now to die,
'Twere now to be most happy. For I fear
My Soul hath her Content so absolute
That not another Comfort like to this
Succeeds in unknown Fate.

DESDEMONA   The Heavens forbid   195
But that our Loves and Comforts should increase
Even as our Days do grow.

OTHELLO   — Amen to that, sweet Powers.

198 **I . . . Content** Othello's repetition of the word *Content* (see the note to line 193) helps make his point. Like *Consent* (I.i.120), it hints at the kind of contentment Othello and Desdemona are yet to experience fully; it also shows that what these lovers feel includes but transcends the kind of 'Joy' Iago alludes to in I.i.70.

199 **It . . . here** Othello may be referring to his throat or his heart, with the implication that he is almost too choked up to go on. But *stops* is also a word that can refer to constipation (see lines 180 and 189), and a word with multiple musical applications (among them the frets on a stringed instrument, the holes on a wind instrument, and the pegs or keys to control a set of organ pipes), and Othello may be alluding to one of those senses when he speaks of *Discord* in line 200. Iago picks up on Othello's musical analogy in the speech that follows, promising to 'set down' and thereby loosen and untune 'The Pegs that make this Music' (line 203) between Othello and Desdemona.

206 **How . . . Isle?** Othello addresses Montano.

207 **well desir'd** Othello means 'greatly favoured, warmly received', with many people desiring (requesting) you to accept their hospitality. Iago is planning to give the phrase another sense.

209 **out of Fashion** in a way that is uncharacteristic of me, and one that does not become a man in my position.

211 **disembark my Coffers** bring my cargo aboard from its 'Bark' (line 189).

212 **Master** ship's captain.
Citadel governor's mansion; administrative capitol.

214 **challenge** stake a claim for. *Respect* recalls I.iii.180–82, 279–81.

215 **well met** I'm glad to have met (been reunited with) you. In the next line Iago picks up on the word *met*.

216 **presently** shortly. Iago probably addresses a subordinate.

219 **native to them** inborn in their characters.

220 **list me** listen to me. But Iago's words can also mean 'list (lean or incline) for me' (compare *Whip me* in I.i.48).

220– **watches . . . Guard** is to stay up and supervise the watch at the
21 guard house. *To night* (tonight) echoes I.iii.379.

222 **directly** overtly, unmistakably.

— I cannot speak enough of this Content,
It stops me here: it is too much of Joy.
And this, and this the greatest Discord be   *They kiss.*   200
That e'er our Hearts shall make.
IAGO   — Oh you are well tun'd now: but I'll set
  down
The Pegs that make this Music, as honest as
I am.
OTHELLO   Come: let us to the Castle.
  — News, Friends, our Wars are done: the Turks
    are drown'd.   205
  — How does my old Acquaintance of this Isle?
  — Honey, you shall be well desir'd in Cyprus,
I have found great Love amongst them. Oh my Sweet,
I prattle out of Fashion, and I dote
In mine own Comforts. — I prythee, good Iago,   210
Go to the Bay, and disembark my Coffers:
Bring thou the Master to the Citadel,
He is a good one, and his Worthiness
Does challenge much Respect. — Come, Desdemona,
Once more well met at Cyprus.   215
IAGO   — Do thou meet me presently at the Harbour.
                    Exeunt Othello and Desdemona
                    [*and all but Iago and Roderigo*].
  — Come thither; if thou be'st Valiant (as they
say Base Men being in love have then a Nobility
in their Natures more than is native to them),
list me. The Lieutenant to night watches on the   220
Court of Guard. First, I must tell thee this:
Desdemona is directly in love with him.
RODERIGO   With him? Why, 'tis not possible.
IAGO   Lay thy Finger thus: and let thy Soul be
instructed. Mark me with what Violence she   225
first lov'd the Moor, but for Bragging, and

---

224   **thus**   over your lips [to keep yourself from talking].
226   **but for**   for no more than [his].

228 **still for Prating** always for prattling and boasting.
discreet both (a) wise, observant (possessed with discretion),
and (b) discrete (individual, and thus self-centred).

229 **Her . . . fed** her appetite for an appealing mate must be
indulged. See the second note to III.iv.66 for another pertinent
sense of *Eye*; compare lines 250–51.

231– **When . . . Sport** when erotic passion has subsided after its
32 initial gratification. *Sport* recalls I.iii.374–76, 390–93; *Blood*
echoes I.iii.328–31, 337; *Delight* (line 230) recalls
I.iii.286–88, 358.

234 **Favour** appearance. Compare I.iii.344–45.

236– **for . . . Conveniences** as a result of his lack of these essential
37 compatibilities. *Conveniences* literally means 'comings-
together'. See the third note to I.i.120, and compare I.iii.331.

238 **abus'd** deceived; misled and misused. *Delicate* (line 237)
echoes I.iii.358; *Tenderness* recalls I.iii.406–9.

238– **heave the Gorge** exhibit the effects of nausea. Compare
39 I.i.147–49. *Disrelish* echoes lines 167–68.

242– **as . . . Position** since it is a hypothesis that emerges as
43 inevitably and naturally as does the offspring of a pregnant
woman. *Unforc'd* echoes I.iii.109–11.

243– **so . . . Fortune** most highly placed to benefit from this fortune.
44 *Stands* echoes lines 50–51.

245 **voluble** loquacious; facile, clever, in his use of words.

246– **Form . . . Seeming** both (a) pretence of civilized and humane
47 character, and (b) appearance of being a well-mannered
human being.

247– **for . . . Affection** the better to accomplish his lustful and
48 skilfully disguised desires. *Salt* (lustful) will recur in III.iii.394;
compass echoes I.iii.365–67; *Affection* recalls I.iii.110–11.

249 **slipper** slippery, cunning; 'subtle'. Compare I.iii.361.

250 **he's** either (a) he has, or (b) he is.

250– **that . . . Advantages** who has an eye that can coin a specious
51 'Occasion' to pursue his salacious purposes. *Counterfeit* is
another word that plays on a vulgar English word for the
female pudendum; see the third note to I.i.120, and compare
Romeo and Juliet, II.iii.50–75, where Mercutio implies that
Romeo has been engaged in 'counter-fitting'.

telling her fantastical Lies. To love him
still for Prating, let not thy discreet
Heart think it. Her Eye must be fed. And what
Delight shall she have to look on the Divel?   230
When the Blood is made dull with the act of
Sport, there should be a Game to enflame
it, and to give Satiety a fresh Appetite.
Loveliness in Favour, Sympathy in Years,
Manners, and Beauties: all which the   235
Moor is defective in. Now for want of these
requir'd Conveniences, her delicate Tenderness
will find it self abus'd, begin to heave the
Gorge, disrelish and abhor the Moor; very
Nature will instruct her in it, and compel   240
her to some second Choice. Now Sir, this
granted (as it is a most pregnant and unforc'd
Position), who stands so eminent in the Degree
of this Fortune as Cassio does: a Knave very
voluble, no further conscionable than in   245
putting on the mere Form of Civil and Humane
Seeming, for the better compass of his salt
and most hidden loose Affection? Why none,
why none: a slipper and subtle Knave, a Finder
of Occasion, that he's an Eye can stamp, and   250
counterfeit Advantages, though true Advantage
never present it self. A divelish Knave:
besides, the Knave is handsome, young, and
hath all those Requisites in him that Folly
and Green Minds look after. A pestilent   255
complete Knave, and the Woman hath found
him already.

---

251   **true Advantage**   a circumstance that would permit him to woo
        her legitimately.

254– **Folly . . . Minds**   wantonness and lusty youth. *Green*, the
55   colour of Venus, figures prominently in *Love's Labour's Lost*;
        see I.i.97, I.ii.89, IV.iii.76–78 of that comedy.

259   **Bless'd Condition**   gracious disposition.

260–   **The Wine . . . Grapes** It is an article of faith with Iago that
61   there is nothing, and no one, that cannot be reduced to the
      lowest common denominator.

263   **Pudding** the mixture of meat, herbs and eggs that fills a
      sausage. As with 'Fig's-end' (line 260, echoing I.iii.319), Iago
      chooses an image with phallic suggestiveness. *Pudding*
      anticipates the sound of *paddle*, a verb that is always erotic in
      Shakespeare (compare *Hamlet*, III.iv.182).

266   **Curtesy** courtesy; courtly manners. See the note to line 178.

267   **an Index** a table of contents. See *Hamlet*, III.iv.50. *Foul* (line
      268) recalls lines 136–44.

272   **Mutabilities** changes and exchanges (see I.iii.350–57). Most
      editions follow the Quarto and adopt *mutualities* (intimate
      manifestations of 'Curtesy', line 266), a reading that suits the
      context more obviously.
      marshal the Way provide an escort to the table (perform the
      function of a marshal at a formal occasion) for the 'Master'
      (either the host or the highest-ranking guest).

272–   **hard at hand** close by, immediately following (with pertinent
73   innuendo). *Hard* echoes I.iii.362.

274   **incorporate Conclusion** corporate merger. See the note to
      I.iii.331, and compare II.i.162, 198 ('Content'), 236–37
      ('Conveniences').

280   **tainting his Discipline** disparaging him for his lack of military
      readiness (bearing, self-control). Compare I.iii.266–72.

282   **minister** provide as your servant. *Minister* derives from
      magister, and it refers to one who assists a master (line 273).
      Time (line 281) echoes I.iii.298, 321–27, 376–77.

284   **sudden in Choler** violent, 'rash'; quick to be angered.

285   **happely** both (a) haply, perchance, and (b) happily (to our
      benefit).

287   **these of Cyprus** the Cypriot soldiers.
      Qualification mollification, pacifying; here, literally, 'dilution'.

288   **shall . . . again** be returned to its proper flavour (solution).
      Taste can also mean 'test' (as in I.iii.106).

RODERIGO I cannot believe that in her, she's
full of most Bless'd Condition.

IAGO Bless'd Fig's-end. The Wine she drinks is 260
made of Grapes. If she had been Bless'd, she
would never have lov'd the Moor. Bless'd
Pudding. Didst thou not see her paddle with
the Palm of his Hand? Didst not mark that?

RODERIGO Yes, that I did: but that was but 265
Curtesy.

IAGO Lechery by this Hand: an Index and obscure
Prologue to the History of Lust and Foul
Thoughts. They met so near with their Lips
that their Breaths embrac'd together. 270
Villainous Thoughts, Roderigo, when these
Mutabilities so marshal the Way, hard at
hand comes the Master, and Main Exercise,
th' incorporate Conclusion. Pish. But Sir,
be you rul'd by me. I have brought you from 275
Venice. Watch you to night: for the Command,
I'll lay't upon you. Cassio knows you not:
I'll not be far from you. Do you find some
Occasion to anger Cassio, either by speaking
too loud, or tainting his Discipline, or from 280
what other Course you please, which the Time
shall more favourably minister.

RODERIGO Well.

IAGO Sir, he's rash, and very sudden in Choler:
and happely may strike at you. Provoke him 285
that he may: for even out of that will I cause
these of Cyprus to Mutiny. Whose Qualification
shall come into no true Taste again but by the
Displanting of Cassio. So shall you have a
shorter Journey to your Desires, by the Means 290

---

289 **Displanting** uprooting, removal (see line 292). Compare lines
173–77.
So thus, in this way.

291   **prefer** promote, advance. Compare I.iii.105–8.

293   **were** would (could) be.

297   **warrant** assure, guarantee.

298   **his Necessaries** Othello's trunks and personal effects.

302   **apt . . . Credit** plausible and easily made credible. *Apt* echoes line 177.

306   **dear** (a) beloved, (b) devoted, and (c) costly (compare I.iii.256–57).

307   **absolute** mere, pure. Compare line 193.
       peradventure either (a) perhaps, or (b) as it happens.

308   **stand accomptant** can be accused of being accountable (guilty). Iago plays on the genital implications of *stand* (male) and *compt* (female); see the third note to I.i.120. *Stand* recalls lines 50–51.

309   **diet** feed.

311   **leap'd . . . Seat** supplanted me in bed with Aemilia; see I.iii.393–95.
       whereof of which.

314   **even'd with him** avenged, requited. *Even'd* recalls I.i.122.

318   **Trash** piece of refuse. Iago has spoken similarly about Roderigo in I.iii.390–94.
       trace pursue (like a hunter). Compare lines 318–19 with I.iii.342–43. Some editions emend *trace* to *trash*, 'leash' or 'harness', and that concept is implicit in Iago's wordplay.

319   **For . . . Hunting** because he is such an obedient hound.
       stand . . . on will endure my manipulating him and spurring him on. *Putting on* echoes I.ii.14–16, II.i.119, 146–49, 244–48, 315–17.

320   **on the Hip** ready for the throw (a wrestling term).

321   **Abuse . . . Garb** deceive the Moor about him while outfitting myself as the kind of responsible, disciplined officer Cassio should have been. The phrase *right Garb* can also refer to the style that will most fittingly repay the Moor for the cuckolding he has supposedly visited upon Iago. One meaning of *right* is 'upright' or 'erect'; see *Measure for Measure*, II.i.103–4, 170–71, II.iv.178, III.i.354–55. Compare lines 64–65, 110, 249–52, for similar metaphors of clothing and counterfeiting. Most editions follow the Quarto and print *rank garb*.

I shall then have to prefer them. And the
Impediment most profitably removed, without
the which there were no Expectation of our
Prosperity.

RODERIGO   I will do this, if you can bring it   295
to any Opportunity.

IAGO   I warrant thee. Meet me by and by at the
Citadel. I must fetch his Necessaries ashore.
Farewell.

RODERIGO   Adieu.   *Exit.* 300

IAGO   That Cassio loves her, I do well believe't;
That she loves him, 'tis apt, and of great
   Credit.
The Moor, howbeit that I endure him not,
Is of a constant, loving, noble Nature,
And I dare think he'll prove to Desdemona   305
A most dear Husband. Now I do love her too,
Not out of absolute Lust (though peradventure
I stand accomptant for as great a Sin)
But partly led to diet my Revenge,
For that I do suspect the lusty Moor   310
Hath leap'd into my Seat. The Thought whereof
Doth (like a poisonous Mineral) gnaw my Inwards:
And nothing can or shall content my Soul
Till I am even'd with him, Wife for Wife.
Or failing so, yet that I put the Moor   315
At least into a Jealousy so strong
That Judgement cannot cure. Which thing to do,
If this poor Trash of Venice, whom I trace
For his quick Hunting, stand the putting on,
I'll have our Michael Cassio on the Hip,   320
Abuse him to the Moor in the right Garb

322   **For . . . too**   because I suspect that Cassio, too, has 'leap'd into my Seat' (line 311).
       Night-cape   Iago probably means *nightcap*, the word that appears in the First Quarto and in most modern editions; like *cappe*, *cape* was a variant spelling for *cap*. But it may also be that Iago is referring to a man's nightwear.

325   **practising upon**   contriving against. *Practising* recalls I.iii.101.

326–   **'Tis . . . us'd**   My plan is here (in my head), but as yet it appears
27   only in an indistinct, inchoate mixture of ingredients, since villainy's proper form cannot be disclosed until its work is complete.

II.ii   This scene takes place in a public place on the island of Cyprus.

3   **importing . . . Perdition**   relating to the complete loss (destruction). *Importing* recalls I.iii.281.

5   **Triumph**   victory celebration; festivity. *Sport* (line 6) recalls II.i.231–33.

6–7   **each . . . him**   with each person to engage in the form of revelry to which he is most inclined and suited. Most editions substitute the Quarto's *mind* for the Folio's *addition*, which here means 'attribute'. Elsewhere Shakespeare uses *addition* to refer not only to titles and honours but to those qualities that distinguish real men from mere pretenders (see *Troilus and Cressida*, I.ii.18–19).

8–9   **So . . . proclaimed**   All of this it pleased him (it was his will as Governor) to have publicly announced. *Pleasure*, echoing line 1, recalls I.i.120 and I.iii.374–76.

10   **Offices**   kitchens and stores of provisions.

12   **have told Eleven**   has tolled eleven (and thus told you it is eleven).

II.iii   We now move to an interior, probably at or adjacent to the Citadel.

1   **look . . . Guard**   be in charge of the security forces. *Look you to* recalls I.iii.290.

2   **Stop**   restraint. This word echoes II.i.199.

3   **Not . . . Discretion**   not to disport ourselves beyond what discretion (judgement, self-control) advises. *Out-sport* echoes II.ii.6–7. *Discretion* recalls II.i.228–29.

4   **hath Direction**   has been instructed. Compare I.iii.297.

(For I fear Cassio with my Night-cape too),
Make the Moor thank me, love me, and reward me,
For making him egregiously an Ass,
And practising upon his Peace and Quiet,   325
Even to Madness. 'Tis here: but yet confus'd,
Knavery's plain Face is never seen till us'd.   *Exit.*

Scene 2

Enter Othello's Herald with a Proclamation.

HERALD   It is Othello's pleasure, our noble and
valiant General, that upon certain Tidings
now arriv'd, importing the mere Perdition of
the Turkish Fleet, every man put himself into
Triumph: some to daunce, some to make Bonfires,   5
each man to what Sport and Revels his Addition
leads him. For besides these beneficial News,
it is the Celebration of his Nuptial. So much
was his pleasure should be proclaimed. All
Offices are open, and there is full Liberty   10
of Feasting, from this present Hour of Five
till the Bell have told Eleven. Heaven bless
the Isle of Cyprus, and our noble General
Othello.   *Exit.*

Scene 3

Enter Othello, Desdemona, Cassio, and Attendants.

OTHELLO   Good Michael, look you to the Guard
    to night.
    Let's teach our selves that honourable Stop
    Not to out-sport Discretion.
CASSIO   Iago hath Direction what to do.

7   **with your earliest**   at your earliest convenience.

9   **The Purchase made**   now that we have obtained the licence to
        engage in our own 'Celebration' (II.ii.8). Othello compares
        himself to a man who has just acquired a garden; he will now
        tend it, hoping thereby to bring forth 'Fruits' (either joys or
        offspring) that will yield 'Profit'. His imagery recalls Iago's
        advice to Roderigo in I.iii.320–35. *Profit* (line 10) echoes
        I.iii.390–93.

14   **cast us**   cast us off, dismissed us from his company. Iago has
        employed this verb in I.i.149. Here his implicit message is
        'now that the General is off to his own revels, it is only to be
        expected that we will enjoy some of our own'. What Iago has
        in mind, of course, is to put Cassio in a position where
        Othello will feel that he must cast him off in reality.

16–17 **made . . . her**   made night unrestrained in its delights.

18   **exquisite**   choice.

19   **Game**   'Sport' (line 17, echoing line 3). Compare II.i.231–33.

20   **fresh**   innocent, unspoiled, like an unplucked flower. *Delicate*
        recalls II.i.238.

22–23 **sounds . . . Provocation**   trumpets a halt to hostilities in order
        to initiate peace negotiations. Iago uses military terminology
        to describe a different type of 'Provocation'. He is attempting
        to provoke (urge on) Cassio; compare I.ii.7, II.i.285.

23   **inviting**   Cassio means 'free and open', but in a way that is
        demure; his replies show that he too is genuinely 'honest'
        (I.iii.406–7).

25   **an . . . Love**   a trumpet call to signal a forthcoming
        engagement.

27   **Stope**   stoup, a two-quart tankard. Having found that Cassio is
        not susceptible to one kind of 'Provocation', Iago shifts to
        another.

28   **brace**   pair. Compare I.iii.24–26.

29   **fain . . . Measure**   gladly pledge a toast.

30   **black Othello**   Iago's racial slur echoes I.i.87–88, I.iii.287–88,
        and II.i.132–34. It is no doubt intended to suggest to Cassio
        that Othello is not a fit match for the 'divine Desdemona'
        (II.i.73), and thus that she would be receptive to an overture
        from 'a Proper Man' (I.iii.399). But Cassio gives no indication
        that he registers Iago's innuendo.

But notwithstanding, with my personal Eye   5
Will I look to't.

OTHELLO   Iago is most honest.
  Michael, goodnight. To morrow with your
      earliest,
  Let me have Speech with you. – Come, my dear
      Love,
  The Purchase made, the Fruits are to ensue;
  That Profit's yet to come 'tween me and you.   10
  – Goodnight.   *Exit [with Desdemona].*

                    Enter Iago.

CASSIO   Welcome, Iago: we must to the Watch.
IAGO   Not this Hour, Lieutenant: 'tis not yet Ten
  o'th' Clock. Our General cast us thus early
  for the love of his Desdemona, who let us not   15
  therefore blame; he hath not yet made wanton
  the Night with her; and she is Sport for Jove.
CASSIO   She's a most exquisite Lady.
IAGO   And I'll warrant her, full of Game.
CASSIO   Indeed she's a most fresh and delicate   20
  Creature.
IAGO   What an Eye she has? Me thinks it sounds a
      Parley
  To Provocation.
CASSIO   An inviting Eye:
  And yet me thinks right modest.
IAGO   And when she speaks,
  Is it not an Alarum to Love?
CASSIO   She is   25
  Indeed Perfection.
IAGO   Well: Happiness to their Sheets.
  Come, Lieutenant, I have a Stope of Wine, and
  here without are a brace of Cyprus Gallants,
  that would fain have a Measure to the Health
  of black Othello.   30

31–32 I . . . **Drinking**   I become intoxicated if I drink even a little. Cassio's reply echoes Othello's counsel in lines 2–3. *Brains* recalls I.iii.328–31 and II.i.126–28. *Curtesy* (courtesy, line 33) echoes II.i.266.

32–34 I . . . **Entertainment**   I wish that social custom would provide some other way for us to provide hospitality and display good fellowship. *Custom* recalls I.iii.228.

38   **craftily qualified**   discreetly and subtly diluted. Cassio has exercised some prudence earlier in the evening. Compare the use of *Qualification* in II.i.287. See the note on *to night* at I.ii.50.

39   **what . . . here**   what a change (insurrection) it has caused in my head.

40   **task my Weakness**   burden my 'Infirmity' (inability to hold my liquor without inebriation).

43   **desire**   both (a) wish, and (b) request. See the note to II.i.207.

46   **it dislikes me**   it is against my better judgement. Iago will soon demonstrate that 'it dislikes' Cassio indeed.

49   **full . . . Offence**   prone to be moved to anger (to take 'Offence') at the slightest challenge to his sense of honour. Compare II.i.278–89, and see lines 58–60.

50   **As . . . Dog**   as the testy dog of a spoiled court favourite.

52–53 **carous'd . . . Pottle-deep**   quaffed drinks to the bottom of the two-quart vessel. Compare line 27.

54   **swelling**   proud, puffed up. Compare II.i.77–82.

55   **That . . . Distance**   who are very touchy lest anyone should encroach upon their space and force them to uphold their honour by drawing their swords.

56   **The . . . Isle**   the very stuff of which this hot-headed island is composed. *Elements* recalls II.i.45.

57   **fluster'd**   agitated and confused. Iago's verb alliterates with *flowing* and *flock* to suggest that the 'Innovation' he has already brought about has turned a company of soldiers into an assortment of prating 'Spirits' with no more restraint than a gaggle of territorial gulls.

58   **watch**   both (a) serve on guard duty (see line 13), and (b) 'look to' (line 6) their honours.

CASSIO Not to night, good Iago, I have very poor
and unhappy Brains for Drinking. I could well
wish Curtesy would invent some other Custom
of Entertainment.

IAGO Oh, they are our Friends: but one Cup, I'll 35
drink for you.

CASSIO I have drunk but one Cup to night, and
that was craftily qualified too: and behold
what Innovation it makes here. I am infortunate
in the Infirmity, and dare not task my Weakness 40
with any more.

IAGO What, Man? 'Tis a Night of Revels, the
Gallants desire it.

CASSIO Where are they?

IAGO Here, at the Door: I pray you call them in. 45

CASSIO I'll do't, but it dislikes me. *Exit.*

IAGO — If I can fasten but one Cup upon him,
With that which he hath drunk to night already,
He'll be as full of Quarrel and Offence
As my young Mistress' Dog. Now my sick Fool
Roderigo, 50
Whom Love hath turn'd almost the Wrong Side
out,
To Desdemona hath to night carous'd
Potations Pottle-deep; and he's to Watch.
Three else of Cyprus, noble swelling Spirits,
That hold their Honours in a wary Distance 55
(The very Elements of this Warlike Isle)
Have I to night fluster'd with flowing Cups,
And they watch too. Now 'mongst this flock of
Drunkards
Am I to put our Cassio in some Action
That may offend the Isle. But here they come. 60

---

59 **put . . . Action** prompt Cassio to some reaction. *Put* echoes
II.i.319, II.ii.4–5; *Action* recalls I.iii.82–84.

61   **If . . . Dream** if what follows will only prove my dream prophetic. Here *Dream* is a metaphor for 'scheme'. *Dream* recalls I.i.142.

63   **given . . . Rouse** imbibed a 'Potation' to my 'Health' (line 29).

65   **past** more than.

68   **Canakin** little can (small tankard).

71   **Span** literally, the width of an outstretched hand. Iago's song alludes to Psalm 39:5, which was rendered 'thou hast made my days as it were a span long' in the Elizabethan Book of Common Prayer.

76   **potent in Potting** proficient (that is, manly) in drinking.

77   **Germaine** German.
        swag-bellied with an engorged, swaying midsection.

78   **to** compared to.

79   **exquisite** choice, distinguished. Compare lines 18, 98.

81   **you** Like *me* (lines 68–69), this pronoun is an example of what grammarians call the ethic dative, a form of colloquial familiarity similar to the use of *your* rather than *the* as an article (lines 76–77). See I.i.48.

82   **overthrow** outdrink. Iago is cleverly challenging Cassio and his companions to prove that they are no less 'potent' than 'your English', let alone 'your Almaine' and 'your Hollander'. *Overthrow* anticipates 'Vomit' (line 83). Compare lines 14–15.

83   **Almaine** German (from *Allemagne*). *Pottle* ('Stope', line 27) echoes lines 52–53.

89   **and a** a. The extra *and* serves as a metrical filler.
        Peer nobleman. But here as in *The Tempest*, IV.i.222–23, the context suggests wordplay on 'pee-er', with the implication that the consequences of King Stephen's 'Potting' (line 76) was that he wet his 'Breeches' (line 90).

90   **cost . . . Crown** cost him only a crown (in England, a coin worth five shillings), with wordplay on the other kind of 'Crown' a king has at his disposal – and with an implicit warning that there may soon be others whose 'breeches' will prove costly. Syphilis caused one's crown to go bald.

91   **He . . . dear** he insisted that they were a sixpence too expensive. *Dear* recalls I.iii.256–57, II.i.305–6.

92   **Lown** literally, low one (as in line 94); worthless rascal.

Enter Cassio, Montano, and Gentlemen.

If Consequence do but approve my Dream,
My Boat sails freely, both with Wind and
   Stream.

CASSIO   'Fore Heaven, they have given me a Rouse
already.

MONTANO   Good faith, a little one: not past a   65
Pint, as I am a Soldier.

IAGO   — Some Wine, ho.
         And let me the Canakin clink, clink:
         And let me the Canakin clink.
            A Soldier's a Man: 70
               Oh Man's Life's but a Span,
            Why then let a Soldier drink.
Some Wine, Boys.

CASSIO   'Fore Heaven, an excellent Song.

IAGO   I learn'd it in England, where indeed they   75
are most potent in Potting. Your Dane, your
Germaine, and your swag-bellied Hollander —
drink, ho — are nothing to your English.

CASSIO   Is your Englishman so exquisite in his
Drinking?   80

IAGO   Why, he drinks you with facility your Dane
dead drunk. He sweats not to overthrow your
Almaine. He gives your Hollander a Vomit, ere
the next Pottle can be fill'd.

CASSIO   To the Health of our General.   85

MONTANO   I am for it, Lieutenant: and I'll do
you Justice.

IAGO   Oh sweet England.
         King Stephen was and a worthy Peer;
            His Breeches cost him but a Crown,   90
         He held them Sixpence all too dear,
            With that he call'd the Tailor Lown.

94

93   **Wight**   person. Compare II.i.134, 160.

95   **Pride**   In the framework of the song, this word means 'ostentation', 'extravagance'. But in the overarching structure of the play as a whole, it can refer to other manifestations of what the New Testament refers to as the 'pride of life' (1 John 2:16), including the 'swelling Spirits' (line 54) now being incited to further proofs of how 'potent' (line 76) they are.

96   **And . . . thee**   therefore content yourself with your old cloak [and don't aspire to 'Breeches' that are too big for you].

102–4 **Well . . . saved**   Cassio alludes to the doctrine of predestination, associated in Shakespeare's time with Calvinism; see Romans 8:28 – 11:36 for the Apostle Paul's exposition of this teaching.

107   **Quality**   'high Renown' (line 93); nobility or elevated station. Cassio is reminding himself that he is 'but of low Degree' (line 94), despite the 'Pride' (line 95) he displays in lines 111–12.

113   **God . . . Sins**   Cassio is probably thinking about his surrender to his 'Weakness' (line 40). But he also knows he is now vulnerable to other 'Sins' that could cost him 'his Place' (lines 101–2) if not his salvation. His theology reflects such passages as Ephesians 2:8, 'by grace are ye saved through faith; and that not of yourselves: it is the gift of God'. See the note to I.i.26.

114   **let's . . . Business**   let's turn our attention to the duties we've been assigned. Compare lines 1, 4–6. *Business* recalls I.i.151–53, I.ii.40, 90, I.iii.13, 52–53, 264–72.

122   **Platform**   ramparts where the watch will be positioned.

124   **that . . . before**   who left a moment ago.

125– **fit . . . Direction**   capable of standing alongside so eminent a
26   general as Caesar and giving instructions as his lieutenant. *Direction* echoes line 4; *stand* recalls II.i.308; *fit* harks back to I.iii.235–38.

127   **a just Equinox**   a precise opposite, a 'nox' (night) side that counterpoises the light-reflecting hemisphere of his nature. Iago refers to the two times each year when day and night are of equal length; he balances two words beginning with *V* to reinforce his meaning. One of them, *Virtue*, derives from the Latin term for man (*vir*); compare I.iii.316–19. By his devious manipulation of 'manhood,' Iago is turning Cassio away from true masculinity towards a vicious perversion of it. Compare I.i.122. *Vice* recalls I.iii.122.

> He was a Wight of high Renown,
> And thou art but of low Degree;
> > 'Tis Pride that pulls the Country down,   95
> > And take thy awl'd Cloak about thee.

– Some Wine ho.

CASSIO   'Fore God, this is a more exquisite
Song than the other.

IAGO   Will you hear't again?   100

CASSIO   No: for I hold him to be unworthy of his
Place that does those things. Well, Heav'n's
above all; and there be Souls must be saved,
and there be Souls must not be saved.

IAGO   It's true, good Lieutenant.   105

CASSIO   For mine own part, no offence to the
General, nor any man of Quality: I hope to
be saved.

IAGO   And so do I too, Lieutenant.

CASSIO   Ay, but by your leave, not before me.   110
The Lieutenant is to be saved before the
Ancient. Let's have no more of this: let's
to our Affairs. God forgive us our Sins.
Gentlemen, let's look to our Business. Do
not think, Gentlemen, I am drunk: this is my   115
Ancient, this is my Right Hand, and this is
my Left. I am not drunk now: I can stand well
enough, and I speak well enough.

GENTLEMEN   Excellent well.

CASSIO   Why very well then: you must not think   120
then that I am drunk.   *Exit.*

MONTANO   To th' Platform, Masters, come, let's
set the Watch.

IAGO   You see this Fellow, that is gone before,
He's a Soldier fit to stand by Caesar   125
And give Direction. And do but see his Vice,
'Tis to his Virtue a just Equinox,

128 'Tis . . . him   It's a pity he has this flaw.

130 On . . . Infirmity   sometime when he is under the influence of
     this 'ingraft' (deeply implanted) debility (line 143). Compare
     II.iii.39–41.

133– He'll . . . Cradle   He'll stay awake long enough for the clock to
34   make two revolutions (mark twenty-four hours) if he is not
     rocked to sleep by alcohol. Here *watch* serves as a pointed
     reminder that Cassio is now supposedly on another kind of
     'watch'.

139 How now   If Roderigo enters before this line (as the Folio
     indicates), Iago asks 'How are you?' and then sends him off to
     watch over the man who should be supervising the watch. If
     Roderigo enters after this line (as the Quarto suggests), Iago
     probably means 'ho now' and is summoning Roderigo. In
     either case, Iago's order is designed to display his own
     discretion and responsibility.

143 ingraft   in-grafted; embedded. Compare the plant imagery in
     II.i.287–89. *Infirmity* echoes line 130; *Action* recalls lines
     58–60, a passage echoed in lines 129–31.

144– It . . . Moor   It would be an honourable gesture to caution
45   Othello.

145 for . . . Island   even if you offered to give me this entire island
     in recompense. Iago pretends to be protecting either (a)
     Cassio, or (b) himself from Othello's wrath; meanwhile he is
     declining an opportunity to perform a genuinely 'Honest
     Action' (line 144).

147 To . . . Evil   to treat his disease [rather than get him in trouble
     because of it]. Iago plans to 'cure' Cassio thoroughly.

148 'Zouns   by God's wounds. Cassio's oath is ironically
     appropriate to the situation in which he finds himself.

150 teach . . . Duty   instruct me in how to do my job (conduct
     myself like an officer in charge of the watch).

151 Twiggen-Bottle   wicker-woven flask (like a modern Chianti
     bottle).

152 prate   make empty threats. Compare II.i.228.

156 Mazzard   head.

The one as long as th' other. 'Tis pity of him:
I fear the Trust Othello puts him in
On some Odd Time of his Infirmity   130
Will shake this Island.
MONTANO   But is he often thus?
IAGO 'Tis evermore his Prologue to his Sleep:
He'll watch the Horologe a double Set
If Drink rock not his Cradle.
MONTANO   It were well
The General were put in Mind of it: 135
Perhaps he sees it not, or his good Nature
Prizes the Virtue that appears in Cassio
And looks not on his Evils. Is not this true?

Enter Roderigo.

IAGO — How now, Roderigo?
I pray you after the Lieutenant, go.   *Exit Roderigo.*   140
MONTANO And 'tis great pity that the noble Moor
Should hazard such a Place as his own Second
With one of an ingraft Infirmity:
It were an Honest Action to say
So to the Moor.
IAGO   Not I, for this fair Island,   145
I do love Cassio well: and would do much
To cure him of this Evil.
[VOICE] *within*   Help, help.
IAGO But hark, what Noise?

Enter Cassio pursuing Roderigo.

CASSIO   'Zouns, you Rogue: you Rascal.
MONTANO What's the matter, Lieutenant?
CASSIO A Knave teach me my Duty? I'll beat the Knave   150
Into a Twiggen-Bottle.
RODERIGO   Beat me?
CASSIO Dost thou prate, Rogue?
MONTANO Nay, good Lieutenant: I pray you, Sir,
hold your Hand.
CASSIO Let me go, Sir, or I'll knock you o'er   155
the Mazzard.

159 — **Away . . . Mutiny** Iago whispers this order to Roderigo, telling him to go yelling that a disturbance has broken out. *Mutiny* echoes II.i.285–87.

162 **Here's . . . indeed** Iago's point is that it's a fine state of affairs when the watch, responsible for maintaining public order, is itself the cause of disorder.

163 **Diablo** the Devil (Italian).

164 **rise** both (a) awaken, and (b) be up in arms (a two-man altercation turning into a general riot).

165 **You'll . . . ever** Your reputation will never recover from this.

169 **Have . . . Duty?** Have you forgotten the place that common sense and your responsibilities should have in your lives? *Sense* recalls I.iii.67–68.

173 **Are . . . Turks?** Have we been transformed into the enemies we've come here to protect the island against? The Muslim Turks were proverbial as infidels. To turn Turk, then, was (a) to become a turncoat (traitor) to God and to Christendom, and (b) to revert from civilization to 'Christian Shame' (line 175), barbarism. Compare II.i.115.

174 **Which . . . Ottamites** which Heaven [because of the tempest] has prevented the Turk from doing to us.

176 **to . . . Rage** to use a blade to indulge and vent his private rage.

177 **Holds . . . light** places little value on his life.
he . . . Motion he condemns himself to death if he 'stirs' to move a hand towards his sword. *Motion* recalls I.iii.93–95, 331–32.

180 **that . . . Grieving** who looks ashen from grief over what has happened.

181 **On . . . thee** For the sake of your devotion to me (and on peril of your losing my own love if you don't obey), I order you.

MONTANO   Come, come: you're drunk.
CASSIO   Drunk?
IAGO   — Away, I say: go out and cry a Mutiny.
                                        [*Exit Roderigo.*]
   — Nay good Lieutenant. — God's will, Gentlemen.   160
   — Help ho. — Lieutenant. — Sir Montano, Sir.
   — Help, Masters. Here's a goodly Watch indeed.
   Who's that which rings the Bell? Diablo, ho.
   The Town will rise. — Fie, fie, Lieutenant,
      hold.
   You'll be asham'd for ever.   165

Enter Othello, and Attendants.

OTHELLO   What is the matter here?
MONTANO   'Zouns, I bleed still,
   I am hurt to th' Death. He dies.
OTHELLO   —   Hold, for your Lives.
IAGO   Hold, ho: Lieutenant, Sir Montano, Gentlemen,
   Have you forgot all place of Sense and Duty?
   Hold. The General speaks to you: hold, hold,   170
   For Shame.
OTHELLO   Why how now ho? From whence ariseth
      this?
   Are we turn'd Turks? and to our selves do that
   Which Heaven hath forbid the Ottamites.
   For Christian Shame, put by this barbarous
      Brawl: 175
   He that stirs next, to carve for his own Rage,
   Holds his Soul light: he dies upon his Motion.
   — Silence that dreadful Bell, it frights the
      Isle
   From her Propriety. — What's the matter,
      Masters?
   — Honest Iago, that looks dead with Grieving,   180
   Speak: who began this? On thy Love I charge
      thee?
IAGO   I do not know: Friends all, but now, even
   now.

183 **In Quarter** Most commentators interpret Iago to mean (a) at their assigned posts. But in view of the wedding-night image that follows (a reminder that Iago has again disturbed a bride and groom who have undressed themselves 'for Bed'), it seems more likely that his primary meaning is (b) in close quarters (celebrating together in accordance with the General's proclamation). *In Quarter* and *in terms* both hint at the 'tilting' that grooms engage in when they draw their 'Swords out' for a more joyous form of 'Opposition bloody' (lines 186–87), as they break the hymens of their virgin brides.

184 **Devesting them** disrobing themselves.

185 **As . . . Men** as if men had lost their minds as a result of the influence of some malign planet.

187– **I . . . it** I am unable to tell you how this stupid conflict began
90 and only wish that I had lost my legs in honourable battle before they brought me here to witness such shameful conduct.

191 **you . . . forgot** you have forgotten yourself (failed to bear in mind the role that defines you as an officer) in this way.

193 **wont . . . civil** always accustomed to be properly behaved (civilized). *Civil* echoes I.i.129–31, II.i.244–48.

194 **Gravity and Stillness** sobriety and calm constancy. Compare I.iii.93–97.

196 **Censure** judgement.

198 **Opinion** reputation, 'Name' (lines 195, 198). Compare I.iii.221–25. Othello compares 'Reputation' to a purse (see I.i.1–3) whose strings Montano has unlaced in profligate spending; compare I.iii.296–98. *Answer* recalls I.iii.348–49.

200 **hurt to Danger** injured to a degree that threatens my life.

202 **which . . . me** which causes me additional pain in my present state. Here *something* means 'somewhat'.

205 **Self-charity** self-love; an instinct for self-preservation. Compare I.i.11, 41–59, I.iii.309–12.

208 **My . . . rule** my unruly emotions begin to oversway my reason. *Blood* recalls II.i.231–33.

209 **collied** blackened (as with coal), with a suggestion of *collared* and *cholered* (overcome with choler, the humour associated with anger).

In Quarter, and in terms like Bride and Groom
Devesting them for Bed: and then, but now
(As if some Planet had unwitted Men),   185
Swords out, and tilting one at other's Breasts,
In Opposition bloody. I cannot speak
Any Beginning to this peevish Odds.
And would in Action glorious I had lost
Those Legs that brought me to a part of it.   190
OTHELLO   How comes it, Michael, you are thus
    forgot?
CASSIO   I pray you pardon me, I cannot speak.
OTHELLO   Worthy Montano, you were wont to be
    civil:
The Gravity and Stillness of your Youth
The World hath noted. And your Name is great   195
In Mouths of wisest Censure. What's the matter
That you unlace your Reputation thus,
And spend your rich Opinion, for the Name
Of a Night-brawler? Give me Answer to it.
MONTANO   Worthy Othello, I am hurt to Danger;   200
Your Officer Iago can inform you,
While I spare Speech which something now
    offends me,
Of all that I do know, nor know I ought
By me that's said or done amiss this Night,
Unless Self-charity be sometimes a Vice,   205
And to defend our selves it be a Sin
When Violence assails us.
OTHELLO   Now by Heaven,
My Blood begins my safer Guides to rule,
And Passion, having my best Judgement collied,
Assays to lead the way. If I once stir,   210

211–
12   **the best . . . Rebuke**   even the most valiant of you shall die at my hands. Compare lines 210–16 with I.iii.64–69.

214   **approv'd . . . Offence**   proven guilty of this outrage. *Offence* echoes line 107; *approv'd* echoes lines 61–62 and recalls II.i.49; *foul* recalls II.i.267–69.

215   **twinn'd with me**   been brought into the world as my twin. Compare lines 214–16 with the Duke's remarks in I.iii.64–69.

216   **loose me**   (a) unleash me, (b) lose me [as a friend], and (c) loosen me [from the bonds that tie me to him]. *Loose* and *lose* were less distinguishable in Shakespeare's time than they are now. Compare I.iii.209.
       of War   under garrison by occupying forces.

218   **manage**   conduct. Such quarrelling is in fact an indication of the combatants' lack of management (self-control).

219   **on . . . Safety**   in the very place (the headquarters of the security detail), and by the very guards, associated with the maintenance of 'domestic' (civil) order.

220   **monstrous**   so extraordinary as to seem like a breach of the natural order of things. *Monstrous* frequently carries overtones of its Latin root, *monstrare*, to signal or warn [of future evils]. Compare I.iii.410–11, II.i.13, III.iii.104–5.

221   **partially . . . Office**   partial [to Cassio] because of your affinity (friendship) with him, or in league with him because you are his ensign. See the third note to I.i.120 and compare I.iii.251–52.

223   **Touch . . . near**   both (a) don't add to the pain I already feel by reminding me of how close I am to Cassio, and (b) don't gall me by implying that, despite those ties, I am unable to do what my honour as a soldier requires and tell the truth.

230–
31   **with . . . him**   with his sword drawn in a manner that displayed his determination to execute the fellow he pursued.

232   **entreats his Pause**   urges him to halt.

234   **Least**   lest. Compare IV.i.211, IV.ii.33.

236   **then rather**   all the more rapidly. *Purpose* recalls I.i.11–12, I.iii.37–39, 397–98.

240   **this was brief**   this all happened very quickly.

Or do but lift this Arm, the best of you
Shall sink in my Rebuke. Give me to know
How this foul Rout began: who set it on,
And he that is approv'd in this Offence,
Though he had twinn'd with me, both at a Birth,   215
Shall loose me. What, in a Town of War,
Yet Wild, the People's Hearts brim-full of
    Fear,
To manage private and domestic Quarrel?
In Night, and on the Court and Guard of
    Safety?
'Tis monstrous: Iago, who began't?   220
MONTANO   If, partially affin'd, or leagu'd in
    Office,
Thou dost deliver more or less than Truth,
Thou art no Soldier.
IAGO   Touch me not so near:
I had rather have this Tongue cut from my Mouth
Than it should do Offence to Michael Cassio.   225
Yet I persuade my self, to speak the Truth
Shall nothing wrong him. – This it is, General:
Montano and my self being in Speech,
There comes a Fellow crying out for Help,
And Cassio following him with determin'd Sword   230
To execute upon him. Sir, this Gentleman
Steps in to Cassio, and entreats his Pause:
My self the crying Fellow did pursue,
Least by his Clamour (as it so fell out)
The Town might fall in Fright. He, swift of
    Foot,   235
Outran my Purpose: and I return'd then rather
For that I heard the Clink and Fall of Swords,
And Cassio high in Oath: which till to night
I ne'er might say before. When I came back
(For this was brief), I found them close
    together   240

241 **At . . . Thrust** striking each other and thrusting their swords in an effort to shed blood. Iago's phrasing is a reminder that while all this was happening outside, Othello and his bride were 'close together' (line 240) in a way that connoted harmony rather than discord. See the note to line 183.

244 **forget** lose control of themselves (literally, forget what is required of 'Men' in the ideal sense because they are subject to the failings common to all of Adam's descendants). Compare lines 169 and 191. *Best* echoes lines 210–12, 246.

248 **some strange Indignity** some insult of an undetermined but no doubt intolerable nature.

249 **Which . . . pass** which was more than a man of honour could bear with patience (passivity). *Patience* recalls II.i.98–99.

250 **mince** understate; literally, chop up to make it easier to swallow.

251 **light** less severe. Compare lines 176–77.

253– **Look . . . Example** Having just upbraided Cassio for engaging
54 in 'private and domestic Quarrel' (line 218), Othello now commits a version of the same offence. By allowing the personal impact of Cassio's crime to affect his judgement of Cassio, Othello gives Iago the wherewithal to initiate another such 'Quarrel' that will touch the General even more 'near' (line 223).

256 **Hurts** injuries. Compare line 200.

259 **vild** vile. *Look* (line 258) echoes lines 114, 253.
   distracted agitated, wrought up.

262 **I** both 'I' and 'Ay'. Compare I.iii.36.
   past all Surgery beyond the power of any physician to heal me.

263 **Marry** truly, indeed. See the note to I.ii.53, and compare II.i.106–8.

267 **bestial** the lower, animal part of my soul (that which is subject to decay and death).

At Blow and Thrust, even as again they were
When you your self did part them.
More of this Matter cannot I report,
But Men are Men, the best sometimes forget;
Though Cassio did some little Wrong to him,   245
As Men in Rage strike those that wish them best,
Yet surely Cassio I believe receiv'd
From him that fled some strange Indignity,
Which Patience could not pass.

OTHELLO   I know, Iago,
Thy Honesty and Love doth mince this Matter,   250
Making it light to Cassio. – Cassio, I love
    thee,
But never more be Officer of mine.

                Enter Desdemona attended.

Look if my gentle Love be not rais'd up:
I'll make thee an Example.

DESDEMONA   What is the matter, Dear?

OTHELLO   All's well now, Sweeting: 255
Come away to Bed. – Sir, for your Hurts,
My self will be your Surgeon. – Lead him off.
– Iago, look with Care about the Town,
And silence those whom this vild Brawl
    distracted.
– Come, Desdemona, 'tis the Soldier's Life   260
To have their balmy Slumbers wak'd with Strife.
                Exit [with Desdemona and Attendants].

IAGO   What, are you hurt, Lieutenant?

CASSIO   I, past all Surgery.

IAGO   Marry, Heaven forbid.

CASSIO   Reputation,
Reputation, Reputation: oh I
Have lost my Reputation. I have lost   265
The Immortal Part, Sir, of my Self, and what
Remains is bestial. My Reputation, Iago,
My Reputation.

IAGO   As I am an Honest Man, I had thought you

271   **Sense** Iago plays on several meanings of this word: (a) reason for concern, (b) physical feeling, and (c) rationality, wisdom.

272   **Imposition** something placed or stamped on a person externally. Here *idle* means 'worthless' or 'trivial'.

272–   **oft . . . Deserving** Iago's words have their most immediate
73   bearing on himself and on Cassio's rise to and fall from favour, but soon they will relate to several other characters. Iago alludes to the Reformation view that salvation is determined not by 'Merit' or 'Deserving' but by Grace; he thus echoes what Cassio has said in lines 102–4, 110–13.

275   **Looser** loser. But here or elsewhere (see I.iii.209), the meanings associated with *loosing* (releasing, divesting) are also pertinent. Compare lines 215–16.

276   **recover** both (a) regain [the esteem of], and (b) cure.

277   **cast . . . Mood** discarded as a result of his anger. Compare line 14.

278   **in Policy** both (a) resulting from Othello's desire to display the political judgement and resolution to be expected of one in his position, and (b) resulting from Iago's own 'Policy' (cunning).
     then than. But here as elsewhere (see *Macbeth*, III.ii.7, III.iv.13), the usual modern sense of *then* can apply as well. The comma preceding *then* is here retained from the Folio text.

280   **Sue to him** plead with him, beg for reinstatement. Compare I.i.6–16. In this line *imperious* means 'haughty' or 'tyrant-like' in manner; *offenceless* echoes line 225.

284   **indiscreet** unwise and undisciplined. Compare lines 1–3.

286–   **discourse . . . Shadow** parrot coarse nonsense to oneself; boast
87   and quarrel over things of no substance. *Fustian* is a rough-textured cloth composed of cotton and flax; like bombast (see the note to I.i.12) it was often used as padding.

290   **What** who; what man.

294   **mass** large quantity.

295   **nothing wherefore** nothing about why it occurred. *Quarrel* echoes lines 49–50.

299   **Applause** Cassio alludes to the boasting and cheering that goes with the kind of 'Potting' where men seek to do 'Justice' to one another (meet each other's challenges in revelry, lines 75–87).

had received some Bodily Wound; there is more 270
Sense in that than in Reputation. Reputation
is an idle and most false Imposition; oft got
without Merit, and lost without Deserving.
You have lost no Reputation at all, unless
you repute your self such a Looser. What, Man, 275
there are more ways to recover the General again.
You are but now cast in his Mood (a Punishment
more in Policy, then in Malice), even so as one
would beat his offenceless Dog to affright an
imperious Lion. Sue to him again, and he's 280
yours.

CASSIO I will rather sue to be despis'd than
to deceive so good a Commander with so slight,
so drunken, and so indiscreet an Officer.
Drunk? And speak Parrot? And Squabble? Swagger? 285
Swear? And discourse Fustian with one's own
Shadow? – Oh thou invisible Spirit of Wine, if
thou hast no Name to be known by, let us call
thee Divel.

IAGO What was he that you follow'd with your 290
Sword? What had he done to you?

CASSIO I know not.

IAGO Is't possible?

CASSIO I remember a mass of things, but nothing
distinctly: a Quarrel, but nothing wherefore. 295
Oh God, that Men should put an Enemy in their
Mouths to steal away their Brains? That we
should with Joy, Pleasance, Revel, and
Applause transform our selves into Beasts.

IAGO Why? But you are now well enough: how came 300
you thus recovered?

CASSIO It hath pleas'd the Divel Drunkenness
to give place to the Divel Wrath; one

304 **Unperfectness** vice (reduction of the human form to that of
'Beasts', line 299), as defined in I.iii.319–35 and II.iii.125–28,
265–67. Compare I.i.43–47, 86–88, 107–12, 114–16.
Unperfectness echoes lines 25–26.

305 **frankly** freely, openly.

308 **hartily** heartily. But here as elsewhere there is potential for
wordplay on *hart* (stag); compare *Hamlet*, I.v.131. *Condition*
(line 307) recalls I.ii.24–28, II.i.258–59.

311 **I will** if I should.

313 **Hydra** a many-headed serpent in Greek mythology who grew
two heads (and thus 'Mouths') for each one that was chopped
off.
stop both (a) stuff, and (b) cause to cease pleading. Compare
II.i.199 and II.iii.2–3. *Answer* echoes line 199.

314 **Sensible** rational, wise. Compare line 271.
by and by in a short time, 'presently' (line 315). *Beast* (line
315) echoes line 299.

316 **inordinate** excessive, unfitting, disorderly.
unbless'd contrary to virtue and grace. Compare II.i.258–64,
II.iii.330–33.

317 **Ingredient** contents, ingredients.

318 **familiar** friendly, serviceable. But Iago is probably alluding to
the idea of a 'familiar spirit' (an accompanying devil); see
lines 316–17. Iago has just shown one way in which that kind
of spirit can be 'well us'd'.

322 **approved it** attested it, proved it by experience. Compare line
214.

324– **Our . . . General** Cassio has spoken similarly in II.i.74, but
25 with no suggestion of uxoriousness. Compare II.i.184.

328 **Mark** marking; attending to, noting.
Devotement of devoting himself to.
Parts attributes, virtues (see the third note to I.i.120, and
compare II.iii.221).

329 **Confess your self** confide your thoughts. Iago plays on various
religious senses of *Confess*, depicting Cassio as a penitent who
is both professing his faith and confessing his sins to a priestly
intercessor; but see *Measure for Measure*, V.i.268, for a
copulative sense of *confess*. As he speaks, Iago is anticipating
the way he will induce Othello to interpret Cassio's
confession.

Unperfectness shews me another, to make me
frankly despise my self.   305
IAGO   Come, you are too severe a Moraller. As the
Time, the Place, and the Condition of this
Country stands, I could hartily wish this
had not befall'n: but since it is as it is,
mend it for your own good.   310
CASSIO   I will ask him for my Place again, he
shall tell me I am a Drunkard: had I as many
Mouths as Hydra, such an Answer would stop
them all. To be now a Sensible Man, by and by
a Fool, and presently a Beast. Oh strange!   315
Every inordinate Cup is unbless'd, and the
Ingredient is a Divel.
IAGO   Come, come, good Wine is a good familiar
Creature, if it be well us'd: exclaim no more
against it. And good Lieutenant, I think you   320
think I love you.
CASSIO   I have well approved it, Sir. I drunk?
IAGO   You, or any man living, may be drunk at a
Time, Man. I tell you what you shall do. Our
General's Wife is now the General. I may say   325
so in this Respect, for that he hath devoted
and given up himself to the Contemplation,
Mark, and Devotement of her Parts and Graces.
Confess your self freely to her: importune

---

329   **importune**   urgently entreat. The Latin root of *importune*
      means 'seek entry to a *portus* [an opening]', and the precision
      of Iago's verb is reinforced by 'put you in your Place again'.
      Virtually every phrase that follows is subliminally provocative
      in comparable ways. Since *Vice* can mean (a) a screw, and (b)
      a clamp or vise (as in *Much Ado About Nothing*, V.ii.21), the
      clause 'she holds it a Vice [flaw] in her Goodness' hints at a
      'Disposition' (literally, a placing apart) that is anything but
      'blessed' in the sense in which Roderigo has introduced that
      word in II.i.259. *Vice* (line 332) echoes lines 126, 205.

336 **Lay** wager (but with a secondary implication that relates to the suggestiveness of 'Joint' and 'this Crack of your Love'). See the note to III.iii.145.

340 **protest** vow, promise; profess.

342 **betimes** early (as in I.iii.382).

344 **undertake for me** take my situation on herself and serve as my agent. Cassio's verb carries unintended implications that relate to Iago's own undertaking; compare *Twelfth Night*, I.iii.60–61, where Sir Andrew Ague-cheek says, 'I would not undertake her in this company.'

345 **check me here** stop my progress at this point in my career. *Check* recalls I.i.147–49; here as there, the sense of the word that relates to chess moves may be pertinent (see lines 348–51).

350– **Probal . . . again** something that analysis would prove to be
51 consistent with sound thinking, and in fact the most direct way to change the General's mind. Compare I.ii.75–76.

352 **inclining** compliant, eager to be of service. See I.ii.82 and I.iii.143–44.

352– **subdue . . . Suit** overcome (win over) in any virtuous request.
53 *Subdue* recalls I.ii.80–81, I.iii.110–11, 248–49.

353– **fram'd . . . Elements** constitutionally disposed to be as
54 generous with her bounty as the elements (earth, water, air, and fire) that freely bestow all that is necessary to sustain life and growth.

355 **were . . . Baptism** even if she requested him to forswear his Christian faith [and embrace an eternity in Hell].

356 **All . . . Sin** all the sacraments and liturgical symbols of [his] redemption from the wages of sin. Compare lines 102–13.

358 **list** wishes. See the note to II.i.220.

360 **Function** vitality. *Appetite* (line 359) recalls I.iii.259–62 and II.i.231–33.

361– **this . . . good** this course, which runs parallel to [whether or
62 not it is identical with] what would seem to be the most direct route to 'his good'. Iago's perverse 'Divinity' (line 362) illustrates 2 Corinthians 11:4.

her Help to put you in your Place again. She   330
is of so free, so kind, so apt, so blessed
a Disposition, she holds it a Vice in her
Goodness not to do more than she is requested.
This Broken Joint between you and her Husband
entreat her to splinter. And my Fortunes   335
against any Lay worth naming, this Crack of
your Love shall grow stronger than it was
before.

CASSIO   You advise me well.

IAGO   I protest in the Sincerity of Love, and   340
honest Kindness.

CASSIO   I think it freely: and betimes in the
Morning I will beseech the virtuous Desdemona
to undertake for me. I am desperate of my
Fortunes if they check me here.   345

IAGO   You are in the right: good night,
    Lieutenant,
I must to the Watch.

CASSIO   Good night, honest Iago.   *Exit.*

IAGO   And what's he, then, that says I play the
    Villain?
When this Advise is free I give, and honest,
Probal to Thinking, and indeed the Course   350
To win the Moor again. For 'tis most easy
Th' inclining Desdemona to subdue
In any honest Suit. She's fram'd as fruitful
As the free Elements. And then for her
To win the Moor, were't to renounce his
    Baptism,
                                                           355
All Seals and Symbols of Redeemed Sin:
His Soul is so enfetter'd to her Love
That she may make, unmake, do what she list,
Even as her Appetite shall play the God,
With his weak Function. How am I then a
    Villain,
                                                           360
To counsel Cassio to this parallel Course,
Directly to his good? Divinity of Hell,

364 **suggest** both (a) plant suggestions, and (b) prompt, tempt. *Shews* (shows) are appearances; compare line 304.

368 **powre** pour (but with more than a hint of 'power'). See the note to I.iii.103.
Pestilence plague, contagion.

369 **repeals him** appeals for his reinstatement.

372 **Pitch** black tar (symbolic of evil at its most foul). *Virtue* (goodness) echoes lines 136–38.

374 **en-mash** both (a) enmesh (the word in the Quarto, adopted here by most editions), and (b) mash (crush and blend together).

376– **fills . . . Cry** serves merely as a supporting member of the
77 chorus of baying dogs. The Prince of Denmark uses a similar image when he refers to himself as a fellow in a 'Cry of Players' who will 'catch' their quarry with stagecraft (*Hamlet*, III.ii.304, II.ii.641–42). Compare Iago's hunting metaphors in II.i.317–20.

379 **Issue** fruit, harvest of my labours.

381 **Wit** wisdom, intelligence (what he will have learned by employing Iago as his go-between). 'Wit' frequently carries genital implications, and Roderigo's phrasing conveys a recognition that the 'Experience' he ends up with will have involved no satisfying 'Issue' of that kind of wit. See the note to II.i.130.

383 **Patience** the ability to bear Fortune's hardships without losing all faith and hope. Compare lines 247–49.

386 **dilatory** expansive (and thus long-delaying); spreading apart, enlarging. Compare I.iii.148–51. *Time* recalls II.i.278–81.

388 **cashier'd** discarded, dismissed from his position. Compare I.i.43–47. The Folio's *hath*, ungrammatical by modern standards, may have been used deliberately here for purposes of balance (see line 387) and of euphony, to forestall an excessive cluster of *s*-sounds. Most of today's editions follow the Quarto and print *hast*.

389 **Though . . . Sun** though other plants appear to be thriving in the sun's light. Here *things grow* and *against* hint at the 'Fruits that blossom first' in Othello's 'garden' (see lines 9–10, and compare I.i.69–70). Meanwhile Roderigo must be 'Content' with Iago's allusions to the 'Pleasure, and Action' that Desdemona's unsuccessful suitor can only dream about (lines 391–92). *Fruits* echoes lines 353–54.

When Divels will the blackest Sins put on,
They do suggest at first with heavenly Shews,
As I do now. For whiles this honest Fool   365
Plies Desdemona to repair his Fortune,
And she for him pleads strongly to the Moor,
I'll powre this Pestilence into his Ear,
That she repeals him for her Body's Lust;
And by how much she strives to do him good,   370
She shall undo her Credit with the Moor.
So will I turn her Virtue into Pitch,
And out of her own Goodness make the Net
That shall en-mash them all.

Enter Roderigo.

           – How now, Roderigo?
RODERIGO   I do follow here in the Chase, not   375
  like a Hound that hunts, but one that fills
  up the Cry. My Money is almost spent; I have
  been to night exceedingly well cudgell'd; and I
  think the Issue will be, I shall have so much
  Experience for my Pains; and, so, with no   380
  Money at all, and a little more Wit, return
  again to Venice.
IAGO   How poor are they that have not Patience?
  What Wound did ever heal but by Degrees?
  Thou know'st we work by Wit, and not by
    Witchcraft,
  And Wit depends on dilatory Time.   385
  Does't not go well? Cassio hath beaten thee,
  And thou by that small Hurt hath cashier'd
    Cassio.
  Though other things grow fair against the Sun,
  Yet Fruits that blossom first will first be
    ripe:
                          390
  Content thy self awhile. By the Mass 'tis
    Morning;
  Pleasure, and Action, make the Hours seem short.

393   **billeted**   lodged, quartered. *Action* echoes lines 58–60, 144–45, 189.

399   **jump**   precisely. The Duke has used this word in I.iii.5.

400   **Soliciting**   entreating assistance from. But Iago plans to persuade Othello that Cassio is wooing Desdemona for other kinds of favours.

401   **Dull . . . Delay**   Don't allow schemes to grow cold by postponing them.

Retire thee, go where thou art billeted;
Away, I say, thou shalt know more hereafter;
Nay get thee gone.   *Exit Roderigo.*
                         – Two things are to be done: 395
My Wife must move for Cassio to her Mistress
(I'll set her on), my self, a while, to draw
The Moor apart,
And bring him jump when he may Cassio find
Soliciting his Wife. Ay, that's the Way: 400
Dull not Device by Coldness and Delay.   *Exit.*

III.i   This scene takes place outside Othello's lodgings at the Citadel.

1   **content your Pains**   reward your labours. Cassio's phrasing
         echoes the discussion of Roderigo's 'Pains' at the end of the
         preceding scene (II.iii.380). It also echoes the previous
         references to *content* in I.i.40, I.iii.225, and II.i.185, 193, 198,
         313. *Brief* (line 2) echoes II.iii.240.

3-4   **Why . . . thus?**   The Clown suggests that the Musicians' music
         resembles the nasal tone of those whose 'Instruments' have
         'been in Naples' and caught syphilis. One manifestation of
         'the Neapolitan Bone-ache' (*Troilus and Cressida*,
         II.iii.21-22) was a deterioration of the nose bridge (see *Timon
         of Athens*, IV.iii.154-56). On the basis of line 20 it is clear
         that the Musicians are playing bagpipes. The shape of these
         instruments had long associated them with the male genitalia,
         and they were proverbial symbols of the lusts of the flesh. For
         Nose as an anatomical protrusion with analogies to the penis,
         see *Antony and Cleopatra*, I.ii.54-56, and *King Lear*,
         I.v.20-25.

7   **marry**   truly, indeed. So also in line 10; compare II.iii.263.

8   **thereby . . . Tale**   What the Clown means is 'there by [near each
         of your "Wind Instruments"] hangs a tail', a male appendage
         (see the note to II.i.157).

13   **for Love's sake**   for the love you bear him. Here as in II.iii.43,
         desires means both (a) wishes, and (b) requests.

16-17   **Music . . . heard**   The Clown probably means 'music that can
         only be smelled'. The phrase *to't again* can be heard as 'toot
         again', another reference to the two types of 'Wind
         Instrument'. Meanwhile *to't* (an abbreviation for the
         copulative sense of 'go to it', as in *King Lear*, IV.vi.113-14)
         keeps us in mind of the activities of those 'Instruments' (line
         3) that 'hang by' men's anal windpipes. The Clown also hints
         sardonically at the Music of the Spheres, a celestial harmony
         too refined for mortal ears to hear.

ACT III

Scene 1

Enter Cassio, Musicians, and Clown.

CASSIO Masters, play here (I will content your
   Pains)
  Something that's brief: and bid 'Good morrow,
   General.'   *[The Musicians play.]*

CLOWN Why Masters, have your Instruments been
  in Naples, that they speak i'th' Nose thus?

MUSICIAN How Sir? How?   5

CLOWN Are these, I pray you, call'd Wind
  Instruments?

MUSICIAN Ay marry are they, Sir.

CLOWN Oh, thereby hangs a Tale.   *pun*

MUSICIAN Whereby hangs a Tale, Sir?

CLOWN Marry Sir, by many a Wind Instrument that   10
  I know. But Masters, here's Money for you:
  and the General so likes your Music that he
  desires you for Love's sake to make no more
  Noise with it.

MUSICIAN Well Sir, we will not.   15

CLOWN If you have any Music that may not be
  heard, to't again. But, as they say, to hear

not ivory

17–18 **to hear . . . care** Othello's disinclination to hear the kind of music the bagpipers play could be regarded as a sign of his superiority to the values their instruments represent. But the Clown's comment also invites comparison with some remarks in *The Merchant of Venice*, V.i.83–88. There Lorenzo says that 'The Man that hath no Music in himself, / Nor is moved with Concord of sweet Sounds, / Is fit for Treasons, Stratagems, and Spoils; / The Motions of his Spirit are dull as Night, / And his Affections dark as Erebus; / Let no such Man be trusted.'

20 **Bag** One meaning of this word was 'codpiece', the bag-like flap that housed a man's 'bagpipe'. *Bag* recalls I.i.79.

25 **Keep . . . Quillets** maintain your quibbles (wordplay). Here Cassio's phrasing gives *Quillets* the same phallic import as *Pipes* in line 20. *Keep up* echoes I.ii.59.

28 **stirring** up and about. In line 31, the Clown gives the word a spin that suggests a different kind of 'stirring' more likely to be applicable to 'the General's Wife' herself.

29 **entreats . . . Speech** requests the privilege of a brief conversation.

32 **I . . . her** I shall find a seemly way to let her know of your wishes.

33 **In happy time** how fortunate to meet you at this opportune moment.

35 **made bold** presumed. Cassio's words recall II.i.98–100. *Suit* (petition), line 36, echoes I.i.7–9, II.iii.280–84, 351–53.

38 **Procure . . . Access** obtain for me an audience. The unintentional suggestiveness of Cassio's wording coheres with the image of the Lieutenant that Iago will soon be offering to Othello. For the sense of *procure* that relates to brothels, see *Measure for Measure*, III.i.341–42. Also see the second note to III.iii.388.

39 **mean** means, way. *Draw* echoes II.iii.396–400.

40–41 **that . . . free** that you may converse with her about your affairs without any of the constraints his presence might impose on you. *Business* recalls II.iii.114; see the note to II.iii.265. *Free* can mean 'liberal' or wanton (see II.i.166, and compare III.iv.39–48).

43 **Florentine** even a citizen of my native Florence. See I.i.18, and the note to I.i.19.

Music the General does not greatly care.

MUSICIAN   We have none such, Sir.

CLOWN   Then put up your Pipes in your Bag, for   20
I'll away. Go, vanish into Air, away.

Exeunt Musicians.

CASSIO   Dost thou hear mine honest Friend?

CLOWN   No, I hear not your honest Friend: I hear
you.

CASSIO   Prythee keep up thy Quillets, there's   25
a poor piece of Gold for thee: if the
Gentlewoman that attends the General's Wife
be stirring, tell her there's one Cassio
entreats her a little favour of Speech. Wilt
thou do this?

CLOWN   She is stirring, Sir: if she will stir   *gobbledygoot* 30
hither, I shall seem to notify unto her.

CASSIO   Do, good my Friend.   *Exit Clown.*

Enter Iago.

In happy time, Iago.

IAGO   You have not been abed then?

CASSIO   Why no: the Day
Had broke before we parted. I have made bold,
Iago,   35
To send in to your Wife. My Suit to her
Is that she will to virtuous Desdemona
Procure me some Access.

IAGO   I'll send her to
You presently, and I'll devise a mean   *appearance vs.*
To draw the Moor out of the way, that your   *reality*   40
Converse and Business may be more free.

CASSIO   I humbly thank you for't.   *Exit [Iago].*

                    I never knew
A Florentine more kind and honest.   *d. irony*

Enter Aemilia.

AEMILIA   Good morrow, good Lieutenant, I am
sorry

45   **For your Displeasure**   that you no longer enjoy the General's good pleasure (favour). *Displeasure* recalls II.ii.1–9, II.iii.392.

47   **stoutly**   strongly (like the General's 'General', II.iii.325). Compare II.i.48, where Cassio says that Othello's 'Bark is stoutly timber'd'.

48   **Fame**   esteem; social standing, reputation, and popularity.

49   **Affinity**   connections (with influential friends and kinsmen). Compare II.iii.221–23.

49–50 **in ... you**   in the exercise of healthy good judgement he had no choice but to cast you off (literally, treat you as 'refuse'). *Protests* (swears) echoes II.iii.340.

52   **safest**   [earliest and] most prudent. Compare I.i.147–49, I.iii.221–25.

53   **Front**   forelock. Aemilia alludes to the conventional image for the seizing of 'Occasion' (opportunity). Compare I.iii.79–80.
     in again   into his employ and fellowship once more. In view of her husband's plans, Aemilia's phrasing in lines 50–53, 56–58 is unwittingly erotic in its imagery.

54   **if ... fit**   if you consider it appropriate. *Fit* recalls I.ii.85–87, I.iii.235–38, II.iii.124–26.

56   **Desdemon**   Desdemona (here, as elsewhere, with the final syllable elided in the Folio text for metrical purposes).

58   **speak ... freely**   say what is in your heart without restraint. Like Iago (lines 38–41), Aemilia promises to arrange a secret meeting.

59   **bound**   indebted. This verb echoes I.ii.65 and I.iii.180, and it anticipates a number of later references to binding.

III.ii   This brief scene takes place elsewhere in the Citadel.

1   **Pilot**   helmsman or ship's captain. Compare II.i.48–51.

2   **And ... Senate**   and by means of him send my dutiful regards to the Senate back in Venice. *Duties* recalls I.iii.39–42.

3   **That ... Works**   by the time you have completed that errand, you will find me walking on the battlements [where our 'Fortification' (line 5) is located]. Othello probably refers to the gun emplacements. See the note to II.i.6.

6   **wait upon**   attend.

For your Displeasure: but all will sure be well.   45
The General and his Wife are talking of it,
And she speaks for you stoutly. The Moor
    replies
That he you hurt is of great Fame in Cyprus,
And great Affinity: and that in wholesome
    Wisdom
He might not but refuse you. But he protests   50
He loves you and needs no other Suitor but
His Likings to take the safest Occasion by
The Front to bring you in again.
CASSIO   Yet I
Beseech you, if you think fit, or that it may
Be done, give me Advantage of some brief   55
Discourse with Desdemon alone.
AEMILIA   Pray you
Come in: I will bestow you where you shall
Have Time to speak your Bosom freely.
CASSIO   I am
Much bound to you.   [*Exeunt.*]

Scene 2

Enter Othello, Iago, and Gentlemen.

OTHELLO   These Letters give, Iago, to the Pilot,
And by him do my Duties to the Senate:
That done, I will be walking on the Works,
Repair there to me.
IAGO   Well, my good Lord, I'll do't.
OTHELLO   – This Fortification, Gentlemen, shall
    we see't?   5
GENTLEMEN   We'll wait upon your Lordship.   *Exeunt.*

III.iii   This scene takes us into a protected place in the Citadel, probably the garden.

2   **All my Abilities** everything I am able to do. The word *ability* derived from the Latin *habere*, 'to have or to hold'. Compare I.iii.24–26.

3   **warrant** guarantee. Compare line 20.

4   **Cause** case, situation. *Cause* and *case* both derive from the Latin word *causa*, and they were virtually interchangeable in Shakespeare's time; in this passage, for example, the Quarto prints *case*. Compare I.ii.95, I.iii.87, 372, II.i.109.

9   **your true Servant** someone who will do anything to repay you. Cassio's phrasing is identical to what a suitor for Desdemona's love might say; compare II.i.98–100, 169–77.

12–13 **He . . . Distance** he shall hold himself in aloof estrangement no longer than prudence demands. *Distance* recalls II.iii.54–58.

14   **Policy** political expediency; cautious governance.

15   **feed . . . Diet** require so limited a menu of nourishment to sustain it. Here *nice* means 'fastidious' and 'careful'.

16   **breed . . . Circumstances** interact with circumstances in such a way as to give birth to a new generation of policy considerations. *Breed* echoes II.i.98–100; *Circumstances* recalls I.i.11–14.

17   **my Place supplied** my position filled by someone else. Compare I.iii.394–95, 400, II.i.310–11, 322, and II.iii.101–2, 302–3, 311, 329–30. *Supplied* recalls I.iii.320–27.

18   **forget** cease to be mindful of. Compare II.iii.169, 191, 244.

19   **doubt** fear, be apprehensive about.

20   **Warrant . . . Place** assurance that you will be reinstated.

23   **watch him tame** keep him from sleep and observe him vigilantly until I wear down his resistance (a technique used in taming hawks, and one employed by Petruchio to train his 'haggard' in *The Taming of the Shrew*). Compare II.i.104–8.

24   **his . . . Shrift** his time at meals (board) a confessional. See the note to II.iii.329.

25–26 **I'll . . . Suit** Little does Desdemona suspect that Iago could now be speaking the same words. Compare II.iii.365–74. Desdemona uses *Suit* to mean 'plea' or 'petition' (as in III.i.35); but Iago will give pertinence to another sense, 'apparel'.

Scene 3

Enter Desdemona, Cassio, and Aemilia.

DESDEMONA   Be thou assur'd, good Cassio, I
    will do
All my Abilities in thy behalf.
AEMILIA   Good Madam, do: I warrant it grieves
    my Husband,
As if the Cause were his.

[handwritten annotation: she does not know how evil iago dramatics is irony]

DESDEMONA   Oh that's an honest Fellow. Do not
    doubt, Cassio,
But I will have my Lord and you again
As friendly as you were.
CASSIO   Bounteous Madam,
What ever shall become of Michael Cassio,
He's never any thing but your true Servant.
DESDEMONA   I know't: I thank you. You do love
    my Lord: 10
You have known him long, and be you well assur'd
He shall in Strangeness stand no farther off
Than in a politic Distance.
CASSIO   Ay, but Lady,
That Policy may either last so long,
Or feed upon such nice and waterish Diet,   15
Or breed it self so out of Circumstances,
That I being absent, and my Place supplied,
My General will forget my Love and Service.

[handwritten annotation: he will be forgotten]

DESDEMONA   Do not doubt that: before Aemilia
    here,
I give thee Warrant of thy Place. Assure thee,   20
If I do vow a Friendship, I'll perform it
To the last Article. My Lord shall never rest,
I'll watch him tame, and talk him out of
    Patience;
His Bed shall seem a School, his Boord a
    Shrift,
I'll intermingle every thing he does   25
With Cassio's Suit. Therefore be merry, Cassio,

27   **Solicitor** agent and advocate. This word was often associated with panderers and other practitioners of 'unlawful Solicitation' (IV.ii.200). But Desdemona's phrasing is a reminder that it could also be applied to the kind of go-between described in Isaiah 53:12, the suffering servant of the Lord who 'was numbered with the transgressors', who 'bare the sin of many', and who 'made intercession for the transgressors'. Desdemona's phrasing echoes what Iago has plotted in II.iii.396–400. Lines 26–28 hint inadvertently at the orgasmic sense of *die* (see *Antony and Cleopatra*, I.iii.136–41) and at the genital sense of *Cause* (see the note to line 4, and compare the wordplay on *Case* in *Romeo and Juliet*, II.iii.56–67).

31–32 **unfit . . . Purposes** in no condition to be of help to my own case. *Purposes* recalls II.iii.236; *unfit* echoes III.i.54.

32   **do your Discretion** act in accordance with your own best judgement. *Discretion* recalls II.iii.1–3, 284.

33   **Hah . . . that** Iago probably speaks this line as if to himself, but in such a way that Othello will overhear it.

36   **sure** surely, certainly.

37–38 **That . . . coming** Iago's interpretation of Cassio's departure is partly correct: Cassio has appeared stealthy in the unseemly haste of his leave-taking, and he is acutely aware of the guilt that has cost him his position as lieutenant.

40   **Suitor** Again Desdemona uses a word that can be construed to mean something other than what she has in mind (that Cassio is soliciting Othello's pardon). Like *languishes* (line 41), *Suitor* was a word that frequently referred to the kind of 'Servant' (line 9) who sought a lady's erotic attentions.

41   **languishes . . . Displeasure** wastes away (like a pining courtly lover) as a result of your rejection of him. *Displeasure* echoes III.i.44–45.

44   **Grace** Desdemona means 'favour with you'. But the theological senses of *Grace* are also relevant: (a) God's grace (as manifested in his devising a way to forgive and reconcile humanity to himself), and (b) the spiritual state of one who has been redeemed (given a new lease on life) through an appropriation of that divine gift. *Grace* recalls I.iii.85–93, II.i.85–87, II.iii.325–28.

45   **His . . . take** accept his repentance and receive him back into your good graces.

For thy Solicitor shall rather die   *foreshadowing*
Than give thy Cause away.

Enter Othello, and Iago.

AEMILIA   Madam, here comes
My Lord.

CASSIO   Madam, I'll take my Leave.

DESDEMONA   Why stay,
And hear me speak.

CASSIO   Madam, not now: I   30
Am very ill at ease, unfit for mine
Own Purposes.

                Well, do your Discretion.   *Exit Cassio.*

IAGO   Hah? I like not that.

OTHELLO   What dost thou say?

IAGO   Nothing, my Lord; or if — I know not what.

OTHELLO   Was not that Cassio parted from my
     Wife?   35

IAGO   Cassio, my Lord? No sure, I cannot think
     it
That he would steal away so Guilty-like,
Seeing your coming.

OTHELLO   I do believe 'twas he.

DESDEMONA   How now, my Lord?
I have been talking with a Suitor here,   40
A man that languishes in your Displeasure.

OTHELLO   Who is't you mean?

DESDEMONA   Why, your Lieutenant Cassio: Good
     my Lord,
If I have any Grace, or Power to move you,
His present Reconciliation take.   45
For if he be not one that truly loves you,

47   **That ... Cunning**   whose error resulted from a lapse in
      'Discretion' (II.iii.3) – reasoned judgement and self-control
      (see the notes to II.iii.191, 244) – rather than from a
      deliberate intention to do wrong (compare lines 394–95).
      Desdemona's use of the present tense is unconsciously apt:
      Cassio and Desdemona are now erring 'in Ignorance' of the
      'Cunning' by which Iago plans to make Othello err (go astray)
      even more egregiously. *Cunning* recalls I.iii.101 (see the note
      to I.iii.104).

48   **I ... Face**   I am unable to distinguish between an 'honest' (true,
      honourable) face and a dishonest one. Compare I.iii.170–71.

50   **humbled**   penitent. In lines 50–52 Desdemona describes herself
      as the kind of solicitor defined in the note to line 27. *Ay sooth*
      means 'yes, truly'.

51   **Grief**   both (a) grievance (sense of having been treated unjustly),
      and (b) sorrow, cause of pain.

52   **suffer**   both (a) bear, endure, and (b) feel agony. Once again
      Desdemona's words are susceptible to erotic constructions
      that would be inconceivable to her.

56   **Dinner**   the main, midday meal.

62   **in ... Reason**   in our ordinary way of judging such a minor
      'Fault' or crime (here a misdemeanour).

64–65 **is ... Check**   is almost too trivial to be considered an offence,
      and if so a minor indiscretion to be reprimanded in private,
      not rebuked with a public punishment. *Check* echoes
      II.iii.344–45.

65   **come**   come to plead with you in his own behalf. Desdemona's
      verb is unknowingly suggestive.

68   **mamm'ring on**   muttering in hesitation about what to do.

69   **woing**   wooing. But here as in *Love's Labour's Lost*, IV.iii.372,
      and *Romeo and Juliet*, III.iv.8, Shakespeare plays on *woe*,
      lament; compare lines 50–52, 61.

71   **ta'en your Part**   stood up for you (pleaded your case). Iago will
      give Desdemona's phrasing an implication that plays on at
      least two other possibilities for *Part*: (a) role (a theatrical
      sense), and (b) the genitalia (referring to Othello and the bride
      with whom he is now 'one flesh', Genesis 2:24). Compare
      I.i.120–21, I.iii.73, II.iii.106, 265–67.

That errs in Ignorance, and not in Cunning,
I have no Judgement in an honest Face.
I prythee call him back.

OTHELLO   Went he hence now?

DESDEMONA   Ay sooth: so humbled   50
That he hath left part of his Grief with me
To suffer with him. Good Love, call him back.

OTHELLO   Not now, sweet Desdemon, some other
    Time.

DESDEMONA   But shall't be shortly?

OTHELLO   The sooner, Sweet, for you.

DESDEMONA   Shall't be to night, at Supper?

OTHELLO   No, not to night.   55

DESDEMONA   To morrow Dinner then?

OTHELLO   I shall not dine at Home:
I meet the Captains at the Citadel.

DESDEMONA   Why then to morrow Night, on Tuesday
    Morn,
On Tuesday Noon, or Night; on Wednesday Morn.
I prythee name the Time, but let it not   60
Exceed three Days. In faith he's penitent:
And yet his Trespass, in our common Reason
(Save that they say the Wars must make Example
Out of her best), is not almost a Fault
T' incur a private Check. When shall he come?   65
Tell me, Othello. I wonder in my Soul
What you would ask me that I should deny,
Or stand so mamm'ring on? What? Michael Cassio,
That came a woing with you? And so many a Time
(When I have spoke of you dispraisingly)   70
Hath ta'en your Part, to have so much to do
To bring him in? Trust me, I could do much.

71–72 **To . . . in?**   to be required to go to so much trouble to bring
    him into your good will again. Desdemona's wording is
    ambiguous in ways that she could hardly imagine. And so is
    Othello's reply in lines 73–74; 'let him come,' he says,
    because 'I will deny thee nothing' [literally, 'no thing'].
    Compare III.i.53, and see the note to line 65.

74   **this . . . Boon**   what I'm requesting is not a special favour for
       myself [but something I ask as a way of promoting your own
       good, lines 77–78].

76   **Or . . . Dishes**   or eat food that will nourish you.

77–78 **sue . . . Person**   urge you to do something that will benefit you
       personally. *Sue* echoes lines 25–26, 40, 78; *Profit* recalls
       I.iii.390–93, *Person* I.iii.404–5, *peculiar* I.i.58–59.

79   **touch . . . indeed**   call on you to prove your love for me. One
       sense of *touch* here is that which relates to the use of a black
       touchstone to test whether a piece of ore is true gold; other
       pertinent senses are (a) affect, as with a particular feeling, (b)
       attain or reach to, (c) get at, strike, impress, and (d) penetrate,
       injure. Compare II.iii.223.

80   **Poise**   both (a) weight, impact, and (b) balance (to weigh your
       love). Compare I.iii.328–31. *Waight* (weight) plays on *wait*,
       to remind us that Othello is finding it 'difficult' to make
       Desdemona wait until a later time to plead Cassio's case.

81   **fearful . . . granted**   something you'll be apprehensive about
       giving me.

86   **strait**   straight away, soon. Othello's phrasing is unwittingly
       erotic. One meaning of *strait* is 'severely', 'sternly', and that
       sense will soon prove pertinent; as a verb, *strait* means 'to put
       in a difficult position (a dire strait)'. *Come* echoes line 65.

89   **Perdition**   damnation (literally, loss). Compare II.ii.3.

91   **Chaos . . . again**   the universe will return to the formless 'void'
       and 'darkness' that existed before 'the Spirit of God moved
       upon the face of the waters' (Genesis 1:2).

93   **woo'd . . . Lady**   either (a) 'came a woing with you' (line 69), or
       (b) wooed Desdemona himself, either on his own behalf (see
       I.ii.67–68, IV.ii.122) or, more likely, as Othello's confidant
       and agent (see lines 69–71, 97–98). Most editions follow the
       Quarto here and substitute *you* for the Folio's *he*. *Know* hints
       at the carnal sense of this verb; compare *Measure for
       Measure*, V.i.204–5.

95   **But . . . Thought**   only to confirm something I was wondering
       about. *Satisfaction* recalls I.iii.261–62.

96   **No further Harm**   nothing more serious than that.

OTHELLO   Prythee no more; let him come when he
  will;
I will deny thee nothing.

DESDEMONA   Why, this is not a Boon:
'Tis as I should entreat you wear your Gloves,   75
Or feed on nourishing Dishes, or keep you warm,
Or sue to you, to do a peculiar Profit
To your own Person. Nay, when I have a Suit
Wherein I mean to touch your Love indeed,
It shall be full of Poise, and difficult Waight,   80
And fearful to be granted.

OTHELLO   I will deny
Thee nothing. Whereon I do beseech thee grant
Me this, to leave me but a little to
My self.

DESDEMONA   Shall I deny you? No, farewell,
My Lord.

OTHELLO   Farewell, my Desdemona; I'll   85
Come to thee strait.

DESDEMONA   – Aemilia, come.
– Be as your Fancies teach you: what e'er you
  be,
I am obedient.   *Exit [with Aemilia]*.

OTHELLO   – Excellent Wretch. Perdition catch my Soul
But I do love thee: and when I love thee not,   90
Chaos is come again.

IAGO   My noble Lord.

OTHELLO   What dost thou say, Iago?

IAGO   Did Michael Cassio,
When he woo'd my Lady, know of your Love?

OTHELLO   He did, from first to last: why dost thou ask?

IAGO   But for a Satisfaction of my Thought,   95
No further Harm.

97   **acquainted with her** In addition to its usual meaning, this phrase could also refer to the kind of intimate knowledge the word *acquainted* suggests; *quaint* was one of many English variations on the Latin word *cunnus*; see the note to I.i.120. Counsaile (counsel, line 108) hints at *coun*, another common form of this word.

98   **went . . . oft** Not yet knowing Iago's drift, Othello uses a phrase that unintentionally hints at both (a) procurement (see the note to line 27, and compare III.i.38), and (b) infidelity. We are thereby reminded of Iago's own role as a supposed go-between for Roderigo and Cassio, and of Desdemona's newly adopted role as a solicitor on Cassio's behalf.

99   **Indeed?** What Othello hears is 'in fact?' But what Iago insinuates is 'in deed?' (with play on the sense of *do* that refers to 'the Deed of Kind', *The Merchant of Venice*, I.iii.86). Compare lines 78–81.
    ought aught; here, 'anything'. In this case *ought* actually means 'zero' or 'nothing'; it thus alludes to the female genitalia in accordance with the notion that a woman has a genital deficiency (an 'O' thing, a 'Fault' (line 64), instead of a protruding male thing). Compare II.iii.203.

100   **honest** trustworthy, honourable, chaste.

104   **Monster** See the note to II.iii.220. Othello's imagery in lines 104–5 recalls what Iago has said in I.iii.410–11.

105   **shewn** shown, disclosed. Here the Folio spelling hints at an aphetic form of *eschewn* (eschewed, shunned or avoided); compare II.i.100, II.iii.304, 364, and see the note to II.i.99.

108   **of my Counsaile** someone I confided in and sought counsel (advice) from. *Counsaile* echoes II.i.165–66.

110   **contract** draw up, pull taut.
    purse . . . together tighten the strings (muscles) of your forehead.

112   **Conceit** 'Thought' (line 113); imagination, concept. See the note to line 97. *Shew* (line 113) echoes line 105.

115   **for** because. In line 121, *For* means 'as for'.

117   **Stops** haltings, which Othello takes to be 'honourable' (see II.iii.2, and compare *mamm'ring*, line 68). *Weigh'st* echoes lines 78–81.

OTHELLO   Why of thy Thought, Iago?
IAGO   I did not think he had been acquainted with
   her.   *Cassio lied to him at the Sagittary*
OTHELLO   O yes, and went between us very oft.
IAGO   Indeed?
OTHELLO   'Indeed?' Ay indeed. Discern'st thou
   ought
   In that? Is he not honest?
IAGO   Honest, my Lord?   100
OTHELLO   'Honest?' Ay, honest.
IAGO   My Lord, for ought I know.   *As far as*
OTHELLO   What dost thou think?   *i know*
IAGO   Think, my Lord?
OTHELLO   'Think, my Lord?' By Heaven, thou echo'st
   me,
   As if there were some <u>Monster</u> in thy Thought   *Metaphor d. irony*
   Too hideous to be shewn. Thou dost mean
      something: 105
   I heard thee say even now, thou lik'st not that,
   When Cassio left my Wife. What didst not like?
   And when I told thee he was of my Counsaile,
   Of my whole course of Wooing, thou criedst
      'Indeed?'
   And didst contract, and purse thy Brow together,   110
   As if thou then hadst shut up in thy Brain
   Some horrible Conceit. If thou dost love me,
   Shew me thy Thought.
IAGO   My Lord, you know I love you.
OTHELLO   I think thou dost.
   And for I know thou'rt full of Love, and Honesty,   115
   And weigh'st thy Words before thou giv'st them   *d. irony*
      Breath,
   Therefore these Stops of thine fright me the
      more:

119 **Tricks of Custom** tricks of the trade (one sense of *custom*, business); the kinds of tricks (mannerisms) all shysters know how to perform in their effort to counterfeit 'a Man that's Just'. *Tricks* recalls II.i.173–77; *Custom* echoes I.iii.228–30, II.iii.32–34.

120 **close Dilations** swellings in the throat that cause momentary blockages of speech. Compare Othello's own inability to continue his discourse in II.i.199; and see the note on *dilatory* at II.iii.386.

121 **That . . . rule** which [referring to 'the Heart'] a passionate condition (in a 'Just' man whose feelings are genuine) is unable to control. Compare *Hamlet*, III.ii.69–78, where the Prince praises Horatio's Stoic imperturbability.

124 **Or . . . none** either (a) or those that are not true (honest) men, if only they would display their actual monstrous natures by not seeming to be true, or (b) or those that are not what they seem, if only they might not seem to be.

125 **Certaine** certainly. Here the final *e* is retained from the Folio to preserve the pronunciation and metre (a regular iamb, in contrast to the normal spelling for *certain*). Compare *A Midsummer Night's Dream*, V.i.130–32.

126 **Why . . . Man** This sentence could be interpreted to mean either (a) because Cassio seems to be an 'Honest Man', he is, or (b) because Cassio does *not* seem to be an 'Honest Man', he is. Iago implies only that Cassio '*should* be' an 'Honest Man'.

127 **this?** Most editions replace the Folio's question mark with either a semicolon or a full stop (the Quarto prints a comma). But Othello appears to be speaking with doubt in his voice.

129 **ruminate** ponder; literally, chew the cud like a cow.

129–30 **give . . . Words** speak with words that answer to the most terrible doubts you harbour.

132 **I . . . free** I am not required to do what even slaves are not constrained to do (utter my inmost thoughts). See the note to III.i.59. Iago alludes to the proverb 'Thought is free' (*Twelfth Night*, I.iii.71), a traditional response to the question (whether implicit or explicit) 'Do you think me a fool?' *Free* recalls III.i.40–41.

133 **say . . . vild** suppose they're vile ('foul', line 134, echoing II.iii.213–16).

For such things in a false disloyal Knave
Are Tricks of Custom, but in a Man that's Just,
They're close Dilations, working from the Heart,   120
That Passion cannot rule.

IAGO   For Michael Cassio,
I dare be sworn, I think that he is honest.

OTHELLO   I think so too.

IAGO   Men should be what they seem,
Or those that be not, would they might seem
none.

OTHELLO   Certaine, Men should be what they seem.   125

IAGO   Why then I think Cassio's an Honest Man.

OTHELLO   Nay, yet there's more in this?
I prythee speak to me, as to thy Thinkings,
As thou dost ruminate, and give thy Worst of
Thoughts
The Worst of Words.

IAGO   Good my Lord, pardon me,   130
Though I am bound to every Act of Duty,
I am not bound to that: all Slaves are free.
Utter my Thoughts? Why, say they are vild and
false?
As where's that Palace whereinto foul things
Sometimes intrude not? Who has that Breast so
pure   135
But some uncleanly Apprehensions
Keep Leets, and Law-days, and in Sessions sit
With Meditations Lawful?

---

134   **As** since. Iago knows that what he says could be applied to
others.

136   **Apprehensions** thoughts. Here the literal Latin senses
('graspings', efforts to 'take hold') are pertinent both to Iago's
aims and to his way of leading Othello on. Compare
I.i.176–77, I.ii.77–79.

137   **Keep ... Law-days** maintains law-courts and days of justice.

137– **in ... Lawful?** attend the same court sessions as do just and
38   legal thoughts.

139– **Thou . . . Thoughts** What Othello doesn't realize is that Iago
41   *does* 'conspire against' him, not because he thinks him
     'wrong'd' but because he wishes to make him think himself
     wronged. Iago will render Othello's 'Ear / A Stranger' to the
     Ancient's real 'Thoughts' while filling it with what Iago
     pretends to be his 'Meditations' (line 138).

142 **vicious . . . Guess** reflecting my own vices in what I guess about
     those of others. Here *vicious* anticipates the usual modern
     sense.

143 **Plague** besetting infirmity.

144 **Jealousy** suspicion (the usual sense in the play).

145 **Shapes Faults** imagines (creates) sins. The literal meaning of
     Faults is 'cracks' or 'defects' (as in geological faults), and here
     that sense is pertinent to Iago's insinuation that Desdemona's
     own genital 'Fault' may have been at fault; see the second
     note to line 99, and compare *King Lear*, I.i.16. *Fault* echoes
     lines 62–65; it also recalls the imagery of II.iii.335–38.

146 **conceits** conjectures, guesses. The Quarto prints *coniects*
     ('conjects'), and most modern editions adopt that reading.
     Conceits echoes line 112. *Imperfectly* recalls II.iii.304.

147– **nor . . . Observance** nor construct something that would
48   trouble you by building on your friend's scattered comments
     and uncertain observations. *Scattering* (here treated as a noun
     rather than as an adjective, as in most editions) recalls the
     imagery of sowing (casting seeds in a random fashion) in
     I.iii.320–35. The comma after *Scattering* is here retained from
     the Folio text.

153 **immediate** most personal and precious. *Jewel* echoes
     I.iii.193–96, and Iago's theft imagery recalls I.i.78–104,
     I.ii.50–51, 62–79, I.iii.59–60, 77–80, III.iii.36–38. *Purse*
     echoes I.iii.343–57, 387–88, 390, and III.iii.110.

154 **Who . . . nothing** Here *who* means 'whoever' or 'anyone who'.
     Trash recalls II.i.317–20; *nothing* is another reminder of the
     'aught', the 'no-thing', to which Iago has alluded in line 145.

156– **But . . . indeed** *Good Name* is equivalent to 'Opinion',
58   'Reputation', and 'Honour'. Iago's apparent shift in subject
     cunningly prompts Othello to demand the 'Thoughts' that
     underlie his generalities. *Indeed* echoes lines 99, 109.

157 **not enriches him** does not increase his own store of wealth.
     Iago's phrasing can be heard as 'naught enriches him'; see the
     notes on *ought* ('aught') at line 99 and *nothing* ('naught') at
     line 154.

OTHELLO   Thou dost conspire against thy Friend,
   Iago,
   If thou but think'st him wrong'd, and mak'st
      his Ear   140
   A Stranger to thy Thoughts.
IAGO   I do beseech you,
   Though I perchance am vicious in my Guess
   (As I confess it is my Nature's Plague
   To spy into Abuses, and oft my Jealousy
   Shapes Faults that are not), that your Wisdom
      then   145
   From one that so imperfectly conceits
   Would take no Notice, nor build your self a
      Trouble
   Out of his Scattering, and unsure Observance:
   It were not for your Quiet, nor your Good,
   Nor for my Manhood, Honesty, and Wisdom,
   To let you know my Thoughts.
OTHELLO   What dost thou mean?
IAGO   Good Name in Man and Woman, dear my Lord,
   Is the immediate Jewel of their Souls.
   Who steals my Purse steals Trash; 'tis
      something, nothing;
   'Twas mine, 'tis his, and has been Slave to
      thousands;
   But he that filches from me my good Name
   Robs me of that which not enriches him
   And makes me poor indeed.
OTHELLO   By Heaven, I'll know
   Thy Thoughts.
IAGO   You cannot, if my Heart were in
   Your Hand, nor shall not whilst 'tis in my
      Custody.   160

Handwritten margin notes: "interprets things in the worst way." · "I don't want to tell you." · "Metaphor" · "extended Metaphor" · "personal possessions aren't important"

159–   **You ... Hand**   you could not, even if you held my heart in
60   your hand. Iago's phrasing echoes I.i.60–64.

162– **It . . . on** Iago personifies Jealousy (a suspicious disposition) as
63   if it were a monster teasing and playing cat-and-mouse with
       its intended prey before it finally seizes and devours it. One
       manifestation of the 'green-ey'd Monster' is Iago himself, of
       course, and he is wryly warning Othello to mistrust the man
       who is about to twist the Moor into a monster; see the note to
       line 104.

163– **That . . . Wronger** What Iago seems to mean is that the
64   cuckold who knows his wife is unfaithful to him is blissfully
       free of jealousy; 'certain of his Fate', he can hate 'his
       Wronger'. But Iago's words apply equally well to the cuckold
       who lives in blissful ignorance, foolishly 'certain' that his love
       is secure, and thus not faced with the need to love the
       'Wronger' (Matthew 6:43–44) he doesn't know about. Here
       Wronger can apply to both the cheating wife and the man
       who is illicitly enjoying her favours.

165   **tells he o'er** does he count one by one. *Tells* recalls II.ii.12.

167   **Poor . . . rich** the man who is content with his poverty is
       actually rich in spirit [because he has nothing to lose, and thus
       no anxieties to trouble him]. Compare Matthew 5:3. *Content*
       echoes III.i.1.

168   **fineless** both (a) endless, boundless, and (b) not 'fine' (not to be
       enjoyed).

173   **To . . . Suspicions** to have new 'Suspicions' take possession of
       me every four weeks. Here *still* means 'continually', and hence
       'perpetually'. *Changes* (recyclings, alterations) recalls
       I.iii.313–15, 350–51, 354–57, 386, II.i.157, and anticipates
       lines 175, 315, 441. *Fresh* (new) recalls II.i.233, II.iii.20–21.

175   **to be resolv'd** either (a) to be given the resolve to end my
       suspicions by seeking the truth, or (b) to be certain ('resolv'd')
       that what I suspect is true and then to act.

175– **Exchange . . . Inference** Consider me to be worth no more than
78   a goat (proverbial for the lechery that breeds jealousy) when
       my soul shall become so base as to entertain such odious and
       fly-blown (disgusting) conjectures as those you are importing.
       Business recalls III.i.40–41; *blow'd* (*blown* in the Quarto and
       in most of today's editions) recalls II.iii.241, and anticipates
       line 434. The coinage *exufflicate* is usually emended to
       exsufflicate, which is construed as a variant of *exsufflate*,
       'blow out' or 'blow away'. But the *-uff* in *exufflicate* could
       derive from *offal* (refuse, 'off-fall', as in *Hamlet*, II.ii.617),
       and thus mean 'discarded' or 'cast off' (see II.iii.14–15, 277)
       as either liquid or solid waste.

OTHELLO   Ha?

IAGO   Oh beware, my Lord, of Jealousy,
It is the green-ey'd Monster which doth mock   *Metaphor*
The Meat it feeds on. That Cuckold lives in
   Bliss
Who, certain of his Fate, loves not his
   Wronger;
But oh, what damned Minutes tells he o'er   *V. irony*   165
Who dotes, yet doubts; suspects, yet soundly
   loves?

OTHELLO   O Misery.

IAGO   Poor, and content, is rich,
And rich enough; but Riches fineless is   *Metaphor*
As poor as Winter to him that ever fears
He shall be poor. Good Heaven, the Souls of all   170
My Tribe defend from Jealousy.

OTHELLO   Why? Why is this?
Thinkst thou I'd make a Life of Jealousy;
To follow still the Changes of the Moon   *Allusion to*
With fresh Suspicions? No. to be once in doubt   *Dian*
Is to be resolv'd. Exchange me for a Goat   175
When I shall turn the Business of my Soul
To such exufflicate and blow'd Surmises
Matching thy Inference. 'Tis not to make me
   jealous
To say my Wife is fair, feeds well, loves
   Company,
Is free of Speech, sings, plays, and dances
   well: 180
Where Virtue is, these are more Virtuous.

---

178   **jealious**   jealous (a common Shakespearean spelling).

182 **weak Merits** inadequacies. Compare I.ii.19–24. *Virtue*
(goodness), line 181, recalls II.iii.372; *free* (line 180) echoes
line 132.

183 **Revolt** betrayal, infidelity. Compare I.i.132–33. *Fear* recalls
II.iii.218.

185 **prove** test and either verify or jettison.

190 **franker** freer, more open and direct. Compare I.iii.38–40.
Reason (line 188) recalls I.iii.328–31, 372–73; *bound* echoes
line 132 and anticipates line 208.

191 **Proof** incontrovertible evidence; compare line 185.

192 **Look to** note well. Compare I.iii.290–91 and II.iii.1–3, 259.

193 **not . . . secure** neither unduly suspicious nor self-assured. Iago
is telling Othello to observe measure, to avoid extremes and
seek the golden mean commended by Aristotle in his
Nicomachean Ethics.

195 **self-Bounty** both (a) security (complacency), and (b)
magnanimity (the generosity of a great-souled nature). *Abus'd*
recalls II.i.321.

196 **Country** native, national (with a suggestion of what the Prince
of Denmark calls 'Country Matters'). See the notes to I.i.120,
I.iii.96, and compare II.iii.95, 306–10. *Know* reinforces the
genital; see the note to line 198.
Disposition character, proclivities (with more than a hint of the
Latin sense, 'to place apart'). Compare I.iii.235, II.iii.306–10,
330–32.

197 **Pranks** tricks, foul deeds. Iago has used this term in II.i.144.

198 **Conscience** both (a) moral sensitivity, and (b) wanton cunning.
Here as in Sonnet 151, *Conscience* plays on *cunnus* (see the
note to I.i.120) and alludes to the kind of consciousness that
derives from carnal knowledge (see the note to line 93).

203 **go to then** there now; that's all you need. See the note to
I.iii.383. Lines 200–2 recall what Brabantio has said in
I.iii.290–91; *shake* echoes II.iii.129–31; *fear* recalls I.ii.71,
II.i.91, 192–95, 322, II.iii.178, 217, 234–35, and
III.iii.182–83, and anticipates lines 229–33, 248–50.

205 **To . . . Oak** to sew up her father's eyes as tightly as close-
grained oak. Compare Othello's phrasing in I.iii.266–68.
Eyes echoes line 184, and recalls II.i.229. *Seeming* (line 204)
means 'deceptive appearance'; compare I.i.58–64, 170–71,
I.iii.105–8, II.i.123–24, 244–48. *Oak* recalls II.i.8.

Nor from mine own weak Merits will I draw
The smallest Fear, or Doubt of her Revolt,
For she had Eyes, and chose me. No, Iago,
I'll see before I doubt; when I doubt, prove;   185
And on the Proof, there is no more but this,
Away at once with Love, or Jealousy.

IAGO   I am glad of this: for now I shall have
    Reason
To shew the Love and Duty that I bear you
With franker Spirit. Therefore, as I am bound,   190
Receive it from me. I speak not yet of Proof.
Look to your Wife, observe her well with
    Cassio,
Wear your Eyes thus: not jealous, nor secure.
I would not have your free and noble Nature,
Out of self-Bounty, be abus'd: look to't.   195
I know our Country Disposition well:
In Venice they do let Heaven see the Pranks
They dare not shew their Husbands. Their best
    Conscience
Is not to leave't undone, but keep't unknown.

[handwritten: they don't think it's wrong as long as they don't get caught]

OTHELLO   Dost thou say so?   200
IAGO   She did deceive her Father, marrying you,
And when she seem'd to shake, and fear your Looks,
She lov'd them most.
OTHELLO   And so she did.
IAGO   Why go to then:
She that so young could give out such a
    Seeming
To seel her Father's Eyes up, close as Oak   *[handwritten: simile]*   205
(He thought 'twas Witchcraft) – But I am much
    too blame:

---

206 **He . . . Witchcraft** Iago cleverly implies that Brabantio thought
    Desdemona a practitioner of witchcraft; Othello fails to note
    that it was the Moor himself whom Brabantio accused of
    using magic.
    too blame too blameworthy.

208   **bound**   Othello means 'indebted'; but he is rapidly becoming
       'fettered' to Iago. Compare III.i.58–59 and III.iii.131–32,
       190, 280.

210   **iot**   jot, iota (the Greek letter corresponding to the Roman *i*).

212   **Consider . . . Love**   Iago's surface meaning is 'regard what I
       have spoken as deriving from my love for you' (line 208). But
       'comes from your Love' can also have pertinent secondary
       implications, among them (a) is designed to address (and
       undo) the kind of love you have for Desdemona, and (b) is a
       result of your past love for my own wife [and my desire to get
       even]; see II.i.301–26.

214–   **strain . . . Suspicion**   construe what I have said to imply
  15   anything greater or to reach further than to a prudent need
       for suspicion. Here *strain* and *larger Reach* hint at the kind of
       phallic extension that gives rise to 'grosser Issues': (a) erection
       and ejaculation, and (b) a vile (illegitimate) issue nine months
       later. Both suggestions are reinforced by 'vild Success' (line
       217). Compare I.iii.368–69, II.iii.378–80. *Grosser* recalls
       I.ii.72–73.

217   **which**   as that for which. *Aim'd* (line 218) recalls I.iii.6–7.

220   **honest**   both (a) truthful, and (b) chaste. This adjective recalls
       I.i.48, 95, I.iii.292, 406–7, II.i.202–4, II.iii.6, 144–45, 180,
       269, 340–41, 348–49, 351–53, III.i.22, 23, 42–43, III.iii.5,
       44–46, 100–1, 121–22, 126, and anticipates lines 237,
       365–68, 371, 373–75, 422.

222   **Nature**   both (a) human nature, and (b) Desdemona's
       disposition.
       erring   wandering departing.

224   **Not . . . Matches**   not to be inclined to the mates offered her.
       Compare I.ii.64–71 and I.iii.93–95, and see the note to line
       93; *bold* echoes III.i.35–36; *affect* recalls I.iii.110–11,
       259–63.

225   **Clime . . . Degree**   country, hue, and station. *Complexion* can
       mean either (a) physiology and psychology, or (b) colour.

227   **such**   one who does not 'affect' (incline to) her own kind.
       a . . . rank   a most foul, loose appetite. *Will* recalls I.iii.400; see
       the note to I.iii.321.

228   **Disproportions**   literally, 'mismatchings' (line 224). Iago plays
       on the Latin sense of *proportion* (before + part), to imply that
       Desdemona has a perverse taste for unfitting 'Matches'
       (dis-proportions) rather than for proper ones. Compare
       I.iii.1–2.

I humbly do beseech you of your Pardon
For too much loving you.

OTHELLO   I am bound to thee
For ever.

IAGO   I see this hath a little dash'd   *understatement*
Your Spirits.

OTHELLO   Not a iot, not a iot.   210

IAGO   Trust me, I fear it has: I hope you will
Consider what is spoke comes from your Love.   *v. irony*
But I do see y'are mov'd. I am to pray
You not to strain my Speech to grosser Issues,
Nor to larger Reach, than to Suspicion.   215

OTHELLO   I will not.

IAGO   Should you do so, my Lord,
my Speech
Should fall into such vild Success which my
Thoughts aim'd not. Cassio's my worthy Friend: *v. irony*
My Lord, I see y'are mov'd.

OTHELLO   No, not much mov'd:
I do not think but Desdemona's honest.   220

IAGO   Long live she so; and long live you to
think so.

OTHELLO   And yet how Nature, erring from it
self —

IAGO   Ay, there's the Point; as (to be bold
with you)
Not to affect many proposed Matches
Of her own Clime, Complexion, and Degree,   225
Whereto we see in all things Nature tends:
Foh, one may smell in such, a Will most rank,
Foul Disproportions, Thoughts Unnatural.
But, pardon me, I do not in Position
Distinctly speak of her, though I may fear   230
Her Will, recoiling to her better Judgement,

---

229   **in Position**   in posing this hypothetical case. See II.i.242–43.

232 **fall to match**   compare. *Fall* echoes *recoiling*.
her Country Forms   the proportions of Venetian men. *Country* echoes line 196.

233 **happily repent**   perhaps be reconverted [to a 'happy', suitable match]. *Happily* recalls II.i.285.

238 **unfolds**   discloses. Compare I.iii.242–45.

241–
42 **Cassio . . . Ability**   Here *Place* can refer not only to Cassio's position as lieutenant but also to the 'great' (enlarged) genitalia of Cassio and, by extension, Desdemona. Compare lines 17, 20. *Ability* recalls line 2.

245 **strain his Entertainment**   should (a) constrain you to entertain his suit, and (b) extend herself (and prevail upon you) to make him welcome. *Strain* echoes lines 214–15; *Entertainment* recalls II.iii.32–34.

246 **vehement Importunity**   insistent imploring on his behalf. *Vehement* derives from a Latin root meaning 'carry'. *Importunity* recalls II.iii.329–30 and anticipates IV.i.115–16.

248 **thought . . . Fears**   considered too much of a busybody.

250 **hold her free**   regard her as free of guilt or suspicion. *Free* recalls lines 132, 180, 194.

251 **Fear . . . Government**   have no concern about my self-control (with a reminder that the governor of Cyprus must first govern his own life).

253 **Quantities**   conditions, types of people.

254 **Humane Dealings**   dealings with humanity. *Humane* was the normal spelling for both *human* and *humane*. Compare II.i.246–47, V.i.60.
Haggard   unruly, wild. Compare line 23. *Prove* echoes line 191.

255 **Iesses**   jesses, the leather straps by which a falcon's legs were attached to the leash. Here the Folio spelling suggests the possibility of wordplay on *yesses* (affectionate, affirmative gestures). *Heart-strings* recalls I.i.1–3, II.iii.196–99.

256 **whistle her off**   send her off (with a falconer's whistle).
down the Wind   wherever the wind carries her.

257 **prey at Fortune**   (a) fend for herself, (b) prey on others, or (c) pray (beg) for sustenance (compare I.iii.242–45, 253–57, and see *Hamlet*, I.v.129).
Haply, for   perhaps because. Compare line 233.

May fall to match you with her Country Forms,
And happily repent.

OTHELLO   Farewell, farewell.
If more thou dost perceive, let me know more:
Set on thy Wife to observe. Leave me, Iago.   235

IAGO   My Lord, I take my leave.

OTHELLO   — Why did I marry? This <u>honest</u> Creature   d. irony
     doubtless
Sees and knows more, much more, than he
     unfolds.

IAGO   My Lord, I would I might entreat your Honour
To scan this thing no farther: leave it to
     Time.   240
Although 'tis fit that Cassio have his Place
(For sure he fills it up with great Ability),
Yet if you please to hold him off awhile,
You shall by that perceive him, and his Means.
Note if your Lady strain his Entertainment   245
With any strong or vehement Importunity,
Much will be seen in that. In the mean time,
Let me be thought too busy in my Fears
(As worthy Cause I have to fear I am),
And hold her free, I do beseech your Honour.   250

OTHELLO   Fear not my Government.

IAGO   I once more take my leave.
                                                   Exit.

OTHELLO   — This Fellow's of exceeding Honesty,
And knows all Quantities with a learn'd Spirit
Of Humane Dealings. If I do prove her Haggard,   Metaphor
Though that her Iesses were my dear Heart-
     strings,   255
I'd whistle her off, and let her down the Wind
To prey at Fortune. Haply, for I am black

258– **those . . . have** the refined manners of pampered gallants of
59   Italy's ducal courts.

260 **Vale . . . much** valley (shadow) of old age, though not very
     much.

263– **That . . . Appetites** that we can think we possess these
64   exquisite creatures but not control their sensual natures.
     Compare II.iii.359–60; *delicate* recalls II.iii.20.

264 **Toad** Othello's image is apt. Toads were regarded as (a) 'ugly
     and venomous' (*As You Like It*, II.i.13), a sense that relates to
     lines 161–63, (b) 'foul' (*Richard III*, IV.iv.81), and (c)
     lecherous (*Troilus and Cressida*, II.iii.171–72, and *Othello*,
     IV.ii.59–60).

268 **Prerogativ'd . . . Base** they are less privileged than the lowly.
     Base recalls II.i.217–20.

270– **Even . . . quicken** We are destined to wear the horns of the
71   cuckold from the moment of our conception. *Quicken* recalls
     II.i.80 (where *quick* means both 'rapid' and 'generative'),
     318–20. *Comes* reinforces Othello's copulative imagery;
     compare lines 65, 90.

272 **If . . . self** She can be untrue only if Heaven scorned its own
     image to deceive us. Othello finds it inconceivable that
     Desdemona is not 'divine' (II.i.73). *Mock'd* echoes lines
     161–63.

274 **generous Islanders** noble (from Latin *generosus*) Cypriots.

275 **attend** await, expect.

276 **too blame** too much to blame, either (a) for marrying a
     'super-subtle Venetian' (I.iii.361), or (b) for allowing myself
     to doubt her. Compare line 206.

278 **Pain . . . Forehead** a headache. Othello fears that his brows are
     sprouting horns. See lines 267–71.

279 **with Watching** Desdemona means 'from too many hours
     awake'; but in fact Othello's pain is a consequence of the new
     kind of 'Watching' Iago has recommended (line 192).
     Compare line 23.

280 **bind it hard** wrap it tightly with this 'Napkin' (handkerchief).

281 **too little** too small to do the job [of easing my 'Pain'].

282 **Let it alone** Don't bother with the 'Napkin'. *Come* echoes line
     271, and *go in with you* recalls such previous passages as
     I.ii.30, I.iii.33–35, II.i.116.

And have not those soft parts of conversation
That Chamberers have, or for I am declin'd
Into the Vale of Years (yet that's not much),   260
She's gone. I am abus'd, and my Relief
Must be to loathe her. Oh Curse of Marriage!
That we can call these delicate Creatures ours,   *Metaphor*
And not their Appetites? I had rather be a Toad,
And live upon the Vapour of a Dungeon,   265
Than keep a Corner in the thing I love
For others' uses. Yet 'tis the Plague to Great
    Ones,
Prerogativ'd are they less than the Base,
'Tis Destiny unshunnable, like Death:
Even then this Forked Plague is Fated to us   270
When we do quicken. Look where she comes.

Enter Desdemona and Aemilia.

If she be false, Heaven mock'd it self:
I'll not believe't.
DESDEMONA   How now, my dear Othello?
Your Dinner, and the generous Islanders
By you invited, do attend your Presence.   275
OTHELLO   — I am too blame.
DESDEMONA   Why do you speak so faintly? Are you
    not well?
OTHELLO   I have a Pain upon my Forehead, here.
DESDEMONA   Why that's with Watching, 'twill
    away again.
Let me but bind it hard, within this Hour   280
It will be well.
OTHELLO   Your Napkin is too little:
Let it alone. Come, I'll go in with you.   *Exit.*
DESDEMONA   I am very sorry that you are not well.
                                                       [*Exit.*]
AEMILIA   I am glad I have found this Napkin:

285   **Remembrance**   memento of his love; keepsake.

286   **wayward**   quirky, odd; a creature of 'Fantasy' (line 293), not Reason. Compare *weyward* in *Macbeth*, I.i.30–35.

288   **conjur'd her**   called upon her; swore to her and made her swear with him.

290   **the . . . out**   the design copied (by an embroideress). Another sense of *ta'en out* (removed, taken away) emerges in III.iv.79–80. Lines 290–91 suggest that Aemilia plans to return Desdemona's 'Napkin' to her as soon as she can have it reproduced for Iago.

296   **common thing**   Iago implies that Aemilia's 'thing' has been handled by so many men that it is now a piece of common currency. Compare Iago's comments in I.iii.393–95 and II.i.115–16, 322. And see the Prince's remark to his mother, 'Ay Madam, it is common', in *Hamlet*, I.ii.74.
      Foolish   wanton. Compare II.i.137–38. Whether there is any basis for Iago's insinuations is left unclear. What we see in Aemilia is a desire to cajole at least a small token of affection from her husband; her effort to do so in lines 297–98 proves to be 'Foolish' in the more usual sense.

302   **by Negligence**   inadvertently; failing to notice it fall or pick it back up. In fact, Othello may have been the one who 'let it drop'; if so, his order (line 282), not Desdemona's 'Negligence', kept it from being retrieved. *Negligence* recalls I.i.74–76.

303   **to th' Advantage**   to my good fortune.

This was her first Remembrance from the Moor,   285
My wayward Husband hath a <u>hundred</u> times
Woo'd me to steal it. But she so loves the
   Token
(For he conjur'd her, she should ever keep it)
That she reserves it evermore about her,
To kiss, and talk to. I'll have the Work ta'en
   out,
And give't Iago. What he will do with it   290
Heaven knows, not I: I nothing, but to
   please
His Fantasy.

hyperbol indication of double time

she'll have it copied + give the fake one to Iago

                    Enter Iago.

IAGO   How now? What do you here
   Alone?
AEMILIA   Do not you chide: I have a thing
   For you.
IAGO   You have a thing for me? It is   295
   A common thing —
AEMILIA   Hah?
IAGO   To have a foolish Wife.
AEMILIA   Oh, is that all? What will you give me
   now
For that same Handkerchief.
IAGO   What Handkerchief?
AEMILIA   What Handkerchief? Why that the Moor
   first gave
To Desdemona, that which so often you   300
Did bid me steal.
IAGO   Hast stol'n it from her?
AEMILIA   No: but she let it drop by Negligence,
And to th' Advantage I, being here, took't up.
Look, here 'tis.
IAGO   A good Wench, give it me.
AEMILIA   What will you do with't, that you have
   been so earnest   305
To have me filch it?

307 **Purpose of import** important purpose. Iago will use the
handkerchief to 'import' (introduce) a specious reason for
Othello to believe that Desdemona has 'imported' Cassio.
Compare line 246, and see the second note to II.iii.329.
Purpose echoes lines 31–32.

309 **lack it** miss it; discover that she is without it. Compare lines
332–33.
Be . . . on't Say or do nothing to acknowledge that you are
aware of how she misplaced it. In III.iv.25 Aemilia obeys her
husband's command. In doing so, she proves herself to be
more loyal to her husband than to her mistress.

311 **loose** both (a) release, let loose, and (b) lose. Compare
II.iii.215–16, 275. *Lodging* recalls I.ii.45, I.iii.381, and
anticipates III.iv.7–13.

314 **Proofs . . . Writ** proofs as authoritative as Scripture. *Proofs*
echoes line 191.

315 **changes** both (a) alters, and (b) exchanges his former self for
the monster I am substituting for it. Compare line 173.

316 **Dangerous Conceits** conceptions (imaginings) of danger.

317 **found to distaste** perceived as tasting bad. *Distaste* echoes
II.i.287–89.

318 **act** acting, working. Compare I.i.60–64, 151, 170–71,
II.i.231–33, III.iii.131.

319 **Mines of Sulphur** Iago alludes to the sulphur mines on the
Aeolian Islands between Italy and Sicily; according to such
authorities as Pliny, they were constantly aflame. *Sulphur* also
suggests Hellfire.

320 **Poppy** opium, a narcotic (sleep-inducing) drug.
Mandragora mandrake, another drug to make one 'drowsy'
(line 321); accented on the second syllable.

323 **ow'dst** owned, enjoyed. See the note to I.i.65.

325 **Avaunt** Away with you.
Rack an instrument of torture that stretched a prisoner until he
broke. *Rack* can also mean 'shelf', as in *The Merchant of
Venice*, I.i.181, and here that sense is a reminder that Iago is
plotting, among other things, to get the Moor 'cashier'd'
(I.i.47).

326 **much abus'd** thoroughly deceived. Compare line 261.

IAGO   Why, what is that to you?
AEMILIA   If it be not for some Purpose of import,
   Give't me again. Poor Lady, she'll run mad
   When she shall lack it.
IAGO   Be not acknown on't: I
   Have use for it. Go, leave me.   *Exit Aemilia.*   310
   — I will in Cassio's Lodging loose this Napkin,
   And let him find it. Trifles light as Air
   Are to the Jealous Confirmations strong   *Simile*
   As Proofs of Holy Writ. This may do something.
   The Moor already changes with my Poison: *Metaphor* 315
   Dangerous Conceits are in their Natures Poisons,
   Which at the first are scarce found to distaste,
   But with a little act upon the Blood
   Burn like the Mines of Sulphur. I did say so.   *Allusion + Simile*

                    Enter Othello.

   Look where he comes. — Not Poppy, nor
        Mandragora,   *hyperbole*
   Nor all the drowsy Syrups of the World,   320
   Shall ever medicine thee to that sweet Sleep
   Which thou ow'dst yesterday.
OTHELLO   — Ha, ha, false to me?
IAGO   Why how now, General? No more of that.
OTHELLO   Avaunt, be gone: thou hast set me on the
   Rack.   *metaphor*   325
   I swear 'tis better to be much abus'd

328   **Sense** awareness (sensation of what was happening to me). See
II.iii.271.

330   **free** carefree. Compare lines 178–81 and III.iv.119–22.

332–   **He . . . all** These lines echo I.iii.200–7.
33

335   **the general Camp** every soldier in the army. Compare I.ii.69.

336   **Pioners** lowest manual labourers; soldiers who dig trenches
and tunnels. *Tasted* echoes line 317.

338   **Content** contentment, peace of mind. See the note to line 167.

339   **plumed Troops** proud armies. Here the disyllabic *plumed*
alludes to the tuft of feathers in a soldier's helmet. Compare
I.iii.400.
big both (a) great, and (b) threatening.

340   **That . . . Virtue** that makes it a virtue, rather than a vice, to
aspire for honour. *Virtue* here means the highest form of
'manliness' as well as 'goodness'. Compare II.iii.126–28, and
see the note to line 182.

341   **Trump** trumpet (here one to call troops into combat).

343   **Quality** nature, character.

344   **Pomp, and Circumstance** splendour, and grandeur. Compare
I.i.12.

345–   **mortal . . . counterfeit** deadly devices (cannons) that imitate
46   Jove's thunder. Here *rude Throats* and *counterfeit* hint at
genital 'Engines'. See the note to II.i.250–51.

347   **Occupation** vocation, calling. Since *occupation* also had a
copulative sense (see *Measure for Measure*, IV.ii.35–41),
Othello speaks more precisely than he realizes.

350   **Ocular Proof** 'Probation' (trial or test) to persuade the eye
(lines 354–55). Compare lines 191, 354–55, 376, for other
references to 'Proof'.

352   **borne** both (a) born, and (b) carried as.

353   **answer** be forced to withstand. Compare II.iii.312–14.

Than but to know't a little.

IAGO   How now, my Lord?

OTHELLO   What Sense had I in her stol'n Hours of
    Lust?—

    I saw't not, thought it not; it harm'd not me;

    I slept the next Night well, fed well, was free
      and merry;   330

    I found not Cassio's Kisses on her Lips.

    He that is robb'd, not wanting what is stol'n,

    Let him not know't, and he's not robb'd at
      all.

IAGO   I am sorry to hear this?

OTHELLO   I had been happy, if the general Camp,   335

    Pioners and all, had tasted her sweet Body,

    So I had nothing known. Oh now for ever

    Farewell the tranquil Mind; farewell Content;

    Farewell the plumed Troops, and the big Wars

    That makes Ambition Virtue! Oh farewell,   340

    Farewell the neighing Steed, and the shrill
      Trump,

    The Spirit-stirring Drum, th' Ear-piercing
      Fife,

    The royal Banner, and all Quality,

    Pride, Pomp, and Circumstance of glorious War.

    And O you mortal Engines, whose rude Throats   345

    Th' immortal Jove's dread Clamours counterfeit,

    Farewell: Othello's Occupation's gone.

IAGO   Is't possible, my Lord?

OTHELLO   Villain, be sure thou prove my Love a
    Whore;

    Be sure of it. Give me the Ocular Proof,

    Or by the Worth of mine eternal Soul,   350

    Thou hadst been better have been borne a Dog

    Than answer my wak'd Wrath.

IAGO   Is't come to this?

OTHELLO   Make me to see't; or (at the least) so
    prove it

    That the Probation bear no Hinge, nor Loop,   355

359 **abandon all Remorse** forsake all compassion, all manifestations of conscience [and give over any hope that you will ever be forgiven and spared from retribution].

360 **On . . . accumulate** pile on one horrible crime after another.

364 **Sense** both (a) intelligence, and (b) sensitivity, feeling. Compare line 328.

365 **God buy you** both (a) God be with you (goodbye to you), and (b) may God buy you and take you hence.
take mine Office take my commission (assigned post) away. *Office* recalls II.iii.221.

366 **That . . . Vice** who are so compulsively honest that you turn honesty into a vice that hurts you [since too much of it is not appreciated]. Compare I.ii.3–4. Iago is pretending to upbraid himself. *Vice* echoes II.iii.332–33.

368 **To . . . Safe** Iago is speaking with private irony; but in due course the principle he states here will prove applicable to those who *are* 'direct and honest'.

369 **this Profit** teaching me this valuable lesson. Iago addresses Othello. *Profit* echoes line 77.

370 **sith . . . Offence** since Love gives birth to so much offence. Again Iago's statement resonates beyond the context that occasions it. *Breeds* recalls line 16.

371 **wise** prudent, self-serving.

372 **looses** both (a) loses, and (b) sets free, unleashes. Before long lines 372–73 will prove applicable to Desdemona and, in different ways, to Cassio, Roderigo, and Othello.

376 **fresh** unspoiled; in its unsullied virginal state. Compare lines 173–74. *Proof* echoes lines 350, 354–55. Most of today's editions follow the Quarto in this line and print *Her name* rather than *My Name*.

377 **Dian's Visage** the face of the Goddess of Chastity and of the Moon.

379 **suffocating Streams** waters to drown her in.

380 **satisfied** contended, at rest. Compare lines 174–87. *Satisfied* echoes line 95.

382 **put . . . you** applied it ('Passion') to you; forced it on you. Compare II.iii.58–60, III.iii.460.

To hang a Doubt on; or woe upon thy Life.

IAGO   My Noble Lord.

OTHELLO   If thou dost slander her, and torture
me,
Never pray more; abandon all Remorse;
On Horror's Head Horrors accumulate;   360
Do Deeds to make Heaven weep, all Earth amaz'd;
For nothing canst thou to Damnation add
Greater than that.

IAGO   O Grace! O Heaven forgive me!   *Apostropho*
Are you a Man? Have you a Soul? or Sense?   *V. irony*
God buy you: take mine Office. – Oh wretched
Fool,   365
That lov'st to make thine Honesty a Vice!
– Oh monstrous World! Take note, take note, O
World,
To be direct and honest is not safe.   *I only told you*
– I thank you for this Profit, and from hence   *what i thought*
I'll love no Friend, sith Love breeds such   *+ now you threaten*
Offence.   *me 370*

OTHELLO   Nay stay: thou shouldst be honest.

IAGO   I should be wise;
For Honesty's a Fool, and looses that
It works for.

OTHELLO   By the World, I think my Wife
Be honest, and think she is not; I think
That thou art just, and think thou art not.   375
I'll have some Proof. My Name, that was as
fresh
As Dian's Visage, is now begrim'd and black   *Allusion +*
As mine own Face. If there be Cords, or Knives,   *simile*
Poison, or Fire, or suffocating Streams,
I'll not endure it. Would I were satisfied.   *I need to*
                                                        act 380
IAGO   I see, Sir, you are eaten up with Passion:
I do repent me that I put it to you.
You would be satisfied?

OTHELLO   Would? Nay, and I will.

IAGO   And may: but how? How satisfied, my Lord?

385 **Super-vision**   This word, spelled as it appears in the Folio text, refers to Cassio's 'topping' Desdemona (line 386): literally viewing her from a 'super' (higher) position. But *vision* also plays on *vice* (screw) and *vise* (see the second note to II.iii.329) to indicate the kind of encounter Iago is describing. Here most editions adopt the Quarto's *supervisor* (observer). *Grossly* (coarsely, stupidly, and flagrantly) echoes lines 214–15.

387 **tedious Difficulty**   wearisome and time-consuming labour. Compare lines 78–81.

388 **Prospect**   both (a) 'Super-vision', and (b) view, place to be observed. The literal meaning of *Prospect* is 'look forward'; it is thus a word whose implications hint at the 'Probal' (II.iii.350–51) instrument Iago is attributing to Cassio.

389 **boulster**   both (a) go to bed (lie together on a bolster, a long pillow), and (b) combine to make a bolster, a variation on 'the Beast with two Backs' (I.i.155–16).

393 **prime**   lustful; 'hot', 'salt', 'in Pride', and 'gross'. *Pride* (line 394) recalls II.iii.95–96.

396 **Imputation . . . Circumstances**   guilt inferred on the basis of firm circumstantial evidence. *Imputation* means 'charge to one's account', and here it plays on the Latin *imputatus* (unpruned, untrimmed), a synonym of *rank* (line 227). Meanwhile *Circumstances*, which derives from *circum* (circle) + *stare* (to stand), hints at that which stands within a circle (compare *Romeo and Juliet*, II.i.23–26) and which may be said to 'lead directly to the Door of Truth' (line 397). Compare lines 13–18, 343–44.

401 **ent'red . . . far**   Here *Cause* means 'case' (see the note to line 4), and Iago's phrasing gives it a genital suggestiveness reinforced by 'Prick'd to't' in line 402 (see Sonnet 20, lines 9–14, for a pertinent sense of *prick'd*). *Reason* (line 399) recalls lines 62–64, 188; see the note to I.i.151. *Office* (commission, vote) echoes line 365.

410 **gripe**   grip, grasp. *Hard* (line 411) echoes line 280.

416 **Monstrous**   inhuman; egregiously foul in its perversity. See the note to II.iii.220, and compare lines 104–5, 161–63, 367.

417 **a fore-gone Conclusion**   an act already performed (literally, a previous coming together); compare II.i.274. Othello's phrase has become a part of our everyday speech; but it now has a meaning quite different from that of its original context. *Conclusion* recalls I.i.14, I.iii.321.

Would you the Super-vision grossly gape on?   385
Behold her topp'd?
OTHELLO   Death and Damnation, oh!
IAGO   It were a tedious Difficulty, I think,
To bring them to that Prospect: damn them then
If ever mortal Eyes do see them boulster
More than their own. What then? How then?   390
What shall I say? Where's Satisfaction?
It is impossible you should see this,
Were they as prime as Goats, as hot as Monkeys,
As salt as Wolves in Pride, and Fools as gross
As Ignorance made drunk. But yet, I say,   395
If Imputation, and strong Circumstances,
Which lead directly to the Door of Truth,
Will give you Satisfaction, you might have't.
OTHELLO   Give me a living Reason she's disloyal.
IAGO   I do not like the Office.   400
But sith I am ent'red in this Cause so far
(Prick'd to't by foolish Honesty and Love),
I will go on. I lay with Cassio lately,
And being troubled with a raging Tooth,
I could not sleep. There are a kind of Men   405
So loose of Soul that in their Sleeps will
     mutter
Their Affairs: one of this kind is Cassio.
In Sleep I heard him say, 'Sweet Desdemona,
Let us be wary, let us hide our Loves.'
And then, Sir, would he gripe, and wring my
     Hand,   410
Cry 'Oh Sweet Creature,' and then kiss me hard,
As if he pluck'd up Kisses by the Roots
That grew upon my Lips; laid his Leg o'er
My Thigh, and sigh'd and kiss'd, and then
Cried 'Cursed Fate, that gave thee to the
     Moor.'   415
OTHELLO   O Monstrous! Monstrous!
IAGO   Nay, this was but his Dream.
OTHELLO   But this denoted a fore-gone Conclusion;

418   **shrewd Doubt**   both (a) well-founded suspicion, and (b) piercing fear (with *shrewd* meaning *shrew'd*, 'made shrewish', sharp, or *beshrew'd*, 'cursed'). *Doubt* echoes lines 172–75, 182–83, 354–56. Most editions follow the Quarto and assign this line to Iago.

420   **demonstrate**   denote. Here demonstrate is accented on the second syllable to reinforce the echo of 'Monstrous', line 416. *Proofs* (line 419) echoes lines 376, 430.

421   **wise**   rational, restrained, prudent. Compare line 371. The phrase *nothing done* alludes to the genital senses of *nothing* and *do* (see the notes to line 99).

424   **Spotted**   dotted. Iago's adjective implies that the handkerchief's spots were an anticipatory symbol of the moral blemishes now being attributed to Desdemona. His phrasing echoes passages such as Jeremiah 13:23 ('Can the Ethiopian change his skin, or the leopard his spots? then may ye also do good, that are accustomed to do evil'), Hebrews 9:14, and 2 Peter 3:14. Strawberries were associated with deception and treachery, based on the notion that serpents lay in wait under strawberries to take their unsuspecting victims; compare *Richard III*, III.iv.32. Othello refers to 'Aspic's Tongues' in line 439.
    Wive's   wife's. Shakespeare normally changes' *f* to *v* before an s.

428   **Beard**   Iago uses this word here as a symbol of superior virility. Compare *Twelfth Night*, III.i.50–51, where the Clown tells a boyish, effeminate 'Cesario' (Viola dressed as a page), 'Now Jove in his next Commodity of Hair send thee a Beard'; also see *Hamlet*, II.ii.453–55, where the Prince uses *beard* as a verb meaning 'confront'. *Beard* can also refer to the pubic hair of either gender, and here that sense is strongly suggested, with the implication that Desdemona's 'Beard' is Cassio's.

431   **Slave**   base wretch (Cassio).

434   **fond**   foolish (based on infatuation). Compare I.iii.316–18, II.i.139.

435   **'Tis gone**   This brief line is here indented to indicate that, like line 400, it would be preceded, and probably followed, by a pause. *Blow* recalls line 177.

'Tis a shrewd Doubt, though it be but a Dream.
IAGO   And this may help to thicken other Proofs
That do demonstrate thinly.
OTHELLO   I'll tear her all to Pieces.   420
IAGO   Nay yet be wise; yet see we nothing done,
She may be honest yet. Tell me but this,
Have you not sometimes seen a Handkerchief
Spotted with Strawberries in your Wive's Hand?
OTHELLO   I gave her such a one: 'twas my first
Gift.   425
IAGO   I know not that: but such a Handkerchief
(I am sure it was your Wive's) did I to day
See Cassio wipe his Beard with.
OTHELLO   If it be that —
IAGO   If it be that, or any, it was hers.
It speaks against her with the other Proofs.   430
OTHELLO   O that the Slave had forty thousand
Lives:
One is too poor, too weak, for my Revenge.
Now do I see 'tis true. Look here, Iago,
All my fond Love thus do I blow to Heaven.
'Tis gone.   435
— Arise, black Vengeance, from the hollow Hell.
— Yield up, O Love, thy Crown, and hearted
Throne

---

436   **hollow Hell**   Othello invokes the powers of Hell because he
realizes that the 'black' deed he is committing himself to is
forbidden by a God who says, 'Vengeance is mine; I will
repay' (Romans 12:19, quoting Deuteronomy 32:35). Here
hollow means both (a) deep, reverberating, and (b) insincere,
false.

437   **hearted Throne**   throne in my heart. Othello describes an
insurrection whereby cruel ('tyrannous') Hate usurps Love's
crown. Compare I.iii.372.

438   **Fraught**   freight. Othello's 'Bosom' (heart) is fraught (burdened) with grief.

439   **Aspic's Tongues**   the tongues of asps (also known as vipers or adders). These venomous snakes were proverbially associated with slander (see Psalm 140:3), and Othello's reference to them here is an indication of the power of Iago's poison. *Content* echoes line 338.

442   **Pontic Sea**   Black Sea, which flows into 'the Propontic and the Hellespont' (the Sea of Marmora and the Bosporus). *Change* (line 441) echoes line 315.

443   **compulsive Course**   unstoppable current. Othello pledges himself to become an irresistible force, without 'retiring Ebb' (pauses and recessions), until he overwhelms his enemies with a 'capable' (all-seizing) 'Revenge'. *Violent* (line 446) recalls I.iii.247, II.i.34.

452   **Witness**   bear witness (so also in line 454). Iago is addressing the stars, whose 'ever-burning Lights above' provide a silent rebuke to the 'icy Current' Iago has released by changing Othello's heart to 'marble' (lines 443, 449).

453   **clip . . . about**   embrace us. But *clip* can also mean 'eclipse' or 'cut'. See V.ii.98–100. The phrase *round about* echoes II.i.85–87. *Elements* recalls II.iii.353–54.

455   **Wit**   mind (here with the implication of 'cunning'). See the note to II.iii.381.

456   **To . . . Service**   Iago's phrasing is ambiguous. What he means privately is 'to the manipulation of the Othello whom Iago "hath turn'd almost the Wrong Side out" ' (II.iii.51).

457   **shall . . . Remorse**   shall be my compelling emotion. Iago's phrasing echoes lines 358–59.

458   **bloody**   both (a) passionate, and (b) violent (line 446). *Business* recalls lines 175–78.

459   **vain Thanks**   empty expressions of gratitude.
      Acceptance bounteous   the most generous reward I can bestow (promotion to the lieutenantry, line 467). Iago has succeeded in his initial objective, to 'get' Cassio's 'Place', I.iii.400.

460   **put . . . to't**   to employ you (put you to the test) in your new role. Othello's phrasing echoes Iago's in line 382.

465   **a-part**   apart, to a separate, private location. The Folio spelling, here retained, illustrates the concept of severance. Compare II.iii.397–98, IV.i.77–78.

To tyrannous Hate. – Swell, Bosom, with thy
   Fraught,
For 'tis of Aspic's Tongues.
IAGO   Yet be content.
OTHELLO Oh Blood, Blood, Blood.   *He kneels.* 440
IAGO   Patience, I say: your Mind perhaps may
   change.
OTHELLO   Never, Iago. <u>Like to the Pontic Sea,</u>   *smile*
   Whose icy Current, and compulsive Course,
   Nev'r feels retiring Ebb, but keeps due on
   To the Propontic, and the Hellespont: 445
   Even so my bloody Thoughts with <u>violent Pace</u> *wants*
   Shall nev'r look back, nev'r ebb to humble *reveng*
   Love,
   Till that a capable and wide Revenge
   Swallow them up. Now by yond marble Heaven,
   In the due Reverence of a sacred Vow,   450
   I here engage my Words.
IAGO   Do not rise yet.
   – Witness you ever-burning Lights above,
   You Elements, that clip us round about,   *Iago kneels.*
   Witness that here Iago doth give up   *dedicate his*
   The Execution of his Wit, Hands, Heart, *life to help* 455
   To wrong'd Othello's Service. Let him command, *othello*
   And to obey shall be in me Remorse,
   What bloody Business ever.
OTHELLO   I greet thy Love,
   Not with vain Thanks, but with Acceptance
   bounteous,
   And will upon the Instant put thee to't.   460
   Within these three Days let me hear thee say
   That Cassio's not alive.   *kill Cassio*
IAGO   My Friend is dead:
   'Tis done at your Request. But let her live.
OTHELLO Damn her, lewd Minx: O damn her,
   damn her.
   Come go with me a-part, I will withdraw *he will* 465
   To furnish me with some swift Means of Death *kill*
                                  Desdemona

468   **I . . . ever** I am eternally bound to you. Iago's chilling
engagement makes it clear that we are to see the 'sacred Vow'
(line 450) the two men have sworn as a grim parody of the
marriage rite (with Iago supplanting Desdemona in Othello's
heart). Othello's commitment to Iago suggests that the Moor
has promised his soul to the Devil, who is now his 'familiar'
(II.iii.318–19).

III.iv This scene takes place elsewhere in the Citadel.

2   **lyes** lies; stays, dwells. It is difficult to determine whether the
variant Folio spellings for *lie(s)* and *lye(s)* in lines 2–13 are
significant. But here as in *Macbeth*, II.iii.24–28, there may be
wordplay (at least in the Clown's speeches in lines 5–13) on
lye as a word for 'urinate'. See the second note to II.iii.89.

6   **'tis Stabbing** (a) it's stabbing him (doing him injury) to say he
lyes (urinates) 'any where' (line 3), (b) it's equivalent to saying
he's 'Stabbing' (with wordplay on the copulative sense of *lies*),
(c) it's enough to get me stabbed for telling a lie (and saying
that he is a liar).

7   **Go to** enough of this evasive jesting. Compare I.iii.387,
III.iii.203.

8   **lodges** both (a) resides, and (b) places himself (in the sense that
relates to lodging something in a receptacle). The Clown
would be spreading scandal about Cassio, he says, if he
implied that he 'lodges' (lies) illicitly. What the Clown hints at
in jest is what Iago has been saying and doing in earnest.
Desdemona's verb recalls III.iii.311–12. Compare line 11,
where *know* hints that Cassio 'lodges' in a carnal sense; see
the notes to III.iii.93, 196.

9   **lye** both (a) emit urine, and (b) lie, lodge.

12   **devise a Lodging** invent (literally, open up) a place of residence
for him. *Devise* derives from a Latin word that means 'divide'.
Compare III.i.39–40, III.iii.385.

14   **enquire him out** seek into where he is and dislodge him.

15   **edified by Report** literally, built up by what you carry back.

16   **catechize** ask pointed, instructive questions. The literal
meaning of this word (which derives from Greek and alludes
to the Church's methods of indoctrinating children and new
converts) is 'sound thoroughly'.

For the fair Divel. Now art thou my Lieutenant.
IAGO   I am your own for ever.   *Exeunt.*

Scene 4

Enter Desdemona, Aemilia, and Clown.

DESDEMONA   Do you know, Sirrah, where
Lieutenant Cassio lyes?
CLOWN   I dare not say he lies any where.   *pun*
DESDEMONA   Why, Man?
CLOWN   He's a Soldier, and for me to say a   5
Soldier lyes, 'tis Stabbing.   *pun*
DESDEMONA   Go to: where lodges he?
CLOWN   To tell you where he lodges is to tell   *pun*
you where I lye.
DESDEMONA   Can any thing be made of this?   10
CLOWN   I know not where he lodges, and for me
to devise a Lodging, and say he lies here, or
he lies there, were to lye in mine own Throat.
DESDEMONA   Can you enquire him out? and be
edified by Report?   15
CLOWN   I will catechize the World for him, that
is, make Questions, and by them Answer.
DESDEMONA   Seek him, bid him come hither:
tell him I have mov'd my Lord on his behalf,
and hope all will be well.   20

---

17   **make . . . Answer**   The kind of catechism the Clown will
undertake 'for' Cassio hints at a copulative sense of *make* and
at genital implications for *Questions* (female) and *Answer*
(male). See the note to I.ii.85–87.

19   **mov'd my Lord**   Desdemona means 'made a motion (proposal)
to my Lord, urging him to relent and reinstate Cassio'. She
doesn't realize that she has moved him to anger. Compare
II.iii.176–77, III.iii.44–45, 213, 219.

21 **Compass** scope; reach or embrace (with wordplay on the genital sense of *Man's Wit* and the copulative meaning of *doing it*). See the notes to II.iii.381, III.iii.99, 421, and compare III.iii.455. *Compass* recalls I.iii.364–67, and anticipates lines 69–74.

23 **loose** both (a) let loose, and (b) misplace, lose.

27 **Cruzadoes** Portuguese coins; so called because they bore a cross.

31 **borne** both (a) born, and (b) carried, reared. Compare III.iii.352.

32 **Humours** psychological imbalances. Compare line 118.

35 **Oh . . . dissemble!** Oh how difficult it is to pretend. Othello probably means that it is no longer appropriate to address Desdemona as 'my good Lady'. *Hardness* (difficulty) can also be construed to refer to an obdurate coldness of heart; see III.iii.436–37, and compare III.iii.410–11.

39 **argues . . . Heart** is an indication of vitality, fertility, and generosity. Under the pernicious influence of Iago, Othello equates *Fruitfulness* with a rank appetite, and *liberal Heart* with gross licentiousness. As the Moor has noted in III.iii.178–81, 'Where Virtue is', traits such as these are all the 'more Virtuous'. But in Othello's eyes, if not in reality, Iago has now turned Desdemona's 'Virtue into Pitch' (II.iii.372). *Fruitfulness* echoes II.iii.353–54, 390; *liberal* recalls II.i.165–66.

41 **A . . . Liberty** a period of confinement to separate it from further temptation. Compare I.iii.349.

42 **Castigation** chastisement, correction (from Latin *castigare*, purify).
Exercise devout devoted religious discipline. Compare II.i.271–74.

CLOWN To do this is within the Compass of
Man's Wit, and therefore I will attempt the
doing it.   *Exit.*

DESDEMONA Where should I loose the
Handkerchief, Aemilia?

AEMILIA I know not, Madam.   25

DESDEMONA Believe me, I had rather have lost
my Purse
Full of Cruzadoes. And but my noble Moor
Is true of Mind, and made of no such Baseness
As jealous Creatures are, it were enough
To put him to ill Thinking.

AEMILIA   Is he not jealous?   30

DESDEMONA Who, he? I think the Sun where he
was borne
Drew all such Humours from him.

Enter Othello.

AEMILIA   Look where he comes.

DESDEMONA I will not leave him now till
Cassio
Be call'd to him. — How is't with you, my Lord?

OTHELLO Well, my good Lady. — Oh hardness to
dissemble!   35
— How do you, Desdemona?

DESDEMONA   Well, my good Lord.

OTHELLO Give me your Hand. This Hand is moist,
my Lady.

DESDEMONA It yet hath felt no Age, nor known
no Sorrow.

OTHELLO This argues Fruitfulness, and liberal
Heart:
Hot, hot, and moist. This Hand of yours
requires
A Sequester from Liberty: Fasting, and Prayer,   40
Much Castigation, Exercise devout,
For here's a young and sweating Divel here
That commonly rebels. 'Tis a good Hand,

45   **frank**   free. This word often means 'guileless' and 'open-hearted', as in lines 45–46. But for Othello it now means 'open to all comers'. See I.iii.38–39, II.iii.304–5, III.iii.188–90. *Indeed* echoes III.iii.156–58; see the note to III.iii.99.

47–48 **The . . . Hearts**   Othello probably means that whereas in the old days hearts (the love of chaste women) gave their hands in holy matrimony, today's wanton women give away their hands without surrendering their hearts. Othello may also be interpreting the 'Heraldry' in line 46 to signify that it was Desdemona's moist 'Hand' that 'gave away' the true state of her 'Heart' (revealing it to be licentious rather than loyal).

49   **I . . . this**   Desdemona means 'I can't say anything on this topic because I am unable to follow what you are saying.' But her words no doubt suggest to Othello that she has something to hide.

50   **Chuck**   like *Chick*, a term of affection.

52   **salt . . . Rheum**   Othello's words could refer to 'distressful runniness in my nose and eyes'; but *salt* can also mean 'lecherous' (as in III.iii.394), and Othello is applying the handkerchief test to see whether the 'Rheum' that has caused the moistness in Desdemona's hand has anything to do with Cassio's beard (III.iii.428).

55   **No faith**   Desdemona means 'No, in faith', but what she says conveys what Othello has been persuaded to believe: that she has no fidelity. This reading derives from the Quarto; the Folio prints *No indeed*. *Fault* recalls III.iii.61–65.

57   **Charmer**   sorceress, magician.

58   **while**   so long as.

59   **amiable**   attractive, lovely, desirable. *Subdue* recalls II.iii.352–53.

62   **hold her loathed**   despise her, regard her as loathsome. Compare III.iii.261–62.

65   **her**   to my wife.

A frank one.

DESDEMONA   You may, indeed, say so: 45
For 'twas that Hand that gave away my Heart.

OTHELLO   A liberal Hand. The Hearts of old gave
   Hands:
But our new Heraldry is Hands, not Hearts.

DESDEMONA   I cannot speak of this: come now,
   your Promise.

OTHELLO   What Promise, Chuck?   50

DESDEMONA   I have sent to bid Cassio come speak
   with you.

OTHELLO   I have a salt and sorry Rheum offends
   me:
Lend me thy Handkerchief.

DESDEMONA   Here, my Lord.

OTHELLO   That which
   I gave you.

DESDEMONA   I have it not about me.

OTHELLO   Not?

DESDEMONA   No faith, my Lord.

OTHELLO   That's a Fault. That Handkerchief   55
Did an Egyptian to my Mother give:
She was a Charmer, and could almost read
The Thoughts of People. She told her, while
   she kept it,
'T would make her amiable, and subdue my Father
Entirely to her Love; but if she lost it,   60
Or made a Gift of it, my Father's Eye
Should hold her loathed, and his Spirits should
   hunt
After new Fancies. She, dying, gave it me,
And bid me, when my Fate would have me Wiv'd,
To give it her. I did so; and take heed on't,   65

66   **Make . . . Darling**   hold it to be a treasure. *Darling* recalls
        I.ii.68.
        precious Eye   Othello refers to Desdemona's eyeball. But *Eye*
        was also a term for the female genitalia (see *Troilus and
        Cressida*, II.i.87), and, whether or not he realizes it, that sense
        relates to Othello's quest for 'the Ocular Proof' (III.iii.350).
        Compare II.i.229, 250–51, II.iii.5–6, 22–24.

67   **loose**   both (a) lose, and (b) let loose.
        Perdition   both (a) loss, and (b) damnation. Compare II.ii.3–4,
        III.iii.88–90.

69   **Web**   texture. Iago will weave this 'Web' into a 'Net' (II.iii.373)
        Web recalls II.i.170–71.

70   **Sybil**   prophetess.

71   **Compasses**   annual revolutions. Compare line 21. In their
        roundabout way, lines 70–71 identify the Sybil as a
        200-year-old woman.

72   **Fury**   ecstasy (in the throes of inspiration).
        sow'd   sewed (but with wordplay on breeding, line 73), and on
        the sowing of seeds to yield the strawberries referred to by
        Iago in III.iii.424).

73   **hallowed**   consecrated, sacred. *Breed* (produce) recalls
        III.iii.370.

74   **Mummy**   the extract from mummified (embalmed) bodies.

75   **Conserv'd of**   preserved from; prepared as a conserve.

76   **veritable**   true; verifiable.
        look . . . well   take special care of it. See III.iii.192, 195.

78   **Wherefore?**   Why?
        startingly   haltingly and impetuously, by fits and starts.
        Compare I.i.98–99, III.iii.117.

79   **rash**   excitedly, passionately. Compare II.i.284.
        out o'th' way   where you can't find it. Compare I.iii.364–65,
        where Iago uses this expression to mean 'off course', and
        III.i.39–40.

81   **and if**   if.

84   **a . . . Suit**   a device to distract me from pleading for Cassio's
        reinstatement. *Suit* recalls III.i.36, III.iii.77–81; *Trick* echoes
        II.i.173–77, III.iii.118–21.

87   **mis-gives**   supplies me with presentiments of woe, fills me with
        doubts and suspicions.

Make it a Darling, like your precious Eye:
To loose't, or give't away, were such Perdition
As nothing else could match.

DESDEMONA   Is't possible?

OTHELLO   'Tis true: there's Magic in the Web of
    it.
A Sybil, that had numb'red in the World   70
The Sun to course two hundred Compasses,
In her Prophetic Fury sow'd the Work:
The Worms were hallowed that did breed the
    Silk,
And it was dy'd in Mummy, which the Skilful
Conserv'd of Maidens' Hearts.

DESDEMONA   Indeed, is't true?   75

OTHELLO   Most veritable, therefore look to't well.

DESDEMONA   Then would to Heaven that I had never
    seen't.

OTHELLO   Ha? Wherefore?

DESDEMONA   Why do you speak so startingly
    And rash?

OTHELLO   Is't lost? Is't gone? Speak, is't out o'th' way?

DESDEMONA   Heaven bless us.

OTHELLO   Say you?   80

DESDEMONA   It is not lost: but what and if it were?

OTHELLO   How?

DESDEMONA   I say it is not lost.

OTHELLO   Fetch't; let me see't.

DESDEMONA   Why so I can, Sir: but I will not now.
This is a Trick to put me from my Suit.
Pray you let Cassio be receiv'd again.   85

OTHELLO   Fetch me the Handkerchief, my Mind
    mis-gives.

88   **sufficient** able, accomplished (compare I.iii.222–23). This word derives from the Latin *facere*, 'to make'; it is related to forms that mean 'lay the foundation for' (see line 90) and 'supply', and it echoes *suffigere*, 'nail up' or 'fasten'. Throughout this exchange we are reminded of what Iago has said in III.iii.239–47.

90   **founded ... Love** Desdemona means 'built all his hopes upon your esteem for him'; but to Othello her words suggest that Cassio has based his erotic 'Fortunes' upon Desdemona as he 'topp'd' (III.iii.386) Othello's 'Love' and in the process the General himself.

91   **Shar'd ... you** Again, it is inevitable that Othello will hear something more than what the innocent Desdemona means here, in part because she herself is associated in his mind with 'Dangers' (see I.iii.165), among them the risk the Moor undertook in wooing her. *Dangers* echoes III.iii.316.

92   **too blame** too much to blame. Compare III.iii.276.
       'Zouns! God's wounds! Given the wounds Othello believes to have been inflicted on him by the 'divine Desdemona' (II.i.73), this oath is painfully apt. See the note to line 88, and compare II.iii.148.

95   **unhappy** unfortunate.

96   **'Tis ... Man** it doesn't take more than a year or two for us to see a man for what he is. *Shews* (shows) recalls III.iii.105, 113, 189, 198.

97   **Stomachs** Aemilia means (sexual) 'appetites'; but the stomach was also considered a seat of the irascible passions (hate and wrath), and she may be alluding to that as well. Compare I.iii.147–48, II.i.229.

101   **And ... Happiness** and behold how fortunate we are [since we see her even as we speak].
       importune her plead with her insistently. Compare II.iii.329–30, III.iii.245–47, IV.i.25.

105   **be ... Love** be restored to my former place in the body (the army) he serves as head. Here imagery that seems sexually suggestive would also have been recognized as theological. In Ephesians 4, the Apostle Paul urges Christians to view themselves as 'members one of another', 'fitly joined together' in their varied offices (duties) as limbs and organs of 'the body of Christ'. *Suit* (line 103) echoes line 84.

DESDEMONA Come, come:
  You'll never meet a more sufficient Man.
OTHELLO The Handkerchief.
DESDEMONA   A Man that all his Time
  Hath founded his good Fortunes on your Love;   90
  Shar'd Dangers with you.
OTHELLO   The Handkerchief.
DESDEMONA   In sooth,
  You are too blame.
OTHELLO   'Zouns!   *Exit.*
AEMILIA Is not this man jealous?
DESDEMONA   I nev'r saw this before.
  Sure there's some Wonder in this Handkerchief:
  I am most unhappy in the Loss of it.   95
AEMILIA 'Tis not a Year or two shews us a Man:
  They are all Stomachs, and we all but Food,   *extended*
  They eat us hungerly, and when they are full   *metaphor*
  They belch us.

                Enter Iago, and Cassio.

          Look you, Cassio and my Husband.
IAGO There is no other way: 'tis she must do't.   100
  And lo the Happiness: go, and importune her.
DESDEMONA How now, good Cassio, what's the
  News with you?
CASSIO Madam, my former Suit. I do beseech you,
  That by your virtuous Means, I may again
  Exist, and be a member of his Love   105
  Whom I with all the Office of my Heart
  Intirely honour. I would not be delay'd.
  If my Offence be of such mortal kind

---

107 **Intirely** entirely. See the note to II.i.64–65. *Office* (duty,
      function), line 106, recalls III.iii.400.

108 **mortal** fatal. Cassio implies that he fetches his 'Life and Being'
      (I.ii.21) from his position as Othello's lieutenant (lines
      104–5).

109–   **nor . . . futurity**   neither my past record, nor my present
10   remorse and repentance, nor my resolve to serve him
          meritoriously in the future. *Merit* recalls I.ii.22–24,
          II.i.147–49, II.iii.271–73, III.iii.182–84.

112   **But . . . Benefit**   merely being assured of that must satisfy me.
          Compare I.iii.309–12.

113–   **So . . . Alms**   So shall I adopt the habit of one who is forced to
15   accept disappointment and direct my energies into some other
          course at Fortune's bestowal. Compare III.iii.254–57. The
          phrase *forc'd Content* is erotically suggestive (see the note to
          II.i.198), and it recalls the imagery of I.iii.109–11.

116   **My . . . Tune**   my advocacy does not now chime (harmonize)
          with his disposition. Compare III.i.1–18.

118   **Were . . . alter'd**   if his face were as changed as his mood.
          Favour recalls I.iii.344–45, II.i.234, III.i.28–29, and
          anticipates IV.iii.18–19; *Humour* echoes lines 31–32.

121   **within the Blank**   in the centre of the target at point-blank
          range. *Displeasure* echoes III.iii.45.

124   **suffice**   satisfy. Compare line 88.

130   **Puff'd**   obliterated. Iago's point is that if personal losses in dire
          battles didn't move Othello to anger, something truly
          momentous must be wrong now. *Blown* (line 128) recalls
          III.iii.175–78, 435.

132   **There's . . . angry**   Iago knows there's *not* 'Matter in't indeed'.
          Matter recalls II.iii.250 and anticipates line 148.

133   **Something . . . State**   surely some political or military matter.
          State recalls I.iii.234–35.

134   **some unhatch'd Practice**   some stratagem that has just been
          detected (removed from the hatch) before it could be hatched.

137–   **Men's . . . Object**   men quarrel over minor matters and take out
38   their anger on their inferiors when their real object is
          elsewhere. Compare Iago's remarks in II.iii.277–80. *Great*
          hints at the implications noted at I.iii.165, II.i.78–82.

139   **endues**   leads, conducts; here, infects. *Members* echoes lines
          103–7.

That nor my Service past, nor present Sorrows,
Nor purpos'd Merit in futurity,   110
Can ransom me into his Love again,
But to know so must be my Benefit:
So shall I clothe me in a forc'd Content,
And shut my self up in some other Course
To Fortune's Alms.
DESDEMONA   Alas, thrice-gentle Cassio, ~~sin remose absolution~~   115
My Advocation is not now in Tune; ~~musical metaphor~~
My Lord is not my Lord; nor should I know him
Were he in Favour as in Humour alter'd.
So help me every Spirit sanctified,
As I have spoken for you all my best,
And stood within the Blank of his Displeasure   120
For my free Speech. You must awhile be patient;
What I can do, I will; and more I will
Than for my self I dare. Let that suffice you.
IAGO   Is my Lord angry?
AEMILIA   He went hence but now,   125
And certainly in strange Unquietness.
IAGO   Can he be angry? I have seen the Cannon
When it hath blown his Ranks into the Air,
And like the Divel from his very Arm
Puff'd his own Brother. And is he angry?   130
Something of Moment then: I will go meet him,
There's Matter in't indeed if he be angry.
DESDEMONA   I prythee do so.   *Exit* [*Iago*].
                    — Something sure of State,
Either from Venice, or some unhatch'd Practice
Made demonstrable here in Cyprus to him,   135
Hath puddled his clear Spirit: and in such
    Cases
Men's Natures wrangle with inferior things,
Though great ones are their Object. 'Tis even
    so.
For let our Finger ache, and it endues
Our other healthful Members even to a sense   140
Of Pain, Nay, we must think Men are not Gods,

[Handwritten marginal notes: "sin remose absolution", "musical metaphor", "Metaphor centre of the target (Archery)"]

142–   **Nor . . . Bridal**   nor expect of them such constant attentiveness
43   as befits a skilful horseman's use of the bridle. Desdemona's
        imagery also relates to another kind of 'Bridal', the marriage
        ceremony; it is thus a reminder of the 'Observancy' (watchful
        care) that husbands and wives were to provide for one
        another (Ephesians 5:21–33). Compare III.iii.278–79.

143   **Beshrew me much**   curse me vehemently.

144   **unhandsome Warrior**   unseemly rebel against my lord's
        authority. *Warrior* (soldier) echoes II.i.184, II.iii.324–25.

145   **Arraigning**   summoning to trial, accusing.

146   **suborn'd**   unduly influenced, bribed to give false testimony.

147   **indited**   both (a) indicted (charged), and (b) recorded (written
        down).

149   **Toy**   foolish 'Conception' (ill-conceived notion). Compare
        I.iii.266–72. *Conception* (line 148) plays on the imagery of
        line 134.

151   **answer'd so**   satisfied with such rational explanations.
        Answer'd echoes lines 16–17 and recalls III.iii.349–53; *Cause*
        (lines 150, 152) echoes III.iii.401–3.

153   **Monster**   Aemilia's image recalls III.iii.104, 162–63, 416.

154   **borne on it self**   borne by and born of its own loins. Compare
        III.iii.352–53, III.iv.31.

157   **fit**   Desdemona means (a) sound in mind and spirit, and (b) 'in
        Tune' (line 116). Compare lines 142–43, and see
        II.iii.124–26, III.i.53–56, III.iii.241.

159   **uttermost**   absolute (literally, outer) limit. Desdemona will
        'utter' (speak out) for Cassio until she drives Othello to his
        uttermost. *Move* recalls line 19; *Suit* echoes line 84.

160   **'Save**   a contraction for 'May God save (preserve and redeem)'.
        make you from   are you doing away from.

165   **Eight score eight**   eight score (160) plus eight. *Lodging* (line
        163) echoes lines 7–14.

166   **tedious**   wearisome, monotonous. Compare III.iii.387.

167   **Reck'ning**   both (a) calculation (enumeration of the hours), and
        (b) punishment (to be sequestered from you).

Nor of them look for such Observancy
As fits the Bridal. Beshrew me much, Aemilia,
I was (unhandsome Warrior as I am)
Arraigning his Unkindness with my Soul:
But now I find I had suborn'd the Witness,
And he's indited falsely.

[margin: extended metaphor]
[margin: misjudged] 145
[margin: Othello]

AEMILIA   Pray Heaven it be
State Matters, as you think, and no Conception,
Nor no jealous Toy, concerning you.

DESDEMONA   Alas the Day, I never gave him Cause.   150

AEMILIA   But jealous Souls will not be answer'd so;
They are not ever jealous for the Cause,
But jealous for they're jealous. It is a
   Monster
Begot upon it self, borne on it self.

[margin: metaphor]

DESDEMONA   Heaven keep the Monster from
   Othello's Mind.

[margin: d. irony] 155

AEMILIA   Lady, Amen.

DESDEMONA   I will go seek him.
                              – Cassio,
Walk here about: if I do find him fit,
I'll move your Suit and seek to effect it to
My uttermost.

CASSIO   I humbly thank your Ladyship.
                    Exeunt Desdemona and Aemilia.

Enter Bianca.

BIANCA   'Save you, Friend Cassio.

CASSIO   What make you from Home?   160
How is't with you, my most fair Bianca?
Indeed, sweet Love, I was coming to your
   House.

BIANCA   And I was going to your Lodging, Cassio.
What? keep a Week away? Seven Days, and Nights?
Eight score eight Hours? And Lovers' absent
   Hours   165
More tedious than the Dial eight score times?
Oh weary Reck'ning.

168   **prest** both (a) prompted, made ready, and (b) pressed, oppressed, burdened (with wordplay on the literal sense of *Leaden*, heavy, here meaning 'dull'). Cassio alludes to pressing, a form of torture applied to those who refused to enter a plea of guilt or innocence when charged with a crime. (Cassio is now being accused, both chidingly by Bianca, and more seriously, without his being aware of it, by Iago.) Cassio may also be alluding to a means of propagation whereby a branch is weighted to the ground until it puts down roots to start a new plant; compare *Romeo and Juliet*, I.i.189–91.

169   **a ... Time** a period uninterruptedly devoted to you. *Continuate* hints at the same part of the female anatomy that is sometimes referred to as a *Score* (line 170); see the third note to I.i.120, and compare *2 Henry IV*, II.i.24, where the Hostess says that Falstaff is 'an infinitive thing upon my Score'.

170   **Strike ... Absence** remove the scores (both notches and sums of twenty) you have tallied in reckoning the hours I owe you. Compare IV.i.128.

171   **Take ... out** copy the design on this handkerchief for me. Compare III.iii.290–91. Here *take out* includes the meaning 'carry away'.

173   **To ... Cause** in keeping with the 'Absence' that has hurt me so deeply, I now feel the pain of the 'Cause' I detect. *Cause* echoes lines 150, 152; *Token* (line 172) recalls III.iii.285–90.

174   **Go to** Oh, come now! Compare III.iii.203.

175   **vild Guesses** vile, worthless inferences. Bianca's jealousy is yet another variation on the dominant theme of *Othello*.

177   **Remembrance** keepsake. Cassio's phrasing is a reminder that the object in question was Desdemona's 'first Remembrance from the Moor' (III.iii.285–88). Compare line 172.

179   **Chamber** bedroom. This word echoes Othello's reference to 'those Soft Parts of Conversation / That Chamberers have' (III.iii.258–59).

181   **like** likely.
    copied imitated. This word derived from *copia* (from which we get the word *copious*), and here it hints that 'there's some Wonder in this Handkerchief' (line 94) that will multiply the effects of a trifle 'light as Air' (III.iii.312) many times over.

CASSIO   Pardon me, Bianca:
  I have this while with Leaden Thoughts been
      prest,
  But I shall in a more Continuate Time
  Strike off this Score of Absence. Sweet Bianca,   170
  Take me this Work out.
BIANCA   Oh Cassio, whence came this?
  This is some Token from a newer Friend,
  To the felt Absence now I feel a Cause:
  Is't come to this? Well, well.
CASSIO   Go to, Woman:
  Throw your vild Guesses in the Divel's Teeth,   175
  From whence you have them. You are jealous now
  That this is from some Mistress, some
      Remembrance;
  No, in good troth, Bianca.
BIANCA   Why, whose is it?
CASSIO   I know not neither: I found it in my
      Chamber,
  I like the Work well. Ere it be demanded   180
  (As like enough it will), I would have it copied:
  Take it, and do't, and leave me for this time.
BIANCA   Leave you? Wherefore?
CASSIO   I do attend here on the General,
  And think it no Addition, nor my Wish,   185

---

184   **attend ... General**   both (a) serve the General as his would-be
      attendant (compare I.iii.294), or (b) await the General's
      arrival (compare III.iii.275).

185   **Addition**   credit; enhancement of my position. *Addition* often
      means 'title' in Shakespeare. Meanwhile it frequently alludes
      to a man's genital endowments, those that pertain to his
      ability to be 'woman'd' (line 186), attractive to and in the
      company of, women; see the note to II.ii.6–7.

188 **bring . . . little** escort me a short distance.

192 **circumstanc'd** subject to circumstances ('manned', ordered off
by a soldier who can't be 'woman'd' now). Compare
III.iii.396 for another sense in which Bianca would 'be
circumstanced'. *Attend* (line 191) echoes line 184.

To have him see me woman'd.
BIANCA   Why, I pray you?
CASSIO   Not that I love you not.
BIANCA   But that you do not love me.
  I pray you bring me on the way a little,
  And say if I shall see you soon at Night?
CASSIO   'Tis but a little way that I can bring
    you,   190
  For I attend here: but I'll see you soon.
BIANCA   'Tis very good. I must be circumstanc'd.
                                   Exeunt omnes.

IV.i   The scene remains at or near the Citadel.

1   **Will you**   does it please you to.

2   **unauthoriz'd**   illicit, adulterous.

6   **Hypocrisy . . . Divel**   the kind of hypocrisy that involves acting like a devil while remaining angelic (an inversion of what is normally meant by hypocrisy). For previous references to preposterous behaviour, see I.iii.61 and III.iii.228. *Harm* (lines 4, 5) echoes III.iii.95–96.

7   **mean . . . so**   have virtuous intentions and yet do thus (referring to what Iago has just hinted at).

8   **they tempt Heaven**   Othello is probably thinking of the clause in the Lord's Prayer in which Christians are taught to say 'lead us not into temptation' (Matthew 6:13). He may also be thinking of the command 'Thou shalt not tempt the Lord thy God' (Deuteronomy 6:16), a passage Jesus quotes to Satan in the wilderness (Luke 4:12). To 'tempt Heaven' is to presume upon one's own spiritual strength, to believe oneself 'all in all Sufficient' (line 269) and thus not in need of divine grace for assistance in conducting a pilgrimage through life that will lead to salvation. *Virtue*, echoing *virtuously* (line 7), recalls III.iii.340, III.iv.104.

9   **Venial Slip**   pardonable misstep (rather than a mortal sin). *Slip* echoes II.i.249–50.

16–17 **they . . . not**   Iago's riddle depends on the distinction between two definitions of *it*: (a) a reputation for 'Honour' (virtue, here referring primarily to chastity), and (b) true honour. Compare III.iii.196–99, and see II.iii.271–73.

18   **forgot it**   forgotten about it. Othello's phrasing recalls other senses of *forgot* (see II.iii.169, 191, 244, where it refers to a negligence that predisposes a person to error), and it provides a reminder that Othello had temporarily forgotten himself when he ordered Desdemona to disregard the handkerchief in III.iii.281–82. Both he and Desdemona have now forgotten what happened at that moment.

20–21 **As . . . all**   Othello alludes to a black bird widely regarded as a harbinger of death; when the raven flew over a house afflicted with infection, it was thought to bode ill (be an omen of bad fortune).

ACT IV

Scene 1

Enter Othello, and Iago.

IAGO   Will you think so?

OTHELLO   Think so, Iago?

IAGO   What,
To kiss in private?

OTHELLO   An unauthoriz'd Kiss?

IAGO   Or to be naked with her Friend in Bed
An Hour, or more, not meaning any Harm?

OTHELLO   Naked in Bed, Iago, and not mean Harm?   5
It is Hypocrisy against the Divel:
They that mean virtuously, and yet do so,
The Divel their Virtue tempts, and they tempt
   Heaven.

IAGO   If they do nothing, 'tis a Venial Slip:
But if I give my Wife a Handkerchief –   10

OTHELLO   What then?

IAGO   Why then 'tis hers, my Lord, and being hers,
She may, I think, bestow't on any Man.

OTHELLO   She is Protectress of her Honour too:
May she give that?

IAGO   Her Honour is an Essence   15
That's not seen: they have it very oft
That have it not. But for the Handkerchief –

OTHELLO   By Heaven, I would most gladly have
   forgot it.
Thou saidst (oh, it comes o'er my Memory,
As doth the Raven o'er the Infectious House,   20
Boding to all) he had my Handkerchief.

IAGO   Ay: what of that?

24–28 **as . . . blab** in the way that irresponsible gallants do when they are out with their fellow males – knaves who, having persuaded 'some Mistress' to grant her favours or having taken advantage of her willingness to proffer them voluntarily, cannot keep themselves from boasting. Iago's syntax is web-like in the intricacy and subtlety of its innuendo. *Mistress* echoes III.iv.176–77; *importunate* recalls III.iv.101 and anticipates lines 115–16; *Suit* echoes III.iv.158–59. *Convinced* here means 'overcame' (persuaded); compare I.iii.109–13. *Supplied* ('fulfilled', 'accommodated') recalls I.iii.321–27, III.iii.17.

30 **unswear** deny if pressed to admit it.

36 **be-lie her** Othello probably means either (a) lie about her, or (b) turn her into a liar (by making her sexually dishonest). But *Be-lie her*, which echoes III.iv.1–13, can also mean 'Lie on her'.

37 **fulsome** lustful, lascivious. Compare *The Merchant of Venice*, I.iii.87, where this adjective is applied to ewes in heat. The context suggests that Othello means 'nauseating', but as he descends into incoherence, the Moor's words come to suggest the images his diseased imagination is casting up. *Fulsome*, for example, is a word that hints at the kind of full-filling that Othello associates with 'Lie on her' (line 35). And in the lines that follow, *Confessions* (see II.iii.329), *hang'd* (see I.iii.365–67), and *Instruction* (see *Measure for Measure*, III.i.546) all hint at copulation.

38–40 **To . . . confess** Othello alludes to a proverb deriving from the practice of urging a condemned criminal to confess his sins and receive absolution before he was put to death. When he says 'First to be hang'd,' Othello means that Cassio should not be allowed this privilege (so that his punishment will be eternal). It probably doesn't occur to Othello that one meaning of 'hanging' is the very crime for which Cassio is to be executed; see the note to I.iii.365, and compare line 67.

41–43 **Nature . . . Instruction** Human nature would not clothe herself in such a shady and character-darkening passion [as the lust Desdemona has manifested with Cassio] without someone to teach her how to do it (literally, to build up her knowledge of it). *Nature* recalls III.iii.222–26.

47 **credulous** gullible.

48 **chast** chaste, virtuous. Compare line 74.

OTHELLO   That's not so good now.
IAGO   What
If I had said I had seen him do you wrong?
Or heard him say (as Knaves be such abroad,
Who, having by their own importunate Suit,   25
Or voluntary Dotage of some Mistress,
Convinced or supplied them, cannot choose
But they must blab) –
OTHELLO   Hath he said any thing?
IAGO   He hath, my Lord, but be you well assur'd,
No more than he'll unswear.
OTHELLO   What hath he said?   30
IAGO   Why, that he did – I know not what he did.
OTHELLO   What? What?
IAGO   Lie.
OTHELLO   With her?
IAGO   With her? On her, what you will.
OTHELLO   Lie with her? Lie on her? We say 'Lie   35
on her', when they be-lie her. Lie with her:
'zouns, that's fulsome. Handkerchief,
Confessions, Handkerchief. To confess, and
be hang'd for his Labour. First to be
hang'd, and then to confess: I tremble   40
at it. Nature would not invest her self
in such shadowing Passion, without some
Instruction. It is not Words that shakes
me thus.
Pish, Noses, Ears, and Lips: is't possible?   45
Confess? Handkerchief? O Divel.   *Falls in a Trance.*
IAGO   Work on,
My Medicine works. Thus credulous Fools are
    caught,
And many worthy and chast Dames even thus,

49   **meet Reproach**   become victims of scandal.

53   **Fit**   seizure. Compare III.iv.157.

54   **forbear**   restrain yourself.

55   **Lethargy**   coma, state of unconsciousness.
    his quiet Course   its uninterrupted way. *Course* (which here suggests *corse*, 'corpse', in a way that parallels *Romeo and Juliet*, III.ii.128) echoes III.iv.113–15 and anticipates IV.ii.91; *stirs* recalls II.iii.176–77, 210–12, III.i.26–32.

59   **straight**   very soon. But like 'withdraw your self a little while' (line 58) and 'great Occasion' (line 60), Iago's phrasing hints at the context of innuendo that charges this moment with tension. Compare I.iii.47–48, III.iii.85–86.

62   **mock me**   Othello thinks that Iago is referring to the horns of a cuckold. Compare III.iii.278. *Mock* recalls I.ii.64–71, III.iii.161–63.

63   **bear**   Iago plays on two senses: (a) endure, and (b) wear, carry. Compare II.i.19, III.iii.188–90.

64   **A . . . Beast**   a cuckold looks like a monster and is reduced to the savagery of a beast. *Monster* (lines 64, 66) echoes III.iv.153–55; *Beast* recalls I.i.114–16, II.iii.314–15.

66   **civil**   both (a) urban (living in a city), and (b) civilized (here meaning politely tolerant in accepting his humiliation). *Populous City* (line 65) recalls I.i.74–76.

68   **Think**   be mindful that. Compare III.iv.141–43.
    bearded Fellow   grown man. But Iago also means a fellow who has permitted himself to be 'bearded' (treated contemptuously) without defending his honour. See the note to III.iii.428.
    but yok'd   subjected to the yoke that horned creatures (here, submissive oxen) bear as they 'draw' (pull) the coaches of their proud, unruly wives and insolent cuckolders.

70   **unproper Beds**   beds that have been violated and are thus no longer their owners' own. Like *peculiar*, *proper* meant 'exclusively one's own'. Here *unproper* also means 'indecent' and 'unchaste'.

71   **Case**   situation (but with a reminder of the genital 'case' that has supposedly been opened up to other men). Compare III.iii.4, 27–28, 401.

72   **arch-Mock**   most egregious, taunting insult. *Mock* echoes line 62. *Spight* (spite) means both 'malice' and 'mortification'.

All Guiltless, meet Reproach. — What ho? My
  Lord?
My Lord, I say: Othello.

              Enter Cassio.

           — How now, Cassio?   50
CASSIO   What's the matter?
IAGO   My Lord is fall'n into an Epilepsy.
  This is his second Fit. He had one yesterday.
CASSIO   Rub him about the Temples.
IAGO   No, forbear:
  The Lethargy must have his quiet Course.   55
  If not, he foams at Mouth: and by and by
  Breaks out to savage Madness. Look, he stirs:
  Do you withdraw your self a little while,
  He will recover straight. When he is gone,
  I would on great Occasion speak with you.   60
                [*Cassio withdraws.*]
  — How is it, General? Have you not hurt your
  Head?
OTHELLO   Dost thou mock me?
IAGO   I mock you not, by Heaven:
  Would you would bear your Fortune like a Man.
OTHELLO   A Horned Man's a Monster, and a Beast.
IAGO   There's many a Beast then in a populous
  City,   65
  And many a civil Monster.
OTHELLO   Did he confess it?
IAGO   Good Sir, be a Man:
  Think every bearded Fellow that's but yok'd
  May draw with you. There's Millions now alive
  That nightly lie in those unproper Beds   70
  Which they dare swear peculiar. Your Case is
    better.
  Oh, 'tis the Spight of Hell, the Fiend's arch-Mock.

73 **To ... Couch** to kiss a wanton in a bed one securely (complacently) thinks 'peculiar'. Compare I.iii.10 and III.iii.193.

78 **patient List** both (a) a quiet listening (if not listing) posture, and (b) a place within whose boundaries you can restrain yourself with patience while you await your call to maintain your honour in chivalric combat. *List* echoes II.iii.358; *apart* recalls III.iii.465.

80 **Passion** surrender to emotional (unmanly) weakness.
resulting demeaning. If the Folio reading is correct (most editors judge it to be a misconstruction of the manuscript and adopt the Quarto's *unsuiting*), Iago is probably adapting a sense of *result* that means 'reverting', springing back into a former position (see II.iii.354–60). It is conceivable that Iago means 're-sulting', resuming a former state that was sullied and foul (see I.i.86–88, 107–12, I.iii.62–71), perhaps with wordplay on 'Sultan', the title of an Islamic ruler (compare I.i.125, where Brabantio refers to 'the gross Clasps of a lascivious Moor', and see the note to line 120).

82 **laid ... Ecstasy** explained your seizure so as to excuse it. *Ecstasy* (from Greek) means 'to be beside oneself'.

83 **bad** 'bade', the past tense of *bid*. Compare II.i.155.

84 **encave** conceal under cover of darkness. This word echoes I.iii.138, and it indicates how far Othello has fallen since he spoke of his heroic adventures in 'Antars vast'.

85 **Fleers** sneers, 'Gibes', and 'Scorns'.

87 **tell ... anew** Once again, Iago draws our attention to how different this Othello is from the majestic warrior whose 'Tale' (I.ii.169) won Desdemona's love and then preserved his 'Prize' (I.ii.51) from her angry father.

89 **hath ... cope** has encountered and is again to encounter.

90 **marry** Modern editions normally place a comma after this adverb (a word that meant 'indeed' and derived from an oath referring to the Virgin Mary). But the lack of punctuation in the original texts permits *marry* to do double duty here as a verb, and one that conveys the impossible situation in which Othello now finds himself: being told to 'marry Patience' by a tormentor who is driving him to a 'Spleen' (raging vengeance) that is the antithesis of patience. *Marry* recalls III.i.7, 10; *Patience* echoes III.iv.122.

To lip a Wanton in a secure Couch,
And to suppose her chast. No, let me know,
And knowing what I am, I know what she   75
Shall be.

OTHELLO   Oh, thou art wise: 'tis certain.

IAGO   Stand you
A while apart,
Confine your self but in a patient List.
Whilst you were here, o'erwhelmed with your
    Grief
(A Passion most resulting such a Man),   80
Cassio came hither. I shifted him away,
And laid good 'Scuses upon your Ecstasy,
Bad him anon return, and here speak with me,
The which he promis'd. Do but encave your self,
And mark the Fleers, the Gibes, and notable
    Scorns   85
That dwell in every Region of his Face.
For I will make him tell the Tale anew:
Where, how, how oft, how long ago, and when
He hath and is again to cope your Wife.
I say, but mark his Gesture: marry Patience,   90
Or I shall say y'are all in all in Spleen,
And nothing of a Man.

OTHELLO   Dost thou hear, Iago,
I will be found most cunning in my Patience.
But (dost thou hear) most bloody.

IAGO   That's not amiss,
But yet keep Time in all: will you withdraw?   95
               [*Othello secludes himself.*]

---

93   **cunning**   Othello means 'crafty', but his words are a reminder
       of how lacking in cunning (literally, 'knowing') he really is.
       Compare III.iii.47, IV.ii.87.

95   **keep Time**   both (a) patiently await your opportunity, and (b)
       be measured, 'in Tune' (III.iv.116). *Withdraw* echoes line 58
       and recalls III.iii.465–67.

97   **Huswife** hussy. Compare II.i.113–14.

98   **Cloath** cloth, clothing. Most of today's editions follow the First Quarto and print *clothes*.

100   **beguile** captivate, ensnare.

104   **unbookish** ignorant, naïve; literally, unread or illiterate. **conserve** register, store away, and preserve. Most editions adopt the Quarto's *conster*, 'construe'. The *con*-form is apt here (see the third note to I.i.120).

105   **light** easy-going, wanton.

107–8 **The . . . me** What Cassio means is that it gives him deadly pain to hear Iago address him by the title ('Addition') he no longer possesses. See the note to III.iv.185. Cassio doesn't realize that the new 'Addition' Iago is giving him (that of a cuckolder who is sharing his private 'Addition' with the General's wife) is designed to kill him in reality. Here *want* means 'lack'.

108   **Ply Desdemona well** Once again Iago prescribes the 'Medicine' (line 47) that will poison his patient most expeditiously.

109   **on't** of it. But Iago plays suggestively on a sense of *on't* (on it) that relates to the play's previous references to covering (I.i.110) and topping (III.iii.386); that innuendo is reinforced by the phrasing of 'if this Suit lay in Bianca's Dow'r'. *Suit* ('petition', but with a hint at 'apparel') echoes lines 24–28.

110   **Dow'r** gift; power to bestow. **speed** prosper (with wordplay on the sense of *speed* that accords with *quickly*). Compare I.iii.273–75, II.i.67, 74–77.

111   **Caitiff** captive (victim of her infatuation for me).

113   **Rogue** wretch; here a term that mixes pity with condescension.

114   **faintly** quietly, modestly (less boastfully than before).

116   **Go . . . said** Keep it up, well done. *Importunes* recalls line 25.

117   **gives it out** spreads it abroad. Again Iago's phrasing is erotically suggestive. Compare line 129.

120   **Roman** This designation makes it excruciatingly clear that Othello is identifying himself with the barbarians conquered and paraded in yoked humiliation by the haughty Romans (here associated with Italians in general). Rather than a prince 'of Royal Siege' (I.ii.22), the Moor now considers himself one of the 'Bondslaves and Pagans' referred to in I.ii.99. *Triumph* recalls II.ii.1–7.

– Now will I question Cassio of Bianca,
A Huswife that by selling her Desires
Buys her self Bread, and Cloath. It is a
    Creature
That dotes on Cassio (as 'tis the Strumpet's
    Plague
To beguile many, and be beguil'd by one);   100
He, when he hears of her, cannot restrain
From the excess of Laughter. Here he comes.

Enter Cassio.

As he shall smile, Othello shall go mad:
And his unbookish Jealousy must conserve
Poor Cassio's Smiles, Gestures, and light
    Behaviours   105
Quite in the wrong. – How do you now,
    Lieutenant?
CASSIO The worser that you give me the Addition
Whose want even kills me.
IAGO   Ply Desdemona well,
And you are sure on't: now if this Suit lay in
Bianca's Dow'r, how quickly should you speed?   110
CASSIO Alas, poor Caitiff.
OTHELLO   – Look how he laughs already.
IAGO I never knew a Woman love Man so.
CASSIO Alas, poor Rogue, I think indeed she
    loves me.
OTHELLO – Now he denies it faintly: and laughs
    it out.
IAGO Do you hear, Cassio?
OTHELLO   – Now he importunes him   115
To tell it o'er. – Go to, well said, well said.
IAGO She gives it out that you shall marry her.
Do you intend it?
CASSIO Ha, ha, ha.
OTHELLO – Do ye triumph, Roman? Do you triumph? 120

121 **I marry** either (a) What, I marry her? or (b) Ay, marry.
Compare line 90.

125 **Cry** rumour. Iago's phrasing implies that Bianca is its source.
Compare II.iii.233, and see the note to II.iii.376–77.

128 **scor'd me** either (a) recorded me as a loser, or (b) striped my
back with scores from a whip. Othello's verb recalls the
wordplay on *score* in III.iv.165–70. The most common
Shakespearean use of *score* is in reference to a tavernkeeper's
tally (a piece of wood in which notches were cut to keep tabs
on each customer's orders). Othello thinks that Cassio is now
boasting of how many scores he has notched with
Desdemona. See the note to III.iv.169.

130– **she . . . Promise** It is Bianca's self-deception (her tendency to
31   flatter herself) that leads her to believe I will marry her. The
play provides no evidence that Bianca is 'giving out' any
stories about an impending marriage; Iago is probably
slandering her too. *Monkey's* (line 129) recalls III.iii.393,
where Iago describes Cassio and Desdemona as 'hot as
Monkeys'.

134 **haunts** follows, pesters. Compare I.i.94 and lines 149–51.
Place recalls III.iii.241–42.

137 **Bauble** empty toy, plaything.

140 **Iesture** Here the unusual spelling suggests a 'Gesture' (line 105)
that is also a 'jesture' (an invitation to laugh).
imports conveys. Compare III.iii.307.

143 **pluck'd him** pulled him (as if he were a grape to be savoured or
a string instrument to be fingered). Compare III.iii.412,
V.ii.13–15.

144 **Nose** Othello is referring to the Roman shape of Cassio's nose.
Nose is often phallic, and Caesar was known for more than
one kind of conquest. See *As You Like It*, IV.ii.3–6, and
compare I.iii.408–9, III.i.4. *Throw* (line 145) recalls I.i.71,
II.i.36–38, III.iv.175.

147 **Before me** a mild oath, probably a euphemism for 'before
God'.

148 **Fitchew** polecat, whose strong 'perfume' (line 149) and sexual
appetite made it a byword for 'whore'.

CASSIO I marry. What? A Customer; prythee bear
  some Charity to my Wit, do not think it so
  unwholesome. Ha, ha, ha.

OTHELLO – So, so, so, so: they laugh that wins.

IAGO Why the Cry goes that you marry her. 125

CASSIO Prythee say true.

IAGO I am a very Villain else.

OTHELLO – Have you scor'd me? Well.

CASSIO This is the Monkey's own giving out:
  she is persuaded I will marry her, out of her 130
  own Love and Flattery, not out of my Promise.

OTHELLO – Iago beckons me: now he begins the
  Story.

CASSIO She was here even now: she haunts me
  in every place. I was the other Day talking 135
  on the Sea-bank with certain Venetians, and
  thither comes the Bauble, and falls me thus
  about my Neck.

OTHELLO – Crying 'Oh dear Cassio', as it were:
  his Iesture imports it. 140

CASSIO So hangs, and lolls, and weeps upon me:
  So shakes and pulls me. Ha, ha, ha.

OTHELLO – Now he tells how she pluck'd him to
  my Chamber. – Oh I see that Nose of yours, but
  not that Dog I shall throw it to. 145

CASSIO Well, I must leave her company.

Enter Bianca.

IAGO Before me: look where she comes.

CASSIO 'Tis such another Fitchew: marry a
  Perfum'd one? – What do you mean by this
  haunting of me? 150

BIANCA Let the Divel and his Dam haunt you:
  what did you mean by that same Handkerchief
  you gave me even now? I was a fine Fool to
  take it: I must take out the work? A likely

155 **Piece of Work** Bianca probably means 'fiction', referring not to the embroidery on the handkerchief but to the story Cassio has told her about how he obtained it. *Piece of Work* may also refer to the 'Mistress' (III.iv.177) Bianca suspects. The phrase *take out* echoes III.iv.171.

157 **some Minx's Token** Bianca's phrasing indicates that she does not regard herself as a minx (hussy or prostitute). She may be more 'bold' (I.iii.93) than Desdemona or Aemilia (though how much more so is left unclear), but she seems to have genuine affection for Cassio, and she also has a sense of personal pride that belies the derogatory remarks that he and Iago make about her. *Token* echoes III.iv.172.

158– **Hobby-horse** easy mount.
59

162 **should be** looks like.

164 **prepar'd for** invited.

166 **rail** upbraid me.

167 **else** otherwise.

171 **fain** eagerly.

173 **Go to** Think no more about it; be on your way. Compare line 116.

175 **laugh'd ... Vice** both (a) showed no shame over his licentious behaviour, (b) heaped scorn on his 'Vice' (here identified with his whore). See the notes to II.iii.329 and III.iii.385.

180 **prizes** values. Two secondary meanings of *prizes* are pertinent: (a) seizes, captures, and (b) forces open with a bar or lever. Compare I.ii.51 and II.iii.136–38.
foolish both (a) wanton (as in II.i.137–44), and (b) silly (foolishly trusting in a gallant's fidelity). Othello responds to the second sense and extends it to a third, (c) abused.

182 **I ... killing** I would subject to an execution that took nine agonizing years to complete.

Piece of Work, that you should find it in   155
your Chamber, and know not who left it there.
This is some Minx's Token, and I must take
out the work? There, give it your Hobby-
horse, wheresoever you had it, I'll take out
no work on't.   160

CASSIO   How now, my sweet Bianca? How now?
    How now?

OTHELLO   – By Heaven, that should be my
    Handkerchief.

BIANCA   If you'll come to Supper to night, you
    may;
    If you will not, come when you are next
    prepar'd for.   *Exit.*

IAGO   After her: after her.   165

CASSIO   Faith I must, she'll rail in the Streets
    else.

IAGO   Will you sup there?

CASSIO   Yes, I intend so.

IAGO   Well, I may chance to see you: for I would   170
    very fain speak with you.

CASSIO   Prythee come: will you?

IAGO   Go to: say no more.   *Exit Cassio.*

      [*Othello comes forward.*]

OTHELLO   How shall I murther him, Iago.

IAGO   Did you perceive how he laugh'd at his
    Vice?   175

OTHELLO   Oh, Iago.

IAGO   And did you see the Handkerchief?

OTHELLO   Was that mine?

IAGO   Yours, by this Hand; and to see how he
    prizes the foolish Woman your Wife; she gave   180
    it him, and he hath giv'n it his Whore.

OTHELLO   I would have him nine Years a killing:
    A fine Woman, a fair Woman, a sweet Woman?

IAGO   Nay, you must forget that.

OTHELLO   Ay, let her rot and perish, and be   185

186 **damn'd to night** both (a) condemned tonight, and (b) cast to the 'outer darkness' (Matthew 25:30).

187 **I strike it** Othello is trying to persuade himself that his heart is as hard as flint. But it keeps rebelling against what Iago insists is a wronged husband's 'way' and reminds the Moor of 'the Pity of it' (lines 191, 201–2). *Stone* echoes III.iii.449.

190 **command him Tasks** order him around as if he were her slave.

194– **sing . . . Bear** For an Iago, Othello's image might refer to the
95 kind of 'song' associated with wantons; for the Moor, however, it is a means of comparing Desdemona to Orpheus and the power his music had to pacify even the fiercest of beasts. For a tragically brief moment, the true Desdemona emerges in all her loveliness, and we are permitted to hope that she may be able to 'sing the Savageness' out of the wounded and frenzied 'Bear' to whom she is married; but it will not be long before Iago disturbs Othello's 'clear Spirit' again (III.iv.136). *Hang* (line 192) echoes lines 38–40; *delicate* (line 193) recalls III.iii.262–64. *Needle* can refer to more than one kind of sewing/sowing instrument (see the note to III.iv.72); compare *Henry V*, II.i.34–38, where the Hostess says 'we cannot lodge and board a dozen or fourteen Gentlewomen that live honestly by the prick of their Needles but it will be thought we keep a Bawdy-house straight', and *Toilus and Cressida*, II.i.87, where Thersites alludes to 'the Eye of Helen's Needle'. See the note to III.iv.66.

195– **high . . . Invention** Elsewhere this phrasing might suggest erotic
96 'Invention' or wit (see the note to II.i.130). Here, though, for Othello it summons up the charisma of a lady who 'paragons Description' (II.i.62). *Wit* recalls III.iii.455.

199 **Condition** (a) breeding, nature, (b) disposition, character, and (c) social standing. Compare I.ii.24–28, II.i.258–59, II.iii.306–10.

203–4 **If . . . offend** If you are so infatuated with what she is doing to you, give her an unlimited charter to dishonour you further.

206 **Messes** bits; mincemeat (compare II.iii.250).

211 **expostulate** reason, argue. *Least* (lest) recalls II.iii.234; *foul* and *fouler* (lines 207–9) recall III.iii.134, 228.

212 **unprovide my Mind** undo the preparations my mind has made for this deed. Compare II.iii.401. *Mind* recalls III.iv.153–55 and anticipates IV.iii.21, 29–30.
   again returning it (a) to the naïvety of its initial affection, and (b) to the compassion to which it kept yielding a moment ago.

damn'd to night, for she shall not live. No,
my Heart is turn'd to Stone: I strike it,
and it hurts my Hand. Oh, the World hath not
a sweeter Creature: she might lie by an
Emperor's side, and command him Tasks.   190
IAGO   Nay, that's not your way.
OTHELLO   Hang her, I do but say what she is:
so delicate with her Needle; an admirable
Musician. Oh she will sing the Savageness out
of a Bear: of so high and plenteous Wit and   195
Invention.
IAGO   She's the worse for all this.
OTHELLO   Oh, a thousand, a thousand times: and
then of so gentle a Condition?
IAGO   Ay, too gentle.   200
OTHELLO   Nay that's certain. But yet the Pity
of it, Iago: oh Iago, the Pity of it, Iago.
IAGO   If you are so fond over her Iniquity,
give her Patent to offend, for if it touch
not you, it comes near no body.   205
OTHELLO   I will chop her into Messes: cuckold me?
IAGO   Oh, 'tis foul in her.
OTHELLO   With mine Officer?
IAGO   That's fouler.
OTHELLO   Get me some Poison, Iago, this Night.   210
I'll not expostulate with her: least her Body
and Beauty unprovide my Mind again. This
Night, Iago.
IAGO   Do it not with Poison, strangle her in
her Bed, even the Bed she hath contaminated.   215
OTHELLO   Good, good; the Justice of it pleases;
very good.

218 **Undertaker** murderer (here, one who will see that he is buried soon). Iago volunteers to undertake a task that will (a) complete the job of taking Cassio out from under Othello (see I.iii.399–401), and (b) repay Cassio for his supposed role as the 'undertaker' of both Aemilia (II.i.322) and Desdemona. See II.iii.344.

221 **warrant** wager; dare say.

223 **'Save you** God save you. At this moment what would ordinarily be a perfunctory greeting becomes charged with significance: this 'worthy General' is much in need of rescue if he is to retain the title with which he has just been addressed. See II.iii.102–13, III.iv.160.

225 **I . . . Pleasures** Othello may be referring to the letter Lodovico has just handed him to convey the greetings of 'The Duke and the Senators of Venice' (line 224); if so, he may kiss its seal as he breaks it to open the document. But he may also be referring to Lodovico (perhaps embracing him), or even – or in addition – to Desdemona (with the implication that she has provided 'Pleasures' not only to Cassio but to 'The Duke and the Senators' as well). In any event, he probably speaks with a tone of Iago-like innuendo that comes across as out of 'Tune' (III.iv.116); compare II.i.200–4. *Pleasures* recalls I.i.119–25, I.iii.374–76, II.ii.1, 8–9; III.iv.121; *Instrument* echoes III.i.3–11.

229 **Lives, Sir** Iago's laconic reply conveys the iciness of official disapproval for a man who has fallen out of grace. In light of line 218, moreover, it has an even more sinister undertone.

231 **unkind Breach** unnatural and unkindly division (with both senses of *kind* pertinent). Little does Desdemona realize that a 'Breach' (fault) of her own is presumed to be the cause of the problem. *Breach* is often a term for the female genitalia (see 2 *Henry IV*, II.iv.53), and Desdemona's phrasing is a reminder that Othello considers her to be guilty of 'an unkind Breach'. Her words call to mind the secondary implications in Iago's song about how King Stephen's 'Breeches cost him but a Crown' (II.iii.90). See the note to III.iii.145.

234 **He . . . Paper** He was not speaking to you: he's busy reading the letter from Venice. *Devision* (line 235) recalls I.i.21.

237 **atone** at-one, reconcile.

238 **Are you wise?** Can you be aware of what you are saying and what it reveals? *Wise* echoes I.i.121, II.i.130–31, 143–44, III.iii.371, IV.i.76.

IAGO   And for Cassio, let me be his Undertaker:
you shall hear more by Midnight.   *A Trumpet.*
OTHELLO   Excellent good. What Trumpet is that
same?   220
IAGO   I warrant something from Venice.

Enter Lodovico, Desdemona, and Attendants.

                                            'Tis Lodovico,
This, comes from the Duke. See, your Wife's
with him.
LODOVICO   'Save you, worthy General.
OTHELLO   With all my Heart, Sir.
LODOVICO   The Duke and the Senators of Venice
greet you.
OTHELLO   I kiss the Instrument of their Pleasures.   225
DESDEMONA   And what's the News, good Cousin
Lodovico?
IAGO   I am very glad to see you, Signior:
Welcome to Cyprus.
LODOVICO   I thank you: how does Lieutenant
Cassio?
IAGO   Lives, Sir.
DESDEMONA   Cousin, there's fall'n between him
and my Lord   230
An unkind Breach: but you shall make all well.
OTHELLO   Are you sure of that?
DESDEMONA   My Lord?
OTHELLO   This fail you not to do, as you will —
LODOVICO   He did not call: he's busy in the
Paper.
Is there Devision 'twixt my Lord and Cassio?   235
DESDEMONA   A most unhappy one: I would do
much
T' atone them, for the Love I bear to Cassio.
OTHELLO   Fire and Brimstone.
DESDEMONA   My Lord?
OTHELLO   Are you wise?
DESDEMONA   — What, is he angry?

241   **Deputing . . . Government** leaving Cassio in charge. Lodovico
      probably believes that the Venetian Senators are trying to
      show favour to Othello, now that the emergency that caused
      them to dispatch him to Cyprus has dissipated; but he also
      seems to be expecting that Othello won't receive the
      command in that spirit. *Government* recalls III.iii.251; *mov'd*
      (line 239) echoes III.iv.158–59.

243   **I . . . mad** Othello appears to interpret Desdemona's 'glad on't'
      (happy about it) as a public announcement that she is pleased
      to see her 'Roman' lover supplant her scorned Moor (see lines
      120, 265). If so, he implies, she deserves all the abuse her
      conqueror is now heaping on her. But *mad* can also mean
      'infatuated with affection or desire' (as in *A Midsummer
      Night's Dream*, III.ii.440–41, and in *Troilus and Cressida*,
      I.i.53–54), and that is probably Othello's primary
      implication. He evidently strikes her as he says 'Divel' in line
      244.

249   **teem with** become impregnated by.

250   **falls** lets fall.
      Crocodile The crocodile was proverbial for its false tears;
      according to fable, it would lure 'relenting Passengers'
      (gullible travellers) to take pity on its plight and then snare
      them (see 2 *Henry VI*, III.i.224–26). *Prove* recalls III.iii.430.

251   **I . . . you** Desdemona's words recall I.iii.240–42. *Offend*
      echoes lines 203–4.

254   **Mistress** Othello's term for Desdemona is coloured by the
      implications this word has acquired in III.iv.176–77, IV.i.26.

256   **turn** turn back, return. Othello goes on to give this word
      several other meanings: (a) alter in her affections, (b) turn
      away from her vows ('Revolt', III.iii.183), and (c) do a
      whore's 'Turns', turn 'tricks'. Compare *Antony and
      Cleopatra*, II.v.56–58.

259   **obedient** Othello twists this word to mean 'compliant', 'easy to
      manage'. Compare II.iii.351–53, III.iv.141–43, IV.i.158–59.

261   **Oh . . . Passion** Othello is probably addressing Desdemona,
      though it is equally possible that he is telling Lodovico what
      kind of thing 'this' is. What he means is that Desdemona is
      counterfeiting true 'Passion' (sincere tears) with all the
      expertise of an artist. No doubt 'well-painted' is also a
      reference to the cosmetics a tainted woman uses to hide her
      blemishes. Compare II.i.110–16. *Passion* recalls line 80.

LODOVICO May be the Letter mov'd him.
  For as I think, they do command him home, 240
  Deputing Cassio in his Government.
DESDEMONA Trust me, I am glad on't.
OTHELLO Indeed?
DESDEMONA My Lord?
OTHELLO I am glad to see you mad.
DESDEMONA Why, sweet Othello?
OTHELLO Divel. — *Othello hits Desdemona*
DESDEMONA I have not deserv'd this. 245
LODOVICO My Lord, this would not be believ'd
  in Venice,
  Though I should swear I saw't. 'Tis very much,
  Make her Amends: she weeps.
OTHELLO — Oh Divel, Divel.
  — If that the Earth could teem with Woman's
  Tears,
  Each Drop she falls would prove a Crocodile. 250
  — Out of my Sight.
DESDEMONA I will not stay to offend you.
LODOVICO Truly an obedient Lady:
  I do beseech your Lordship call her back.
OTHELLO Mistress.
DESDEMONA My Lord?
OTHELLO — What would you with her, Sir?
LODOVICO Who I, my Lord? 255
OTHELLO Ay, you did wish that I would make her
  turn:
  Sir, she can turn, and turn, and yet go on
  And turn again. And she can weep, Sir, weep.
  And she's obedient: as you say, obedient,
  Very obedient. — Proceed you in your Tears. 260
  — Concerning this, Sir — oh well-painted
  Passion —
  I am commanded home. — Get you away:

263   **I'll . . . anon** I'll send for you to follow me shortly. This line is a poignant reminder of how much things have changed since Othello first arranged 'Conveyance' for his wife (I.iii.281–85).

264   **avaunt** begone. Othello is speaking to Desdemona.

265   **Place** post, command. But of course Othello is also thinking about both (a) the 'Place' (role and position) he has had as his wife's bed partner, and (b) the 'Place' (Desdemona's genitalia) he believes that she has now surrendered to a cuckolder. *Place* echoes lines 134–35.

267   **Goats and Monkeys** Othello is referring to Cassio and Desdemona. Compare III.iii.392–95, IV.i.129–31.

269   **all . . . sufficient** capable in every way. Compare I.iii.221–25, III.iii.241–44, and III.iv.88. *Nature* recalls lines 41–43; *Passion* (line 270) echoes line 261.

271   **The . . . Chance** neither the shot fired by Accident nor the arrow aimed by Chance. *Virtue* (line 270) echoes lines 7–8.

272   **chang'd** transformed; converted from what he was. *Change* is a potent word in this play, and Iago's use of it here recalls such earlier passages as I.iii.313–15, 350–51, 354, 386, and III.iii.315, 441.

273   **safe** in a healthy condition. Compare I.iii.223–25, II.i.32–33, II.iii.208, and III.iii.368. *Wits* echoes lines 195–96.

274   **He's . . . is** Iago's phrasing echoes 'I am not what I am' (I.i.64). It also recalls Desdemona's remarks in II.i.123–24; compare III.iii.123–26.
        breath give breath to; breathe.
        Censure judgement, opinion.

275   **What . . . be** What Iago conveys to his listeners is 'the kind of man he should be'; but what he means privately is 'the kind of man he will be after I have finished my work on him'. Compare Iago's phrasing in III.iii.123–24, and his insinuations in II.iii.124–47.

278   **Use** custom, habitual practice. *Prove* echoes lines 249–50.

279   **Blood** emotions, passion. Compare I.iii.122, 328–33, and II.iii.207–10, III.iii.316–19, 442–49, 456–58.

280   **Fault** breach (crack) in his normal demeanour. Compare lines 230–31, and see the note to III.iii.145.

I'll send for you anon. – Sir, I obey the
   Mandate,
And will return to Venice. – Hence, avaunt:
Cassio shall have my Place.   [*Exit Desdemona.*]
                         – And Sir, to night   265
I do entreat that we may sup together.
You are welcome, Sir, to Cyprus. – Goats and
   Monkeys.   *Exit.*
LODOVICO   Is this the Noble Moor, whom our
   full Senate
Call all in all sufficient? Is this the Nature
Whom Passion could not shake? Whose solid
   Virtue   270
The shot of Accident nor dart of Chance
Could neither graze nor pierce?
IAGO   He is much chang'd.
LODOVICO   Are his Wits safe? Is he not light
   of Brain?
IAGO   He's that he is; I may not breath my
   Censure.
What he might be; if what he might he is not,   275
I would to Heaven he were.
LODOVICO   What? Strike his Wife?
IAGO   'Faith that was not so well: yet would I
   knew
That Stroke would prove the worst.
LODOVICO   Is it his Use?
Or did the Letters work upon his Blood,
And new create his Fault?
IAGO   Alas, alas: 280
It is not Honesty in me to speak
What I have seen, and known. You shall observe
   him,
And his own Courses will denote him so
That I may save my Speech: do but go after
And mark how he continues.   285
LODOVICO   I am sorry that I am deceiv'd in him.
                                   Exeunt.

IV.ii This scene occurs inside the Citadel.

1 **You . . . then?** Here as so often happens, Shakespeare begins the scene not only in mid-conversation but in mid-line.

4 **no Harm** nothing illicit or suspicious in their behaviour. Compare IV.i.3–6.

5 **Breath** This word echoes IV.i.274; it also recalls Iago's phrasing in II.i.269–70, when he tells Roderigo that Cassio and Desdemona 'met so near with their Lips that their Breaths embrac'd together'.

7 **out . . . way** away (to leave them alone). Compare III.i.39–40 and III.iv.79.

11 **at Stake** as the stakes to be surrendered if I lose (am proven wrong). The phrase 'Lay down my Soul at Stake' is a reminder of what Othello believes Desdemona to have done with Cassio. And Aemilia's pledge recalls what Desdemona has said to Cassio in III.iii.19–28. Compare I.iii.292, where Othello says, 'My Life upon her Faith', and III.iii.272–73.

12 **abuse your Bosom** deceive and misuse your heat. *Bosom* echoes I.ii.70–71, III.i.57–58, III.iii.438.

14 **Let . . . Curse** let God punish it with the same curse he laid on the serpent that tempted Eve in the Garden of Eden: 'Because thou hast done this, thou art cursed above all cattle, and above every beast of the field; upon thy belly shalt thou go, and dust shalt thou eat all the days of thy life; and I will put enmity between thee and the woman, and between thy seed and her seed; it shall bruise thy head, and thou shalt bruise his heel' (Genesis 3:14–15).
requit requite; recompense, repay.

16–17 **The . . . Slander** Aemilia doesn't realize that she is here describing the 'foul' Desdemona that Iago's 'Slander' (false witness) has planted in Othello's mind. *Foul* echoes IV.i.207–9. Here *happy* (line 16) means both (a) contented and (b) fortunate (compare line 42).

18–19 **She . . . much** Othello means that Aemilia says enough to make it appear that Desdemona is chaste, but even the most simple-minded go-between would be able to cover for her mistress just as capably.

19 **This . . . Whore** Othello is probably referring to Aemilia; but his words recall Iago's description of Desdemona in I.iii.361. Here *subtile* means 'deceitful', and it recalls the description of the Serpent in Genesis 3:1; see the note to line 14.

Scene 2

Enter Othello, and Aemilia.

OTHELLO   You have seen nothing then?

AEMILIA   Nor ever heard: nor ever did suspect.

OTHELLO   Yes, you have seen Cassio and she
together.

AEMILIA   But then I saw no Harm: and then I
heard
Each Syllable that Breath made up between them.   5

OTHELLO   What? Did they never whisper?

AEMILIA   Never, my Lord.

OTHELLO   Nor send you out o'th' way?

AEMILIA   Never.

OTHELLO   To fetch
Her Fan, her Gloves, her Mask, nor nothing?

AEMILIA   Never,
My Lord.

OTHELLO   That's strange.

AEMILIA   I durst, my Lord, to wager she is Honest: 10
Lay down my Soul at Stake. If you think other,
Remove your Thought: it doth abuse your Bosom.
If any Wretch have put this in your Head,
Let Heaven requit it with the Serpent's Curse,
For if she be not honest, chaste, and true,   15
There's no Man happy. The purest of their
Wives
Is foul as Slander.

OTHELLO   Bid her come hither: go.   *Exit Aemilia.*
— She says enough: yet she's a simple Bawd
That cannot say as much. This is a subtile
Whore,
A Closet Lock and Key of villainous Secrets,   20

---

20   **Closet**   private chamber, here one that can be closed to conceal
       evil secrets but at the same time one whose 'Lock' can be
       opened by anyone with the right 'Key'. The phrase 'Lock and
       Key' has obvious genital implications, but it could also apply
       to a bawd; see *Troilus and Cressida*, V.x.52.

25 **Some . . . Mistress** Busy yourself with some of your
accustomed work, madam. In line 28 Othello derisively refers
to Aemilia's 'Function' as a 'Mystery' (a skilled trade).
Compare *Measure for Measure*, IV.ii.33–56. *Function* recalls
II.iii.358–60.

26 **Procreants** those who are about to engage in procreational
activity. Othello's phrasing is a reminder that under normal
circumstances a husband would legitimately desire privacy
with his 'true and loyal Wife' (line 32) for the kind of
lovemaking that conceives a child.

29 **import** signify (literally, 'bring in' or introduce). See the second
note to II.iii.329, and compare I.iii.280–81, II.ii.3–4,
III.iii.307, IV.i.140, V.ii.304–5.

33–34 **like . . . Heaven** like one of Heaven's own. Othello is probably
thinking of 2 Corinthians 11:14, where Christians are warned
that 'Satan himself is transformed into an angel of light.'
Compare II.iii.362–65. Othello's implication is that
Desdemona is so cunning that even the devils might not
recognize her for one of their own. *Least* means 'lest'
(compare IV.i.211), but here it plays ironically on the usual
modern sense of 'least'.

38 **Desdemon** This metrically abbreviated form of Desdemona's
name plays poignantly on *moan*; compare III.i.56, III.iii.53,
V.ii.26, 197, 275.

41 **Motive** mover, cause.

And yet she'll kneel and pray: I have seen her
  do't.

        Enter Desdemona, and Aemilia.

DESDEMONA   My Lord, what is your Will?
OTHELLO   Pray you, Chuck, come hither.
DESDEMONA   What is your Pleasure?
OTHELLO   Let me see your Eyes:
  Look in my Face.
DESDEMONA   What horrible Fancy's this?
OTHELLO – Some of your Function, Mistress;   25
  Leave Procreants alone, and shut the Door;
  Cough, or cry Hem, if any body come.
  Your Mystery, your Mystery: nay dispatch.
                  Exit Aemilia.
DESDEMONA   Upon my Knee, what doth your
  Speech import?
  I understand a Fury in your Words,   30
  But not the Words.
OTHELLO   Why? What art thou?
DESDEMONA   Your Wife, my Lord: your true and
  loyal Wife.
OTHELLO   Come swear it: damn thy self, least
  being like one
  Of Heaven, the Divels themselves should fear
  to seize thee.
  Therefore be double damn'd: swear thou art
  honest.   35
DESDEMONA   Heaven doth truly know it.
OTHELLO   Heaven truly knows
  That thou art false as Hell.
DESDEMONA   To whom, my Lord?
  With whom? How am I false?
OTHELLO   Ah Desdemon,
  Away, away, away.
DESDEMONA   Alas the heavy Day: why do you
  weep?
  Am I the Motive of these Tears, my Lord?   40

42   **happely** by chance.

45   **Why . . . too** This line is a reminder that Desdemona has sacrificed everything (her father's love and blessing, as well as a substantial inheritance) by casting her lot with the Moor. She has made her husband her 'all in all' (IV.i.269). Compare I.iii.242–45, IV.ii.122–24.

46   **try . . . Affliction** test my faith and 'Patience' (uncomplaining endurance) by subjecting me to unmerited suffering. Othello is alluding to Job, who was plagued with 'Sores and Shames' and 'Poverty' (lines 47, 48) so that God could prove to Satan that there was at least one man on earth who loved his Lord for himself rather than for the good fortune that God bestowed on his servants.
    they Heaven (here treated as 'the Heavens').

52–53 **The . . . at** Othello seems to be thinking of himself as a figure (either a number or a human image) on a clock face. What points to him with 'Scorn' is probably one of the clock hands, which is both 'fixed' and 'moving', like a finger wagging mockingly. Compare Othello's remarks about the 'Roman' Cassio in IV.i.120, 124. *Time* echoes IV.i.95. *Scorn* recalls IV.i.84–86; *moving* echoes line 41.

57   **Fountain** fountainhead, spring. Othello implies that he fetches his 'Life and Being' (I.ii.21) from Desdemona; see his remarks in I.iii.292 and in III.iii.89–90, and compare III.iv.103–7.

59   **Cestern** cistern. Whereas a 'Fountain' is overflowing with life-giving 'Current', a cistern merely catches everything that comes into it; it is thus an apt analogy for a foul 'public Commoner' (line 71), a pasture open to anyone.

60   **knot and gender** copulate and procreate. See the notes to III.iii.264, 271, and compare I.iii.410–11.

60–61 **Turn . . . Cherubin** Take your sweet 'Rose-lipp'd' face ('Complexion') and turn it there, Patience. Othello addresses his Good Angel, his cherubin, and implies that if she simply peers into this 'Cestern' with her own eyes, she too will 'look grim as Hell' (line 62) and counsel vengeance rather than forbearance or pity. *Patience* echoes line 51; *Complexion* harks back to III.iii.224–25.

62   **I** both 'I' and 'ay'. This line can be read at least two ways: either (a) 'I [Othello] here look grim as Hell', or (b) 'Ay, here look grim as Hell'.

64   **Shambles** slaughterhouse.

If happely you my Father do suspect,
An Instrument of this your calling back,
Lay not your Blame on me: if you have lost him,
Why I have lost him too.
OTHELLO   Had it pleas'd Heaven   45
To try me with Affliction, had they rain'd
All kind of Sores and Shames on my bare Head,
Steep'd me in Poverty to the very Lips,
Given to Captivity me and my utmost Hopes,
I should have found in some place of my Soul   50
A drop of Patience. But alas, to make me
The fixed Figure for the Time of Scorn
To point his slow and moving Finger at.
Yet could I bear that too, well, very well;
But there where I have garner'd up my Heart,   55
Where either I must live, or bear no Life,
The Fountain from the which my Current runs,
Or else dries up: to be discarded thence,
Or keep it as a Cestern, for foul Toads
To knot and gender in. – Turn thy Complexion
    there,   60
Patience, thou young and Rose-lipp'd Cherubin,
I here look grim as Hell.
DESDEMONA   I hope my noble Lord esteems me
    honest.
OTHELLO   Oh I, as summer Flies are in the
    Shambles,
That quicken even with Blowing. Oh thou Weed,   65
Who art so lovely fair, and smell'st so sweet,
That the Sense aches at thee, would thou hadst
    never been borne.

---

65   **quicken ... Blowing**   hatch and start reproducing as soon as
        their eggs are deposited on the raw meat. *Blowing* recalls
        III.iii.435, III.iv.127–30.

67   **borne**   both (a) carried, and (b) born.

68   **ignorant**   Desdemona means 'unknowing' or 'unintended'; but ignorance has earlier been associated with a wilful surrender to lust or mindless passion (compare II.i.145 and III.iii.46–48, 392–95).

69   **fair Paper**   a metaphor for Desdemona's light-skinned countenance.

72   **make . . . Cheeks**   turn my wrathful cheeks fire-red (like a blacksmith's forge).

75   **the Moon winks**   The Goddess of Chastity shuts (hides) her eyes. See III.iii.376–78. *Stops* recalls III.iii.117, and *Nose* echoes IV.i.144–45. *Modesty* (line 73) harks back to II.iii.22–23.

76   **bawdy**   wanton, promiscuous.

77   **hush'd**   hiding away in a cave (rather than blowing lustily outside). *Mine* recalls III.iii.319; *hollow* echoes III.iii.436.

81   **Vessel**   body. Desdemona's image recalls such biblical phrases as 'chosen vessel' (Acts 9:15), 'earthen vessels' (2 Corinthians 4:7), and 'weaker vessel' (1 Peter 3:7). Compare 1 Corinthians 3:16–17.

84   **sav'd**   redeemed. See the note to IV.i.223. *Touch* recalls IV.i.203–5; *foul* echoes lines 16–17.

87   **cunning**   deceitful, crafty; but with wordplay on *cunnus* (see the third note to I.i.120). To Othello, this 'Commoner' has now become so thoroughly identified with the 'Cestern' (line 59) that defines her that she is little more than 'a Corner in the thing' Othello once loved (III.iii.266). Compare IV.i.93, V.ii.11, 327.

89   **Office . . . Peter**   position that serves as the counterpart to Saint Peter's as keeper of 'the keys to the kingdom of Heaven' (Matthew 16:19). Othello is varying the 'Lock and Key' image of line 20. *Office* recalls II.iv.106–7; *Mistress* echoes IV.i.254.

91   **done our Course**   both (a) concluded our meal (speaking figuratively), and (b) run our course (with an implicit comparison between Desdemona and the kind of 'Hobby-horse' Bianca refers to in IV.i.158–59). Othello also plays on the copulative sense of *done* (compare *Titus Andronicus*, IV.ii.76). *Course* echoes IV.i.55; *Pains* (efforts) recalls III.i.1.

DESDEMONA   Alas, what ignorant Sin have I
    committed?
OTHELLO   Was this fair Paper, this most goodly
    Book,
    Made to write 'Whore' upon? What committed,   70
    Committed? Oh thou public Commoner,
    I should make very Forges of my Cheeks,
    That would to Cinders burn up Modesty,
    Did I but speak thy Deeds. What committed?
    Heaven stops the Nose at it, and the Moon
      winks: 75
    The bawdy Wind, that kisses all it meets,
    Is hush'd within the hollow Mine of Earth
    And will not hear't. What committed?
    Impudent Strumpet.
DESDEMONA   By Heaven you do me wrong.
OTHELLO   Are you not a Strumpet?
DESDEMONA   No, as I am a Christian.   80
    If to preserve this Vessel for my Lord
    From any other foul unlawful Touch
    Be not to be a Strumpet, I am none.
OTHELLO   What, not a Whore?
DESDEMONA   No, as I shall be sav'd.
OTHELLO   Is't possible?   85
DESDEMONA   Oh Heaven forgive us.
OTHELLO   I cry you Mercy then.
    I took you for that cunning Whore of Venice,
    That married with Othello. — You, Mistress,

Enter Aemilia.

    That have the Office opposite to Saint Peter,
    And keeps the Gate of Hell. You, you: ay you.   90
    We have done our Course; there's Money for your
      Pains;

92　**turn ... Counsaile** both (a) open the door and keep quiet
about what you've witnessed, and (b) lock your lips to keep
our secret safe. Like *conceive* (line 93), *Counsaile* (counsel)
echoes *cunnus*, and Othello's innuendo probably includes the
idea that Aemilia is a 'profane and liberal Counsailor'
(II.i.166) whose job is to 'keep' (watch over) her merchandise
in the way that will allow her to turn the most profit as a
'coun-seller'. *Turn* echoes IV.i.256–58.

93　**conceive** imagine, conjure up in his distraught mind. Compare
III.iv.147–49, V.ii.56–57.

95　**half asleep** stunned almost into a daze; groggy.

101　**go by Water** (a) be transported on a sea of tears, (b) be washed
away by the sea rather than put on record. See the note to
V.ii.129–30. *Answers* (line 100) recalls III.iv.151.

103　**Change** Once again this word registers a world of difference;
see the note to IV.i.272.

104　**'Tis ... so** It's appropriate that I should be treated this way.
This is one of the few moments in the play in which we see
Desdemona surrender to an outburst of anger. But she speaks
only to herself.

105–6 **How ... Misuse?** What have I ever done that would justify his
attaching the smallest negative judgement to my tiniest
misconduct? Desdemona alludes to the practice of punishing
offenders by sticking signs on their backs and forcing them to
walk barefoot through the streets in public disgrace; this
happens to Elianor, the Duchess of Gloucester, in *2 Henry VI*,
II.iv. But *stick* also provides an inadvertent but piercing
reminder of the kind of 'Misuse' that Othello believes
Desdemona to have undertaken. *Opinion* recalls I.iii.223–25,
II.iii.196–99.

109　**easy Tasks** both (a) light reproofs (taking them to task in a
gentle way), and (b) forms of penance that children are able to
bear (such as being given a repetitive task to perform as a
reminder to avoid some type of naughty behaviour).

111　**a ... Chiding** like a child being scolded for the first time.

112　**bewhor'd her** both (a) called her, and (b) treated her like, a
whore.

113　**Dispight** abuse. The Shakespearean spelling, here retained,
combines *dis-* (negation or separation) and *spight* (spite,
malice).
　　heavy Terms strong language, foul names.

I pray you turn the Key, and keep our Counsaile. *Exit.*
AEMILIA   Alas, what does this Gentleman conceive?
   How do you, Madam? How do you, my good
      Lady?
DESDEMONA   Faith, half asleep.   95
AEMILIA   Good Madam, what's the matter with my Lord?
DESDEMONA   With who?
AEMILIA   Why, with my Lord, Madam?
DESDEMONA   Who is thy Lord?
AEMILIA   He that is yours, sweet Lady.
DESDEMONA   I have none; do not talk to me, Aemilia,
   I cannot weep; nor Answers have I none,   100
   But what should go by Water Prythee to night
   Lay on my Bed my Wedding Sheets, remember,
   And call thy Husband hither.
AEMILIA   Here's a Change indeed.   *Exit.*
DESDEMONA   'Tis meet I should be us'd so:
      very meet.
   How have I been behav'd that he might stick   105
   The small'st Opinion on my least Misuse?

           Enter Iago, and Aemilia.

IAGO   What is your Pleasure, Madam? How is't
   with you?
DESDEMONA   I cannot tell: those that do teach
      young Babes
   Do it with gentle Means, and easy Tasks.
   He might have chid me so: for in good faith   110
   I am a Child to Chiding.
IAGO   What is the matter, Lady?
AEMILIA   Alas, Iago, my Lord hath so bewhor'd
      her,
   Thrown such Dispight and heavy Terms upon her

118 **Callet** slut.

122 **Hath . . . Matches?** Has she turned down so many proposed matches with noble Venetians? Aemilia echoes III.iii.223–33. Compare III.iii.175–78, III.iv.67–68, V.ii.198.

123 **Her . . . Friends?** Compare Desdemona's remarks in lines 42–45.

125 **Beshrew** curse. Iago both means and doesn't mean what he says here. His words imply that he is at a loss to understand how a man could mistreat a lovely wife the way Othello is doing; what he knows privately is that Othello will be beshrewed for his actions. Compare III.iv.143, IV.iii.77–78.

126 **Trick** compulsion; fit of irrational behaviour. This word echoes III.iv.84.

128 **busy** meddling (like a busybody). Compare III.iii.248.

129 **cogging, cozening** cheating and deceiving.
Slave . . . Office boot-licking sycophant, trying to win his way into Othello's favour as a way of obtaining a promotion. *Office* (position) echoes line 89; *hang'd* (lines 127, 130) recalls IV.i.38–40.

131 **impossible** inconceivable.

133 **A . . . him** May the only 'pardon' he hears be that of the hangman who asks his forgiveness before he places the fatal halter (noose) around his neck. Unlike the forgiving Desdemona, Aemilia has an ordinary mortal's lust for vengeance.

134 **keeps her company** spends time with her.

135 **What Form?** Under the cover of what pretext ('Likelihood')?

138 **unfold** disclose; reveal [for the slanderous hypocrites they are]. *Scurvy* (line 137), vile, recalls I.ii.7.

That True Hearts cannot bear it.
DESDEMONA   Am I that Name, Iago?
IAGO   What Name, fair Lady?   115
DESDEMONA   Such as she said my Lord did say I was.
AEMILIA   He call'd her Whore: a Beggar in his
   Drink
Could not have laid such Terms upon his Callet.
IAGO   Why did he so?
DESDEMONA   I do not know: I am sure I am none
   such.   120
IAGO   Do not weep, do not weep: alas the Day.
AEMILIA   Hath she forsook so many Noble Matches?
Her Father? And her Country? And her Friends?
To be call'd Whore? Would it not make one weep?
DESDEMONA   It is my wretched Fortune.
IAGO   Beshrew him for't: 125
How comes this Trick upon him?
DESDEMONA   Nay, Heaven doth know.
AEMILIA   I will be hang'd if some eternal Villain,
Some busy and insinuating Rogue,
Some cogging, cozening Slave, to get some
   Office,
Have not devis'd this Slander: I will be hang'd
   else.   130
IAGO   Fie, there is no such Man: it is impossible.
DESDEMONA   If any such there be, Heaven pardon
   him.
AEMILIA   A Halter pardon him: and Hell gnaw his
   Bones.
Why should he call her Whore? Who keeps her
   company?
What Place? What Time? What Form? What
   Likelihood?   135
The Moor's abus'd by some most villainous Knave,
Some base notorious Knave, some scurvy Fellow.
− Oh heavens, that such Companions thou'dst
   unfold,
And put in every honest Hand a Whip

141 **Speak within Door** Restrain yourself, and speak in an 'inside' voice, or be silent until we can speak privately. Compare II.i.101–13.

142 **Squire** villainous valet; companion in quest of special favour.

143 **the Seamy-side without** Aemilia puns on the tailor's sense of 'Seamy-side' (the inside lining of a garment) to describe another kind of seaminess (foulness, filth). Compare II.iii.50–51. *Wit* echoes IV.i.195–96, 273.

145 **go to** no more of this nonsense. Compare IV.i.173.

148 **how . . . him** what I did to lose his love. Desdemona's words recall what she has said in lines 42–45.

149 **ere** both (a) before, and (b) e'er (ever).
my Will even so much as my will. Desdemona refers to a wayward intent, such as the lust in the heart referred to by Jesus in Matthew 5:28. It would never occur to her to commit her genital 'Will' to a 'trespass' in 'actual Deed' (line 150). Desdemona's kneeling posture is a poignant reminder of the swearing ceremony in III.iii.449–68.

150 **actual Deed** Desdemona alludes to the sense of *deed* that relates to the 'Act of Sport' (II.i.231–32); see the note to III.iii.99 (on *deed*), and compare the references to action in III.iii.318, IV.ii.159–61.

152 **or . . . Form** or looked illicitly on any male form.

154– **though . . . Divorcement** even if he should discard me and
55 leave me a disgraced beggar. Compare I.ii.14 and III.iii.254–57. *Shake* recalls II.iii.129–31, III.iii.202–3, IV.i.43–44, 269–70.

156 **Comfort forswear me** either (a) may comfort forsake me, or (b) may I repudiate and deny myself any further comfort.
Unkindness mistreatment (resulting from the actions of one who is acting unlike the kind of man Desdemona married).

157 **defeat** undo, destroy. Compare I.iii.344–45.

160 **Addition** title, designation ('Whore', with wordplay on *abhor*, lines 158–59). Compare III.iv.184–86 and IV.i.107–8.

161 **mass of Vanity** store of vainglorious riches and honours.

162 **content** patient, resolved. See the note to III.iv.113–15. *Humour* recalls III.iv.117–18; *Business* harks back to III.iii.456–58; *State* echoes III.iv.133, 148; *Offence* recalls III.iv.108–12, IV.i.203–4.

To lash the Rascals naked through the World,   140
Even from the East to th' West.

IAGO   Speak within Door.

AEMILIA   Oh fie upon them: some such Squire he
    was
That turn'd your Wit the Seamy-side without,
And made you to suspect me with the Moor.

IAGO   You are a Fool: go to.

DESDEMONA   Alas, Iago,   145
What shall I do to win my Lord again?
Good Friend, go to him: for by this Light of
    Heaven,
I know not how I lost him. Here I kneel:
If ere my Will did trespass 'gainst his Love,
Either in discourse of Thought or actual Deed,   150
Or that mine Eyes, mine Ears, or any Sense
Delighted them, or any other Form,
Or that I do not yet, and ever did,
And ever will (though he do shake me off
To beggarly Divorcement) love him dearly,   155
Comfort forswear me. Unkindness may do much,
And his Unkindness may defeat my Life,
But never taint my Love. I cannot say 'Whore',
It does abhor me now I speak the Word;
To do the Act that might the Addition earn   160
Not the World's mass of Vanity could make me.

IAGO   I pray you be content: 'tis but his Humour.
The Business of the State does him Offence,
And he does chide with you.

DESDEMONA   If 'twere no other.

IAGO   It is but so, I warrant.   165
Hark how these Instruments summon you to Supper:

---

165   **I warrant**   I'm sure.

166   **these Instruments**   Iago probably refers to an off-stage trumpet
        call. *Instruments* echoes IV.i.225.

167 **The ... Meat** your Venetian guests await your arrival for supper. *Meat* means 'solid food'; in Shakespeare's time the word was not limited to its usual modern sense.

170 **find** determine [having scrutinized the evidence in the way a jury judges a legal case]. Compare line 190.

172 **dafts** daffest (like one doffing, putting off, his hat).

173 **Devise** device. Compare II.iii.401.

174 **keep'st ... Conveniency** [you] stand in the way of my coming together [with Desdemona]. Roderigo uses *Conveniency* in something approximating the original Latin sense; compare II.i.236–37. *Advantage* (line 175) recalls III.iii.302–4. In this sentence as in II.iii.278, *then* can mean both 'than' (its primary sense) and 'then'.

177 **put ... Peace** pocket (put up with) without retaliation. Compare the phrasing in III.i.20.

178 **foolishly suff'red** endured like a fool. Here *foolishly* is a reminder that Roderigo has been hoping to get Desdemona to act 'foolishly', in the sense of II.i.137–44 and IV.i.180. Meanwhile *suff'red* means both (a) been the victim of pain, and (b) put up with it patiently (a sense that echoes lines 45–62). Compare I.iii.155–56, II.i.22–24, III.iii.50–52, V.ii.249–50.

181–
82 **your ... together** Roderigo speaks more than he knows here. *Performances* recalls III.iii.20–22.

184–
85 **I ... Means** I have thrown away all my money. Roderigo's words recall IV.ii.108–9.

186 **had** received; been given. *Deliver* recalls I.iii.89, 376–77, II.i.128–29, II.iii.221–23.

187 **corrupted a Votarist** seduced a nun (a woman who has vowed herself to celibacy).

189–
90 **Expectations ... Acquaintance** the comforting expectation that I would soon be given her respectful attention and intimate 'Acquaintance' (compare III.iii.97). *Comforts* echoes line 156 and recalls II.i.192–97, 208–10; *Respect* recalls II.i.213–14.

191 **go to** hush now, that's enough. Compare line 145.

194 **scurvy** vile, contemptible. See line 137.
fopp'd gulled, turned into a fop (fool).

The Messengers of Venice stays the Meat,
Go in, and weep not. All things shall be well.

Exeunt Desdemona and Aemilia.

Enter Roderigo.

– How now, Roderigo?

RODERIGO   I do not find that thou deal'st justly
   with me.   170

IAGO   What in the contrary?

RODERIGO   Every Day thou dafts me with some
   Devise, Iago, and rather, as it seems to me
   now, keep'st from me all Conveniency, then
   suppliest me with the least Advantage of Hope.   175
   I will indeed no longer endure it. Nor am I
   yet persuaded to put up in Peace what already
   I have foolishly suff'red.

IAGO   Will you hear me, Roderigo?

RODERIGO   Faith I have heard too much: and   180
   your Words and Performances are no Kin
   together.

IAGO   You charge me most unjustly.

RODERIGO   With naught but Truth: I have wasted
   my self out of my Means. The Jewels you have   185
   had from me to deliver Desdemona would half
   have corrupted a Votarist. You have told me
   she hath receiv'd them, and return'd me
   Expectations and Comforts of sudden Respect,
   and Acquaintance, but I find none.   190

IAGO   Well, go to: very well.

RODERIGO   'Very well, go to': I cannot go to,
   Man, nor 'tis not very well. Nay, I think
   it is scurvy, and begin to find my self fopp'd
   in it.   195

IAGO   Very well.

RODERIGO   I tell you, 'tis not very well: I
   will make my self known to Desdemona. If she

199–   **give ... Suit**   put an end to my pursuit of her favour. *Suit*
200   recalls IV.i.109–10.

200   **unlawful Solicitation**   illicit courtship. Compare III.iii.25–28,
     IV.ii.82–84.

202   **Satisfaction of you**   either (a) repayment of all that I have given
     you [on the understanding that you were offering love-tokens
     to her on my behalf], or (b) revenge [by means of a challenge
     that will allow me to satisfy the demands of my honour].
     Compare the references to 'Satisfaction' in III.iii.380–98. Iago
     promises Roderigo satisfaction in line 252.

203   **You ... now**   I presume you've said your piece now?

204   **I**   both 'I' [have], and 'Ay' (yes). Compare lines 62, 64, 237.

205   **protest ... Doing**   vow an intent to do. Here *Doing* provides a
     reminder of the kind of 'Deed' (line 150) Roderigo has been
     thwarted in his attempts to accomplish.

206   **Mettle in thee**   real manhood here. Iago's shift from 'you' (line
     183) to the more familar 'thee' is meant to imply a new
     warmth and intimacy; Roderigo eventually takes it that way;
     but for the private Iago it is a familiarity that masks the
     contempt a man of cunning has for a naïve dupe.

207   **Instant**   moment. But Iago is playing on the Latin roots of this
     word (*in* plus *stare*, to stand) to keep the audience focused on
     the erections Roderigo has been unable to 'build on' his hopes
     for Desdemona. Compare I.ii.36–38, III.iii.458–60, IV.iii.6.

210   **just Exception**   justifiable criticism. *Opinion* (line 208) echoes
     lines 105–6.

214   **Wit**   intelligence. Compare line 143.

218   **shew**   show. Compare III.iv.96, IV.ii.246. *Reason* (line 216)
     recalls III.iii.399 and anticipates lines 222–23, 251. *Purpose*
     (line 217) echoes III.iii.307–8.

221   **devise ... Life**   plot devices to kill me. *Engines* (weapons)
     recalls III.iii.345–47.

225   **depute**   appoint as the Duke's deputy (representative). *Depute*
     derives from the Latin *deputare* (to cut off, prune, cleanse, or
     detach), and that sense will prove prophetic. *Place* echoes
     IV.i.265, IV.ii.50–51, 135, 225; and *Compass* (achievability)
     recalls III.iv.21–23, 69–74.

will return me my Jewels, I will give over
my Suit, and repent my unlawful Solicitation.   200
If not, assure your self, I will seek
Satisfaction of you.

IAGO   You have said now.

RODERIGO   I: and said nothing but what I
protest Intendment of Doing.   205

IAGO   Why, now I see there's Mettle in thee:
and even from this Instant do build on thee
a better Opinion than ever before. Give me
thy Hand, Roderigo. Thou hast taken against
me a most just Exception: but yet I protest   210
I have dealt most directly in thy Affair.

RODERIGO   It hath not appear'd.

IAGO   I grant indeed it hath not appear'd: and
your Suspicion is not without Wit and
Judgement. But Roderigo, if thou hast that   215
in thee indeed which I have greater Reason
to believe now than ever (I mean Purpose,
Courage, and Valour), this Night shew it.
If thou the next Night following enjoy not
Desdemona, take me from this World with   220
Treachery, and devise Engines for my Life.

RODERIGO   Well: what is it? Is it within
Reason and Compass?

IAGO   Sir, there is especial Commission come from
Venice to depute Cassio in Othello's place.   225

RODERIGO   Is that true? Why then Othello and
Desdemona return again to Venice.

IAGO   Oh no: he goes into Mauritania and taketh
away with him the fair Desdemona, unless his

---

228   **Mauritania**   the area of north-west Africa that was thought to
be the original home of the Moors. Whether Iago tells the
truth is unclear. It is hard to see why he would lie here; but it
is of some interest that this is the first time we have heard of
such a posting. See IV.i.239–41, IV.ii.42–44.

230   **Abode**   abiding, continued residence.

231   **determinate**   determining, causative. *Determinate* derives from
       the Latin word *terminus* (end); it thus anticipates Iago's
       answer to the question Roderigo asks in line 233. Compare
       II.iii.230.

234–   **uncapable ... place**   unable to fill the vacancy that would be
35   created by Othello's departure. *Uncapable* recalls
       III.iii.448–49; *Brains* harks back to II.iii.296–97.

237–   **do ... Right**   do for yourself something that you both deserve
38   and will find to your advantage. *Profit* recalls III.iii.369.
       Harlotry   slut (a woman little better than a common whore).

241   **watch ... thence**   watch for his departure from there. *Watch*
       echoes III.iii.279.

241–   **fashion ... out**   arrange to take place. *Fashion* recalls
42   II.i.208–9.

244   **second**   assist (the way a second helps his friend with the
       arrangements for a duel). Iago's phrasing emphasizes that
       what he and Roderigo are planning is an ambush, not an
       honourable combat.

247   **a ... Death**   a rationale for regarding his death as necessary
       (required by Roderigo's 'Right' to have Cassio removed, lines
       237–38). *Bound* (line 248) recalls III.iii.208.

249   **high Supper time**   both (a) fully time for supper, and (b) time
       for 'high supper' (a feast, as opposed to the normal light
       meal).

251   **I ... this**   I need to hear more persuasive arguments for this
       course before I'll proceed.

IV.iii This scene takes place inside the Citadel. The high supper in
       honour of Lodovico and the other visiting Venetians has just
       concluded, and Othello has offered to escort Lodovico to his
       quarters.

Abode be ling'red here by some Accident.   230
Wherein none can be so determinate as the
removing of Cassio.
RODERIGO   How do you mean removing him?
IAGO   Why, by making him uncapable of Othello's
place: knocking out his Brains.   235
RODERIGO   And that you would have me to do.
IAGO   I: if you dare do your self a Profit,
and a Right. He sups to night with a Harlotry:
and thither will I go to him. He knows not
yet of his honourable Fortune: if you will   240
watch his going thence (which I will fashion
to fall out between Twelve and One), you may
take him at your pleasure. I will be near
to second your Attempt, and he shall fall
between us. Come, stand not amaz'd at it,   245
but go along with me: I will shew you such
a Necessity in his Death that you shall
think your self bound to put it on him. It
is now high Supper time: and the Night grows
to wast. About it.   250
RODERIGO   I will hear further Reason for this.
IAGO   And you shall be satisfied.   *Exeunt.*

Scene 3

Enter Othello, Lodovico, Desdemona, Aemilia,
and Attendants.

LODOVICO   I do beseech you, Sir, trouble your
   self
No further.
OTHELLO   Oh pardon me: 'twill do me good
   To walk.
LODOVICO   Madam, good night: I humbly thank
   Your Ladyship.
DESDEMONA   Your Honour is most welcome.

6   **on th' Instant** at once. Compare IV.ii.207.

7   **forthwith** very quickly.

8   **Look't be done** See that it is taken care of before I get back. Othello's phrasing echoes I.iii.290, II.iii.1–3, 259, III.iii.192, 195, III.iv.76.

10   **incontinent** Desdemona means 'forthwith' (line 7); but *incontinent* could also mean 'incapable of containing (restraining) his passion'. Compare Roderigo's use of 'incontinently' in I.iii.303. *Gentler* (milder, more tender) recalls I.ii.24–28, I.iii.49, 176, II.i.119, II.iii.253, IV.i.198–200, IV.ii.108–9.

12   **bid** hath bid.

14   **Nightly Wearing** bed smock, nightdress.

17   **approve him** both (a) approve of him, and (b) prove him worthy. *Approve* recalls II.iii.322 and anticipates line 49.

18   **Stubbornness** gruffness, rough manner.
       Checks rebukes.

19   **Grace and Favour** the loving care of a father who chastises his child for its own good. Desdemona is probably thinking of such teachings as Proverbs 13:24, 19:18, and 22:6, and especially Hebrews 12:5–15. Characteristically, she herself bestows grace and favour on her husband, even though 'it hath not appear'd' (IV.ii.212) that he is in fact treating her in the way she chooses to believe he is. *Favour* recalls III.iv.118.

21   **All's one** This expression normally means 'that's all the same; it doesn't matter'. Here it seems to be Desdemona's way of assuring herself that she should make light of her sudden misgivings. The expression *good Father* probably invokes God the Father, and is thus to be construed as a prayer; most editions follow the Quarto and print *good faith*.

22   **shrowd** shroud. The spelling in the original texts is one that sometimes occurs for *shrewd* or *shrew'd* (an aphetic form for *beshrewed*, cursed); compare *Hamlet*, I.iv.1, where the Second Quarto prints *shroudly* for what the Folio spells *shrewdly*.

OTHELLO   Will you walk, Sir? – Oh Desdemona.
DESDEMONA   My Lord.   5
OTHELLO   Get you to Bed on th' Instant, I will be
  Return'd forthwith. Dismiss your Attendant
      there:
  Look't be done.
DESDEMONA   I will, my Lord.
              Exit [Othello, with Lodovico and Attendants].
AEMILIA   How goes it now? He looks gentler
  than he did.
DESDEMONA   He says he will return incontinent,   10
  And hath commanded me to go to Bed,
  And bid me to dismiss you.
AEMILIA   Dismiss me?
DESDEMONA   It was his Bidding: therefore, good
      Aemilia,
  Give me my Nightly Wearing, and adieu.
  We must not now displease him.   15
AEMILIA   I would you had never seen him.
DESDEMONA   So would not I: my Love doth so
      approve him,
  That even his Stubbornness, his Checks, his
      Frowns
  (Prythee unpin me) have Grace and Favour in
      them.
AEMILIA   I have laid those Sheets you bad me on
  the Bed.   20
DESDEMONA   All's one: good Father, how foolish
  are our Minds?
  If I do die before thee, prythee shrowd me
  In one of these same Sheets.

24 **Barbary** The maid's name recalls an epithet Iago has levelled at Othello in I.i.110. It probably indicates that the maid in question was either an Arabian or a North African from the Barbary Coast. Her exoticism and prophetic powers resemble those of the Egyptian 'Charmer' who gave Othello's mother the handkerchief that Desdemona has now misplaced (see III.iv.55–75).

28 **to night** tonight. Here the original orthography allows 'Willow' to be construed, appropriately, as a 'Song to Night'. Compare IV.ii.238, where *sups to night* is similarly ambiguous.

29–30 **I . . . hang** it's all I can do to keep myself from hanging. *Hang* echoes IV.ii.127, 130.

31 **dispatch** hurry, and then be on your way [so as not to 'displease' Othello, line 15]. *Dispatch* recalls I.iii.45, 146–48, IV.ii.28.

32 **Night-gown** dressing gown. Compare line 14.

33 **proper** both (a) handsome, and (b) well-mannered, courtly. Desdemona's observation is yet another reminder of the 'proposed Matches' (III.iii.224) she might have responded to had she not given her all to the Moor. *Proper* recalls I.iii.68–69, 262, 399.

36 **a . . . Venice** Aemilia may be suggesting that Desdemona now wishes she had married Lodovico; but what she implies even more strongly is that she herself would have undertaken an arduous pilgrimage for a mere 'Touch of his nether [lower] Lip'.

39 **Sycamour** Here as in *Romeo and Juliet*, I.i.124, the original spelling plays on 'sick-amour'. The Willow symbolized unrequited love, and willow garlands were worn by forlorn or forsaken lovers. *Bosom* (line 41) recalls IV.ii.12.

45 **Her . . . Stones** The song's phrasing reminds us that Iago has used *salt* in a very different sense in II.i.247 and III.iii.394. It also recalls IV.i.186–95 and encourages us to hope that Desdemona's tears will be able to soften the stony heart that Iago has planted in her husband's breast.

47 **high** hie, hasten. Compare the play on *hie* and *high* in *Romeo and Juliet*, II.iv.69, 79, and in *Macbeth*, I.v.22, 27, and see V.i.34.

49 **Let . . . approve** Barbary's song echoes lines 17–19.

AEMILIA   Come, come: you talk.
DESDEMONA   My Mother had a Maid call'd Barbary,
  She was in love: and he she lov'd prov'd mad,   25
  And did forsake her. She had a Song of Willow,
  An old thing 'twas: but it express'd her Fortune,
  And she died singing it. That Song to night
  Will not go from my Mind: I have much to do
  But to go hang my Head all at one side   30
  And sing it like poor Barbary. Prythee
    dispatch.
AEMILIA   Shall I go fetch your Night-gown?
DESDEMONA   No, unpin me here.
  This Lodovico is a proper Man.
AEMILIA   A very handsome Man.
DESDEMONA   He speaks well.   35
AEMILIA   I know a Lady in Venice would have
  walk'd barefoot to Palestine for a Touch of
  his nether Lip.
DESDEMONA   *The poor Soul sat singing by*
      a Sycamour Tree,
    Sing all a green Willow;   40
      Her Hand on her Bosom,
      her Head on her Knee,
    Sing Willow, Willow, Willow.
      The fresh Streams ran by her,
      and murmur'd her Moans:
    Sing Willow, Willow, Willow.
      Her salt Tears fell from her,
      and soft'ned the Stones: 45
    Sing Willow –
        Lay by these.
               – *Willow, Willow.*
Prythee high thee: he'll come anon.
    Sing all a green Willow
      must be my Garland.
    Let no body blame him,
      his Scorn I approve.

52   **I . . . Love** Here we are reminded of what Desdemona has not done. The original Willow Song was in the voice of a forsaken man, and the line that followed this one was 'She was born to be false, and I to die for her love.' An audience knowing this might have applied the omitted words to the situations of both Othello and Desdemona.

54   **couch** go to bed. Compare IV.i.73–74.
    moe more.

56   **bode** portend, forecast. This word echoes IV.i.19–21, IV.ii.229–30 (*Abode*).
    'Tis . . . there It has nothing to do with it. Compare I.i.136.

58   **in Conscience** in the deepest part of your mind. See I.ii.2–3, III.iii.198–99.

60   **in . . . kind** in so egregiously foul a way. *Gross* recalls III.iii.385, 394–95.

62   **this Heavenly Light** Desdemona swears by the Moon, ruled by Diana, the Goddess of Chastity. Compare III.iii.173 and IV.ii.75. *Deed* (lines 61, 65) echoes IV.ii.150; compare line 69.

65   **for . . . World** Desdemona's question relates to the one posed by Jesus in Mark 8:36, 'what shall it profit a man, if he shall gain the whole world, and lose his own soul?' It also echoes 1 John 2:15, 'Love not the world, neither the things that are in the world.'

67   **Price** Aemilia's phrasing hints at the 'pearl of great price' that Jesus likens to himself and to 'the kingdom of heaven' (Matthew 13:45–46).
    Vice sin. See the second note to II.iii.329, and compare III.iii.365–66, IV.i.175.

69   **troth** faith, truth. *Undo't* plays on the copulative sense of *do*; see the note to IV.ii.91.

71   **Joint-ring** a ring of detachable halves, and thus frequently employed as a love-token. Here the word's parts hint at the genital and moral 'Vice' under consideration.

72   **Lawn** fine linen.

73   **petty Exhibition** small gift. Compare I.iii.235–38.

76   **Monarch** ruler of the whole world.
    venture run the risk of having to endure.

Nay that's not next. Hark, who is't that
   knocks?   50
AEMILIA   It's the Wind.
DESDEMONA   *I call'd my Love False Love:*
            but what said he then?
       Sing Willow, Willow, Willow.
       If I court moe Women,
            you'll couch with moe Men.
So get thee gone, good night. Mine Eyes do
   itch: 55
Doth that bode Weeping?
AEMILIA   'Tis neither here nor there.
DESDEMONA   I have heard it said so. O these Men,
   these Men!
Dost thou in Conscience think (tell me,
   Aemilia)
That there be Women do abuse their Husbands
In such gross kind?
AEMILIA   There be some such, no question.   60
DESDEMONA   Wouldst thou do such a Deed for all
   the World?
AEMILIA   Why, would not you?
DESDEMONA   No, by this Heavenly Light.
AEMILIA   Nor I neither, by this Heavenly Light:
   I might do't as well i'th' Dark.
DESDEMONA   Wouldst thou do such a Deed for
   all the World?   65
AEMILIA   The World's a huge thing: it is a great
   Price for a small Vice.
DESDEMONA   In troth, I think thou wouldst not.
AEMILIA   In troth I think I should, and undo't
   when I had done. Marry, I would not do such a   70
   thing for a Joint-ring, nor for measures of
   Lawn, nor for Gowns, Petticoats, nor Caps,
   nor any petty Exhibition. But for all the
   whole World: why who would not
   make her Husband a Cuckold to make him a   75
   Monarch? I should venture Purgatory for't.

79–80 **but ... World** a wrong that is limited to the realm in which it
occurs [and thus subject to whoever executes the laws in that
realm]. *Beshrew* (line 77) recalls IV.ii.125.

80 **for your Labour** in exchange for your efforts. But Aemilia's
phrase can also mean (a) as a result of your bearing a man
and enduring the labour of childbirth to bring forth 'the
World' (compare III.iv.134), and (b) to do your labour for
you. Compare II.i.128–29.

84 **a Dozen** The worldly Aemilia jests by choosing a number that
she knows to be ludicrously small, but one that will seem
incredibly large to the chaste Desdemona.

84–85 **to / The Vantage** in addition; over and above that number.
Vantage echoes IV.ii.172–75.

85 **store** populate, stock; restore.

87 **fall** fall into sin; literally, fall on their backs. *Faults* recalls
IV.i.279–80.
Say ... Duties suppose husbands fail to fulfil their marital
duties to their wives. Here *slack* can mean both (a) neglect,
and (b) lack the virile wherewithal to bestow 'Treasures' (as
noted in line 88).

88 **foreign Laps** the 'jewelboxes' of other women. *Powre* (pour)
echoes II.iii.368.

89 **peevish Jealousies** unreasonable suspicions.

90 **Restraint** restrictions.

91 **scant ... despight** reduce what they formerly provided us in
retaliation. *Despight* echoes IV.ii.112–14.

92 **Galls** feelings [too]; bitterness. Compare I.iii.214–15, II.i.98.
Here *Grace* means 'forgiveness' and 'compassionate love'.
Compare III.iii.44–45, 363, IV.iii.17–19.

94 **Sense** both (a) sensuality ('Affection', line 98), and (b) passions
(such as 'Sweet' lust and 'Sowre' anger, line 95). Compare
III.iii.364, IV.ii.65–67, 149–52.

95 **Sowre** both (a) sour, and (b) sore. Compare *powre*, line 88.

97 **change** exchange. But the usual sense of *change* (alter) is also
pertinent. Compare IV.ii.103.

DESDEMONA   Beshrew me, if I would do such a
   Wrong
For the whole World.

AEMILIA   Why, the Wrong is but a Wrong i'th'
World; and having the World for your Labour,   80
'tis a Wrong in your own World, and you might
quickly make it Right.

DESDEMONA   I do not think there is any such
   Woman.

AEMILIA   Yes, a Dozen: and as many to
The Vantage as would store the World they
   play'd for.   85
But I do think it is their Husbands' Faults
If Wives do fall. Say that they slack their Duties,
And powre our Treasures into foreign Laps;
Or else break out in peevish Jealousies,
Throwing Restraint upon us; or say they
   strike us,   90
Or scant our former Having in despight.
Why we have Galls: and though we have some
   Grace,
Yet have we some Revenge. Let Husbands know,
Their Wives have Sense like them: they see,
   and smell,
And have their Palates both for Sweet and Sowre,   95
As Husbands have. What is it that they do
When they change us for others? Is it Sport?
I think it is: and doth Affection breed it?
I think it doth. Is't Frailty that thus errs?

100   **It . . . too** That is true as well. By *Frailty* (lines 99, 101), Aemilia means the human proclivity to succumb to temptation. She is rebelling against the male tendency to ascribe frailty primarily to women. *Sport* (lines 97, 101) refers to a gamesome desire to seek out opportunities for sensual gratification; compare II.i.231–33, II.ii.5–7. By *Affection* (lines 98, 100) Aemilia probably means strong sexual drives and emotional attractions to particular individuals; her nouns echo II.i.247–48.

102   **use** treat. See I.iii.172–73, 289, II.i.130–31, II.iii.318–19, IV.i.278, IV.ii.104–6, V.i.105.

103   **Ills** evils.
    instruct us so teach us to do [by their own bad examples]. Compare II.i.224–25, 234–41, IV.i.41–43.

104   **Uses** practices, behaviour. This word echoes III.iii.264–67.

105   **Not . . . mend** not to pick up evil tendencies from the evil done to me, but to use the suffering I endure to grow in grace. What Desdemona describes is the Job-like patience invoked by Othello in IV.ii.45–62 only to be spurned in favour of the revenge advocated by his bad angel, Iago. By Iago's standards, there is no one so 'impotent' (II.i.163) and foolish as a 'Deserving Woman' (II.i.147) who seeks to 'mend' herself by accepting 'Bad' fortune as something ordained by God to test and refine her character. And judging by what Aemilia has just said, she looks at the world in much the same way as her husband. For Desdemona, however, the only way to respond to 'Bad' treatment is to 'overcome evil with good' (Romans 12:2), to 'love your enemies, bless them that curse you, do good to them that hate you, and pray for them which despitefully use you' (Matthew 5:44). Lines 104–5 echoes I.iii.198–217, II.i.145–62, II.iii.306–10.

It is so too. And have not we Affections,   100
Desires for Sport, and Frailty, as Men have?
Then let them use us well: else let them know,
The Ills we do, their Ills instruct us so.
DESDEMONA   Good night, good night: Heaven me
  such Uses send
Not to pick Bad from Bad, but by Bad mend.   *Exeunt.*   105

V.i.   This scene takes place on a street near Bianca's house; it is
       shortly after midnight (as indicated in IV.ii.240–44).

1   **Bark**   probably a bark-house or tan-house (a structure in which
       bark is stored), but possibly a tree (with *Bark* used
       metronymically to epitomize it) or a docked ship (if this scene
       takes place at the 'Bay', II.i.211). Most editions adopt the
       Quarto's *Bulk*, a vendor's stall projecting from a larger
       building. Compare II.i.48–49.

2   **put it home**   sheathe it in Cassio's body. *Put* echoes III.iii.382,
       460, IV.ii.246–48; *home* recalls II.i.167.

4   **It . . . mars us**   what happens now will either make our fortunes
       or ruin them.

5   **fix . . . Resolution**   Iago's description of 'Resolution' (manly
       resolve, determination) implicitly likens it both to an
       unbending blade and to the kind of male assertion for which
       Roderigo's intended victim stands accused by Iago. Compare
       Hamlet, III.i.80–85, and *Macbeth*, I.vii.59–61, 79–80.

6   **miscarry in't**   fail to carry it off successfully.

7   **take thy stand**   both (a) assume your position, and (b) stand
       firm in your purpose. Again Iago's phrasing suggests more
       than one kind of 'bold' readiness; compare I.iii.93 and
       II.i.50–51, 98–100.

9   **satisfying Reasons**   reasons that answer any questions I pose
       about a 'Deed' that neither my mind nor my heart can
       embrace with any 'Devotion'. See the note to IV.ii.202;
       Reasons echoes IV.ii.215–20.

10   **'Tis . . . gone**   One effect of Iago's 'satisfying Reasons' is to put
       out of Roderigo's mind any thought of the commandment
       against murder (Exodus 20:13).

11   **I . . . Sense**   I have rubbed and chafed this pimple-like dupe
       almost to the quick. *Sense* echoes IV.iii.93–94.

14   **makes my Gain**   will be to my advantage.
       Live Roderigo   if Roderigo survives.

15   **Restitution**   restoration, repayment.

16   **bobb'd**   swindled.

18–19 **he . . . ugly**   his personal appeal will put me in the shade again
       [and deny me the lieutenancy I've been conditionally promised
       (III.iii.458–67) by the same General who originally promoted
       him over me].

ACT V

Scene 1

Enter Iago and Roderigo.

IAGO Here, stand behind this Bark, straight
      will he come:
Wear thy good Rapier bare, and put it home.
Quick, quick, fear nothing; I'll be at thy
      Elbow.
It makes us, or it mars us, think on that,
And fix most firm thy Resolution.   5
RODERIGO Be near at hand, I may miscarry in't.
IAGO Here, at thy hand: be bold, and take thy
      stand.   [*He withdraws.*]
RODERIGO — I have no great Devotion to the Deed,
And yet he hath given me satisfying Reasons:
'Tis but a Man gone. Forth my Sword: he dies.   10
IAGO I have rubb'd this young Quat almost to the
      Sense,
And he grows angry. Now, whether he kill
      Cassio,
Or Cassio him, or each do kill the other,
Every way makes my Gain. Live Roderigo,
He calls me to a Restitution large   15
Of Gold, and Jewels, that I bobb'd from him,
As Gifts to Desdemona. It must not be.
If Cassio do remain, he hath a daily
Beauty in his Life that makes me ugly.
And besides, the Moor may unfold me to him: 20

---

20   **unfold . . . him**   disclose to him what I have insinuated about
      him. Compare IV.ii.138.

25   **Coat** Cassio is apparently wearing a 'privy coat' (a coat of
       mail concealed under the doublet) to protect his torso.

26   **make . . . thine** test your 'Coat' to see whether it can prevent
       penetration by a similar thrust. *Proof* recalls IV.i.277–78.

27   **I am maim'd** Though the early texts do not so specify with a
       stage direction, editors assume that the stab that maims
       Cassio is delivered from behind by Iago. Support for that
       inference is provided by Cassio's reference to 'Villains' in line
       52.

33   **Thou teachest me** What Othello means is 'You instruct me by
       your example'; but his words could be applied to Iago's
       assumed role as 'counsellor' not only for the Moor but for
       Roderigo, Cassio, Desdemona, and others. See IV.iii.102–3.
       Sense of (sensitivity to) echoes line 11.
       Minion spoiled darling (here meaning 'courtesan').
       Deer both (a) stag, and (b) dear one.

34   **highs** both (a) is now at its height [with the implication that
       such an 'unblest Fate' (fortune) will now fall precipitously
       from its seeming bliss], and (b) hies, hastens. Othello's
       phrasing recalls II.i.85–87, 186–201. *Highs* echoes IV.iii.47.
       I come Othello's verb echoes what another man might say to a
       real 'Strumpet'; and it provides a tragic evocation of how a
       devoted husband might normally be planning to conclude an
       evening. See the note to III.iii.71–72, and compare III.iii.65,
       73, 85–86, IV.ii.25–28, V.i.1, 45.

35   **For . . . blotted** Othello's words suggest a kind of exorcism: he
       is wilfully ejecting from his heart the 'Charms' by which he
       believes evil 'Eyes' to have taken his soul captive. Compare
       I.i.171–73, I.ii.62–75, I.iii.88–93, III.iii.204–6, and
       III.iv.55–75.

36   **Thy . . . spotted** Othello's reference to Desdemona's
       'Lust-stain'd' bed is a reminder of the Renaissance view that if
       the sheets were *not* blood-stained after a couple's wedding
       night, the bride was not a virgin. For the tragically deluded
       Othello, Desdemona's spotted sheets will carry the opposite
       implication. See the notes to II.iii.183 and III.iii.424.

There stand I in much Peril. No, he must die:
But so, I heard him coming.

Enter Cassio.

RODERIGO   I know his Gait,
  'Tis he. – Villain, thou diest.   [*He stabs Cassio.*]
CASSIO   That Thrust had been mine Enemy indeed,
  But that my Coat is better than thou know'st: 25
  I will make Proof of thine.   [*He stabs Roderigo.*]
RODERIGO   Oh, I am slain.
CASSIO   I am maim'd for ever! – Help, ho: Murther,
  Murther.

Enter Othello.

OTHELLO   The Voice of Cassio, Iago keeps his
  Word.
RODERIGO   O Villain that I am.
OTHELLO   It is even so.
CASSIO   Oh help, ho: Light, a Surgeon.   30
OTHELLO   'Tis he. – O brave Iago, honest and
  just,
  That hast such Noble Sense of thy Friend's
  Wrong,
  Thou teachest me. – Minion, your Deer lies
  dead,
  And your unblest Fate highs: Strumpet, I come.
  For of my Heart, those Charms, thine Eyes,
  are blotted: 35
  Thy Bed, Lust-stain'd, shall with Lust's Blood
  be spotted.   *Exit.*

Enter Lodovico and Gratiano.

37 **No Passage?** No one passing by?

40 **heavy** darkest, most impenetrable and leaden (like a thick curtain). Compare I.iii.253–57, II.i.145, IV.ii.40, 112–14.

41 **Counterfeits** decoys. See II.i.250–51, III.iii.345–47.

42 **Cry** both (a) place where the cry of anguish is heard, and (b) possible cry of dog-like villains eager to capture their prey. Compare II.iii.375–77, IV.i.125.

45 **Shirt** nightshirt. As usual, Iago has thought of everything; he now presents himself as a man who has been awakened from his slumbers in 'heavy Night' (line 40).

46 **cries on Murther** cries out that someone has been murdered.

47 **Cry** Here as in line 42, this word suggests a hunting cry: the baying of dogs in pursuit of a quarry that is now wounded.

52 **spoil'd** turned into one of the spoils (bleeding victims) of the pack of 'Villains' who have ambushed me. Here *spoil* implies that Cassio has fallen, not in an honourable duel or military encounter, but in the manner of a game animal stalked from a concealed position.
undone defeated, grievously wounded. Compare IV.iii.69–70.

56 **make away** get away. Compare I.i.67, I.iii.270–72, III.iv.160.

CASSIO   What ho? No Watch? No Passage? Murther, Murther.

GRATIANO   'Tis some Mischance, the Voice is very direful.

CASSIO   Oh help.

LODOVICO   Hark.

RODERIGO   Oh wretched Villain.

LODOVICO   Two or three groan. 'Tis heavy Night;   40
These may be Counterfeits: let's think't unsafe
To come into the Cry without more Help.

RODERIGO   Nobody come: then shall I bleed to death.

Enter Iago with a Light.

LODOVICO   Hark.

GRATIANO   Here's one comes in his Shirt, with
Light, and Weapons.   45

IAGO   Who's there? Whose Noise is this that cries
on Murther?

LODOVICO   We do not know.

IAGO   Do not you hear a Cry?

CASSIO   Here, here: for Heaven sake help me.

IAGO   What's the matter?

GRATIANO   This is Othello's Ancient, as I take
it.

LODOVICO   The same indeed, a very valiant
Fellow.   50

IAGO   What are you here that cry so grievously?

CASSIO   Iago? Oh I am spoil'd, undone by
Villains:
Give me some Help.

IAGO   O me, Lieutenant! What Villains have done
this?

CASSIO   I think that one of them is hereabout,   55
And cannot make away.

IAGO   Oh treacherous Villains.
— What are you there? Come in, and give some
Help.

60   **inhumane**   Here the Elizabethan spelling conveys two modern meanings: Iago is so inhumane as to be an 'inhuman Dog'. Compare II.i.246–47, III.iii.254.

62   **How . . . Town?**   How can everyone remain asleep when such terrible deeds are taking place on the town's streets? Iago's phrasing echoes II.i.53. And the outcry he raises here recalls two earlier ones for which he has also been responsible: (a) the rousing of Brabantio in I.i.78–80, and (b) the rousing of Cyprus in II.iii.159–65. The kind of 'order' that permits Iago to work his mischief most effectively is a cunningly choreographed chaos.

63   **Are . . . Evil?**   Iago pretends to be exercising the same kind of prudence that Lodovico and Gratiano exhibited in lines 40–42; with private irony, he asks whether they are 'Counterfeits' (line 41).

64   **prove us**   demonstrate us to be [by holding up your light to our faces]. Iago's posture is probably meant to suggest the legendary story of Diogenes the Cynic (412–323 BC), who carried a lantern in his search for an honest man. *Cynic* derives from the Greek word for 'Dog' (line 60). *Prove* echoes line 26.
    praise   both (a) appraise, evaluate, and (b) praise, commend.

65   **cry you Mercy**   beg your pardon [for questioning your integrity]. Compare IV.ii.86.

69   **bind**   bandage. Compare III.iii.278–81.

76–77 **I . . . you**   Gratiano has probably been looking for Cassio to tell him that he has just been appointed Governor of Cyprus (see IV.ii.239–40). Like Othello at the beginning of the play, however, the man of the hour has been engaged in 'a Business of some Heat' (I.ii.40) that has taken him away from the post where those with 'serious and great Business' (I.iii.265) of the state could find him. As in II.iii, Iago will seek to use what he knows to tarnish Cassio's reputation a second time.

78   **easily**   gently; comfortably and expeditiously, without jolting.

80   **this Trash**   Iago's name for Bianca echoes what he has earlier said about Roderigo (II.i.318) and about reputation (III.iii.152–58). As the compassionate Bianca falls victim to Iago, what remains of her 'Good Name' is converted into 'Trash'; compare II.iii.372–74.

RODERIGO   O help me there.
CASSIO   That's one of them.
IAGO   Oh murd'rous Slave! O Villain!
                              [*He stabs Roderigo.*]
RODERIGO   O damn'd Iago! O inhumane Dog!   60
IAGO   Kill Men i'th' Dark? – Where be these
   bloody Thieves?
 How silent is this Town? – Ho, Murther,
   Murther.
 – What may you be? Are you of good, or evil?
LODOVICO   As you shall prove us, praise us.
IAGO   Signior Lodovico?
LODOVICO   He, Sir.
IAGO   I cry you Mercy: 65
 Here's Cassio hurt by Villains.
GRATIANO   Cassio?
IAGO   How is't, Brother?
CASSIO   My Leg is cut in two.
IAGO   Marry Heav'n forbid.
 – Light, Gentlemen, I'll bind it with my Shirt.

                Enter Bianca.

BIANCA   What is the matter, ho? Who is't that
   cried?   70
IAGO   Who is't that cried?
BIANCA   Oh my dear Cassio,
 O my sweet Cassio: oh Cassio, Cassio, Cassio.
IAGO   O notable Strumpet. – Cassio, may you
   suspect
 Who they should be that have thus mangled you?
CASSIO   No.   75
GRATIANO   I am sorry to find you thus; I
 Have been to seek you.
IAGO   Lend me a Garter. So.
 Oh for a Chair to bear him easily hence.
BIANCA   Alas he faints: Oh Cassio, Cassio, Cassio.
IAGO   Gentlemen all, I do suspect this Trash   80
 To be a Party in this Injury.

82 **Patience . . . Cassio** Cassio is probably trying to protest. *Patience* recalls IV.ii.45–51, 60–62.

83 **know . . . no?** The answer Iago provides to this question is, as usual, two-faced (see I.ii.33). He 'knows' Roderigo far better than he lets on; and yet he has treated Roderigo like anything but what 'my Friend' implies.

84 **dear Countryman** Iago's implied meaning is 'beloved fellow Venetian'; but he is probably smirking over how 'dear' (costly, as in I.iii.256–57, II.i.306, II.iii.8–10, 91) it has been to Roderigo to have Iago as the agent who would make him a 'Countryman' with Desdemona. See the note to I.iii.96, and compare IV.ii.122–23.

88–90 **Signior . . . you** Iago's apology recalls I.iii.49–50. *Neglected* recalls III.iii.302.

93 **said** done. Compare II.i.169, IV.i.116.

95 **I'll . . . Surgeon** Iago's offer echoes II.iii.256–57. *Mistress* echoes IV.ii.88 and anticipates lines 100, 120.

96 **Save . . . Labour** cease your ministrations. Iago's implication is (a) that Bianca's tears are hypocritical, and (b) that the kind of 'Labour' Cassio needs now is that of a physician, not a strumpet. *Labour* echoes IV.iii.80.

99 **Look you pale?** Iago's repetition of this question in the next line suggests that he is here addressing Bianca; but it is conceivable that he first asks Cassio if he is fading. It would be characteristic of Iago to improvise as it occurs to him that the same words could be directed to Bianca with a different implication.

100 **Stay . . . Gentlemen** Iago wants to be sure that an audience (Lodovico and Gratiano) remains to hear him accuse Bianca. Many editions follow the Quarto and adopt *Gentlewoman* here; compare line 104.

101 **Gastness** ghastliness; a paleness suggesting that she is aghast with terror (her blood having made a cowardly retreat from its colours).

102 **stare** look wide-eyed. Whether Bianca is frightened or is glaring back with silent anger is a matter of interpretation. *Look* (line 103), 'observe watchfully', recalls III.iv.76.

104–5 **Nay . . . use** Iago implies that Bianca's expression will 'speak' even more eloquently than her 'Tongue' would if it were disposed to confess her 'Guiltiness'. Compare *Hamlet*, II.ii.625–36.

— Patience awhile, good Cassio. — Come, come;
Lend me a Light: know we this Face, or no?
Alas, my Friend, and my dear Countryman
Roderigo? No: yes, sure. Yes, 'tis Roderigo.   85
GRATIANO   What, of Venice?
IAGO   Even he, Sir: did you know him?
GRATIANO   Know him? Ay.
IAGO   Signior Gratiano? I cry your gentle Pardon:
These bloody Accidents must excuse my Manners,
That so neglected you.
GRATIANO   I am glad to see you.   90
IAGO   How do you, Cassio? — Oh, a Chair, a Chair.
GRATIANO   Roderigo?
IAGO   He, he, 'tis he. — Oh that's well said, the
   Chair.
— Some good Man bear him carefully from hence,
I'll fetch the General's Surgeon. — For you,
   Mistress,   95
Save you your Labour. — He that lies slain here,
   Cassio,
Was my dear Friend. What Malice was between
   you?
CASSIO   None in the World: nor do I know the Man.
IAGO   What? Look you pale? — Oh, bear him out o'
   th' Air.   [*Carry off Cassio in the Chair.*]
— Stay you, good Gentlemen. — Look you pale,
   Mistress?   100
— Do you perceive the Gastness of her Eye?
— Nay, if you stare, we shall hear more anon.
— Behold her well: I pray you look upon her.
Do you see, Gentlemen? Nay, Guiltiness
Will speak though Tongues were out of use.

Enter Aemilia.

AEMILIA   Alas,   105
What is the matter? — What is the matter,
   Husband?
IAGO   Cassio hath here been set on in the Dark

108 **are scap'd** have escaped.

111 **Fruits of Whoring** Iago implies that Cassio has received his just deserts (see the note to lines 76–77). *Fruits* recalls II.iii.9.

112 **know of** find out from.

114 **He . . . not** Depending on one's reading of Bianca, she could mean either (a) though I tremble with fear, it is not because I feel any guilt about his having had supper at my house, or (b) though I shake, it is not with fear or guilt, but with anger at your insinuation that I am somehow involved in what has happened to Cassio. *Shake* (lines 113–14) recalls IV.ii.154–55.

115 **charge** command.

116 **Strumpet** Aemilia accepts Iago's assessment of Bianca's character; but the play provides little evidence that Aemilia's 'Life' is more 'honest' than Bianca's (lines 116–18). See the notes to IV.i.130–31, 157, and compare IV.iii.61–105.

119 **let's . . . dress'd** let's go and make sure that Cassio's wounds are dressed (treated and bandaged) properly.

120 **tell's . . . Tale** give us a different account than the lie you've just told.

122 **happ'd** chanced to happen.

123 **afore** before me. Iago is probably addressing the men who now have Bianca in custody.

124 **makes . . . quite** makes my fortune or undoes me completely (compare line 4). At this point, with Othello about to commit an act that will undo *him* completely, and with Cassio blemished a second time, Iago stands a chance to vault all the way to the top of the military hierarchy.
foredoes fordoes; does in thoroughly, destroys.

V.ii This scene takes us into the Governor's bedchamber.

1 **It . . . Cause** It is because of the case against her. Othello is assuring his soul that the guilty Desdemona must be executed. Compare III.iii.3–4, 401–3, III.iv.173.

2 **you chaste Stars** Othello is probably thinking of the Moon and the stars that attend on her like Diana's votaries. Compare IV.ii.75.

By Roderigo, and Fellows that are scap'd:
He's almost slain, and Roderigo quite dead.

AEMILIA Alas, good Gentleman: alas, good
Cassio.   110

IAGO This is the Fruits of Whoring. Prythee,
Aemilia,
Go know of Cassio where he supp'd to night.
— What, do you shake at that?

BIANCA He supp'd at my House, but I therefore
shake not.

IAGO O did he so? I charge you go with me.   115

AEMILIA Oh fie upon thee, Strumpet.

BIANCA   I am no Strumpet,
But of Life as honest as you that thus
Abuse me.

AEMILIA As I? Fough, fie upon thee.

IAGO Kind Gentlemen: let's go see poor Cassio
dress'd.
— Come, Mistress, you must tell's another
Tale.   120
— Aemilia, run you to the Citadel,
And tell my Lord and Lady what hath happ'd.
— Will you go on afore? — This is the Night
That either makes me, or foredoes me quite.   *Exeunt.*

Scene 2

Enter Othello with a Light, and Desdemona in her Bed.

OTHELLO It is the Cause, it is the Cause, my
Soul.
— Let me not name it to you, you chaste Stars,
It is the Cause. Yet I'll not shed her Blood,
Nor scar that whiter Skin of hers than Snow,

5 **smooth ... Alablaster** as polished as the supine alabaster figures sculpted for the lids of tombs. As Othello looks at Desdemona's snow-white skin, he imagines her as the recumbent effigy that will soon adorn her funerary monument. Compare IV.ii.185–87, and see III.iii.449–51, IV.i.187, IV.iii.45.

7 **Put ... Light** The first 'Light' is the candle ('flaming Minister') in Othello's hand; see the note to V.i.64. The second 'Light' is Desdemona's life. Compare John 1:1–4.

8 **quench** extinguish.

10 **repent me** regret my action and wish to undo it (compare V.i.123–24). *Repent* echoes III.iii.229–33, 381–82, IV.ii.198–202.

11 **Thou ... Nature** you, the most intricate design that ever excelled Nature while yet being one of Nature's creations. Compare IV.ii.87. *Nature* recalls IV.i.269–70.

12 **Promethean Heat** divine fire (here signifying the spark of life). The god Prometheus brought fire from Heaven and gave it to mankind; for this act of love he was tied to a rock and afflicted by Zeus. *Pluck'd* (line 13) recalls IV.i.143–44.

17 **balmy** fragrant, perfumed with balsam. *Balmy* suggests both (a) a healing ointment, and (b) the embalming of corpses. *Justice* (line 18) recalls I.i.137–39, II.iii.86–87, IV.i.216.

20 **after** afterwards.

21 **Fatal** both (a) death-dealing, and (b) doomed. Compare V.i.33–34, and see lines 38–39.

22 **cruel Tears** the tears of an executioner who grieves over what he must do but is firmly resolved against relenting.

22–23 **This ... love** Othello likens himself to a loving parent who must chastise his child (see the note to IV.iii.19). But an Elizabethan audience would also have heard a tragically ironic echo of the New Testament counterpart to the story of Prometheus: the gospel of a gracious God who sacrificed his own Son to redeem a fallen human race.

24 **I** both 'I' and 'Ay'. See IV.ii.237, and compare lines 27, 35, 53, 184, 292.

26 **Desdemon** Here as in IV.ii.38, the abbreviated form of Desdemona's name puts the stress on *moan*; compare lines 197, 275. Here as elsewhere, *to night* (tonight) can also mean 'to Night'; see V.i.112, and compare lines 80, 81.

And smooth as monumental Alablaster: 5
Yet she must die, else she'll betray more Men.
– Put out the Light, and then put out the Light.
– If I quench thee, thou flaming Minister,
I can again thy former Light restore,
Should I repent me. – But once put out thy Light,   10
Thou cunning'st Pattern of excelling Nature,
I know not where is that Promethean Heat
That can thy Light relume. When I have pluck'd
Thy Rose, I cannot give it vital Growth
Again, it needs must wither. I'll smell thee on   15
The Tree.
– Oh balmy Breath, that dost almost persuade
Justice to break her Sword. One more, one more.
– Be thus when thou art dead, and I will kill
    thee,
And love thee after. One more, and that's the
    last.   20
So Sweet was ne'er so Fatal. I must weep,
But they are cruel Tears: this Sorrow's
    Heavenly,
It strikes where it doth love. – She wakes.
DESDEMONA   Who's there? Othello?
OTHELLO   I, Desdemona.
DESDEMONA   Will you come to Bed, my Lord?   25
OTHELLO   Have you pray'd to night, Desdemon?
DESDEMONA   I, my Lord.
OTHELLO   If you bethink your self of any Crime
Unreconcil'd as yet to Heaven, and Grace,
Solicit for it straight.

---

29   **Unreconcil'd ... Grace**   for which you have yet to reconcile
      yourself to God (by confessing it, repenting of it, and seeking
      forgiveness for it). *Grace* echoes IV.iii.92–93.

30   **Solicit ... straight**   ask the Lord's mercy for it immediately.
      Othello's words echo III.iii.25–28, IV.ii.198–200; *straight*
      recalls IV.i.57–59.

32   **walk by**   walk nearby [so as not to intrude on your privacy].

33   **forefend**   forfend; forbid, prevent. Compare V.i.124.

35   **I, I**   both (a) I, I, and (b) Ay, I. Compare lines 24, 27, 53.

36   **Amen**   Othello endorses Desdemona's prayer because he
      assumes that she will need all the 'Mercy' Heaven can grant
      her.

39   **rowle**   roll. The Folio spelling hints at play on two other words:
      (a) *roule* (the Quarto spelling) or *roulette*, a small ball; and
      (b) *rowel*, the wheel of a spur. *Fatal* (line 38) echoes line 21.

40   **I know not**   I have no awareness or experience of. Here *know*
      hints at the 'Sins' (line 41) Othello believes Desdemona to
      have committed.

41   **They . . . you**   If I have any sins on my soul, they result from
      my loving you too much. Desdemona may be suggesting that
      her love for the Moor has bordered on the idolatrous because
      it has been so absolute. Othello assumes that she is referring
      to her other adulterous 'Loves'.

44   **nether-Lip**   Desdemona echoes what Aemilia has said in
      IV.iii.36–38. *Passion shakes* recalls IV.i.269–70; compare
      V.i.113–14. *Frame* harks back to I.iii.404–5, II.iii.353–54.

46   **Portents**   omens, premonitions. The literal meaning of *portend*
      is 'stretch forth', or 'point' (line 47).

47   **Peace . . . still**   In another ironic echo of the New Testament,
      Othello uses the words that Jesus spoke to the stormy Sea of
      Galilee before he rebuked the fearful, faithless disciples who
      had said, 'Master, carest thou not that we perish?' (Mark
      4:37–40). In the Gospel story, 'the wind ceased, and there
      was a great calm'.

52   **Perjury**   lying under oath (here before the highest tribunal, God
      himself).
      thy Death-bed   Desdemona wants to interpret this to mean 'the
      bed you will eventually die in'.

53   **presently**   right now. *I* (both 'I' and 'Ay') echoes line 34.

DESDEMONA   Alack, my Lord,   30
What may you mean by that?
OTHELLO   Well, do it, and
Be brief. I will walk by: I would not kill
Thy unprepared Spirit, no, Heavens forefend,
I would not kill thy Soul.
DESDEMONA   Talk you of Killing?
OTHELLO   I, I do.
DESDEMONA   Then Heaven have Mercy on me.   35
OTHELLO   Amen, with all my Heart.
DESDEMONA   If you say so,
I hope you will not kill me.
OTHELLO   Humh.
DESDEMONA   And yet I fear you: for you're
  Fatal then
When your Eyes rowle so. Why I should fear I
  know not,
Since Guiltiness I know not. But yet I feel I fear.   40
OTHELLO   Think on thy Sins.
DESDEMONA   They are Loves I bear to you.
OTHELLO   Ay, and for that thou diest.
DESDEMONA   That Death's unnatural that kills
  for Loving.
Alas, why gnaw you so your nether-Lip?
Some bloody Passion shakes your very Frame.
These are Portents: but yet I hope, I hope,   45
They do not point on me.
OTHELLO   Peace, and be still.
DESDEMONA   I will so: what's the matter?
OTHELLO   That Handkerchief which I so lov'd, and
  gave thee,
Thou gav'st to Cassio.
DESDEMONA   No, by my Life and Soul: 50
Send for the Man, and ask him.
OTHELLO   Sweet Soul, take heed,
Take heed of Perjury, thou art on thy Death-bed.
DESDEMONA   I, but not yet to die.
OTHELLO   Yes, presently.

55   **Article**   charge, accusation. Compare I.iii.10–12, III.iii.20–22. *Confess* (line 54) recalls IV.i.38–40, 46, 67.

56   **choke**   This word will be a portent (omen) too; see line 46.

56–57 **Conception . . . withal**   persuasion of your guilt that makes me groan with agony and fury. Othello's imagery hints at the kind of conception that leads to the throes of childbirth. It thus recalls I.iii.410–11, III.iv.134. *Conception* echoes III.iv.147–48, IV.ii.93; *groan* echoes V.i.40.

61   **such . . . Heaven**   the kind of love that Heaven not only authorizes but urges us to show to all our neighbours: Christian charity. *Warranty* recalls I.ii.77–79, III.iii.20, IV.ii.165. *Offend* (line 60) echoes IV.ii.162–63; compare II.iii.201–3, III.iv.52.

64   **stone my Heart**   turn my heart to stone. Compare line 5, and see IV.i.187 and IV.iii.45. This and the play's other references to stone would probably have reminded Shakespearean playgoers of Jesus' words, 'The stone which the builders rejected, the same is become the head of the corner: this is the Lord's doing, and it is marvellous in our eyes' (Matthew 21:42). *Perjur'd* echoes line 52.

66   **which . . . Sacrifice**   Othello is probably thinking of the way he was conceiving of the deed in lines 17–23, with himself as the embodiment of Heaven's sword of justice (God the Father) and Desdemona as the pure white lamb who would satisfy the demands of divine law. But an Elizabethan audience would have recognized the fatal flaw in a theology that perceived the sacrificial victim as both sinner and redeemer. Brutus engages in similarly erroneous thinking when he depicts the conspirators as 'Sacrificers but not Butchers' in *Julius Caesar*, II.i.164. In both instances well-meaning, noble men are naïvely presuming to take upon themselves the role that God has reserved to himself (see Romans 12:17–13:7).

71   **Unlawfully**   illicitly. Compare IV.ii.81–84, 198–202. *Us'd* (copulated with) recalls IV.iii.102–5. *Confess* and *confess'd* (line 69) echo IV.i.38–40, 67.

73   **ta'en . . . for't**   seen that it was done (on Othello's order, III.iii.458–62 and IV.i.218–20). *Stopp'd* (silenced), line 72, recalls II.i.199, II.iii.1–3, 313, III.iii.117, IV.ii.75, and anticipates lines 255–58.

74   **interprets**   prophesies accurately. Compare lines 43–47.

Therefore confess thee freely of thy Sin:
For to deny each Article with Oath   55
Cannot remove nor choke the strong Conception
That I do groan withal. Thou art to die.

DESDEMONA   O Heaven have Mercy on me.

OTHELLO   I say, Amen.

DESDEMONA   And have you Mercy too. I never did
Offend you in my Life: never lov'd Cassio,   60
But with such general Warranty of Heaven
As I might love. I never gave him Token.

OTHELLO   By Heaven I saw my Handkerchief in's
Hand.
O perjur'd Woman, thou dost stone my Heart,
And makes me call what I intend to do   65
A Murther, which I thought a Sacrifice.
I saw the Handkerchief.

DESDEMONA   He found it then:
I never gave it him. Send for him hither:
Let him confess a Truth.

OTHELLO   He hath confess'd.

DESDEMONA   What, my Lord?   70

OTHELLO   That he hath us'd thee.

DESDEMONA   How? Unlawfully?

OTHELLO   Ay.

DESDEMONA   He will not say so.

OTHELLO   No, his Mouth is stopp'd:
Honest Iago hath ta'en order for't.

DESDEMONA   Oh, my Fear interprets. What, is
he dead?

OTHELLO   Had all his Hairs been Lives, my great
Revenge   75
Had Stomach for them all.

DESDEMONA   Alas, he is betray'd, and I undone.

OTHELLO   Out, Strumpet: weep'st thou for him to
my Face?

76   **Stomach**   (a) appetite, (b) disposition, (c) courage, and (d)
wrath. Compare III.iv.97.

81   **strive** resist, struggle.

82   **Being done** Now that 'Justice' has passed sentence; see lines
17–18. *Pause* recalls II.iii.231–32.
But . . . say just long enough for me to say.

86   **I . . . merciful** The Prince addresses similar words to his mother
in *Hamlet*, III.iv.175: 'I must be cruel only to be kind.'
Compare lines 21–22.

91   **like** likely.

92   **high** loud. Othello may be referring to all the commotion Iago
stirred up. It is also possible, however, that he is wondering if
the noise of Desdemona's struggle was heard outside the
bedchamber, so that it was because of that rather than 'to
speak of Cassio's Death' that Aemilia came to the door.
Compare V.i.33–34.

94   **stirs** moves. Compare IV.i.57.

97   **insupportable** unbearable, unendurable pain. Compare
I.iii.253–57. *Heavy* recalls V.i.40; compare lines 364–65.

98–   **Me . . . Alteration** It seems to me that there should now be a
100   total eclipse of light, blocking out both the Sun and the
Moon, and that the frightened Globe should gape (*yawn*) in
terror at the sudden change. Here *yawn* probably refers to
earthquakes, which were thought to accompany eclipses.
Eclipse echoes III.iii.453.

DESDEMONA   O banish me, my Lord, but kill me
  not.

OTHELLO   Down, Strumpet.

DESDEMONA   Kill me to morrow, let me live   80
  To night.

OTHELLO   Nay, if you strive —

DESDEMONA   But half an Hour.

OTHELLO   Being done, there is no Pause.

DESDEMONA   But while I say
  One Prayer.

OTHELLO   It is too late.   *Smothers her.*

DESDEMONA   O Lord, Lord, Lord.

Aemilia at the Door.

AEMILIA   My Lord, my Lord? What ho? My Lord,
  my Lord.

OTHELLO   What Noise is this? — Not dead? Not yet
  quite dead?   85
  I that am cruel am yet merciful,
  I would not have thee linger in thy Pain.
  So, so.

AEMILIA *within*.   What ho? My Lord, my Lord?

OTHELLO   Who's there?

AEMILIA   Oh good my Lord, I would speak a Word
  with you.

OTHELLO   Yes. — 'Tis Aemilia. — By and by.
  — She's dead.   90
  'Tis like she comes to speak of Cassio's Death:
  The Noise was high. — Hah, no more Moving?
  Still as the Grave. — Shall she come in? Were't good?
  I think she stirs again. No, what's best to do?
  If she come in, she'll sure speak to my Wife.   95
  My Wife, my Wife: what Wife? I have no Wife.
  Oh insupportable! Oh heavy Hour!
  Me thinks it should be now a huge Eclipse
  Of Sun and Moon; and that th' affrighted Globe
  Did yawn at Alteration.
                     I do beseech you   100

102   **I ... thee**   Compare I.iii.49–50 and V.i.88–90 for earlier instances of similar forgetting. *Forgot* recalls II.iii.169, 191, 244, III.iii.13–18, IV.i.18, 184.

107   **Error ... Moon**   errant (straying) course of the Moon. Othello's phrase also means 'error caused by the Moon' (widely associated with lunacy). Both notions are implicit in what he goes on to say. Meanwhile, his reference to the Moon echoes line 2 and reminds us of how grievously the Moor has erred in his reading of 'Dian's Visage' (III.iii.377) when he saw it displayed in Desdemona. The Moon is frequently depicted as cold (see *A Midsummer Night's Dream*, I.i.73), and Othello may be associating it with Desdemona's 'cold' chastity in lines 269–70.

108   **wont**   accustomed to do.

113   **Tune**   harmony. Othello probably refers to a breakdown of the plan to have the deaths of Desdemona and her lover occur simultaneously. What he probably doesn't realize is that his imagery is self-contradictory: in Renaissance philosophy, murder is by definition 'out of Tune', because it represents a breach in the cosmic harmony that Music symbolizes. Compare II.i.200–4, III.i.1–18, III.iv.116, and IV.i.95, 194–95.

116   **Out**   oh.

120   **No body: I my self**   This utterance would seem to be a contradiction of 'A guiltless Death I die' (line 119), in part because (a) it implies suicide (a damnable sin), and (b) it is a lie. But it gives *Guiltless* (line 119, echoing lines 39–40) two meanings that epitomize the grace of the 'divine Desdemona' (II.i.73). First, it redefines as a 'Sacrifice' what Othello committed as a 'Murther' (line 66); Desdemona commends herself to her 'kind Lord' by attempting to assume responsibility for his deed. And second, it demonstrates Desdemona's exemplary fidelity to the man whose doubts about her faith have led him to commit the most heinous of crimes. As Aemilia notes in line 126, Desdemona's apparent sin proves her to be 'the more Angel'. And it transfigures what might seem like 'Pitch' into the most exalted 'Virtue' (II.iii.372). In the sense noted in III.iii.27–28 and IV.iii.105, Desdemona proves herself to be 'Heavenly True' (line 131).

AEMILIA　　　　　　　That I may speak with you.
Oh good my Lord.
OTHELLO　I had forgot thee: oh come in, Aemilia.
　Soft, by and by, let me the Curtains draw.
　Where art thou? What's the matter with thee now?

Enter Aemilia.

AEMILIA　Oh my good Lord, yonder's foul Murthers
　done.　　　　　　　　　　　　　　　　　　　105
OTIIELLO　What? Now?
AEMILIA　　　　　　　But now, my Lord.
OTHELLO　It is the very Error of the Moon,
　She comes more nearer Earth than she was wont,
　And makes men mad.
AEMILIA　　　　　　　Cassio, my Lord, hath kill'd
　A young Venetian, call'd Roderigo.　　　　　110
OTHELLO　Roderigo kill'd? And Cassio kill'd?
AEMILIA　No, Cassio is not kill'd.
OTHELLO　　　　　　　Not Cassio kill'd?
　Then Murther's out of Tune, and sweet Revenge
　Grows harsh.
DESDEMONA　O falsely, falsely murder'd.
AEMILIA　Alas! what Cry is that?
OTHELLO　　　　　　　That? What?　　　　115
AEMILIA　Out, and alas, that was my Lady's Voice.
　– Help, help, ho, help. – Oh Lady, speak again,
　Sweet Desdemona, oh sweet Mistress, speak.
DESDEMONA　A guiltless Death I die.
AEMILIA　　　　　　　Oh who hath done
　This Deed?
DESDEMONA　No body: I my self, farewell.　　120
　Commend me to my kind Lord: oh farewell.　*She dies.*
OTHELLO　Why, how should she be murd'red?
AEMILIA　　　　　　　Alas: who knows?
OTHELLO　You hear her say her self, it was not I.
AEMILIA　She said so: I must needs report the
　Truth.
OTHELLO　She's like a Liar gone to burning Hell,　125
　'Twas I that kill'd her.

127 **She . . . Folly** Othello means that she gave herself over to
wantonness (see II.i.136–44). But in fact she 'turn'd to Folly'
of another kind: 'the foolishness of God' as defined in 1
Corinthians 1:26–31 and expounded by Desiderius Erasmus
in his *In Praise of Folly* (1509). Here *turn'd* recalls
IV.i.256–58 and IV.ii.92. *Belie* (line 128) recalls IV.i.32–37.

129– **false / As Water** Water was proverbially unreliable. Compare
30 IV.ii.100–1.

130 **rash as Fire** as impulsive and destructive as the element that
symbolizes (and, in Elizabethan psychology, causes) wrath.

132 **top** cover sexually. Compare III.iii.384–85.

133– **I . . . Extremity** I would be damned to the lowest part of Hell if
35 I were not justified in this extreme measure.

137 **true** true to her wedding vows; truthful. What Othello fails to
register is that Desdemona *has* been 'true' to him, and never
more so than in the falsehood with which she ended her life.

138 **World** Othello's image recalls IV.iii.64–85.

139 **Chrysolite** topaz. Chrysolite was the largest and one of the
hardest of precious stones, and according to legend it would
crack if it had any flaws; it was thus a symbol of spiritual
purity. Othello's reference to selling such a 'World' evokes the
image of Judas, who bartered Jesus, 'a pearl of great price'
(Matthew 13:46), for 'thirty pieces of silver' (Matthew
26:15). Shortly before they describe Judas' betrayal, the
Gospels tell of a woman who came with 'an alabaster box of
very precious ointment, and poured it on [Jesus'] head as he
sat at meat'. Jesus explained to his disciples that 'she did it for
my burial' (Matthew 26:7–12). See the notes to lines 5, 64,
and to IV.iii.67.

144 **Iterance** repetition.

145 **made Mocks with** made a mockery of. *Mocks* recalls IV.i.62,
72. *Mistress* echoes line 118 and recalls V.i.95–96, 100, 120.

147 **Dost . . . Word?** Othello's question is to the point in a way he
doesn't realize. He himself has just given the word *Husband*
one definition with his actions; but what he says about Iago
makes the word seem even more 'pernicious' (line 149), an
adjective whose root meaning is 'killing thoroughly'.
Aemilia's dawning recognition of who her 'Husband' has been
parallels line 96, where Othello suddenly realizes he has 'no
Wife'.

AEMILIA   Oh the more Angel she,
  And you the blacker Divel.
OTHELLO   She turn'd to Folly:
  And she was a Whore.
AEMILIA   Thou dost belie her,
  And thou art a Divel.
OTHELLO   She was false
  As Water.
AEMILIA   Thou art rash as Fire, to say   130
  That she was false. Oh she was Heavenly True.
OTHELLO   Cassio did top her: ask thy Husband
    else.
  O, I were damn'd beneath all Depth in Hell
  But that I did proceed upon Just Grounds
  To this Extremity. Thy Husband knew it all.   135
AEMILIA   My Husband?
OTHELLO   Thy Husband.
AEMILIA   That she was false to Wedlock?
OTHELLO   Ay, with Cassio. Nay, had she been true,
  If Heaven would make me such another World,
  Of one entire and perfect Chrysolite,
  I'd not have sold her for it.
AEMILIA   My Husband?
OTHELLO   Ay,   140
  'Twas he that told me on her first.
  An Honest Man he is, and hates the Slime
  That sticks on Filthy Deeds.
AEMILIA   My Husband?
OTHELLO   What needs
  This Iterance, Woman? I say, thy Husband.
AEMILIA   — Oh Mistress, Villainy hath made Mocks
    with Love.   145
  — My Husband say she was false?
OTHELLO   He, Woman;
  I say thy Husband. Dost understand the Word?
  My Friend, thy Husband; honest, honest Iago.
AEMILIA   If he say so, may his pernicious Soul
  Rot half a Grain a Day: he lies to th' Heart,   150

151 **She . . . Bargain** She was too foolishly attached to the foul transaction she made when she contracted herself to you.

154 **you were best** you would be well advised. Compare line 300.

155 **Powre** power. Compare IV.iii.88, V.ii.211.

156 **Gull** dupe. Aemilia tells Othello that *he* 'turn'd to Folly'.

157 **ignorant** naïve, gullible. See the note to IV.ii.68.

158 **make thee known** expose you as a murderer. See the note to line 40. *Deed* echoes lines 119–20, 142–43.

160 **The . . . Mistress** Aemilia's outcry recalls the earlier ones that have been instigated by her husband; see the note to V.i.62. For the first time in the play, however, the person who rouses the town is doing so with worthy motives. Up to this point Aemilia has resembled Iago more than Desdemona. She has reflected much of his worldly cynicism. She has been a trifle obtuse about the possible consequences of giving her husband Desdemona's handkerchief. She has even lied when her mistress asked where she might have lost the handkerchief (see III.iv.24–25). But now any loyalty to her husband and any instinct for self-preservation have vanished. Aemilia disregards Othello's threats (lines 154–59), and she is prepared to forsake her wedding vows and expose her spouse if he turns out to be guilty of instigating her mistress's murder. *Mistress* echoes line 145.

165 **if . . . Man** This phrasing would normally mean 'if you have the courage to prove your masculinity' (see the note to II.iii.127). But here her words suggest a moral and spiritual distinction between a man and either a beast (such as the 'inhumane Dog' Iago has been called in V.i.60) or a devil.

170 **apt** credible, plausible. Compare II.i.302, II.iii.330–33.

176 **charm** control, as with a magical spell. See the note to V.i.35. *Go to* (come now, hush) recalls IV.ii.191.

177 **bound** obliged. Aemilia is asserting that her bond to Desdemona now takes precedence over her matrimonial bonds. Compare I.iii.177–87, III.i.58–59, and III.iii.131–32, 190–91, 208–9, 468.

She was too fond of her most filthy Bargain.

OTHELLO   Hah?

AEMILIA   Do thy worst:
This Deed of thine is no more worthy Heaven
Than thou wast worthy her.

OTHELLO   Peace, you were best.

AEMILIA   Thou hast not half that Powre to do me
  Harm   155
  As I have to be hurt. Oh Gull, oh Dolt,
  As ignorant as Dirt: thou hast done a Deed —
  I care not for thy Sword — I'll make thee known,
  Though I lost twenty Lives. — Help, help, ho, help:
  The Moor hath kill'd my Mistress. Murther,
    Murther.   160

  Enter Montano, Gratiano, and Iago [with Others].

MONTANO   What is the matter? How now, General?

AEMILIA   Oh, are you come, Iago? You have done well,
  That Men must lay their Murthers on your Neck.

GRATIANO   What is the matter?

AEMILIA   Disprove this Villain, if thou be'st
  a Man: 165
  He says thou told'st him that his Wife was
    false.
  I know thou didst not: thou'rt not such a
    Villain.
  Speak, for my Heart is full.

IAGO   I told him what I thought, and told no more
  Than what he found himself was apt and true.   170

AEMILIA   But did you ever tell him she was false?

IAGO   I did.

AEMILIA   You told a Lie, an odious damned Lie:
  Upon my Soul, a Lie, a wicked Lie.
  She false with Cassio? Did you say with Cassio?   175

IAGO   With Cassio, Mistress. Go to, charm your
    Tongue.

AEMILIA   I will not charm my Tongue; I am bound
    to speak,

179   **forefend**   forfend; forbid, defend. Compare line 33.

181   **stare**   look at me in amazement. Compare V.i.102.

182   **strange**   incredible, amazing. Compare I.iii.158.

183   **monstrous**   This word has occurred on a number of previous occasions (see I.iii.411, II.i.13, II.iii.220, and III.iii.104–5, 161–63, 367, 416), and here as before it applies to something so extraordinary in its perversity as to suggest an ominous disruption in the cosmic order.

184   **I**   both 'I' and 'Ay', as in lines 24, 27, 35, 53, 292.

187   **What . . . mad?**   Iago's question recalls Othello's statement to Desdemona in IV.i.243. What Iago means is 'crazy', of course; but *mad* could also mean 'infuriated' in the modern sense, and that sense is applicable to Aemilia's rage. *Charge* (command), line 187, recalls II.iii.181, V.i.115.

188   **leave**   permission, liberty.

189   **'Tis . . . now**   It would ordinarily be a wife's place to obey her husband, but not in circumstances when he has done such violence to the very institution of matrimony (compare lines 147, 177). *Proper* recalls IV.iii.33.

193   **lift up Eye**   Aemilia probably means 'raise her eyes to Heaven in prayer'. But the phrase she uses could also apply to the wanton eye of the 'foul' woman Othello thought Desdemona to be. Compare II.i.229, 249–52, II.iii.22–23, and V.i.35. Here *ere* can mean both (a) before, and (b) e'er (ever). Compare IV.ii.149.

196   **shews**   shows, appears to be. Compare III.iv.96, IV.ii.218, 245–48. *Stopp'd* (line 195) echoes line 72.

198   **mortal**   fatal. This is Brabantio's most sympathetic moment, and one that is made even more poignant by the truncated form of his daughter's name in line 197; see the note to line 26.

199   **Shore**   sheared, cut.

200   **do . . . Turn**   commit suicide. *Turn* echoes line 127.

201   **curse . . . side**   This line recalls Othello's resolve to dismiss 'Patience' in favour of vengeance (IV.ii.45–62). It also reminds us that in another sense Desdemona was Othello's 'Better Angel' (compare line 126) and that in cursing her from his side to make room for Iago (III.iii.442–51) the Moor has fallen 'to Reprobance' (line 202), reprobation or damnation. *Pitiful* (line 203) recalls IV.i.201–2.

My Mistress here lies murthered in her Bed.
ALL   Oh Heavens, forefend.
AEMILIA   And your Reports have set the Murder on.   180
OTHELLO   Nay stare not, Masters, it is true
    indeed.
GRATIANO   'Tis a strange Truth.
MONTANO   O monstrous Act.
AEMILIA   Villainy, Villainy, Villainy:
    I think upon't, I think, I smell't: O Villainy.
    I thought so then. I'll kill my self for Grief.   185
    O Villainy! Villainy!
IAGO   What, are you mad? I charge you get you Home.
AEMILIA   Good Gentlemen, let me have leave to
    speak.
    'Tis proper I obey him; but not now.
    – Perchance, Iago, I will ne'er go home.   190
OTHELLO   Oh, oh, oh.   *Othello falls on the Bed.*
AEMILIA   Nay, lay thee down, and roar:
    For thou hast kill'd the sweetest Innocent
    That ere did lift up Eye.
OTHELLO   Oh she was foul!
    – I scarce did know you, Uncle, there lies
    your Niece,
    Whose Breath indeed these Hands have newly
    stopp'd: 195
    I know this Act shews horrible and grim.
GRATIANO   Poor Desdemon: I am glad thy
    Father's dead.
    Thy Match was mortal to him: and pure Grief
    Shore his old Thread in twain. Did he live now,
    This Sight would make him do a Desperate Turn: 200
    Yea, curse his Better Angel from his side,
    And fall to Reprobance.
OTHELLO   'Tis pitiful: but yet Iago knows

204   **Shame**   dishonour, disgrace. Compare I.i.85, I.iii.316–18, II.iii.165, 171, 175, IV.ii.45–51, V.ii.215. *Act* recalls IV.ii.150, 159–61.

206   **gratify . . . Works**   reward him for his lovemaking labours. Compare III.iii.241–44.

207   **Recognizance**   remembrance, love-token. Compare III.iii.285–88, III.iv.177.

211   **Powres**   powers. Compare line 155.

213   **as . . . North**   as unrestrainedly as the North Wind. Aemilia gives *liberal* a connotation very different from that associated with it in II.i.165–66 and III.iv.39, 47. Othello has earlier depicted the wind as so 'bawdy' that it 'kisses all it meets', but yet as too modest to 'hear' of Desdemona's deeds (IV.ii.76–78). Now Aemilia announces that it will be released from 'the hollow Mine of Earth' (IV.ii.77) to proclaim the far more shameful deeds of Iago.

216   **Be wise**   take prudent measures to save your own skin. Compare IV.i.238. When Aemilia defies Iago yet again, he draws on her and has to be restrained (line 217).

221   **Trifle**   Aemilia's noun recalls Iago's remarks in III.iii.312–14; compare I.i.129–31.

226   **Coxcomb**   fool. Aemilia's term derives from the red crest atop the cap of a professional jester.

227–   **Are . . . Thunder?**   Othello's ultimate question (which echoes
28   that of Job) is how Heaven could have permitted such an injustice as Iago's crime to be committed. But Othello also means that if he had one of Heaven's lightning bolts, he would use it like Zeus the Thunderbearer. *Stones* (here the boulders suggested by thunder) echoes a number of previous passages, among them lines 64, 139.

231   **I, I**   both (a) 'I, I', and (b) 'Ay, ay'. Compare line 184.
       oh . . . side   Aemilia's last request is in keeping with the conversion she has experienced. Unlike Othello, who has turned from Desdemona to Iago, Aemilia has been transformed from Iago's wife into a martyred servant of Desdemona and her gracious spirit. See II.i.164–65.

That she with Cassio hath the Act of Shame
A thousand times committed. Cassio confess'd it,   205
And she did gratify his Amorous Works
With that Recognizance and Pledge of Love
Which I first gave her. I saw it in his Hand:
It was a Handkerchief, an antique Token
My Father gave my Mother.   210
AEMILIA   Oh Heaven, oh Heavenly Powres!
IAGO   Come, hold your Peace.
AEMILIA   'Twill out, 'twill out. I Peace?
No, I will speak as liberal as the North;
Let Heaven, and Men, and Divels, let them all,
All, all, cry Shame against me, yet I'll speak.   215
IAGO   Be wise, and get you Home.
AEMILIA   I will not.
GRATIANO   — Fie,
Your Sword upon a Woman.
AEMILIA   Oh thou dull Moor, that Handkerchief
     thou speak'st of
I found by Fortune, and did give my Husband:
For often, with a solemn Earnestness   220
(More than indeed belong'd to such a Trifle),
He begg'd of me to steal't.
IAGO   Villainous Whore.
AEMILIA   She give it Cassio? No, alas, I found it,
And I did give't my Husband.
IAGO   Filth, thou liest.
AEMILIA   — By Heaven I do not, I do not,
     Gentlemen.   225
— Oh murd'rous Coxcomb, what should such a Fool
Do with so good a Wife?
OTHELLO   Are there no Stones
In Heaven but what serves for the Thunder?
— Precious Villain.   *The Moor runs at Iago.*
                                   Iago stabs his Wife.
GRATIANO   The Woman falls: sure he hath kill'd
     his Wife.   *Exit Iago.*   230
AEMILIA   I, I: oh lay me by my Mistress' side.

235–36 **Come . . . rather** Guard the door to keep Othello from leaving.

237 **I . . . neither** I've lost my valour as well as my wife.

238 **puny Whipster** novice whipper. Othello may be thinking of (a) petty officers who flogged thieves and whores, (b) carters and drovers who used whips to drive their horses and mules, or (c) boys whipping their tops to make them spin. In any event, his image is a reminder that he has declined dramatically from the kind of soldier who once commanded the swords of his adversaries without even drawing his own (I.ii.59–61). His words anticipate lines 271–75.

244 **Bliss** blessing; Heaven. *Bode* (line 240) echoes IV.iii.55–56.

247 **the Ice-brook's Temper** its steel made hard and durable by ice-water. Compare Othello's phrasing in III.iii.442–49.

249 **dear** dearly, grievously.

250 **perforce must suffer** will be forced to suffer for it.

252 **naked** unarmed, reduced to defencelessness.

258 **your Stop** the obstacle you represent. Compare lines 72–73. *Impediments* (line 257) recalls II.i.289–94.
vain empty, idle; presumptuous.

259 **Who . . . Fate?** Othello implies that no one has any power to affect his or her fortune or destiny. Most Elizabethans would have seen his assertion as at best a half-truth. To some degree, they would have agreed, everyone is subject to circumstances beyond his or her control; at the same time, however, they would have said that everyone is responsible for the way he or she responds to those circumstances. As Iago points out in I.iii.319–35, 'Our Bodies are our Gardens, to the which our Wills are Gardeners.' And 'we have Reason to cool our raging Motions, our carnal Stings, or unbitted Lusts'. If, like Cassio in II.iii and Othello in III.iii, we fail to use our reason properly, we put our wills and our bodies at the mercy of destructive 'Motions' that will become their 'Fate'. *Boast* recalls I.ii.20–21; *Fate* echoes lines 21, 38–39.

260 **weapon'd** with a weapon. Compare 'woman'd' in III.iv.186.

GRATIANO   He's gone, but his Wife's kill'd.

MONTANO   'Tis a notorious Villain: take you this
   Weapon
Which I have here recover'd from the Moor.
Come, guard the Door without, let them not pass,   235
But kill him rather. I'll after that same
   Villain,
For 'tis a damned Slave.

                      Exeunt Montano and Gratiano.

OTHELLO   — I am not Valiant neither:
But every puny Whipster gets my Sword.
But why should Honour outlive Honesty?
Let it go all.

AEMILIA   — What did thy Song bode, Lady?   240
Hark, canst thou hear me? I will play the Swan,
And die in Music: *Willow, Willow, Willow*.
— Moor, she was chaste: she lov'd thee, cruel
   Moor,
So come my Soul to Bliss, as I speak true:
So speaking as I think, alas, I die.   *She dies.* 245

OTHELLO   — I have another Weapon in this Chamber,
It was a Sword of Spain, the Ice-brook's
   Temper:
Oh here it is. — Uncle, I must come forth.

GRATIANO   If thou attempt it, it will cost thee
   dear;
Thou hast no Weapon, and perforce must suffer.   250

OTHELLO   Look in upon me then, and speak with me,
Or naked as I am I will assault thee.

GRATIANO   What is the matter?

OTHELLO   Behold, I have a Weapon:
A better never did it self sustain
Upon a Soldier's Thigh. I have seen the Day   255
That with this little Arm, and this good Sword,
I have made my way through more Impediments
Than twenty times your Stop. But, oh vain Boast,
Who can control his Fate? 'Tis not so now.
Be not afraid, though you do see me weapon'd: 260

261 **Butt** target (in archery).

262 **And . . . Sail** and the beacon marking the entrance into my final harbour.

263 **lost** wasted; unnecessary. Compare IV.ii.147–48, V.ii.158–59.

264– **Man . . . retires** if you should mount a quick attack on me, I
65 would be forced either (a) to beat a hasty retreat, or (b) to conclude my military career forever (see III.iii.337–47).

266 **ill-Starr'd** doomed by a malign influence from the stars and planets ('Star-cross'd', *Romeo and Juliet*, Prologue, line 6). *Starr'd* echoes lines 1–3, and it indicates once more that Othello is inclined to blame 'Fate' (line 259) rather than himself for what has befallen Desdemona.

267 **Compt** account (the Last Judgement). Compare I.iii.5, II.i.308. *Pale* echoes V.i.99–100. *Smock* (woman's undergarment) here refers to Desdemona's 'Nightly Wearing' (IV.iii.14).

273 **Sulphur** the 'Fire and Brimstone' (IV.i.238) of Hell.

274 **Steep-down Gulfs** deep and precipitous whirlpools. *Desdemon* (line 275) echoes line 197.

277 **That's . . . am** You refer to the man who was Othello; here is someone other than that person. See the notes to IV.i.274–76. *Rash* (impulsively violent) echoes line 130.

278 **Viper** a small poisonous snake. Compare III.iii.439.

279 **I . . . Feet** Othello means that he is looking at Iago's feet to see if they are the cloven hooves of the Devil.

282 **I . . . kill'd** The 'Divel' speaks this sentence tauntingly.

284 **in my Sense** as I view the matter, given the agony I feel. Compare I.iii.12, III.iii.328, and V.i.31–33.

286 **Fall'n . . . Slave** brought low through the intrigue of a base villain. *Practice* recalls III.iv.134.

Here is my Journey's End, here is my Butt
And very Sea-mark of my utmost Sail.
Do you go back dismay'd? 'Tis a lost Fear:
Man but a Rush against Othello's Breast,
And he retires. Where should Othello go?   265
– Now: how dost thou look now? Oh ill-Starr'd
   Wench,
Pale as thy Smock: when we shall meet at Compt,
This Look of thine will hurl my Soul from
   Heaven,
And Fiends will snatch at it. Cold, cold, my
   Girl?
Even like thy Chastity.   270
– O cursed, cursed Slave! – Whip me, ye Divels,
From the Possession of this Heavenly Sight:
Blow me about in Winds, roast me in Sulphur,
Wash me in Steep-down Gulfs of liquid Fire.
– Oh Desdemon! Dead Desdemon: dead. Oh, oh!   275

Enter Lodovico, Montano, Iago, and Officers,
Cassio in a Chair.

LODOVICO   Where is this rash, and most
   unfortunate Man?
OTHELLO   That's he that was Othello: here I am.
LODOVICO   Where is that Viper? Bring the
   Villain forth.
OTHELLO   I look down towards his Feet; but
   that's a Fable.
   – If that thou be'st a Divel, I cannot kill thee.
                               [*He stabs Iago.*]   280
LODOVICO   Wrench his Sword from him.
IAGO   I bleed, Sir, but not kill'd.
OTHELLO   I am not sorry neither, I'd have thee
   live:
   For in my Sense, 'tis Happiness to die.
LODOVICO   Oh thou Othello, that was once so good,   285
   Fall'n in the Practice of a cursed Slave,
   What shall be said to thee?

288   **A honourable Murderer**   What Othello says is true in at least two ways: (a) he honestly believed that his wife and his former lieutenant had committed adultery, and (b) he was persuaded by Iago that the only way he could restore his own reputation was to murder those who had sullied it. Tragically, the kind of honour Desdemona has won Othello has sold to the Devil.

289   **nought . . . Honour**   nothing I did was motivated by malice, but only by the dictates of honour and the 'Justice' it demanded (see lines 17–18). *Nought* (naught, nothing) recalls I.i.47, 162, IV.ii.183–84; see the note to III.iii.99. *Did* echoes lines 119–20.

290   **part**   in part.

292   **I**   both 'ay' and 'I' [did]. Compare lines 184, 231.

293   **Cause**   reason, justification. This word reverberates with the implications it has accumulated in such previous passages as V.ii.1–3.

295   **demand**   ask, question.

296   **ensnar'd**   Othello's verb recalls the 'Net' (II.iii.373) and 'Web' (III.iv.69) that Iago has used as weapons. *Know* (line 297) echoes lines 40, 158.

300   **thou dost best**   you are probably wise (compare line 154). Othello implies that crimes so unspeakable as Iago's are best contemplated in an appalled silence. *Lips* (line 299) echoes line 44.

304   **imports**   conveys instructions for. Compare IV.ii.29.

306   **gross**   (a) foul, monstrous, and (b) flagrant. Compare IV.iii.60.

307   **discontented Paper**   letter expressing Roderigo's discontent with the way Iago has mistreated him and challenging Iago to a duel.

310   **belike**   in all likelihood. *Interim* recalls I.iii.253–56.

311   **Came . . . him**   stepped in and addressed his complaints. Here *satisfi'd* is a euphemism for 'stabbed'. See the notes to IV.ii.202 and V.i.9, and compare IV.ii.202, 251–52.

314   **Wive's**   wife's. *Pernicious* (line 312) echoes lines 149–50.

OTHELLO   Why any thing;
   An honourable Murderer, if you will:
   For nought I did in Hate, but all in Honour.
LODOVICO   This Wretch hath part confess'd his
     Villainy: 290
   Did you and he consent in Cassio's Death?
OTHELLO   I.
CASSIO   Dear General, I never gave you Cause.
OTHELLO   I do believe it, and I ask your Pardon:
   Will you, I pray, demand that demi-Divel   295
   Why he hath thus ensnar'd my Soul and Body.
IAGO   Demand me nothing: what you know, you know.
   From this time forth, I never will speak Word.
LODOVICO   What? Not to pray?
GRATIANO   Torments will ope your Lips.
OTHELLO   Well, thou dost best.   300
LODOVICO   Sir, you shall understand what hath
     befall'n,
   Which, as I think, you know not. Here is a
     Letter
   Found in the Pocket of the slain Roderigo,
   And here another; the one of them imports
   The Death of Cassio, to be undertook   305
   By Roderigo.
OTHELLO   O Villain!
CASSIO   Most Heathenish, and most gross.
LODOVICO   Now here's another discontented Paper
   Found in his Pocket too: and this it seems
   Roderigo meant t' have sent this damned Villain,
   But that, belike, Iago in the Interim   310
   Came in and satisfi'd him.
OTHELLO   Oh thou pernicious Caitiff.
   – How came you, Cassio, by that Handkerchief
   That was my Wive's?

317   **wrought ... Desire** worked to advance what he wanted to accomplish. The word *wrought* will recur in line 339, and it goes a long way towards summing up Iago's role in the action. It also defines the completion of a circle. In I.iii.105, Brabantio has charged that Othello 'wrought upon' Desdemona: fortunately, the old man didn't live to see that what he spoke would prove true in an even grimmer sense. *Purpose* (line 316) recalls IV.ii.217–18; *confess'd* (line 315) echoes lines 69, 290.

320   **Brave** defy, insult.

321   **cast** cast off; removed from office. See II.iii.277.

325   **taken off** divested (like a garment).

327   **cunning** well-crafted. Since Iago has himself engaged in 'Cruelty' that fits various senses of *cunning* (see IV.ii.87), this sentence is exquisitely appropriate. Compare III.iii.46–48, V.ii.11.

329   **You ... rest** you shall remain under tight security. *Fault* (line 330), offence, recalls IV.iii.86–87.

335   **unlucky** unfortunate. Here again Othello's wording would appear to place the blame for his 'Deeds' on ill fortune rather than on his own agency. See the notes to lines 259, 266, 277.

336   **as I am** Othello has used similar phrasing in line 277; compare II.ii.123–24, IV.i.274–76.

337   **ought** aught; anything. Compare III.iii.99–101, and see line 289.

340   **Perplexed** bewildered (literally, 'twisted thoroughly', wrought). *Extreme* recalls lines 133–35; *wrought* (line 339) echoes line 317.

341   **base Judean** Most editions adopt the Quarto's 'base Indian' (referring to an ignorant savage); the Folio reading, which may result from an authorial revision, suggests the low-minded Judas, who squandered 'a pearl of great price' (see the note to line 139, and compare I.i.10) and lost his soul. The word 'Tribe' (line 342) could refer to a group of any kind; Iago uses the word in I.iii.362 and III.iii.171.

342   **subdu'd** humbled; dew-filled. Compare III.iv.59–60. *Eyes* recalls V.ii.38–39, 191–93.

343   **unus'd ... Mood** unaccustomed to emotional states that cause them to dissolve. *Unus'd* echoes line 71; *melting* recalls II.i.8; *Mood* harks back to II.iii.277.

CASSIO   I found it in my Chamber:
  And he himself confess'd it but even now   315
  That there he dropp'd it for a special Purpose,
  Which wrought to his Desire.
OTHELLO   — O Fool, Fool, Fool!
CASSIO There is besides, in Roderigo's Letter,
  How he upbraids Iago, that he made him
  Brave me upon the Watch: whereon it came   320
  That I was cast. And even but now he spake,
  After long seeming dead, Iago hurt him,
  Iago set him on.
LODOVICO You must forsake this Room, and go
    with us:
  Your Power and your Command is taken off,   325
  And Cassio rules in Cyprus. For this Slave,
  If there be any cunning Cruelty
  That can torment him much, and hold him long,
  It shall be his. You shall close Prisoner rest,
  Till that the nature of your Fault be known   330
  To the Venetian State. — Come, bring away.
OTHELLO Soft you; a Word or two before you go.
  I have done the State some Service, and they
    know't:
  No more of that. I pray you in your Letters,
  When you shall these unlucky Deeds relate,   335
  Speak of me as I am. Nothing extenuate,
  Nor set down ought in Malice. Then must you
    speak
  Of one that lov'd not wisely, but too well;
  Of one not easily jealous, but, being wrought,
  Perplexed in the extreme; of one whose Hand,   340
  Like the base Judean, threw a Pearl away
  Richer than all his Tribe; of one whose subdu'd
    Eyes,
  Albeit unus'd to the melting Mood,

345   **Medicinable Gum** medicinal resin. Othello probably refers to the balm of the balsam tree, a fragrant juice associated with physical healing and spiritual renewal. See the note to line 17. *Medicinable* recalls III.iii.320–23, IV.i.46–47.

346   **Aleppo** a city in Turkey, where it was a capital crime for a Christian to strike, let alone kill, a Turk.

347   **malignant . . . Turk** malicious and turban-attired Turk. For Shakespeare's European contemporaries the turban signified a defiance of all things Christian.

348   **traduc'd the State** insulted Venice (and hence Christendom).

349   **circumcised Dog** The word *Dog* recalls Roderigo's epithet for Iago in V.i.60; in the process it suggests that in recalling what he did to the Turk, Othello is symbolically slaying the 'inhumane' wretch who has brought him to this new 'Aleppo'. The adjective *circumcised* was applied contemptuously to both Turks and Jews, and it symbolized the stubborn infidelity of those who refused the 'circumcision of Christ', a spiritual operation 'made without hands, in putting off the body of the sins of the flesh' (Colossians 2:11). Othello is implicitly acknowledging that he himself has 'turn'd Turk' (II.iii.173); the 'Hellish' Iago (line 362) has driven the Moor to 'renounce his Baptism' (II.iii.355) like the 'base Judean' (line 341). Compare Matthew 27:3–5.

351   **Period** conclusion (here the punctuation at the end of Othello's speech). *Bloody* recalls V.i.35–36; compare I.iii.66, II.iii.187, III.iii.446, 458, IV.i.93–94, V.i.61, 89–90, V.ii.45. *Marr'd* (disfigured, undone) echoes V.i.4.

355   **Spartan Dog** both (a) a fierce breed of dogs from Sparta, and (b) a harsh, flint-like, cruel Spartan. Lodovico addresses Iago. *Dog* echoes line 349. *Work* (line 357) recalls I.iii.397–99, II.i.116, II.iii.385–86, III.iii.118–21, 290–91, 371–73, III.iv.70–72, 179–80, IV.i.46–47, 154–56, 278–80, V.ii.205–8.

359   **keep** secure, guard.

361   **succeed on you** are to be inherited by you.

362   **Censure** judgement, sentencing. Compare II.iii.194–96, IV.i.274–76.

364   **aboord** aboard. *Straight* echoes line 30; *State* (Venetian ruling body) echoes lines 329–34, 348, and recalls III.iv.133, 148; *heavy* echoes line 97.

Drops Tears as fast as the Arabian Trees
Their Medicinable Gum. Set you down this: 345
And say besides, that in Aleppo once,
Where a malignant and a Turban'd Turk
Beat a Venetian, and traduc'd the State,
I took by th' Throat the circumcised Dog,
And smote him, thus.   *He stabs himself.* 350
LODOVICO   Oh bloody Period.
GRATIANO   All that is spoke is marr'd.
OTHELLO   — I kiss'd thee ere I kill'd thee: no
    way but this,
Killing my self, to die upon a Kiss.   *He dies.*
CASSIO   This did I fear, but thought he had no
    Weapon:
For he was great of Heart.
LODOVICO   — Oh Spartan Dog,   355
More fell than Anguish, Hunger, or the Sea,
Look on the Tragic Loading of this Bed:
This is thy Work. — The Object poisons Sight,
Let it be hid. — Gratiano, keep the House,
And seize upon the Fortunes of the Moor,   360
For they succeed on you. — To you, Lord
    Governor,
Remains the Censure of this Hellish Villain:
The Time, the Place, the Torture, oh enforce it.
My self will straight aboord, and to the State
This heavy Act with heavy Heart relate.   *Exeunt.* 365

FINIS

PERSPECTIVES ON OTHELLO

Extended commentary on *Othello*, and indeed on Shakespeare generally, began in the final decade of the seventeenth century when a historian and literary critic named Thomas Rymer published *A Short View of Tragedy* (London, 1692). A strict neoclassicist,* Rymer assailed his eminent predecessor for a wanton disregard of the 'rules' that were thought to give dramatic works verisimilitude and instruct audiences in 'poetic justice' (a rational distribution of rewards and punishments that represented the cosmos as designed and controlled by a benign Providence).

From all the Tragedies acted on our English Stage *Othello* is said to bear the Bell away. The Subject is more of a piece, and there is indeed something like, there is, as it were, some phantom of a Fable. The Fable is always accounted the Soul of Tragedy. And it is the Fable which is properly the Poets part. Because the other three parts of Tragedy, to wit the Characters, are taken from the Moral Philosopher; the Thoughts or scene, from them that teach Rhetorick; and the last part, which is the Expression, we learn from the Grammarians.

This Fable is drawn from a Novel, compos'd in Italian by Giraldi Cinthio, who also was a Writer of Tragedies. And to that use employ'd such of his Tales, as he judged proper for the Stage. But with this of the Moor, he meddl'd no farther.

Shakespear alters it from the Original in several particulars, but always, unfortunately, for the worse. He bestows a name on his Moor; and styles him the Moor of Venice: a Note of pre-eminence, which neither History nor Heraldry can allow him. Cinthio, who

---

* Through an over rigid reading of Aristotle's *Poetics*, many critics (and indeed a prestigious school of playwrights, particularly in Renaissance Italy and France) had concluded that a dramatic work which was formally 'correct' would focus on a single action (with no subplots to distract the audience's attention from the main event), in a single setting, within the confines of a single day. We now refer to those who adhered to the doctrine of 'the three unities' (unity of time, unity of place, and unity of action) as neoclassicists. By the beginning of the eighteenth century they reigned supreme in England.

knew him best, and whose creature he was, calls him simply a Moor. We say the Piper of Strasburgh; the Jew of Florence; and, if you please, the Pindar of Wakefield: all upon Record, and memorable in their Places. But we see no such Cause for the Moors preferment to that dignity. And it is an affront to all Chroniclers, and Antiquaries, to top upon 'um a Moor, who yet had never faln within the Sphere of their Cognisance.

Then is the Moors Wife, from a simple Citizen, in Cinthio, dress'd up with her Top knots, and rais'd to be Desdemona, a Senators Daughter. All this is very strange; and therefore pleases such as reflect not on the improbability. This match might well be without the Parents Consent. Old Horace long ago forbad the Banes [when he said that] 'Savage should not mate with gentle, nor serpents pair with birds, lambs with tigers' [in his] *Ars Poetica.*

What ever rubs or difficulty may stick on the Bark, the Moral, sure, of this Fable is very instructive. First, this may be a caution to all Maidens of Quality how, without their Parents consent, they run away with Black-amoors. Secondly, this may be a warning to all good Wives, that they look well to their Linnen. Thirdly, this may be a lesson to Husbands, that before their Jealousie be Tragical, the proofs may be Mathematical.

Cinthio affirms that *She was not overcome by a Womanish Appetite, but by the Vertue of the Moor.* It must be a good-natur'd Reader that takes Cinthio's word in this case, tho' in a Novel. Shakespear, who is accountable both to the Eyes, and to the Ears, and to convince the very Heart of an Audience, shews that Desdemona was won, by hearing Othello talk. . . . This was the Charm, this was the philtre, the love-powder that took the Daughter of this Noble Venetian. This was sufficient to make the Black-amoor White, and reconcile all, tho' there had been a Cloven-foot into the bargain. . . .

Shakespear in this Play calls 'em the *supersubtle Venetians.* Yet examine throughout the Tragedy there is nothing in the noble Desdemona, that is not below any Countrey Chambermaid with us. . . .

The Character of that State is to employ strangers in their Wars; but shall a Poet thence fancy that they will set a Negro to be their General; or trust a Moor to defend them against the Turk? With us a Black-amoor might rise to be a Trumpeter; but Shakespear would not have him less than Lieutenant-General. With us a Moor might marry some little drab, or Small-coal Wench: Shakespear would provide him the Daughter and Heir of some great Lord, or Privy-Councellor; and all the Town should reckon it a very suitable match. Yet the English are not bred up with that hatred and aversion to the Moors, as are the Venetians, who suffer by a perpetual Hostility from them. . . .

Nothing is more odious in Nature than an improbable lye; and, certainly, never was any Play fraught, like this of *Othello*, with improbabilities.

The Characters or Manners, which are the second part in a Tragedy, are not less unnatural and improper, than the Fable was improbable and absurd.

Othello is made a Venetian General. We see nothing done by him, nor related concerning him, that comports with the condition of a General, or, indeed, of a Man, unless the killing himself, to avoid a death the Law was about to inflict upon him. When his Jealousy had wrought him up to a resolution of's taking revenge for the suppos'd injury, he sets Jago to the fighting part, to kill Cassio; and chuses himself to murder the silly Woman his Wife, that was like to make no resistance.

His Love and his Jealousy are no part of a Souldiers Character, unless for Comedy.

But what is most intolerable is Jago. He is no Black-amoor Souldier, so we may be sure he should be like other Souldiers of our acquaintance; yet never in Tragedy, nor in Comedy, nor in Nature was a Souldier with his Character. . . . Shakespear knew his character of Jago was inconsistent. . . . This he knew, but to entertain the Audience with something new and surprising, against common sense, and Nature, he would pass upon us a close, dissembling, false, insinuating rascal, instead of an open-hearted, frank, plain-dealing Souldier, a character constantly worn by them for some thousands of years in the World. . . .

Nor is our Poet more discreet in his Desdemona. He had chosen a Souldier for his Knave; and a Venetian Lady is to be the Fool. This Senators Daughter runs away to a Carriers Inn, the Sagittary, with a Black-amoor; is no sooner wedded to him, but the very night she Beds him, is importuning and teizing him for a young smock-fac'd Lieutenant, Cassio. And tho' she perceives the Moor Jealous of Cassio, yet will she not forbear, but still rings *Cassio, Cassio* in both his Ears. . . .

In the neighing of an Horse, or in the growling of a Mastiff, there is a meaning, there is as lively expression, and, may I say, more humanity, than many times in the Tragical flights of Shakespear. . . .

Here we see the meanest woman in the Play takes this Handkerchief for a trifle below her Husband to trouble his head about it. Yet we find, it entered into our Poets head, to make a Tragedy of this Trifle. . . .

There is in this Play, some burlesk, some humour, and ramble of Comical Wit, some shew, and some Mimickry to divert the spectators; but the tragical part is, plainly none other, than a Bloody Farce, without salt or savour.

Within two years of Rymer's attack upon the play, a fellow

neoclassicist, Charles Gildon, defended *Othello* from many of his contemporary's charges. By the time Gildon penned his more fully considered *Remarks on the Plays of Shakespear* (London, 1710), however, he had come to see most of the tragedy through the same lens that had refracted Rymer's perception of it.

> If Othello had been made deformed, and not over young but no Black, it had removed most of the Absurdities, but now it pleases only by Prescription. 'Tis possible, that an innocent tender young Woman, who knew little of the World, might be won by the brave Actions of a gallant Man not to regard his Age or Deformities, but Nature, or what is all one in this Case, Custom, having put such a Bar as so opposite a Colour, it takes away our Pity from her, and only raises our Indignation against him. . . . It must be own'd that Shakespear drew Men better than Women; to whom indeed he has seldom given any considerable Place in his Plays; here and in *Romeo and Juliet* he has done most in this matter, but here he has not given any graceful Touches to Desdemona in many places of her Part.
>
> Whether the Motives of Othello's Jealousie be strong enough to free him from the Imputation of Levity and Folly I will not determine; since Jealousie is born often of very slight Occasions, especially in the Breasts of Men of those warmer Climates. Yet this must be said, Shakespear has manag'd the Scene so well, that it is that alone which supports his Play, and imposes on the Audience so very successfully, that till a Reformation of the Stage comes, I believe it will always be kindly receiv'd.

Three years after Gildon's *Remarks* John Hughes wrote an astonishingly sensitive and sympathetic essay on *Othello* for *The Guardian* (April, 1713). After noting that he had long perceived the tragedy as 'a noble but irregular Production of a Genius which had the power of animating the Theatre beyond any writer we have ever known', Hughes observed that

> The chief Subject of this Piece is the Passion of Jealousie, which the Poet has represented at large in its Birth, its various Workings and Agonies, and its horrid Consequences. From this Passion, and the Innocence and Simplicity of the Person suspected, arises a very moving Distress.
>
> It is a Remark, as I remember, of a Modern Writer, who is thought to have penetrated deeply into the Nature of the Passions, that *the most extravagant Love is nearest to the strongest Hatred*. The Moor is furious in both these Extremes. His Love is tempestuous, and mingled with a Wildness peculiar to his Character which seems very artfully to prepare for the Change which is to follow.

How savage, yet how ardent is that Expression of the Raptures of his Heart when, looking after Desdemona as she withdraws, he breaks out,

> Excellent Wretch! Perdition catch my Soul
> But I do love thee; and when I love thee not,
> Chaos is come again.

The deep and subtle Villainy of Iago, in working this Change from Love to Jealousie in so tumultuous a Mind as that of Othello, prepossessed with a Confidence in the disinterested Affection of the Man who is leading him on insensibly to his Ruin, is likewise drawn with a Masterly Hand. Iago's broken Hints, Questions, and seeming Care to hide the Reason of them; his obscure Suggestions to raise the Curiosity of the Moor; his personated Confusion and refusing to explain himself while Othello is drawn on and held in suspence till he grows impatient and angry, then his throwing in the Poyson, and naming to him in a Caution the Passion he would raise

> – O beware of Jealousie!

are inimitable Strokes of Art in that Scene which has always been justly esteemed one of the best which was ever represented on the Theatre.

To return to the Character of Othello; his Strife of Passions, his Starts, his Returns of Love, and Threatnings to Iago who had put his Mind on the Rack; his Relapses afterwards to Jealousie, his Rage against his Wife, and his asking Pardon of Iago, whom he thinks he had abused for his Fidelity to him, are Touches which no one can overlook that has the Sentiments of Human Nature, or has consider'd the Heart of Man in its Frailties, its Penances, and all the Variety of its Agitations. The Torments which the Moor suffers are so exquisitely drawn as to render him as much an Object of Compassion, even in the barbarous Action of murdering Desdemona, as the innocent Person her self who falls under his Hand.

But there is nothing in which the Poet has more shewn his Judgment in this Play, than in the Circumstances of the Handkerchief, which is employ'd as a Confirmation to the Jealousie of Othello already raised. What I would here observe is that the slightness of this Circumstance is the Beauty of it. . . . It would be easie for a tasteless Critick to turn any of the Beauties I have here mentioned into Ridicule; but such an one would only betray a Mechanical Judgment formed out of borrow'd Rules and Commonplace Reading, and not arising from any true Discernment in Human Nature and its Passions.

The Moral of this Tragedy is an admirable Caution against hasty Suspicions and the giving way to the first Transports of Rage and Jealousie, which may plunge a Man in a few Minutes in all the Horrors of Guilt, Distraction and Ruin.

In the wake of Hughes's article, other readers of *Othello* began taking a similar view of the Moor and his calamity. Among the most influential of these commentators was scholar Lewis Theobald, who published an appraisal of Othello in *The Censor* (January 1717):

> I have frequently perus'd with Satisfaction the *Othello* of Shakespeare, a Play most faulty and irregular in many Points but Excellent in one Particular. For the Crimes and Misfortunes of the Moor are owing to an impetuous Desire of having his Doubts clear'd, and a Jealousie and Rage, native to him, which he cannot controul and which push him on to Revenge. He is otherwise in his Character brave and open, generous and full of Love for Desdemona, but stung with the subtle Suggestions of Iago and impatient of a Wrong done to his Love and Honour. Passion at once o'erbears his Reason and gives him up to Thoughts of bloody Reparation. Yet after he has determin'd to murther his Wife his Sentiments of her suppos'd Injury and his Misfortune are so pathetick that we cannot but forget his barbarous Resolution, and pity the Agonies which he so strongly seems to feel.

A decade and a half later, in the notes to *Othello* that accompanied his edition of *The Works of Shakespeare* (London, 1733), Theobald noted that the 'Groundwork' of the play is 'built upon a Novel of Cinthio Giraldi', a writer 'who seems to have design'd his Tale' as 'a Document to young Ladies against disproportion'd Marriages' and a warning that 'they should not link themselves to such, against whom Nature, Providence, and a different way of Living have interpos'd a Bar'.

> Our Poet inculcates no such Moral: but rather, that a Woman may fall in Love with the Virtues and shining Qualities of a Man; and therein overlook the Difference of Complexion and Colour. Mr Rymer has run riot against the Conduct, Manners, Sentiments, and Diction of this Play: but in such a Strain, that one is mov'd rather to laugh at the Freedom and Coarseness of his Raillery, than provok'd to be downright angry at his Censures. . . .
>
> Besides this, let us see how finely the Poet has made his Handkerchief of Significancy and Importance. Cinthio Giraldi, from whom he has borrowed the Incident, only says that it was the Moor's Gift, upon his Wedding, to Desdemona; that it was most curiously wrought after the Moorish Fashion, and very dear both to him and his Wife. . . . But our Author, who wrote in a suspicious Age (when Philtres were in Vogue for procuring Love, and Amulets for preserving it) makes his Handkerchief deriv'd from an Inchantress; Magick and Mystery are

in its Materials and Workmanship; its Qualities and Attributes are solemnly laid down; and the Gift recommended to be cherish'd by its Owners on the most inducing Terms imaginable, *viz.* the making the Party amiable to her Husband, and the keeping his Affections steady. Such Circumstances, if I know any thing of the Matter, are the very Soul and Essence of Poetry: Fancy here exerts its great creating Power, and adds a Dignity, that surprizes, to its Subject.

By the middle of the eighteenth century Charlotte Lennox was following Theobald's lead and comparing *Othello* favourably with the source from which Shakespeare had drawn his principal plot. In *Shakespear Illustrated* (London, 1753–54), Lennox noted that

In Cinthio the Moor is mentioned without any Mark of Distinction; Shakespear makes him descended from a Race of Kings; his Person is therefore made more considerable in the Play than in the Novel, and the dignity which the Venetian Senate bestows upon him is less to be wondered at. . . .

Cinthio might perhaps think it necessary to give his Villain a pleasing Person and insinuating Address, in order to make his Artifices less suspected; but to give Probability to the Jealousy of the Moor, was it not also as necessary to make the suspected Rival possess some of those Qualities with which the Minds of young Ladies are soonest captivated. Shakespear therefore paints Cassio young, handsome, and brave; and Othello, who feeds his Jealousy by reflecting that he himself is neither young nor handsome, by the same Train of Thought falls naturally into a Suspicion that what he loses for want of those Qualities will be gained by another who possesses them.

But on the other hand Shakespear has made a very ill Use of the Lieutenant's Wife. Cinthio shews this Woman privy, much against her Will, to the Design on Desdemona; and though she dares not discover it to her, for fear of her Husband's Resentment, yet she endeavours to put her upon her Guard, and gives her such Advice as she thinks will render all his Schemes ineffectual. Shakespear calls this Woman Emilia, and makes her the Attendant and Friend of Desdemona, yet shews her stealing a Handkerchief from her, which she gives to her Husband, telling him at the same Time that the Lady will run mad when she misses it; therefore, if it is not for some Purpose of Importance that he wants it, desires him to return it to her again. If her Husband wants it for any Purpose of Importance, that Purpose cannot be very good; this Suspicion however never enters her Mind, but she gives it him only upon that very Condition which ought to have made her refuse it. Yet this Woman is the first who perceives Othello to be jealous, and repeats this Observation to her Mistress, upon hearing him so often demand the Handkerchief she had stolen, and fly into a

Rage when he finds his Wife cannot produce it. Emilia pronounces him jealous, perceives the Loss of that fatal Handkerchief, confirms some Suspicions he had entertained, and though she loves her Mistress to Excess, chuses rather to let her suffer all the bad Consequences of his Jealousy, than confess she had taken the Handkerchief, which might have set all right again; and yet this same Woman, who could act so base and cruel a Part against her Mistress, has no greater Care in dying, than to be laid by her Side.

Responding to Thomas Rymer's assertion that Desdemona's affection for Othello 'is out of Nature', Lennox allowed that

Such Affections are not very common indeed; but a very few Instances of them prove that they are not impossible; and even in England we see some very handsome Women married to Blacks, where their Colour is less familiar than at Venice; besides the Italian Ladies are remarkable for such Sallies of irregular Passions. Cinthio, it is true, says that Desdemona was not overcome by a womanish Appetite, but represents her, as Shakespear does likewise, subdued by the great Qualities of the Moor. . . .

The Outlines of Iago, Desdemona, and Cassio's Characters are taken from the Novel; but that of Othello is entirely the Poet's own. In Cinthio we have a Moor, valiant indeed, as we are told, but suspicious, sullen, cunning, obstinate and cruel. Such a Character married to the fair Desdemona must have given Disgust on the Stage; the Audience would have been his Enemies, and Desdemona herself would have sunk into Contempt for chusing him. With that Judgment then has Shakespear changed the horrid Moor of Cinthio into the amiable Othello, and made the same Action which we detest in one, excite our Compassion in the other!

The Virtues of Shakespear's Moor are no less characteristic than the Vices of Cinthio's; they are the wild Growth of an uncultivated Mind, barbarous and rude as the Clime he is born in; thus, his Love is almost Phrensy; his Friendship Simplicity; his Justice cruel; and his Remorse Self-Murder.

The greatest of the eighteenth-century critics shared Charlotte Lennox's high opinion of *Othello*. In the comments upon the play that accompanied his edition of Shakespeare's works (London, 1765), Samuel Johnson declared that the 'beauties' of the drama 'impress themselves so strongly upon the attention of the reader, that they can draw no aid from critical illustration'. According to Johnson

The fiery openness of Othello, magnanimous, artless, and credulous, boundless in his confidence, ardent in his affection, inflexible in his resolution, and obdurate in his revenge; the cool malignity of Iago, silent in his resentment, subtle in his designs, and studious at once of his interest and his vengeance; the soft simplicity of Desdemona, confident of merit, and conscious of innocence, her artless persever-ance in her suit, and her slowness to suspect that she can be suspected, are such proofs of Shakespeare's skill in human nature, as, I suppose, it is vain to seek in any modern writer. The gradual progress which Iago makes in the Moor's conviction, and the circumstances which he employs to inflame him, are so artfully natural, that, though it will perhaps not be said of him as he says of himself, that he is 'a man not easily jealous', yet we cannot but pity him when at last we find him 'perplexed in the extreme'. . . .

The scenes from the beginning to the end are busy, varied by happy interchanges, and regularly promoting the progress of the story; and the narrative in the end, though it tells but what is known already, yet is necessary to produce the death of Othello.

Had the scene opened in Cyprus, and the preceding incidents been occasionally related, there had been little wanting to a drama of the most exact and scrupulous regularity.

By 1808, when Samuel Taylor Coleridge began a decade of lectures and incidental remarks on *Othello* and other works – quoted here from the second edition of Thomas Middleton Raysor's collection of the poet's *Shakespearean Criticism* (London, 1960) – the inductive exegetical approaches of German Romantics such as August Wilhelm Schlegel had begun to undermine the stern, deductic orthodoxy of the seventeenth- and eighteenth-century theorists. But it took a writer of Coleridge's insight and eloquence to demolish what remained of the neoclassi-cism that had long been used to denigrate Shakespeare's flexible artistry.

Dr. Johnson has remarked that little or nothing is wanting to render the *Othello* a regular tragedy but to have opened the play with the arrival of Othello in Cyprus, and to have thrown the preceding act into the form of narration. Here then is the place to determine whether such a change would or would not be an improvement, nay (to throw down the glove with a full challenge), whether or no the tragedy would by such an arrangement become *more regular*; i.e., more consonant with the rules dictated by universal reason or the true common sense of mankind in its application to the particular case. For surely we may safely leave it to common sense whether to reply to or laugh at such a remark as, for instance – suppose a man had described a rhomboid or parallelogram and a critic were with great gravity to observe, 'If the lines had only been in true right angles, or if the horizontal parallels had been but of the same length as the two perpendicular parallels that form the sides, the diagram would have been according to the strictest rules of geometry.' For in all acts of judgement it [can] never be too often recollected and scarcely too often repeated, that rules are means to ends, – consequently, that the end must be determined and understood before it can be known what the rules are or ought to be.

To Coleridge we are also indebted for a description of Iago's soliloquy at the end of Act I, scene iii as 'the motive-hunting of motiveless malignity'; for the author of 'The Rime of the Ancient Mariner', as for later interpreters of *Othello*, Iago was best summed up as 'fiendish' – 'a being next to devil, only *not* quite devil'.

For one of Coleridge's contemporaries, Charles Lamb, it was difficult if not impossible to countenance a performance of the drama. In his work *On the Tragedies of Shakespeare, Considered with Reference to their Fitness for Stage Representation* (London, 1811), Lamb wrote that

Nothing can be more soothing, more flattering to the nobler parts of our natures, than to read of a young Venetian lady of highest extraction, through the force of love and from a sense of merit in him whom she loved, laying aside every consideration of kindred, and country, and colour, and wedding with *a coal-black Moor* – (for such he is represented, in the imperfect state of knowledge respecting foreign countries in those days, compared with our own, or in compliance with popular notions, though the Moors are now well enough known to be by many shades less unworthy of a white woman's fancy) – it is the perfect triumph of virtue over accidents, or the imagination over the senses. She sees Othello's colour in his mind. But upon the stage, when the imagination is no longer the ruling faculty, but we are left to our poor unassisted senses, I appeal to every one that has seen *Othello* played, whether he did not, on the contrary, sink Othello's mind in his colour; whether he did not find something extremely revolting in the courtship and wedded caresses of Othello and Desdemona; and whether the actual sight of the thing did not over-weigh all that beautiful compromise which we make in reading: – and the reason it should do so is obvious, because there is just so much reality presented to our senses as to give a perception of disagreement, with not enough of belief in the internal motives, – all that which is unseen, – to over-power and reconcile the first and obvious prejudices. What we see upon a stage is body and bodily action; what we are conscious of in reading is almost exclusively the mind, and its movements: and this I think may sufficiently account for the very different sort of delight with which the same play so often affects us in the reading and the seeing.

On the other side of the Atlantic a former President of the United States spoke even more vehemently about the racial aspects of the play. In an essay on 'Misconceptions of Shakespeare upon the Stage' (*New England Magazine*, 1835), John Quincy Adams asserted that

There are several of the most admired plays of Shakespeare which give more pleasure to read than to see performed upon the stage. For instance, *Othello* and *Lear*, both of which abound in beauty of detail, in poetical passages, in highly wrought and consistently preserved characters. But the pleasure that we take in witnessing a performance upon the stage depends much upon the sympathy that we feel with the sufferings and enjoyments of the good characters represented, and upon the punishment of the bad. We never can sympathize much with Desdemona or with Lear, because we never can separate them from the estimate that the lady is little less than a wanton, and the old king nothing less than a dotard. Who can sympathize with the love of Desdemona? – the daughter of a Venetian nobleman, born and educated to a splendid and lofty station in the community. She falls in love and makes a runaway match with a blackamoor, for no better reason than that he has told her a braggart story of his hair-breadth escapes in war. For this, she not only violates her duties to her father, her family, her sex, and her country, but she makes the first advances. She tells Othello she wished Heaven had made her such a man, and informs him how any friend of his may win her by telling her again his story. On that hint, says he, I spoke; and well he might. The blood must circulate briskly in the veins of a young woman so fascinated, and so coming to the tale of a rude, unbleached African soldier.

The great moral lesson of the tragedy of *Othello* is, that black and white blood cannot be intermingled in marriage without a gross outrage upon the law of Nature; and that, in such violations, Nature will vindicate her laws. The moral of *Othello* is not to beware of jealousy, for jealousy is well founded in the character and conduct of his wife, though not in the fact of her infidelity with Cassio. Desdemona is not false to her husband, but she has been false to the purity and delicacy of her sex and condition when she married him; and the last words spoken by her father on parting from them, after he has forgiven her and acquiesced in the marriage, are –

Look to her, Moor; have a quick eye to see:
She has deceived her father, and may thee.

Whatever sympathy we feel for the sufferings of Desdemona flows from the consideration that she is innocent of the particular crime imputed to her, and that she is the victim of a treacherous and artful intriguer. But, while compassionating her melancholy fate, we cannot forget the vice of her character. Upon the stage, her fondling with Othello is disgusting. Who, in real life, would have her for a sister, daughter, or wife? She is not guilty of infidelity to her husband, but she forfeits all the affection of her father and all her own filial affection for him. . . .

The character of Desdemona is admirably drawn and faithfully preserved throughout the play. It is always deficient in delicacy. Her conversations with Emilia indicate unsettled principles, even with regard to the obligations of the nuptial tie, and she allows Iago, almost unrebuked, to banter with her very coarsely upon women. This character takes from us so much of the sympathetic interest in her sufferings, that when Othello smothers her in bed, the terror and the pity subside immediately into the sentiment that she has her deserts.

As if in reply to Lamb and in anticipation of Adams, William Hazlitt emphasized 'the picturesque contrasts' that dominate the tragedy. In *Characters of Shakespear's Plays*. (London, 1817) Hazlitt said that

The Moor Othello, the gentle Desdemona, the villain Iago, the good-natured Cassio, the fool Roderigo, present a range and variety of character as striking and palpable as that produced by the opposition of costume in a picture. Their distinguishing qualities stand out to the mind's eye, so that even when we are not thinking of their actions or sentiments, the idea of their persons is still as present to us as ever. These characters and the images they stamp upon the mind are the farthest asunder possible, the distance between them is immense: yet the compass of knowledge and invention which the poet has shewn in embodying these extreme creations of his genius is only greater than the truth and felicity with which he has identified each character with itself, or blended their different qualities together in the same story. What a contrast the character of Othello forms to that of Iago! . . . The making one black and the other white, the one unprincipled, the other unfortunate in the extreme, would have answered the common purposes of effect, and satisfied the ambition of an ordinary painter of character. Shakespear has laboured the finer shades of difference in both with as much care and skill as if he had had to depend on the execution alone for the success of his design.

For Victor Hugo, the prominent French poet and novelist, what Hazlitt had described as 'picturesque' effects were illustrations of

Shakespeare's penetration of 'the mystery of things'. Writing in his book *William Shakespeare*, translated by Melville B. Anderson (London, 1887), Hugo defined Othello as 'the night'.

An immense fatal figure. Night is amorous of day. Darkness loves the dawn. The African adores the white woman. Othello has for his light and for his frenzy, Desdemona. And then, how easy to him is jealousy! He is great, he is dignified, he is majestic, he soars above all heads; he has as an escort bravery, battle, the braying of trumpets, the banners of war, renown, glory; he is radiant with twenty victories, he is studded with stars, this Othello; but he is black. And thus how soon, when jealous, the hero becomes the monster, the black becomes the negro! How speedily has night beckoned to death!

By the side of Othello, who is night, there is Iago, who is evil – evil, the other form of darkness. Night is but the night of the world; evil is the night of the soul. How deeply black are perfidy and falsehood! It is all one whether what courses through the veins be ink or treason. . . . Pour hypocrisy upon the break of day, and you put out the sun; and this, thanks to false religions, is what happens to God.

Iago near Othello is the precipice near the landslip. 'This way!' he says in a low voice. The snare advises blindness. The lover of darkness guides the black. Deceit takes upon itself to give what light may be required by night. Falsehood serves as a blind man's dog to jealousy. . . . These ferocities of darkness act in unison. These two incarnations of the eclipse conspire, the one roaring, the other sneering, for the tragic suffocation of light.

Sound this profound thing. Othello is the night, and being night, and wishing to kill, what does he take to slay with? Poison? the club? the axe? the knife? No; the pillow. To kill is to lull to sleep. . . . And it is thus that Desdemona, spouse of the man Night, dies, stifled by the pillow upon which the first kiss was given, and which receives the last sigh.

A decade and a half after the publication of Hugo's volume, Algernon Charles Swinburne produced *A Study of Shakespeare* (London, 1880) in which he reflected upon 'the fatalism of *Othello*'.

[U]pon the head of the very noblest man whom even omnipotence or Shakespeare could ever call to life he has laid a burden in one sense heavier than the burden of Lear, insomuch as the sufferer can with somewhat less confidence of universal appeal proclaim himself a man more sinned against than sinning. . . .

[But] as surely as Othello is the noblest man of man's making, Iago is the most perfect evildoer, the most potent demi-devil. It is of course the merest commonplace to say as much, and would be no less a waste of speech to add the half comfortable reflection that it is in any case no shame to fall by such a hand. But this subtlest and strangest work of Shakespeare's admits and requires some closer than common scrutiny. Coleridge has admirably described the first great soliloquy which opens to us the pit of hell within as 'the motive-hunting of a motiveless malignity'. But subtle and profound and just as is this definitive appreciation, there is more in the matter yet than even this. It is not only that Iago, so to speak, half tries to make himself half believe that Othello has wronged him, and that the thought of it gnaws him inly like a poisonous mineral: though this also be true, it is not half the truth – nor half that half again. Malignant as he is, the very subtlest and strongest component of his complex nature is not even malignity. It is the instinct of what Mr. Carlyle would call an inarticulate poet. . . . A genuine and thorough capacity for human lust or hate would diminish and degrade the supremacy of his evil. He is almost as far above or beyond vice as he is beneath or beyond virtue. And this it is that makes him impregnable and invulnerable. When once he has said it, we know as well as he that thenceforth he never will speak word. We could smile almost as we can see him to have smiled at Gratiano's most ignorant and empty threat, being well assured that torments will in no wise ope his lips: that as surely and as truthfully as ever did the tortured philosopher before him, he might have told his tormentors that they did but bruise the coating, batter the crust, or break the shell of Iago.

As the nineteenth century drew to a close, a later playwright assessed the work of his most eminent predecessor and concluded that *Othello* was best described as 'pure melodrama'. Writing 'Mainly about Shakespeare' in London's *Saturday Review* (May 1897), George Bernard Shaw denied that there was so much as 'a touch of character' in *Othello* 'that goes below the skin'. Even worse, Shaw said,

the fitful attempts to make Iago something better than a melodramatic villain only make a hopeless mess of him and his motives. To any one capable of reading the play with an open mind as to its merits, it is obvious that Shakespeare plunged through it so impetuously that he had it finished before he had made up his mind as to the character and motives of a single person in it. Probably it was not until he stumbled into the sentimental fit in which he introduced the willow song that he saw his way through without making Desdemona enough of the 'supersubtle Venetian' of Iago's description to strengthen the case for Othello's jealousy. That jealousy, by the way, is purely melodramatic jealousy. The real article is to be found later on in 'A Winter's Tale', where Leontes is an unmistakable study of a jealous man from life. But when the worst has been said of 'Othello' that can be provoked by its superficiality and staginess, it remains magnificent by the volume of its passion and the splendour of its word-music, which sweep across the scenes up to a plane on which sense is drowned in sound. The words do not convey ideas: they are streaming ensigns and tossing branches to make the tempest of passion visible. . . . The actor cannot help himself by studying his part acutely; for there is nothing to study in it. Tested by the brain, it is ridiculous: tested by the ear, it is sublime. He must have the orchestral quality in him; and as that is a matter largely of physical endowment, it follows that only an actor of certain physical endowments can play Othello. Let him be as crafty as he likes without that, he can no more get the effect than he can sound the bottom C on a violoncello. The note is not there, that is all; and he had better be content to play Iago, which is within the compass of any clever actor of normal endowments.

The twentieth century opened with a now-famous analysis of *Shakespearean Tragedy* (London, 1904) by A. C. Bradley. It was Bradley who established the canon of four 'great' tragedies (*Hamlet*, *Othello*, *King Lear*, and *Macbeth*), and it was Bradley who would exert the strongest critical influence upon the way most of the commentators who followed him would think about the plays he chose to examine. In his view

Othello's description of himself as

> one not easily jealous, but, being wrought,
> Perplexed in the extreme,

is perfectly just. His tragedy lies in this – that his whole nature was indisposed to jealousy, and yet was such that he was unusually open to deception, and, if once wrought to passion, likely to act with little reflection, with no delay, and in the most decisive manner conceivable. . . .

Othello is, in one sense of the word, by far the most romantic figure among Shakespeare's heroes; and he is so partly from the strange life of war and adventure which he has lived from childhood. He does not belong to our world, and he seems to enter it we know not whence – almost as if from wonderland. There is something mysterious in his descent from men of royal siege; in his wanderings in vast deserts and among marvellous peoples; in his tales of magic handkerchiefs and prophetic Sibyls; in the sudden vague glimpses we get of numberless battles and sieges in which he has played the hero and has borne a charmed life; even in chance references to his baptism, his being sold to slavery, his sojourn in Aleppo.

And he is not merely a romantic figure; his own nature is romantic. He has not, indeed, the meditative or speculative imagination of Hamlet; but in the strictest sense of the word he is more poetic than Hamlet. Indeed, if one recalls Othello's most famous speeches – those that begin, 'Her father loved me,' 'O now for ever,' 'Never Iago,' 'Had it pleased Heaven,' 'It is the cause,' 'Behold, I have a weapon,' 'Soft you, a word or two before you go' – if one places side by side with these speeches an equal number by any other hero, one will not doubt that Othello is the greatest poet of them all. . . .

The sources of danger in this character are revealed but too clearly by the story. In the first place, Othello's mind, for all its poetry, is very simple. He is not observant. His nature tends outward. He is quite free from introspection, and is not given to reflection. Emotion excites his imagination, but it confuses and dulls his intellect. On this side he is the very opposite of Hamlet, with whom, however, he shares a great openness and trustfulness of nature. In addition, he has little experience of the corrupt products of civilised life, and is ignorant of European women.

In the second place, for all his dignity and massive calm (and he has greater dignity than any other of Shakespeare's men), he is by nature full of the most vehement passion. . . .

Lastly, Othello's nature is all of one piece. His trust, where he trusts, is absolute. Hesitation is almost impossible to him. He is extremely self-reliant, and decides and acts instantaneously. If stirred to indignation, as 'in Aleppo once', he answers with one lightning stroke. Love, if he loves, must be to him the heaven where either he must live or bear no life. If such a passion as jealousy seizes him, it will swell into a well-nigh incontrollable flood. He will press for immediate conviction or immediate relief. Convinced, he will act with the authority of a judge and the swiftness of a man in mortal pain. Undeceived, he will do like execution on himself.

This character is so noble, Othello's feelings and actions follow so inevitably from it and from the forces brought to bear on it, and his sufferings are so heart-rending, that he stirs, I believe, in most readers a passion of mingled love and pity which they feel for no other hero in Shakespeare. . . . And pity itself vanishes, and love and admiration alone remain, in the majestic dignity and sovereign ascendancy of the close. Chaos has come and gone; and the Othello of the Council-chamber and the quay of Cyprus has returned, or a greater and nobler Othello still. As he speaks those final words in which all the glory and agony of his life – long ago in India and Arabia and Aleppo, and afterwards in Venice, and now in Cyprus – seem to pass before us, like the pictures that flash before the eyes of a drowning man, a triumphant scorn for the fetters of the flesh and the littleness of all the lives that must survive him sweeps our grief away, and when he dies upon a kiss the most painful of all tragedies leaves us for the moment free from pain, and exulting in the power of 'love and man's unconquerable mind' [Wordsworth].

But what of Iago? Bradley refused to accept without scepticism anything that Othello's nemesis says about himself. At the same time he rejected Coleridge's explanation that Iago was impelled purely by 'motiveless malignity'; no, Bradley said,

> The most delightful thing to such a man would be something that gave an extreme satisfaction to his sense of power and superiority; and if it involved, secondly, the triumphant exertion of his abilities, and, thirdly, the excitement of danger, his delight would be consummated. And the moment most dangerous to such a man would be one when his sense of superiority had met with an affront, so that its habitual craving was reinforced by resentment, while at the same time he saw an opportunity of satisfying it by subjecting to his will the very persons who had affronted it. . . . At *any* time he would have enjoyed befooling and tormenting Othello. Under ordinary circumstances he was restrained, chiefly by self-interest, in some slight degree perhaps by the faint pulsations of conscience or humanity. But disappointment at the loss of the lieutenancy supplied the touch of lively resentment that was required to overcome these obstacles; and the prospect of satisfying the sense of power by mastering Othello through an intricate and hazardous intrigue now became irresistible. Iago did not clearly understand what was moving his desire; though he tried to give himself reasons for his action, even those that had some reality made but a small part of the motive force; one may almost say they were no more than the turning of the handle which admits the driving power into the machine. Only once does he appear to see something of the truth. It is when he uses the phrase 'to *plume up my will* in double knavery'.
>
> To 'plume up the will,' to heighten the sense of power or superiority – this seems to be the unconscious motive of many acts of cruelty which evidently do not spring chiefly from ill-will, and which therefore puzzle and sometimes horrify us most. It is often this that makes a man bully the wife or children of whom he is fond. The boy who torments another boy, as we say, 'for no reason,' or who without any hatred for frogs tortures a frog, is pleased with his victim's pain, not from any disinterested love of evil or pleasure in pain, but mainly because this pain is the unmistakable proof of his own power over his victim. So it is with Iago. His thwarted sense of superiority wants satisfaction. What fuller satisfaction could it find than the consciousness that he is the master of the General who has undervalued him and of the rival who has been preferred to him; that these worthy people, who are so successful and popular and stupid, are mere puppets in his

hands, but living puppets, who at the motion of his finger must contort themselves in agony, while all the time they believe that he is their one true friend and comforter? It must have been an ecstasy of bliss to him. And this, granted a most abnormal deadness of human feeling, is, however horrible, perfectly intelligible.

For all his craft, however, Iago is undone by a 'failure in perception' that is 'closely connected with his badness'.

He was destroyed by the power that he attacked, the power of love; and he was destroyed by it because he could not understand it; and he could not understand it because it was not in him. Iago never meant his plot to be so dangerous to himself. He knew that jealousy is painful, but the jealousy of a love like Othello's he could not imagine, and he found himself involved in murders which were no part of his original design. That difficulty he surmounted, and his changed plot still seemed to prosper. Roderigo and Cassio once dead, all will be well. Nay, when he fails to kill Cassio, all may still be well. He will avow that he told Othello of the adultery, and persist that he told the truth, and Cassio will deny it in vain. And then, in a moment, his plot is shattered by a blow from a quarter where he never dreamt of danger. He knows his wife, he thinks. She is not over-scrupulous, she will do anything to please him, and she has learnt obedience. But one thing he does not know – that she *loves* her mistress and would face a hundred deaths sooner than see her fair fame darkened. There is genuine astonishment in his outburst 'What! Are you mad?' as it dawns upon him that she means to speak the truth about the handkerchief . . . The foulness of his own soul made him so ignorant that he built into the marvellous structure of his plot a piece of crass stupidity.

To the thinking mind the divorce of unusual intellect from goodness is a thing to startle; and Shakespeare clearly felt it so. The combination of unusual intellect with extreme evil is more than startling, it is frightful. It is rare, but it exists; and Shakespeare represented it in Iago. But the alliance of evil like Iago's with *supreme* intellect is an impossible fiction; and Shakespeare's fictions were truth.

Almost a quarter of a century after Bradley published his study of *Othello*, T. S. Eliot commented upon the play in a 1927 essay on 'Shakespeare and the Stoicism of Seneca', republished in his *Selected Essays* (London, 1932).

I have always felt that I have never read a more terrible exposure of human weakness – of universal human weakness – than the last great speech of Othello. I am ignorant whether any one else has ever adopted this view, and it may appear subjective and fantastic in the extreme. It is usually taken on its face value, as expressing the greatness in defeat of a noble but erring nature. . . . [But] what Othello seems to me to be doing in making this speech is *cheering himself up*. He is endeavouring to escape reality; he has ceased to think about Desdemona, and is thinking about himself. Humility is the most difficult of all virtues to achieve; nothing dies harder than the desire to think well of oneself. Othello succeeds in turning himself into a pathetic figure, by adopting an *aesthetic* rather than a moral attitude, dramatising himself against his environment. He takes in the spectator, but the human motive is primarily to take in himself. I do not believe that any writer has ever exposed this bovarysme, the human will to see things as they are not, more clearly than Shakespeare.

For another writer contemporaneous with Eliot, Othello's concluding remarks carried a different significance. In *The Lion and the Fox* (London, 1927), Wyndham Lewis argued that

Of all the colossi, Othello is the most characteristic, because he is the simplest, and he is seen in an unequal duel throughout with a perfect specimen of the appointed enemy of the giant – the representative of the race of men at war with the race of titans. The hero comes straight from a world where Machiavelli's black necessities – the obligation, for animal survival, for the lion to couple with the fox – are not known. He is absolutely defenceless: it is as though he were meeting one of his appointed enemies, disguised of course, as a friend, for the first time. He seems possessed of no instinct by which he might scent his antagonist, and so be put on his guard. . . .

The great spectacular 'pugnacious' male ideal is represented perfectly by Othello; who was led out to the slaughter on the Elizabethan stage just as the bull is thrust into the Spanish bull-ring. . . . Othello is of the race of Christs, or of the race of 'bulls'; he is the hero with all the magnificent helplessness of the animal, or all the beauty and ultimate resignation of the god. From the moment he arrives on the scene of his execution, or when his execution is being prepared, he speaks with an unmatched grandeur and beauty. To the troop that is come to look for him, armed and snarling, he says: 'Put up your bright swords or the dew will rust them!' And when at last he has been brought to bay he dies by that significant contrivance of remembering how he had defended the state when it was traduced, and in reviving this distant blow for his own demise. . . . [We] feel, in all our dealings with this simplest and grandest of his creations, that we are meant to be in the presence of an absolute purity of human guilelessness, a generosity as grand and unaffected, although quick and, 'being wrought, Perplexed in the extreme', as deep as that of his divine inventor.

There is no utterance in the whole of Shakespeare's plays that reveals the nobleness of his genius and of its intentions in the same way as the speech with which Othello closes . . . it is the speech of a military hero, as simple-hearted as Hotspur. The tremendous and childlike pathos of this simple creature, broken by intrigue so easily and completely, is one of the most significant things for the comprehension of Shakespeare's true thought.

'Simple' and 'simple-hearted' were not the adjectives that G. Wilson Knight found most apposite when he set out to define the stylistic characteristics of Othello's discourse. In *The Wheel of Fire: Essays in Interpretation of Shakespeare's Sombre Tragedies* (London, 1930), Knight observed that

... When Othello is represented as enduring loss of control he is, as Macbeth and Lear never are, ugly, idiotic; but when he has full control he attains an architectural stateliness of quarried speech, a silver rhetoric of a kind unique in Shakespeare. . . . This is the noble Othello music: highly-coloured, rich in sound and phrase, stately. Each solidifies as it takes its place in the pattern. . . .

Othello radiates a world of romantic, heroic, and picturesque adventure. All about him is highly coloured. He is a Moor; he is noble and generally respected; he is proud in the riches of his achievement. . . . Othello tells us:

> Rude am I in my speech,
> And little bless'd with the soft phrase of peace.

Yet the dominant quality in this play is the exquisitely moulded language, the noble cadence and chiselled phrase, of Othello's poetry. Othello's speech, therefore, reflects not a soldier's language, but the quality of soldiership in all its glamour of romantic adventure: it holds an imaginative realism. It has a certain exotic beauty, is a storied and romantic treasure-house of rich, colourful experiences.

By the late 1930s commentary on *Othello* was beginning to focus on the theological significance of the tragedy. According to one school of thought, exemplified by E. M. W. Tillyard in *Shakespeare's Last Plays* (London, 1938), the playwright set out to do 'something more than picture with unflinching courage and accuracy a number of people crushed by the universe'. In Tillyard's view *Othello*

pictures through the hero not only the destruction of an established way of life, but the birth of a new order. Othello in his final soliloquy is a man of a more capacious mind than the Othello who first meets us. Dover Wilson has the same feeling about Shakespearean tragedy when he says: 'The Lear that dies is not a Lear defiant, but a Lear redeemed. His education is complete, his regeneration accomplished.' True, the new order is cut short in both plays, but its creation is an essential part of the tragic pattern.

. . . Othello recognizes his errors and transmutes them into his new state of mind; [by contrast] Antony, Cleopatra, and Coriolanus abandon their errors without transmuting them. Hence reconciliation is not the word to apply to their states of mind. It is a different thing to pass from A to B, and to fuse A and B into an amalgam C. Antony does the first, Othello the second. When St. Paul was converted he may have freed himself from a kind of devil, but the fierce angel that was born in the conversion incorporated, among other things, that very devil from which he had broken free. That is true reconciliation.

Like Tillyard, Kenneth O. Myrick saw Othello as a character who commits a grievous crime but who emerges in the end as a regenerated sinner. In 'The Theme of Damnation in Shakespearean Tragedy' (*Studies in Philology*, 1941), Myrick asked:

How, then, did Shakespeare expect us to feel toward the Moor when thoughts of heaven and hell are suggested to our minds? At times during his jealousy – as when he loses consciousness in the paroxysm of his passion, or strikes his wife before the emissaries of Venice, or calls her an impudent strumpet – part of our tragic terror is [that he will] sink into entire spiritual ruin. And the dread lest he incur damnation as well as the horrors of jealousy is, I think, not far from our minds. When he furiously curses his wife, bitterly urges her to double-damn herself by swearing innocence, and then begs her on her deathbed to confess and save her soul, the thought must cross our minds that it is Othello who is in danger of perdition. Immediately after the death of Desdemona the thought is brought home to us with unmistakable emphasis in the words of both Othello and Emilia. . . . But though his life is in ruins, the final impression which the great Moor leaves with us is not that of a ruined soul, but of a man ennobled by contrition. The phrases of conventional piety do not intrude here to reduce a tragic moment to commonplace. But what the theologians would call repentance is here – the utterly humble grief of heart, which is *contrition*; the making of amends to the injured party (in this instance the manly apology to Cassio) which is one part of what is called *satisfaction*. 'In the majestic dignity and sovereign ascendancy of the close' no doubt the Elizabethan, as the modern, felt the renewed nobility of the hero and rejoiced 'in the power of "love and man's unconquerable mind" ' [Bradley]. But mingled with that feeling would be another, which can have as much meaning for us as for our ancestors. For Othello's story is the perfect illustration of man's tragic vulnerability. At his first appearance, his magnificent poise, his modesty, his justice, his genius for command, his elevation of soul all seemed to raise him above the fallibility of the other sons of Adam. His downfall gives the lie to the Stoic boast in the strength of his own virtue, and demonstrates the inability of unaided human nature to govern its own life. In him we see exemplified in the highest degree alike the spiritual greatness and the tragic weakness of men, in both of which the age of Shakespeare had a profound belief.

For the great theatrical producer Harley Granville-Barker it was impossible to arrive at so optimistic a reading of the hero's final moments. In his *Prefaces to Shakespeare*, Fourth Series (London, 1945), Granville-Barker observed that

Of vanity, envy, self-seeking and distrust, which are the seeds of jealousy in general, Othello, it is insisted from the beginning, is notably free, so free that he will not readily remark these qualities in others – in Iago, for instance, in whom they so richly abound. And he has never yet cared enough for a woman to be jealous of her; that also is made clear. It is a nature, then, taught by no earlier minor failings of this kind to resist a gross attack on it, should that come.

But sexual jealousy, once given rein, is a passion like no other. It is pathological, a moral lesion, a monomania. Facts and reason become its playthings. Othello does at first put up a feeble intellectual resistance, in a single soliloquy he struggles a little with himself; but, after this, every defence is swept away, and the poison rages in him unchecked. Here, then, is the sudden and swift descent to catastrophe, which the story, as Shakespeare dramatises it, demands. A bad business, certainly; yet, to this extent, shocking rather than tragic. Indeed, did not Othello suffer so and dispense suffering, the spectacle of his wholly baseless duping and befooling would be more comic than otherwise, the mere upsetting of his confidence and dignity as enjoyable to us as to Iago; and, in a ghastly fashion, it for a few moments becomes so when he is set eavesdropping upon Cassio and Bianca. Shocking, that is, and pitiful, for all perplexed suffering is pitiful. But there is more to tragedy than this.

. . . [Othello] cannot reason with himself about something which is in its very nature unreasonable, nor can Shakespeare set him searching for the significance of events which exist only in Iago's lies – we, the audience, should resent such futility. He is betrayed and goes ignorantly to his doom. And when, at last, Desdemona dead, he learns the truth, what can he have to say – or we! – but 'O, fool, fool, fool!' The mere sight of such beauty and nobility and happiness, all wickedly destroyed, must be a harrowing one. Yet the pity and terror of it come short of serving for the purgation of our souls, since Othello's own soul stays unpurged. Hamlet dies spiritually at peace; Lear's madness has been the means to his salvation; by interpreting his life's hell to us even Macbeth stirs us to some compassion. But what alchemy can bring the once noble Moor and the savage murderer into unity again? The 'cruel tears' and the kiss and the talk of justice are more intolerable than the savagery itself. Nor can remorse bridge the gulf between the two. Othello wakes as from a nightmare only to kill himself, his prospect hell. And the play's last word is, significantly, not of him, but of tortures for Iago; punishment as barren as the crime. It is a tragedy without meaning, and that is the ultimate horror of it.

Unlike Granville-Barker, Winifred M. T. Nowottny saw the Moor's fate as a tragedy with considerable 'meaning', and in her article on 'Justice and Love in *Othello*' (*University of Toronto Quarterly*, 1952) she argued that 'Shakespeare intends in this play an evaluation of justice in its relation to love'.

In *Othello* jealousy is treated as a state in which man experiences the opposition of two kinds of belief – belief in 'evidence' and belief in the person one loves – and the opposition of the value of justice (as he conceives it) to the value of love. What is tragic in *Othello* derives from these oppositions.

[When Iago begins undermining the Moor's confidence in Desdemona in Act III, scene iii] Shakespeare . . . deliberately forces upon the audience the question, In what strength could Othello reject Iago? The answer would seem to be, By an affirmation of faith which is beyond reason, by the act of choosing to believe in Desdemona. Shakespeare's point is that love is beyond reason. Desdemona's love for Othello has been made 'unreasonable' in a way which permits discussion of it in the drama, as when Brabantio tries to bring it to the bar of reason and to punishment by the law, but Othello's race and strangeness (which constitute Brabantio's case) are after all only dramatic heightenings of a simple truism which it is Shakespeare's peculiar excellence to have thought remarkable enough for repeated dramatization: the truism that love, any love, is a miracle. Being a daily miracle, it is not often seen as miraculous; to arrive at that valuation of it costs something, as in *King Lear*; to fail to arrive at it costs even more, as in *Othello*. With love, reason and justice have ultimately nothing to do. . . .

It is one of the finest strokes in the construction of the play that Shakespeare puts the vow of revenge before the test of the handkerchief. By so doing, he makes clear in the action what he has already suggested in the poetry: that the idea of revenge, though it seems to Othello to follow from what he now thinks of Desdemona and offers him the illusion of release from the conflict of his emotions, is not in fact Othello's whole bent. If he could only unify himself by revenge, that would be one way out, but he cannot; the test of the handkerchief is a desperate attempt to unify himself in the opposite way – by having Desdemona prove that what Iago has said is false. Othello's description to Desdemona of the mystic nature of the handkerchief . . . is not an irrelevance; he is in reality asking Desdemona to restore to him the sacredness of love. After the failure of this attempt, he is not seen until Act IV, and Act IV concentrates on showing the dreadful interim within Othello when the disjunction of his personality rages for expression and cannot find the means. . . .

The scene of the murder of Desdemona is a visible demonstration of the laws inherent in the process that led up to it. This is a drama of an error of judgment, the error being in the application of judgment to love. It is not, however, surprising, that the relation of Act V to all that goes before has been imperfectly seen, for the perception about human justice which Shakespeare laid down for himself to work by: as, that justice, however it is conceived of, cannot be executed in love; that love and justice differ in their natures, their processes, and their conclusions; that justice, though ideally conceived of as an expiating sacrifice or as the only cure for a wound in the fitness of things, may be, in its human origin and motivation, indistinguishable from man's need to find redress for what he cannot bear to find in human nature; that, finally, the man who accepts justice as the supreme value in life will, if he be wholly consistent, at last execute himself. . . .

[In Act V] it is in the growing intensity of Othello's realization of his continuing love, counterpointed by the growing compulsiveness of the sanctions of justice which he must allege to outdo it, that Shakespeare expresses the major conflict of the drama. Faced by the fact that love continues, even in this extremity, Othello is driven to urge higher and higher the claims of that justice which shall destroy it. Justice has already been called in under its aspect of safeguard of society: 'Yet she must die, else she'll betray more men.' Love persists. Justice is then called in as an abstract ideal. Love, still, can almost persuade her to break her sword, and hints that the threatened act of destruction is at heart the act of possession, of plucking the rose. Justice, in a final terrifying aggrandisement, claims the ultimate possible sanction, the sanction of love: '. . . this sorrow's heavenly; It strikes where it doth love.' The process is complete. Justice overrides love by presenting itself as love. In this parallel ascent, where the claims of justice rise with the claims of love, Shakespeare has manifested their tragic contestation, and through the form of the poetry he has shown how the act of killing is related at one level to the tension of opposites in Othello and at a deeper level to the fundamental and eternal opposition of justice and love.

. . . In human justice as it is commonly ordered the executioner need not question the motive of the judge, nor the judge question his own. With Desdemona, Othello is judge and executioner; he is also plaintiff, and the only possible witness for the defence. In him justice confounds itself by the concentration of all its persons in one, and in being so confounded by unity, throws into relief the indivisible and unconfounded unity of love.

There remains the revelation of the truth. . . . Othello has killed Desdemona for betraying their love; he kills himself for the same reason. He surveys his life, judges it, passes sentence, and executes it, as long ago he did in Aleppo. . . . Othello's death is perfectly consistent with his life. From first to last, he is the judge.

In an article that reinforced Nowottny's thesis, Paul N. Siegel discussed 'The Damnation of Othello' (*PMLA: Publications of the Modern Language Association of America*, 1953) in terms of a dramatic structure that evolved, ultimately, from the biblical story of Man's dealings with his Creator.

Of Shakespeare's four great tragedies the Christian overtones of *Othello* have been least apprehended. Critics have seen in it a noble soul caught in the toils of a diabolically cunning being, who tempts him to doubt the divine goodness of one in whom he has absolute faith, but they have failed to see the symbolic force of the characters and the action. For the Elizabethans, however, the noble soul of Othello, the diabolic cunning of Iago, and the divine goodness of Desdemona would not have had a loosely metaphoric meaning. Desdemona, who in her forgiveness and perfect love, a love requited by death, is reminiscent of Christ, would have represented Christian values; Iago, who in his envious hatred and destructive negativism is reminiscent of Satan, would have represented anti-Christian values. The choice that Othello had to make was between Christian love and forgiveness and Satanic hate and vengefulness. When he exclaimed, 'Arise, black vengeance, from thy hollow cell! / Yield up, O love, thy crown and hearted throne / To tyrannous hate,' he was succumbing to the devil, and, like all men who succumb to the devil, his fall was reminiscent of that of Adam.

Elizabethans were habituated to regard human actions in terms of such analogy. In the homilies Adam's choice in disobeying God and Christ's choice in sacrificing Himself to redeem mankind were presented again and again as setting a basic pattern for our conduct. Writing for an audience accustomed to think analogically and to regard the history of humanity as a repeated illustration of the truths of the Bible story, Shakespeare implied the great Christian scheme of things in the pattern of events of a specific action, appealing to the poetic imagination rather than outlining it in detail, as the morality plays do. *Othello* is not a retelling of the story of man's fall in allegorical form; it is a drama of human passion which is given deeper significance by the analogies that are suggested in the course of its action. . . .

When Othello comes to kill Desdemona, he does so in the exalted mood of being about to render justice, not to perform revenge. And this justice is to include clemency. Desdemona is to be given the opportunity to pray and ask for heaven's forgiveness: 'I would not kill thy unprepared spirit; / No; heaven forfend! I would not kill thy soul.' But the soul that he is about to kill, the divine light that he is about to quench, is his own. In the mood of elevated pity in which he offers Desdemona the opportunity to confess her misdeeds lies Othello's last hope for escaping damnation. 'This sorrow's heavenly' indeed. When he says 'amen' in reply to Desdemona's 'Then Lord have mercy on me,' Desdemona cries, 'And have you mercy too!' But Othello cannot call up from within him the forgiveness of Christ and, forgetting the Lord's Prayer and Christ's injunction (Matt. vi.15), 'If ye forgive not men their trespasses, neither will your Father forgive your trespass,' loses his own claim to God's mercy. When Desdemona denies having been unfaithful to him, his rage is rekindled: 'O perjured woman! thou dost stone my heart, / And makest me call what I intend to do / A murder, which I thought a sacrifice.' In his oscillation of feeling he is back to the vengeful spirit in which he had told Iago, 'My heart is turning to stone; / I strike it, and it hurts my hand.' No more does he speak of 'justice' but of his 'great revenge.' Desdemona is now not 'sweet soul' but 'strumpet.' When she entreats, 'But while I say one prayer,' he refuses her what he believes to be the opportunity for salvation which he had previously offered her and stifles her, saying, 'It is too late.' . . .

[But if the ensign succeeds in getting the Moorish general to 'renounce his baptism'] the victory of Iago is seen to be, like all victories of the devil, a pyrrhic victory. Although he triumphs over Othello, it is at the same time demonstrated that his values cannot triumph. His view of reality is false: Desdemona is pure. She remains heavenly true to Othello, although the cynically worldly Emilia lightheartedly suggests that she revenge herself by cuckolding her husband. 'Wouldst thou do such a deed for all the world?' asks Desdemona. We are reminded of Christ's rejection of the temptation to possess the world. . . . 'Marry, I would not do such a thing for a joint-ring,' Emilia replies, 'nor for measures of lawn, nor for gowns, petticoats, nor caps, nor any petty exhibition; but, for the whole world – why, who would not make her husband a cuckold to make him a monarch?' . . . Although she is speaking jestingly to divert her mistress, it is clear that Christ's words (Mark viii.36) 'What shall it profit a man to gain the whole world and lose his soul?' have no great significance for her.

This is Desdemona's temptation scene, the counterpart of Othello's temptation scene, as Bradley calls it. Unlike Othello, she does not follow her preceptor's ethic of revenge; she obeys the vow she had made, kneeling in the presence of Iago as Othello had kneeled to vow hatred and revenge, that she would continue in her love and devotion for Othello no matter what he does to her. In doing so she follows the Christian ethic of returning good for evil, accepting ill treatment as a discipline enabling her to grow in virtue: 'Good night, good night: heaven me such uses send, / Not to pick bad from bad, but by bad mend!' . . . The words in which she accepts her misfortune echo the centuries-long praise of adversity as a teacher of Christian patience. . . . They help to reconcile the audience to her suffering and death, as through her Griselda-like patience and devotion she becomes a saint and a martyr in her love, dying with a divine lie upon her lips, ironically committing the deathbed perjury against which Othello had warned her, but a perjury which makes her, as Emilia says, 'the more angel.'

If Othello loses Desdemona for eternity, the faithful Emilia joins her mistress in death, as did the repentant thief who acknowledged Christ as his Lord as he died by His side and was told by Him (Luke xxiii.43), 'Today shalt thou be with me in paradise.' In her easy-going tolerance of her husband, the depths of whose iniquity she does not realize, in her theft of the handkerchief at his behest, Emilia has played a part in her mistress' calamity, but she redeems herself by her trust in Desdemona and her loyalty to her. . . . She does indeed stake her soul on the purity of Desdemona. 'Moor, she was chaste,' she says as she lies dying, 'she loved thee, cruel Moor, / So come my soul to bliss, as I speak true.' These words, at the supreme moment of death, carry the assurance that in losing her life by heroically defying Iago and revealing the truth she has won her soul.

Desdemona raises and redeems such earthly souls as Emilia. Belief in her, like belief in Christ, is a means of salvation.

Following closely upon Siegel's analysis of the biblical themes implicit in *Othello*, Irving Ribner published an article on the play's debt to medieval drama. Writing on '*Othello* and the Pattern of Shakespearean Tragedy' (*TSE: Tulane Studies in English*, 1955), Ribner noted that

At the basis of *Othello* is a traditional philosophy of man's relation to the forces of evil in the world. It goes back to the virtual beginnings of Christianity, and in the Middle Ages it had given rise to a distinctive dramatic form: the morality play. It was a basically simple philosophy which held that all men were surrounded by the forces of evil and that any man, no matter how great or noble, could be seduced by evil; man's reason being defective, he was capable of delusion, and the forces of evil could delude man into thinking they were good. Once he had succumbed, however, man was always capable of recognizing his error, recovering from his delusion and casting off evil. If he did so, after a period of penance, he could still triumph over evil and attain salvation. It is in essence an optimistic philosophy of life, and I believe that it is implicit in *Othello*.

With this traditional worldview to express, it was almost inevitable that Shakespeare's dramatic pattern in *Othello* should be the very pattern traditionally used to express that philosophy, that of the morality play. . . . Iago is, as many critics have pointed out, Shakespeare's adaptation of the morality Vice. It is only with this awareness that we can grasp the essential relation between Othello and his ensign. It is not enough, however, to call Iago a mere primitive survival of the morality drama, as those who have identified him as a Vice have done. That he is a Vice is essential to the framework of the entire play, for Shakespeare did not just incorporate a morality play relic in *Othello*. He cast his entire drama in the morality pattern. . . .

The story of *Othello* is that of a man of great potential goodness who chooses evil through deception, suffers the horrible consequences of his choice, and at the end realizes his error and undergoes repentance before death. . . .

The Vice of the morality play developed a definite pattern of action which is easily recognizable. He usually appeared early and made his true nature clear to the audience, just as Iago does. He almost always had a dupe – and often more than one – whom he gulled, and who provided comic interludes between the more serious moments of the play; it is clear that Roderigo performs this function in *Othello*. The Vice's most common trait, however, was that of the masquer or dissimulator. After making clear his true identity, the Vice always pretended to be something which he was not. . . . Man chooses evil because he mistakes it for the good, and thus the task of the devil becomes to pose as good. . . . The devil must disguise himself as the friend of man and thus cause man to forsake the true good and to accept disguised evil in its stead. This essentially is what Iago does for Othello. . . .

The early morality drama, because it was concerned essentially with the religious problem of man's salvation, and because the religious doctrine from which it emerged offered the hope of salvation to all, never allowed its hero to be damned; he always recognized his error and attained a new and greater felicity by reunion with the good. But as the morality developed in the early sixteenth century, perhaps under the influence of the Reformation, it came more and more to embody the notion of an inexorable retribution for sin, with the erring mortal suffering final damnation for his evil choice. Out of this ultimately evolved a concept of tragedy as final retribution visited upon man for his sins. . . .

[But] Shakespeare's *Othello* . . . is concerned not with the damnation of a soul, but rather with a Christian plan for salvation which had been depicted upon the stage since Medieval times. The design of the play is an expression of Shakespeare's belief that salvation for the sinner who recognized his sin and underwent penance was always possible, a belief equally implicit in the mercy extended to Angelo in *Measure for Measure*, a play almost certainly written in 1604, the very year of *Othello*.

In her British Academy Shakespeare Lecture on 'The Noble Moor' (London, 1955), Helen Gardner argued that

Among the tragedies of Shakespeare *Othello* is supreme in one quality: beauty. Much of its poetry, in imagery, perfection of phrase, and steadiness of rhythm, soaring yet firm, enchants the sensuous imagination. . . . But *Othello* is also remarkable for another kind of beauty. . . . The play has a rare intellectual beauty, satisfying the desire of the imagination for order and harmony between the parts and the whole. Finally, the play has intense moral beauty. . . . These three kinds of beauty are interdependent, since all arise from the nature of the hero. . . .

Othello is like a hero of the ancient world in that he is not a man like us, but a man recognized as extraordinary. He seems born to do great deeds and live in legend. He has the obvious heroic qualities of courage and strength, and no actor can attempt the role who is not physically impressive. He has the heroic capacity for passion. But the thing which most sets him apart is his solitariness. He is a stranger, a man of alien race, without ties of nature or natural duties. His value is not in what the world thinks of him, although the world rates him highly, and does not derive in any way from his station. It is inherent. He is, in a sense, a 'self-made man', the product of a certain kind of life which he has chosen to lead. . . .

The love between Othello and Desdemona is a great venture of faith. He is free; she achieves her freedom, and at a great cost. Shakespeare, in creating the figure of her wronged father, who dies of grief at her revolt, sharpened and heightened, as everywhere, the story in the source. Her disobedience and deception of him perhaps cross her mind at Othello's ominous 'Think on thy sins.' If so, she puts the thought aside with 'They are loves I bear you.' . . .

The famous double time [the fact that Shakespeare sometimes implies the passage of weeks, and even months, even though the action of the play appears limited to a few intense days], which has so vexed critics, though it does not trouble spectators, is in accord with the conception of love as beyond nature. That lovers' time is not the time of the seasons is a commonplace. . . .

Tragic responsibility can only be savoured within a fixed field of moral reference. Mercy killings, honour slayings and innocent adulteries are not the stuff of tragedy. But tragic responsibility is not the same as moral guilt. It shows itself in Hamlet's acceptance of the imperative to stay at his post, although this involves many deaths and his own commission of acts which outrage the very conscience which impels him; in Lear's flinging out into the storm to take upon himself the role of universal sufferer and universal judge; and in Macbeth's perseverance in 'knowing the deed'. It shows itself in Othello's destruction of an idol, his decision to regain his freedom by destroying what he must desire, but cannot honour. The baser passions mingled with this imperative to sacrifice, that in the final moment Othello kills his wife in rage, only means that in presenting man as 'an animal that worships', Shakespeare, keeping to 'the truth of human passions', presents both terms. But, in its mixture of primitive animality and agonizing renunciation, the murder of Desdemona has upon it the stamp of the heroic. . . .

The act is heroic because Othello acts from inner necessity. Although the thought of social dishonour plays a part in his agony, it has no place in this final scene. He kills her because he cannot 'digest the poison of her flesh'; and also to save her from herself, to restore meaning to her beauty. The act is also heroic in its absoluteness, disinterestedness, and finality. Othello does not look beyond it. It must be done. The tragic hero usurps the function of the gods and attempts to remake the world. The *hubris*, which arouses awe and terror, appears in an extreme form in Othello's assumption of the role of a god who chastises where he loves, and of a priest who must present a perfect victim. He tries to confess her, so that in her last moment she may be true, and suffering the death of the body as expiation may escape the death of the soul. Her persistence in what he believes to be a lie and her tears at the news of Cassio's death turn the priest into the murderer. The heroic is rooted in reality here: the godlike mingled with the brutal, which Aristotle saw as its true opposite, and Desdemona, love's martyr, dies like a frightened child, pleading for 'but half an hour' more of life.

'I am glad I have ended my revisal of this dreadful scene. It is not to be endured,' said Johnson. And yet, this terrible act has wonderful tragic rightness. Only by it can the tragic situation be finally resolved, and in tragedy it is the peace of finality which we look for. Living, Desdemona cannot ever prove her innocence. There is nothing she can do to 'win her lord again.' She could, of course, save herself, and in so doing save her husband from a crime, dishonour, and death. She could leave this terrifying monster and ask for the protection of her own countrymen, the messengers of Venice. This sensible solution never crosses her mind. She remains with the man her 'love approves', and since 'There is a comfort in the strength of love,' for all her bewilderment and distress she falls asleep, to wake to find her faith rewarded by death. But in death she does 'win her lord again.'

Emilia's silence while her mistress lived is fully explicable in terms of her character. She shares with her husband the generalizing trick and is well used to domestic scenes. The jealous, she knows,

> are not ever jealous for the cause,
> But jealous for they are jealous.

If it was not the handkerchief it would be something else. Why disobey her husband and risk his fury? It would not do any good. This is what men are like. But Desdemona dead sweeps away all such generalities and all caution. At this sight, Emilia though 'the world is a huge thing' finds that there is a thing she will not do for it. By her heroic disregard for death she gives the only 'proof' there can only be of Desdemona's innocence: the testimony of faith. For falseness can be proved, innocence can only be believed. Faith, not evidence, begets faith.

The revival of faith in Othello which rings through his last speech overrides that sense of his own guilt which we have been told he ought to be dwelling on. His own worth he sees in the services he has rendered. It is right that he should be conscious of what has given his life value when he is about to take it, as he was conscious of her beauty when about to sacrifice that. His error he cannot explain. He sees in it an image which asserts her infinite value and his supreme good fortune, which in ignorance he did not realize, accepting and translating into his own characteristic mode of thought Emilia's characteristic 'O gull! O dolt! As ignorant as dirt!' The tears he weeps now are not 'cruel tears' but good tears, natural and healing. He communicates this by an image drawn from his life of adventure. Perhaps the Arabian tree comes to his mind because in that land of marvels 'the Phoenix builds her spicy nest.' Then, as he nerves himself to end everything, there flashes across his mind an image from his past which seems to epitomize his whole life and will 'report him and his cause aright'; an act of suicidal daring, inspired by his chosen loyalty to Venice. With the same swiftness he does justice on himself, traducer and murderer of his Venetian wife. As, at their reunion, after the tempest, his joy stopped his speech, so now his grief and worship express themselves finally in an act, the same act: he dies 'upon a kiss.' . . .

Each of Shakespeare's great tragedies has its own design. The ground plan of the tragedy of *Othello* is that of a tragedy of fortune, the fall of a great man from a visible height of happiness to utter loss. This is not at all the shape the story has in the source; but this is how Shakespeare saw Cinthio's powerful but sordid story of a garrison intrigue. . . .

Fortune has been said to be the mistress of comedy, as opposed to Destiny, the mistress of tragedy. The vision of life which Shakespeare embodied in *Othello* cannot be analysed in terms of either destiny or fortune, and this is, I think, why more than one critic has complained that the play, although thrilling, lacks 'meaning'. The hero is a great individual, with all the qualities of a tragic hero, who expresses the strength of his nature in a terrible deed. But he finds the value of his life not within himself but without himself. He is the most obviously heroic of the tragic heroes, but he is unlike the great-hearted man of Aristotle, who is 'unable to make his life revolve around another' and is not 'given to admiration'. His nobility lies in his capacity to recognize value and give loyalty. The rhythm of pure tragedy is of a single life fulfilling itself and coming to an end in death. The rhythm of pure comedy is of relationships dissolved and reformed. The truth of tragedy is that each of us is finally alone. The truth of comedy is that man's final end is union with others, that he is 'in unitie defective'. . . .

In *Othello* the two rhythms are so finely poised against each other that if we listen to either without the other we impoverish the whole. Othello is the tragic hero, fulfilling his destiny, who comes to the limit, 'the very sea-mark of his utmost sail', expressing his whole nature in a tragic act. He is the comic hero, discovering at the close a truth he knew at the beginning, and so he appears, dazed and blundering beneath the scourge of Emilia's tongue, remote for the time from our sympathy. Should the course of his life be described as a pilgrimage to a goal, or is it a straying from the centre which he finds again in death? Such straying is the rhythm of life, whose law is change. Failures and recoveries of faith are the rhythm of the heart, whose movement is here objectified and magnified for our contemplation. . . .

The significance of *Othello* is not to be found in the hero's nobility alone, in his capacity to know ecstasy, in his vision of the world, and in the terrible act to which he is driven by his anguish at the loss of that vision. It lies also in the fact that the vision was true. I cannot agree to find lacking in meaning this most beautiful play which seems to have arisen out of the same mood as made Keats declare: 'I am certain of nothing but of the holiness of the Heart's affections and the truth of Imagination.'

For Robert B. Heilman the key to *Othello* lay less in 'the holiness of the Heart's affections' than in the right use of 'the truth of Imagination'. In an essay on 'Wit and Witchcraft: Thematic Form in *Othello*' (*Arizona Quarterly*, 1956), Heilman stressed the acuity with which Iago uses his 'head' to outsmart most of the play's other characters.

Making a fool of someone else is an aesthetic demonstration of intellectual superiority. It is implicitly partial, temporary; a comic episode after which life goes on. Let this exploit in self-aggrandizement expand with the full pressure of passion, and that attack becomes an ultimate one against sanity: Iago's design to put Othello 'into a jealousy so strong / That judgment cannot cure,' driving him 'even to madness' (2.1.310–11, 320). It is the extreme revenge possible to the man of 'reason,' a chaos that logically extends and completes the other modes of chaos which Iago instinctively seeks, in a variety of ways, at all stages of the action. Twice again he speaks of Othello's madness as a likelihood or as a formal objective (4.1.56, 101), and his program works well enough to make Lodovico inquire about Othello's mental soundness (4.1.280) and to make Othello express a doubt about his own sanity (5.2.111). Madness spreads: Emilia fears lest Desdemona 'run mad' (3.3.317), Othello cries to her that he is 'glad to see you mad' (4.1.250), and she in turn fears his 'fury' (4.1.32). But the planned madness eventually recoils upon its creator: 'What, are you mad?' is Iago's response when Emilia tells the truth about what he has done (5.2.194).

Such points in the auxiliary theme of madness (a slender anticipation of what will be done in *Lear*) mark the course of rational Iago. Insofar as he identifies rationality and wisdom with his own purpose, he is close enough to Everyman; but he is sharply individualized, and at the same time made the representative of a recognizable human class, when the drama reveals that his purposes require the irrationalizing of life for everyone else. Of the insights that create Iago, none is deeper than the recognition that a cool rationality may itself bring about or serve the irrational.... This is a basic Shakespearean definition of evil: the sharp mind in the service of uncriticized passion. And the final irony, as Shakespeare sees it, is that the owner of the sharp mind is eventually destroyed by the passion his mind serves. ... When Othello decides to follow Iago and be 'wise' and 'cunning,' he adopts a new code: he will 'see' the facts, get the 'evidence,' 'prove' his case against Desdemona, and execute 'justice' upon her. This is the program of 'wit.' Now this is not only utterly inappropriate to the occasion on which, under Iago's tutelage, Othello elects to use it, nor is it simply one of several possible errors; rather he adopts an attitude or belief or style which is the direct antithesis of another mode of thought and feeling which is open to him. ... He essays to reason when reason is not relevant: he substitutes a disastrous wit for a saving witchcraft [a metaphor for love]. He could reject Iago's 'proof' against Desdemona by an 'affirmation of faith,' as Winifred Nowottny has put it, 'which is beyond reason, by the act of choosing to believe in Desdemona.' ... His final failure is that, though he comes to recognize that he has been witless, he is never capacious enough in spirit to know how fully he has failed or how much he has thrown away.

In Heilman's view Othello's undoing derived ultimately from

his inability to plumb, and nurture himself from, the depths of his own mind and spirit. Heilman returned to this theme several years later in "Twere Best not Know Myself: Othello, Lear, Macbeth' (*Shakespeare Quarterly*, 1964).

Whatever theoretical status may be assigned to self-knowledge in the tragic process, the historic fact is that major tragedies characteristically deal in some part with the action of the hero's mind as it turns upon, or toward, or away from, himself. It is this interaction of the hero's mind with the least yielding of all materials that contributes some of the necessary toughness of the tragic substance. . . .

. . . Not to have the talent for self-knowledge is one thing; to have the talent and be unable or unwilling to use it is another. . . .

What strikes Shakespeare is two main manifestations of that strange disastrous chasm, predictable yet irrational, between man as creature of will and as possessor of knowledge. There is the one chasm that man has to create to pursue an end; he denies, pushes back, closes off the knowing self and what it knows. Purpose needs ignorance; and the protagonist is driven to a quest for ignorance more taxing than the quest for knowledge, since for the tragic hero it means trying to deny a trait essential to the hero. It is the Faustus way and, with variations, the Macbeth way. The other chasm is created by the violent rush of emotion, a rush so powerful and self-justifying that it seems truth itself, and makes invisible the very chasm it creates; this chasm is not needed by the hero for his own protection, but rather has to be discovered by him as a shocking distortion in the terrain of existence that he knows and accepts. Slowly the mind discovers the split between action and reality, and gains, as well as it can, perspective on both. It is the way of Othello, and Lear.

. . . The clarification of Othello, as Shakespeare presents it, has both a psychological and a moral side. The psychological, which is traced in the middle third of V.ii, is the wrenching from disbelief to assent as his initial faith is breached by the inexorable pressure of facts. Othello's assurance in his error so resists correction that it takes all of Emilia's verbal violence and Iago's murderous attempt upon her to break Othello's set closure against the truth. Once he regains the power to grasp what others are, what they have been and have done, he must move on to the more punishing task – seeing what he has done and what he is. This moral side of his enlightenment, occupying the final third of a uniquely compressed scene, is the seat of ambiguity. In the traditional view, and probably the majority view, Othello nobly decrees justice against himself. . . . In executing himself, it is felt, Othello judges and identifies himself. But there have been various dissents, ranging from the argument that Othello is to be seen as a damned soul to the argument that he is far more bent on cheering himself up than on seeing himself in a moral glass. These conflicting interpretations reveal less an impasse than an ambivalence in the rendering of Othello's final hour, as if Shakespeare were hovering imaginatively over dual possibilities and in the end committed himself to something of both. To propose this is not to decry artistic uncertainty but rather to give credit for a sense of ambiguity, that is, for full apprehension of latent meanings, of doubleness in the personality itself.

The more 'modern' view of Othello is that he fails to think of himself as a vain and self-righteous man who has acted evilly, but appears in his own eyes as no more than a rather worthy fellow who has made a foolish mistake and thereby lost a valuable possession; that he is prone less to notice his shortcomings than to list extenuating circumstances; and that he is at some pains to make a histrionic exit, not as a criminal on the gallows, but as a substantial Venetian patriot. . . . Whoever believes that [this] reading embodies at least an important part of a complex truth will point, naturally, to the high incidence of defensive, self-explaining or self-lauding lines that Othello speaks and the relatively small number, and the rather unfocused, slanting vocabulary, of the lines that give him an opportunity to identify himself as a vengeful wife-murderer.

The situation is at least ambiguous; some of the internal evidence forces one to doubt the completeness of Othello's self-recognition. This doubt gains in probability if we look at external evidence: Othello acts like other Shakespearean heroes at the point where self-knowledge is a necessary or possible form of action. They do not easily experience anagnorisis [self-discovery]. . . .

'Know thyself', one of western man's oldest moral exhortations, comes easily and frequently into the preceptorial mouth; hence it may seem to name a routine obligation that, as long as it is not forgotten, may be easily fulfilled. To Shakespeare the dramatist, carrying out that command is indispensable to well being; yet carrying it out is so difficult as to border on the impossible. . . . Not that what one has done and been does not get into the consciousness; Shakespeare never takes the cynical view that man is totally obtuse or insulated against self-knowledge. Rather he knows the difficulty of coming to it, and likewise of evading it. Othello appears to hurry over his evil act and to spend most of his few remaining words on sketching the most favorable possible portrait of himself. Lear needs a civil war, a terrible storm, and madness before he can shift from abuse of villains to acknowledgment that it is he who needs forgiveness; and even after that he cannot see that the death of Cordelia is due, ultimately, to the forces that he set in motion. Unlike the others, Macbeth does know himself from the start; for him the task is not slowly yielding to knowledge, but getting away from it, making it ever less effective, and escaping, as well as this may be done, into a frenzy of total action that will eventually relieve consciousness by destroying it. It would be supererogatory to praise these different dramatizations of a psychological realm whose validity we sense even more strongly, perhaps, after four hundred years.

In '*Othello* and the Pattern of Shakespearean Tragedy' (*Shakespeare Survey*, 1968) G. R. Hibbard observed that

The twelve lines that conclude *Othello* provide an ending that is radically different from the ending of any other of the tragedies. Lodovico's main concern is with Iago and his punishment. There is no formal praise of the hero, the only tribute he receives being Cassio's laconic comment on his suicide: 'For he was great of heart'. His body, and that of Desdemona, are not carried off in state, but hurriedly hidden from view by the drawing of the curtain around the bed on which they lie, because the spectacle they offer is felt as something monstrous and obscene. Nothing is left to be settled and disposed of except the house and fortunes of the Moor, which pass in one brief clipped sentence to Gratiano, Desdemona's next of kin. No interpretation of the events that have led up to the disaster is given, or even promised. Faced with actions which they find shocking and unintelligible, the surviving characters seek, with a haste that is almost indecent, to put them out of sight and out of mind. Their reaction is that of the normal ordinary man, and, as such, serves to underline for the last time the remoteness of Othello from those among whom he has lived and moved. The most immediately and impressively heroic of all the tragic heroes is granted no epic valediction from the mouths of others, no ceremonious rites of funeral; primarily, of course, because he has forfeited all claim to them through his crime in murdering Desdemona, but also, I think, because he is, and always has been, a mystery and a challenge to the unheroic world in which fate and circumstance have placed him. His relationship to that world, and his isolation from it, are both stated in the final couplet. The Venetian state must be acquainted with the death of its greatest soldier and servant; but there is no indication that it will, in any real sense, be seriously affected by that death. . . .

The unique quality of Shakespearean tragedy, in general, distinguishing it from all other tragedy written at the time, is due in no small measure, it seems to me, to the fact that Shakespeare came to tragedy by way of the history play. It was through the continuous exploration of historical matter that he discovered and penetrated into the intimate connexions between the private decision and its public consequences, between the political action and its repercussions on the individual psyche. . . .

It is exactly this close interconnexion of the public and the private that is not present in *Othello* – at least not in its usual form – though this fact is by no means evident at the play's opening. In Act I the imminence of a Turkish attack in Cyprus and preparations for the defence of the island demand as much attention from the audience as the marriage of Othello and Desdemona, on which they have a considerable impact, or as Iago's gulling of Roderigo. . . . But before Act II begins there have already been indications of the direction in which the action is moving. One of the most striking features of Act I is the frequency with which public affairs of the utmost consequence give way in it to private matters. The third scene opens with the Venetian Senate hurriedly gathered together at night for an extraordinary meeting in order to decide what measures are to be taken to counter the imminent invasion of Cyprus. Yet, despite the extreme urgency of the business, they break off their deliberations to listen, first to Brabantio's complaint against Othello, then to the Moor's defence of himself and his actions, and finally to Desdemona's assertion of her love for him. Only after all this has happened does the Duke invest Othello with the supreme command in Cyprus; and no sooner has Othello accepted this office than the discussion in the Senate turns to the question of whether his wife shall accompany him or not. . . .

Acting in his customary capacity of counsel for the prosecution, [Thomas] Rymer, the lawyer and historian, has made a point that more recent criticism of the play has tended to ignore: by all normal standards of behaviour the actions of the Venetian Senate are highly improbable. Yet they are clearly an essential part of Shakespeare's design, since there is no counterpart to them in the story he was drawing on. The wars between Venice and the Turks have no place in Cinthio's narrative. There Othello merely goes to Cyprus in the regular course of duty as the replacement for a governor whose term of office has expired, not as the man who is best fitted to cope with a great crisis. . . . Improbable though the scene in the Senate may appear when viewed in isolation, it works superbly well within the context of the play, where it has a complex function. It establishes the superior worth and dignity of the hero over those whom he serves; he is the indispensable man in complete control of an ugly situation. It brings out the total devotion of Desdemona to him, since she is prepared to face not only her father's displeasure but also the hazards of war in order to be with the man of her choice. And it leaves the audience with at least a suspicion that, were it not for the military crisis, the attitude of the Duke and the Senate might well be rather different. Rymer is wrong when he says that so far as the Senate is concerned 'The publick may sink or swim'; the point of the scene is that they can see no hope for the state except in Othello.

Once public matters have fulfilled this purpose of helping to define the supreme importance and value of the hero, and of establishing the depth of the love that exists between him and Desdemona, they are dismissed as quickly as possible. They receive their quietus in the brief scene (II, ii) which is given over to the Herald's proclamation that the wars are done and that the night is to be devoted to general rejoicing. . . .

. . . At the heart of *Othello* there is a kind of darkness. Only Iago knows what is true and what is false, and he does his best to confuse the distinction between them in his own mind as well as in the minds of others. Misled and misinformed by him, the rest of the characters misinterpret the events in which they are caught up. Alone of Shakespeare's tragic heroes Othello does not even know who his true antagonist is until the play is within fewer than a hundred and fifty lines of its conclusion. . . .

Othello is about the wanton destruction of happiness – something so precious and so fragile that its loss is felt as quite irredeemable. This, I think, is the fundamental source of the peculiar sense of pain and anguish that this tragedy, more than any of the others, leaves in the consciousness of a spectator or a reader. But there are two other related features of the play which add to and sharpen the pain. The relationship of the hero and the heroine is – and one of the miracles of *Othello* is the unobtrusive artistry with which Shakespeare produces this effect – a thing of rare and extraordinary beauty. Warm, moving, and vital, it has at the same time some of the qualities of an artifact. The mutual passion of Romeo and Juliet is spontaneous and instinctive; that of Antony and Cleopatra is the fruit of knowledge and experience – there has been an element of deliberate calculation on both sides. But the love of Othello and Desdemona is something that has grown gradually, then been discovered intuitively, then fashioned consciously, and, finally, achieved by them in the face of all the obstacles to it set up by their differences of race and colour, their disparity in years, and the opposition to it of the society to which they belong. Drawn by the fascination of Othello's story of his life into the strange, remote, heroic world which he inhabits, Desdemona has become part of that world, which is itself a work of art created by the hero out of his own experience. Listening to the Moor, as he relates his history to the Senate and re-enacts the drama of his wooing, one is aware of the story as a romantic epic of love and war. There is also a trace of the myth of Pygmalion and Galatea about it all as Othello, first unconsciously, then with a growing awareness of what he is doing, converts the 'maiden never bold, / Of spirit so still and quiet that her motion / Blush'd at herself', into his 'fair warrior', ready to make a 'storm of fortunes', to defy her father and public opinion, and to avow her love in the Senate. And just as Othello has, in part at least, created the Desdemona that he loves, actualizing possibilities within her that have hitherto lain dormant, so she, in her love for him, has, as it were, completed him by recognizing in him a beauty invisible to other eyes yet indubitably there. . . . It is not only the value of what is destroyed in *Othello* that gives pain, but also the sheer loveliness and perfection of what is destroyed. To a far greater extent than in any other of the tragedies the aesthetic sense is directly involved in and affected by the tragic experience that the play provides.

The distinctive feature of the destructive process in *Othello* is its ugliness, for what the hero is subjected to is a deliberate and calculated degradation such as no other of Shakespeare's tragic heroes undergoes. . . .

. . . The Moor's speech before he stabs himself is not, as T. S. Eliot suggested, an attempt at cheering himself up. It is rather the ultimate defeat of Iago, for it shows that the Ancient has not, after all, ensnared the hero's soul. Enough of the servant of the Venetian republic survives to enable Othello to reaffirm the values by which he once lived and to execute justice on himself. Unlike the other tragic heroes, he speaks his own valediction. He has to, because he is the only character left, now that Desdemona is dead, who is fitted and qualified to do so. The unusual ending of this tragedy is dictated by its unusual nature.

To Susan Snyder the 'unusual nature' of *Othello* appeared to be dictated by its peculiar mixture of generic expectations. In an article on '*Othello* and the Conventions of Romantic Comedy' (*Renaissance Drama*, 1972), Snyder began by noting that

The motives are sexual love and jealousy; intrigue and deception propel the plot; the outcome is engineered by a clever manipulator; the impact is personal, 'domestic,' rather than political and cosmic. These features strike us as appropriate to Shakespeare's comedies. Yet they also characterize one of his greatest tragedies. *Othello* is based, not on the chronicles and lives of the great that supply plots for most of the other Shakespearean tragedies, but on a *novella* in Giraldi [Cinthio]'s *Hecatommithi*. Shakespeare often turned to tales of this sort for the plots and situations of his comedies; in fact, Giraldi's own collection, the certain source of *Othello*, is a probable source for *Measure for Measure* and a possible one for *Twelfth Night*. Yet *Othello* is overwhelmingly tragic in movement and effect. Are the close ties to comedy at all significant, then? I shall argue that they are, that the tragedy is generated and heightened *through* the relation to comedy rather than in spite of it, and that *Othello* develops a tragic view of love by moving from the assumptions of romantic comedy to the darker vision articulated in some of Shakespeare's lyric poetry. . . .

Shakespearean comedy invariably presents as all or part of its initial situation individual characters in a single and unsatisfied state and directs them through plot complications toward appropriate pairings-off at the end. Plays like *The Merchant of Venice, As You Like It,*

Twelfth Night, even *The Taming of the Shrew*, find their generating tension in barriers between characters, and they stress the uneasiness of isolation even when those barriers are self-imposed. . . . The marriage-endings operate as symbols for full participation in life. Marriageable young people who deny or hesitate on the brink are all pushed in. . . .

Love is natural, then, as well as right. Comedy answers to our wishes in this respect, not our fears. But comedy also affirms that love is irrational and arbitrary. Here the fear is dealt with not by ignoring but by disarming it. . . .

The tragic truth of *Othello* develops out of a closer look at these very assumptions about love, nature, reason. Just as such a scrutiny logically comes *after* the first questioning acceptance, so Othello's story is deliberately presented as post-comic. Courtship and ratified marriage, the staple of comic plots, appear in *Othello* as preliminary to tragedy. The play's action up until the reunion of Othello and Desdemona in Act II, scene i, is a perfect comic structure in miniature. The wooing that Othello and Desdemona describe in the council scene (I.iii) has succeeded in spite of barriers of age, color, and condition of life; the machinations of villain and frustrated rival have come to nothing; the blocking father is overruled by the good Duke; and nature has cooperated in the general movement with a storm that disperses the last external threat, the Turks, while preserving the favored lovers. Othello's reunion speech to Desdemona in Cyprus underlines this sense of a movement accomplished, a still point of happiness like the final scene of a comedy. . . . But at the same time that Othello celebrates his peak of joy so markedly, his invocations of death, fear, and unknown fate [in II.i] make us apprehensive about the post-comic future. . . . The happy ending is completed, but Othello and Desdemona are left to go on from there.

If I am right to see Othello's tragedy as developing from a questioning of comic assumptions, then this initial comic movement ought to contain the seeds of tragedy. And it does, in various ways. Othello's account of their shy, storytelling-and-listening courtship, however moving and beautiful, is in retrospect slightly disturbing. . . .

In the comedies love was a strength, but in *Othello* it is vulnerable to attacks of reason, arguments from nature. More than that, vulnerability is its very essence. Before falling in love with Desdemona, Othello was self-sufficient, master of himself and the battlefield. After he believes her to be false, his occupation is gone. Why? Love has created a dependency, a yielding of the separate, sufficient self to incorporation with another. What comedy treated as a new completeness becomes in *Othello* the heart of tragedy. Tragic vulnerability is there, even in the play's comic phase. . . . To love totally is to give up the freedom of self for the perils of union and the expansive great world for a personal and contingent one. . . . 'My life upon her faith!' is literally true. Desdemona has become Othello's world. . . .

What I am suggesting is that the action of *Othello* moves us not only as a chain of events involving particular people as initiators and victims, but as an acting out of the tragic implications in any love relationship. Iago is a human being who generates the catastrophe out of his own needs and hatreds, but he is also the catalyst who activates destructive forces not of his own creation, forces present in the love itself. His image of 'monstrous birth' . . . has special significance in this regard: coming at the end of a resolved marriage scene, it suggests that the monster is a product of the marriage. He says, 'it is engender'd,' not 'I have engendered it,' because he is not parent but midwife. 'Hell and night,' embodied in this demidevil who works in the dark, will bring the monster forth, but it is the fruit of love itself.

Since the mid-1970s much of the commentary on *Othello* has focused on the sexual and racial questions the play evokes. In an article on 'Shakespeare's Desdemona', for example (*Shakespeare Studies*, 1976), Shirley Nelson Garner points out that critics have tended to avoid comment on the passage in Act IV, scene iii where Desdemona comments on the attractiveness of a man who has just arrived in Cyprus from Venice.

The reason for these efforts to get rid of Desdemona's lines about Lodovico seems obvious. Many critics and scholars come to Shakespeare's play with the idea that Desdemona ought to be pure and virtuous and, above all, unwavering in her faithfulness and loyalty to Othello. The notion is so tenacious that when Desdemona even appears to threaten it, they cannot contemplate her character with the usual care and imagination.

At what appears to be the other extreme is such a critic as W. H. Auden, one of the few who notice the passage and see it as a significant revelation of Desdemona's character. Viewing her cynically partly on account of it, he remarks: 'It is worth noting that, in the willow-song scene with Emilia, she speaks with admiration of Ludovico [sic] and then turns to the topic of adultery. . . . It is as if she had suddenly realized that she had made a *mésalliance* and that the sort of man she ought to have married was someone of her own class and colour like Ludovico. Given a few more years of Othello and Emilia's influence and she might well, one feels, have taken a lover' ['The Alienated City: Reflections on *Othello*', *Encounter*, 1961]. But isn't Auden finally making the same assumption as the others? Doesn't his . . . dismissal of Desdemona imply that he has expected her to be perfect? If she is not, then she must be corrupt. Isn't this Othello's mistake exactly?

Either Desdemona is pure or she is the 'cunning whore of Venice' (IV.ii.88). . . .

That Desdemona is neither goddess nor slut Shakespeare makes very clear. He evidently realized that he would have to defend his characterization of her more against the idealization of the essentially good characters than the denigration of the villain. Consequently, though he undermines both extremes, he expends his main efforts in disarming Desdemona's champions rather than her enemy. In her first two appearances, Shakespeare establishes her character and thus holds in balance the diverging views, but he goes out of his way to make her human rather than divine.

He carefully shapes Othello's account of Desdemona to counter Brabantio's initial description of her as 'A maiden never bold, / Of spirit so still and quiet that her motion / Blushed at herself' (I.iii.94–96). Because Brabantio is unwilling to believe that Desdemona's 'perfection so could err' (l. 100) that she would elope with Othello, he accuses him of seducing her by witchcraft or drugs. In Othello's eloquent defense (ll. 127–29), he shows not only that Brabantio's accusations are false but also that it was Desdemona who invited his courtship. . . . So far is Desdemona from being Brabantio's 'maiden never bold' that she gave Othello 'a world of kisses' for his pains and clearly indicated that she would welcome his suit. . . . The scene is carefully managed so as to create sympathy for both Othello and Desdemona. Because Desdemona initiates the courtship, Othello is absolutely exonerated of Brabantio's charge. His cautiousness acknowledges the tenuousness of his position as a black man in Venetian society and is appropriate and even admirable. . . .

When Desdemona finally appears, she strengthens the image Othello has presented. Before the senators, she answers her father's charges forcefully and persuasively, without shyness or reticence. More significantly, it is she, and not Othello, who first raises the possibility of her going to Cyprus. . . . As though she might have overheard Brabantio tell Othello that she would not have run to his 'sooty bosom' (I.ii.69), she confirms her sexual attraction to him as well as her own sexuality by insisting that she wants the full 'rites' of marriage.

Shakespeare must have wanted to make doubly sure of establishing Desdemona's sensuality, for he underscores it the next time she appears. At the beginning of Act II, while she awaits Othello on the shore of Cyprus, her jesting with Iago displays the kind of sexual playfulness that we might have anticipated from Othello's description of their courtship. . . .

Shakespeare's delicately poised portrayal of Desdemona to this point prepares us for the splendid antithesis between Iago and Cassio in the middle of the second act. . . . Iago distorts Desdemona's character by suppressing the side of it that Cassio insists on and emphasizing her sensuality. . . . But Cassio's view is limited as well. He idealizes Desdemona as much as her father did. . . .

Desdemona's liveliness, assertiveness, and sensuality are corroborated in her marrying Othello. The crucial fact of her marriage is not that she elopes but that she, a white woman, weds a black man. Though many critics focus on the universality of experience in *Othello*, we cannot forget the play's racial context. Othello's blackness is as important as Shylock's Jewishness, and indeed the play dwells relentlessly upon it. . . .

Desdemona's marrying a man different from Roderigo, Cassio, and other 'curled darlings' of Italy is to her credit. She must recognize in Othello a dignity, energy, excitement, and power that all around her lack. . . . When she says she saw Othello's visage in his mind, she suggests that she saw beneath the surface to those realities that seemed to offer more promise of life. If the myth of black sexuality (which Othello's character denies at every turn) operates for Desdemona, as it does for some of the other characters, it can only enhance Othello's attractiveness for her as she compares him with the pale men around her.

Because Desdemona cuts herself off from her father and friends and marries someone from a vastly different culture, she is even more alone on Cyprus than she would ordinarily have been in a strange place and as a woman in a military camp besides. These circumstances, as well as her character and experience, account in part for the turn the tragedy takes.

Writing on 'Women and Men in *Othello*: "what should such a fool / Do with a good a woman?" ' (*Shakespeare Studies*, 1977), Carol Thomas Neely buttresses Garner's argument that Desdemona has generally been misunderstood by the commentators who have written about her.

Othello critics idealize her along with the hero, but like him they have a tendency to see her as an object. The source of her sainthood seems a passivity verging on catatonia. . . . Iago critics, finding the same trait, condemn Desdemona for it. . . . When Desdemona is credited with activity, she is condemned for that too; she is accused of being domineering, of using witchcraft, of rebelliousness, disobedience, wantonness. [But] whatever view critics take, discussion of her is virtually an afterthought to the analysis of the men. Emilia and Bianca are still more neglected and are invariably contrasted with Desdemona. . . .

The women in *Othello* are not murderous, and they are not foolishly idealistic or foolishly cynical as the men are. From the start they, like the comedy heroines, combine realism with romance, mockery with affection. Bianca comically reflects the qualities of the women as Roderigo does those of the men. The play explicitly identifies her with the other women in the overheard conversation about her which Othello takes to be about Desdemona and in her response to Emilia's attack: 'I am no strumpet, but of life as honest / As you, that thus abuse me' (V.i.120–21). At this point, Iago tries to fabricate evidence against her just as Othello, in the scene immediately following, fabricates a case against Desdemona. Bianca's active, open-eyed, enduring affection is similar to that of the other women. She neither romanticizes love nor degrades sex. She sees Cassio's callousness but accepts it wryly. . . . She mocks him to his face, but not behind his back as he does her. . . . When jealous, she accuses Cassio openly and continues to feel affection for him. The play's humanization of her, much like, for example, that of the bourgeois characters at the end of *Love's Labor's Lost*, underlines the folly of the male characters who see her as merely whore.

Emilia articulates the balanced view which Bianca embodies. . . . She, like other Shakespearean shrews, especially Beatrice and Paulina, combines sharp-tongued honesty with warm affection. . . . She rejects the identification with Bianca yet sympathizes with female promiscuity. She corrects Desdemona's occasional naiveté but defends her chastity. . . . She understands but tolerates male fancy; the dangers of such tolerance become evident in this play as they never do in the comedies.

Desdemona's and Emilia's contrasting viewpoints in the willow scene [IV.iii] have led critics to think of them as opposites, but they have much in common. When we first see them together, they encourage and participate in Iago's misogynist banter but reject his stereotypes. Desdemona here defends Emilia from Iago's insults just as Emilia will ultimately defend Desdemona from Othello's calumny. While Desdemona is no shrew (though she might be said to approach one in the matter of Cassio's reinstatement), her love is everywhere tempered by realism and wit like that of the comedy heroines. . . .

Desdemona's spirit, clarity, and realism do not desert her entirely in the latter half of the play as many critics and performances imply. In the brothel scene [IV.ii], she persistently questions Othello to discover exactly what he accuses her of and even advances a hypothesis about her father, linking with herself the 'state-matters' which may have transformed Othello. Throughout the scene she defends herself as 'stoutly' as she had earlier defended Cassio. . . . Her naiveté and docility in the willow scene are partly a result of her confusion and exhaustion but perhaps also partly a protective facade behind which she waits, as she did during courtship, while determining the most appropriate and fruitful reaction to Othello's rage. The conversation and the song with its alternate last verses explore alternate responses to male perfidy – acceptance . . . or retaliation. Emilia supports retaliation . . . though, like Bianca, she practices acceptance. Desdemona's final couplet suggests that she is groping for a third response, one that is midway between 'grace' and 'revenge,' one that would be more active than acceptance yet more loving than retaliation: 'God me such usage send, / Not to pick bad from bad, but by bad mend!' (ll. 104–5). The lines are a reply to Emilia and a transformation of an earlier couplet of Iago's: 'fairness and wit, / The one's for use, the other using it' (II.i.129–30). Desdemona will put fairness and wit to 'use' in a sense that includes and goes beyond the sexual one, acknowledging and using 'bad' to heal it. . . . Just before her death, as in the brothel scene, she strives to 'mend' Othello's debased view of her, transforming the 'sins' he accuses her of into 'loves I bear to you'; but he recorrupts them: 'And for that thou diest' (V.ii.40–41).

Vanity is the central characteristic of coxcombs and is at the root of the men's murderousness in *Othello*. . . . Since the reputation and manliness which the men covet is achieved in competition with others, all of them are 'jealous in honor' – indeed are 'easily jealous' in every sense of the word. Brabantio is possessive, watchful, enraged to have the object of his esteem taken from him. Iago is critical and envious and resentful – of Cassio's position and 'daily beauty,' of Othello's love and power, perhaps even of Roderigo's wealth and rank. Othello is sexually possessive and envious and suspicious – of Cassio, of Emilia, and (too briefly) of Iago as well as of Desdemona. . . .

The women, in contrast, are indifferent to reputation and partially free of vanity, jealousy, and competitiveness. Desdemona's willingness 'to incur a general mock' is evident in her elopement and her defense of it, and her request to go to Cyprus. Emilia braves scorn to defend her mistress. . . . If Cassio's description of Bianca corresponds at all to fact, she too ignores reputation . . . to pursue him. . . .

The play's ending is less like tragedy than like cankered comedy. . . . As in the comedies, the men are chastened and their rhetoric somewhat subdued, but they remain relatively unchanged. . . . The conflict between the men and the women has not been eliminated or resolved. The men have been unable to turn the women's virtue into pitch, but the women have been unable to mend male fancy. So the comic resolution of male with female, idealism with realism, wit with sex is never achieved. The play concludes, not with symmetrical pairing off, but with one final triangle: Emilia, Desdemona, and Othello dead on the wedding sheets. . . . 'The object poisons sight'; it signifies destruction without catharsis, release without resolution. The pain and division of the ending are unmitigated, and the clarification it offers is intolerable. 'Let it be hid' is our inevitable response.

In ' "This That You Call Love": Sexual and Social Tragedy in *Othello*' (*Journal of Women's Studies in Literature*, 1979) Gayle

Greene offers an even broader discussion of the gender relations in what has been described as Shakespeare's most wrenching tragedy.

Bianca provides a reflection of what Desdemona is, Emilia a potential of what she might be: an autonomous being capable of speaking from her own center of self and finding a language which is strong and clear because it does come from that center. Desdemona needs more of the one, less of the other. As Desdemona's defenselessness is explicable in terms of a 'feminine' docility, so too are Othello's limitations traceable to the 'manly' ideal of character and conduct involved in his 'occupation.' As with Lear, Hamlet, and Antony, the experience of betrayal makes the tragic protagonist doubt his very identity, but unlike the others, Othello assumes that selfhood can be recovered by an act of physical violence and destruction of the loved one. . . .

Othello's investment of his 'manhood' in his 'honesty,' in an ideal of honor as reputation that requires Desdemona's death, and in his confusion of her character with her 'chastity,' points to an error . . . not only of Othello, but of society as a whole. Though to the end Othello is still thinking in such terms, justifying himself as 'an honorable murderer' who 'did all in honor,' . . . Shakespeare is suggesting that woman's virtue need be defined as a more active and positive quality than chastity, 'the preservation of this vessel for my lord,' and that the 'honor' for which Othello so readily kills be made of sterner stuff than 'the bubble reputation.' The ideal of manly and womanly behavior that the play finally affirms is something closer to a combination of masculine and feminine than that recognized or represented by Desdemona or Othello: it is the ideal, familiar elsewhere in Shakespeare, that the best of women has something of man in her, and the best of men something of woman. . . .

This is not to imply that the complexities of this tragedy are reducible to a tract on the subject of women. The sense we are left with is one of woe and wonder, the paradox that we kill what we most love, and that what is grand about these characters, their faith and absolute commitment, is also their doom. . . . It is equally possible to see man's ambivalence toward woman in terms of his suspicion that he has wronged her: binding her to a double standard [permitting promiscuity to men but denying it to women] in which she has not been consulted, to which she has not consented, he expects her revenge to take the form of sexual betrayal. The social dimension in this play is prominent by virtue of Othello's blackness and the carefully delineated backgrounds, classes, and 'occupations' of each of the characters. This man of action, who has never looked within, and his obedient lady are fatally interlocked in the ancient rite of love and death. Though Desdemona comes closer than he does to recognizing the human being and adjusting her ideal accordingly, theirs is not a marriage of true minds, not based on a recognition of persons, and though touching and wondrous, is fatally flawed. . . . Shakespeare is suggesting, in his radical critique of some of society's most cherished notions, that accepted ideals of manly and womanly behavior are distortive and destructive of the human reality, and that relations be based on saner and more certain ground than 'this that you call love.'

Though he approaches the topic from a different direction, Stephen Greenblatt confirms Gayle Greene's suspicion that there is something in 'this that you call love' that makes Othello susceptible to Iago's insinuation that Desdemona is adulterous. For Greenblatt, however, the underlying psychology has less to do with the double standard than with an ecclesiastical teaching, traceable to St Jerome (if not ultimately to St Paul), that 'adultery' can take place inside as well as outside matrimony. In an essay on 'The Improvisation of Power' in *Renaissance Self-Fashioning* (Chicago, 1980), Greenblatt notes that even though both Catholic and Protestant theologians acknowledged 'the legitimate role of sexual pleasure' in matrimony, they did so only 'with warnings and restrictions'.

. . . The conjugal act may be without sin, writes the rigorist Nicolaus of Ausimo, but only 'if in the performance of this act there is no enjoyment of pleasure.' Few *summas* and no marriage manuals take so extreme a position, but virtually all are in agreement that the active *pursuit* of pleasure in sexuality is damnable, for as Jacobus Ungarelli writes in the sixteenth century, those who undertake intercourse for pleasure 'exclude God from their minds, act as brute beasts, lack reason, and if they begin marriage for this reason, are given over to the power of the devil.' . . .

These anxieties, rich in implication for *Othello*, are frequently tempered in Protestant writings by a recognition of the joyful ardor of young married couples, but there remains a constant fear of excess, and, as Ambrose observed centuries earlier, even the most plausible excuse for sexual passion is shameful in the old: 'Youths generally assert the desire for generation. How much more shameful for the old to do what is shameful for the young to confess.' Othello himself seems eager to ward off this shame; he denies before the Senate that he seeks

> To please the palate of my appetite,
> Nor to comply with heat, the young affects
> In me defunct . . .
>
> (1.3.262–64)

But Desdemona makes no such disclaimer; indeed her declaration of passion is frankly, though by no means exclusively, sexual:

> That I did love the Moor, to live with him,
> My downright violence, and scorn of fortunes,
> May trumpet to the world: my heart's subdued
> Even to the utmost pleasure of my lord.
>
> (1.3.248–51)

This moment of erotic intensity, this frank acceptance of pleasure and submission to her spouse's pleasure, is, I would argue, as much as Iago's slander the cause of Desdemona's death, for it awakens the deep current of sexual anxiety in Othello, anxiety that with Iago's help expresses itself in quite orthodox fashion as the perception of adultery. Othello unleashes upon Cassio – 'Michael Cassio, / That came a-wooing with you' (3.3.71–72) – the fear of pollution, defilement, brutish violence that is bound up with his own experience of pleasure and for awakening such sensations in himself. . . . Othello transforms his complicity in erotic excess and his fear of engulfment into a 'purifying,' saving violence. . . . His insupportable sexual experience has been, as it were, displaced and absorbed by the act of revenge which can swallow up not only the guilty lovers but – as the syntax suggests – his own 'bloody thoughts.'

Building on Greenblatt's insights in an article on 'Sexual Anxiety and the Male Order of Things in *Othello*' (*English Literary Renaissance*, 1980), Edward A. Snow argues that

One component of Othello's jealousy . . . is a patriarchal conscience telling him that Desdemona's illicit behavior with Cassio is only a repetition of what she first did with Othello, and that he himself has released in her the boundless appetite she now satisfies with Cassio. . . .

Yet the play also stresses how little these male fantasies have to do with Desdemona's mundane reality as a specific woman. Even when her suit on Cassio's behalf starts to wear on our nerves as well as Othello's, the focus is not so much on a fault in her character as on the pathological reverberations that even a woman's trivial indiscretions have in the minds of men. . . .

. . . The underlying male fear is thralldom to the demands of an unsatisfiable sexual appetite in women. It is crucial to recognize, however, that the threat appears not when something intrinsically evil emerges in Desdemona's will, but when the conventional boundaries of marriage close in upon it. . . .

The tragedy of the play, then, is the inability of Desdemona to escape or triumph over restraints and Oedipal prohibitions that domesticate women to the conventional male order of things.

Michael Neill opens his essay on 'Unproper Beds: Race, Adultery, and the Hideous in *Othello*' (*Shakespeare Quarterly*, 1989) with the observation that

> If the first act of *Othello*, as Susan Snyder has shown, is structured as a miniature romantic comedy, then the last act returns to comic conventions in the form of cruel travesty. For the tragedy ends as it began with a bedding – the first clandestine and offstage, the second appallingly public; one callously interrupted, the other murderously consummated. A bedding, after all, is the desired end of every romantic plot; and Desdemona's 'Will you come to bed, my lord' (5.2.24) sounds as a poignant echo of the erotic invitations which close up comedies like *A Midsummer Night's Dream*: 'Lovers to bed' (5.1.364). But where comic decorum kept the bed itself offstage, consigning love's consummation to the illimitable end beyond the stage-ending, the bed in *Othello* is shamelessly displayed as the site of a blood-wedding which improperly appropriates the rites of comedy to a tragic conclusion.
>
> The result, from the point of view of seventeenth-century orthodoxy, is a generic monster. Indeed, just such a sense of the monstrosity of the play, its promiscuous yoking of the comic with the tragic, lay at the heart of Rymer's objections to it. Jealousy and cuckoldry, after all, like the misalliance of age and youth, were themes proper to comedy; and the triviality of the handkerchief plot epitomized for Rymer the generic disproportion that must result from transposing them into a tragic design. . . . Much of the force of Rymer's invective stems from the way in which he was able to insinuate a direct connection between what he sensed as the generic monstrosity of the tragedy and the social and moral deformity he discovered in its action. . . . It is clear, moreover, that for Rymer ideas of a literary and biological kind were inseparable, so that the indecorum of the design was consequential upon the impropriety of choosing a hero whose racially defined inferiority must render him incapable of the lofty world of tragedy. . . .
>
> Jealousy can work as it does in this tragedy because of its complex entanglement with the sense that Iago so carefully nurtures in Othello of his own marriage as an adulterous transgression – an improper mixture from which Desdemona's unnatural counterfeiting naturally follows. . . .
>
> In the seventeenth century adultery was conceived (as the history of the two words reminds us) to be quite literally a kind of *adulteration* – the pollution or corruption of the divinely ordained bond of marriage, and thus in the profoundest sense a violation of the natural order of things. Its unnaturalness was traditionally expressed in the monstrous qualities attributed to its illicit offspring, the anomalous creatures stigmatized as bastards. . . .

It is Iago's special triumph to expose Othello's color as the apparent sign of just such monstrous impropriety. He can do this partly by playing on the same fears of racial and religious otherness that had led medieval theologians to define marriage with Jews, Mahometans, or pagans as 'interpretative adultery.' More generally, any mixture of racial 'kinds' seems to have been popularly thought of as in some sense adulterous – a prejudice that survives in the use of such expressions as 'bastard race' to denote the 'unnatural' offspring of miscegenation.... In the Elizabethan popular imagination, of course, the association of African races with the monsters supposed to inhabit their continent made it easy for blackness to be imagined as a symptom of the monstrous – not least because the color itself could be derived from an adulterous history. According to a widely circulated explanation for the existence of black peoples (available in both Leo Africanus and Hakluyt), blackness was originally visited upon the offspring of Noah's son Cham as a punishment for adulterate disobedience of his father.

In such a context the elopement of Othello and Desdemona, in defiance of her father's wishes, might resemble a repetition of the ancestral crime, confirmation of the adulterous history written upon the Moor's face. Thus if he sees Desdemona as the fair page defaced by the adulterate slander of whoredom, Othello feels this defacement, at a deeper and more painful level, to be a taint contracted from him.... Tragedy, in Chapman's metaphor, is always 'black-fac'd'; but Othello's dark countenance is like an inscription of his tragic destiny for more reasons than the traditional metaphoric associations of blackness with evil and death. Iago's genius is to articulate the loosely assorted prejudices and superstitions that make it so and to fashion from them the monster of racial animus and revulsion that devours everything of value in the play. Iago's trick is to make this piece of counterfeiting appear like a revelation, drawing into the light of day the hidden truths of his society....

If the ending of this tragedy is unendurable, it is because it first tempts us with the redemptive vision of Desdemona's sacrificial self abnegation and then insists, with all the power of its swelling rhetorical music, upon the hero's magnificence as he dismantles himself for death – only to capitulate to Iago's poisoned vision at the very moment when it has seemed poised to reaffirm the transcendent claims of their love – the claims of kind and kindness figured in the union between a black man and a white woman and the bed on which it was made.

SUGGESTIONS FOR FURTHER READING

Many of the works quoted in the preceding survey, or excerpts from those works, can be found in modern collections of criticism. Of particular interest or convenience are the following anthologies:

Bloom, Harold (ed.), *Iago* (Major Literary Characters), New York: Chelsea House, 1992.

—— (ed.), *William Shakespeare's 'Othello'* (Modern Critical Interpretations), New York: Chelsea House, 1987.

Cookson, Linda, and Bryan Loughrey (eds), *Critical Essays on 'Othello'* (Longman Critical Essays), Harlow, Essex: Longman, 1991.

Dean, Leonard F. (ed.), *A Casebook on 'Othello'*, New York: Crowell, 1961.

Muir, Kenneth, and Philip Edwards (eds), *Aspects of 'Othello'* (articles reprinted from *Shakespeare Survey*), Cambridge: Cambridge University Press, 1977.

Scott, Mark W. (ed.), *Shakespearean Criticism*, vol. 4, Detroit: Gale, 1987.

Snyder, Susan (ed.), *'Othello': Critical Essays*, New York: Garland, 1988.

Vaughan, Virginia M., and Kent Cartwright (eds), *'Othello': New Perspectives*, Rutherford, NJ: Farleigh Dickinson University Press, 1991.

Other studies that include valuable discussions of *Othello*:

Adamson, Jane, *'Othello' as Tragedy*, Cambridge: Cambridge University Press, 1980.

Altman, Joel B., ' "Preposterous Conclusions": Eros, *Enargeia*, and the Composition of *Othello*', *Representations*, 18 (1987), 129–57.

Auden, W. H. 'The Joker in the Pack', in *The Dyer's Hand*, London: Faber & Faber, 1962.

Battenhouse, Roy W., *Shakespearean Tragedy: Its Art and Its Christian Premises*, Bloomington: Indiana University Press, 1969.

Bayley, John, *Shakespeare and Tragedy*, London: Routledge & Kegan Paul, 1981.

Belsey, Catherine, *The Subject of Tragedy: Identity and Difference in Renaissance Drama*, London: Methuen, 1985.

Bristol, Michael E., 'Charivari and the Comedy of Abjection in *Othello*', in *True Rites and Maimed Rites: Ritual and Anti-Ritual in Shakespeare and his Age*, ed. Linda Woodbridge and Edward Berry, Urbana: University of Illinois Press, 1992.

Brodwin, Leonora Leet, *Elizabethan Love Tragedy 1587–1625*, London: University of London Press, 1971.

Bulman, James C., *The Heroic Idiom of Shakespearean Tragedy*, Newark, Del.: University of Delaware Press, 1985.

Calderwood, James L., *The Properties of 'Othello'*, Amherst: University of Massachusetts Press, 1989.

Campbell, Lily B., *Shakespeare's Tragic Heroes: Slaves of Passion*, Cambridge: Cambridge University Press, 1930.

Cartwright, Kent, *Shakespearean Tragedy and its Double: The Rhythms of Audience Response*, University Park: Pennsylvania State University Press, 1991.

Cavell, Stanley, '*Othello* and the Stake of the Other', in *Disowning Knowledge in Six Plays by Shakespeare*, Cambridge: Cambridge University Press, 1987.

Cook, Ann Jennalie, 'The Design of Desdemona: Doubt Raised and Resolved', *Shakespeare Studies*, 13 (1980), 187–96.

Davison, Peter, '*Othello*': *An Introduction to the Variety of Criticism* (Critics Debate Series), Basingstoke: Macmillan, 1988.

Dickey, Franklin M., *Not Wisely But Too Well: Shakespeare's Love Tragedies*, San Marino, Cal.: Huntington Library, 1957.

Dollimore, Jonathan, *Radical Tragedy: Religion, Ideology, and Power in the Drama of Shakespeare and his Contemporaries*, Chicago: University of Chicago Press, 1983.

Eliot, T. S. 'Shakespeare and the Stoicism of Seneca', in *Selected Essays*, 1932, repr. London: Faber & Faber, 1950.

Elliott, Martin, *Shakespeare's Invention of Othello: A Study in Early Modern English*, Basingstoke: Macmillan, 1988.

Fineman, Joel, 'The Sound of O in *Othello*: The Real Tragedy of Desire', *Psychoanalysis*, ed. Richard Feldstein and Henry Sussman, London: Routledge, 1990.

Grennan, Eamon, 'The Women's Voices in *Othello*: Speech, Song, Silence', *Shakespeare Quarterly*, 38 (1987), 275–92.

Hall, Michael, *The Structure of Love: Representational Patterns and Shakespeare's Love Tragedies*, Charlottesville: University Press of Virginia, 1989.

Hankey, Julie (ed.), *Othello* (Plays in Performance), Bristol: Bristol Classical Press, 1987.

Heilman, Robert B., *Magic in the Web*, Lexington: University of Kentucky Press, 1956.

Holloway, John, *The Story of the Night*, London: Routledge & Kegan Paul, 1961.

Honigmann, E. A. J., *Shakespeare: Seven Tragedies. The Dramatist's Manipulation of Response*, Basingstoke: Macmillan, 1985.

Hunter, G. K., *Shakespeare and Colour Prejudice* (British Academy Lecture), London: Oxford University Press, 1968.

Hyman, Stanley E., *Iago: Some Approaches to the Illusion of his Motivation*, London: Atheneum, 1970.

Jardine, Lisa, ' "Why should he call her whore?": Defamation and Desdemona's Case', in *Addressing Frank Kermode: Essays in Criticism and Interpretation*, ed. Margaret Tudeau-Clayton and Martin Warner, Urbana: University of Illinois Press, 1991.

Jeffrey, David L., and J. Patrick Grant, 'Reputation in *Othello*', *Shakespeare Studies*, 6 (1970), 197–208.

Jones, Eldred, *Othello's Countrymen: The African in English Renaissance Drama*, London: Oxford University Press, 1965.

King, Rosalind, ' "Then Murder's Out of Tune": The Music and Structure of *Othello*', *Shakespeare Survey*, 39 (1987), 149–58.

Kirsch, Arthur C., *The Passions of Shakespeare's Tragic Heroes*, Charlottesville: University Press of Virginia, 1990.

Little, Arthur L., Jr., ' "An essence that's not seen": The Primal Scene of Racism in *Othello*', *Shakespeare Quarterly*, 44 (1993), 304–24.

McDonald, Russ, 'Othello, Thorello, and the Problem of the Foolish Hero', *Shakespeare Quarterly*, 30 (1979), 51–67.

Mikesell, Margaret Lael, and Virginia Mason Vaughan (eds), '*Othello': An Annotated Bibliography*, New York: Garland, 1990.

Newman, Karen, ' "And wash the Ethiop white": Femininity and the Monstrous in *Othello*', in *Shakespeare Reproduced*, ed. Jean E. Howard and Marion O'Connor, London: Methuen, 1987.

Parker, Patricia, 'Shakespeare and Rhetoric: "Dilation" and "Delation" in *Othello*', in *Shakespeare and the Question of Theory*, ed. Patricia Parker and Geoffrey Hartman, London: Methuen, 1985.

Ridley, M. R., *Othello* (The Arden Shakespeare), London: Methuen, 1958.

Rose, Mary Beth, *The Expense of Spirit: Love and Sexuality in English Renaissance Drama*, Ithaca, NY: Cornell University Press, 1988.

Rosenberg, Marvin, *The Masks of 'Othello': The Search for the Identity* of *Othello, Iago, and Desdemona by Three Centuries of Actors and Critics*, Berkeley: University of California Press, 1961.

Rozett, Martha Tuck, *The Doctrine of Election and the Emergence of Elizabethan Tragedy*, Princeton: Princeton University Press, 1984.

Sanders, Norman (ed.), *Othello* (New Cambridge Shakespeare), Cambridge: Cambridge University Press, 1984.

Siemon, James R., ' "Nay, that's not next": *Othello*, V.ii in Performance, 1760–1900', *Shakespeare Quarterly*, 37 (1986), 38–51.

Slights, Camille Wells, *The Casuitical Tradition in Shakespeare, Donne, Herbert, and Milton*, Princeton: Princeton University Press, 1981.

Snyder, Susan, *The Comic Matrix of Shakespeare's Tragedies*, Princeton: Princeton University Press, 1979.

Spivack, Bernard, *Shakespeare and the Allegory of Evil*, New York: Columbia University Press, 1958.

Stallybrass, Peter, 'Patriarchal Territories: The Body Enclosed', in *Rewriting the Renaissance: The Discourses of Sexual Difference in Early Modern Europe*, ed. Margaret W. Ferguson, Maureen Quilligan, and Nancy J. Vickers, Chicago: University of Chicago Press, 1986.

Wayne, Valerie, 'Historical Differences: Misogyny and *Othello*', in *The Matter of Difference: Materialist Feminist Criticism of Shakespeare*, ed. Valerie Wayne, Ithaca, NY: Cornell University Press, 1991.

Wine, Martin L., *Othello* (Text and Performance Series), Basingstoke: Macmillan, 1984.

Young, David, *The Action to the Word: Structure and Style in Shakespearean Tragedy*, New Haven: Yale University Press, 1990.

Background and general critical studies and useful reference works:

Abbott, E. A., *A Shakespearian Grammar*, New York: Haskell House, 1972 (information on how Shakespeare's grammar differs from ours).

Allen, Michael J. B., and Kenneth Muir (eds), *Shakespeare's Plays in Quarto: A Facsimile Edition*, Berkeley: University of California Press, 1981.

Andrews, John F. (ed.), *William Shakespeare: His World, His Work, His Influence*, 3 vols, New York: Scribners, 1985 (articles on 60 topics).

Barroll, Leeds, *Politics, Plague, and Shakespeare's Theater*, Ithaca: Cornell University Press, 1992.

Bentley, G. E., *The Profession of Player in Shakespeare's Time, 1590–1642*, Princeton: Princeton University Press, 1984.

Blake, Norman, *Shakespeare's Language: An Introduction*, New York: St Martin's Press, 1983.

Campbell, O. J., and Edward G. Quinn (eds), *The Reader's Encyclopaedia of Shakespeare*, New York: Crowell, 1966.

Eastman, Arthur M., *A Short History of Shakespearean Criticism*, New York: Random House, 1968.

Hinman, Charlton (ed.), *The Norton Facsimile: The First Folio of Shakespeare's Plays*, New York: Norton, 1968.

Muir, Kenneth, *The Sources of Shakespeare's Plays*, New Haven: Yale University Press, 1978 (a concise account of how Shakespeare used his sources).

Onions, C. T., *A Shakespeare Glossary*, 2nd edn, London: Oxford University Press, 1953.

Partridge, Eric, *Shakespeare's Bawdy*, London: Routledge & Kegan Paul, 1955 (indispensable guide to Shakespeare's direct and indirect ways of referring to 'indecent' subjects).

Schoenbaum, S., *Shakespeare: The Globe and the World*, New York: Oxford University Press, 1979 (lively illustrated book on Shakespeare's world).

—— *Shakespeare's Lives*, 2nd edn, Oxford: Oxford University Press, 1992 (readable, informative survey of the many biographers of Shakespeare, including those believing that someone else wrote the works).

—— *William Shakespeare: A Compact Documentary Life*, New York: Oxford University Press, 1977 (presentation of all the biographical documents, with assessments of what they tell us about the playwright).

Spevack, Marvin, *The Harvard Concordance to Shakespeare*, Cambridge, Mass.: Harvard University Press, 1973.

Vickers, Brian (ed.), *Shakespeare: The Critical Heritage, 1623–1801*, 6 vols, London: Routledge & Kegan Paul, 1974–81.

PLOT SUMMARY

I.1   It is night. In a street in Venice, Iago assures Roderigo that he knew nothing about Othello's marriage to Desdemona, the daughter of a Senator. Roderigo, a gentleman, had wished to marry Desdemona himself and had been paying Iago to further his interests. Iago argues that he would not have helped Othello, who is a Moor, since he hates Othello for making Cassio his Lieutenant. Iago, who is Othello's Ancient or Ensign, believes that the Lieutenancy was rightly his.

     The two men rouse Desdemona's father, Brabantio, to warn him that his daughter has left him. Brabantio sets out to find the eloped couple.

I.2   At the Sagittary, Iago talks with Othello. Cassio arrives with a summons for Othello from the Duke of Venice. Brabantio enters and tries to have Othello arrested for bewitching his daughter. A compromise is struck; the father agrees to accompany Othello to the Duke.

I.3   In the Council chamber they find the Duke and his Senators discussing the Turkish fleet, which is heading towards Cyprus. Brabantio asks the Duke to punish the Moor for bewitching Desdemona. Othello defends himself by telling the story of his and Desdemona's courtship. Desdemona arrives, and confirms that Othello is her husband.

     The Council moves on to consider matters of war. The Duke orders Othello to leave that night to oversee the defence of Cyprus. Desdemona will follow, with Iago, in the morning.

     Left on stage with Iago, Roderigo bemoans how hopeless his love for Desdemona has become. Iago persuades him to go to Cyprus in the hope that the newly-weds' love will not last. After he has left, Iago decides to try to make Othello believe that Cassio is having an affair with Desdemona.

II.1   On a jutting headland of Cyprus, Montano, the island's present Governor, learns that the storm that is raging has wrecked the Turkish fleet. Gradually the Venetians arrive and disembark; first

Cassio, and then Desdemona, Iago and Iago's wife, Aemilia. Iago jokes coarsely with the ladies.

Finally Othello arrives, and takes most of the company off to the Citadel. Iago tells Roderigo that Cassio and Desdemona are in love. Roderigo agrees to help Iago in his plans to disgrace Cassio.

II.2–3 A Herald announces Othello's declaration of a night of celebration. At the Citadel, Othello puts Cassio in charge of the men on guard, and retires to bed with Desdemona. Iago persuades Cassio to drink some wine in the company of Montano. Cassio is drunk when he leaves to check the sentries.

Roderigo enters, and Iago directs him after Cassio. Roderigo provokes Cassio, who chases him. Montano tries to calm the Lieutenant, but is attacked by him. Othello arrives and dismisses Cassio from his service. When the Moor has left, Iago advises Cassio to ask Desdemona to help him get his position back.

Alone, Iago enjoys the success of his plans. Next he will try to arrange it so that Othello comes upon Cassio asking for Desdemona's help.

III.1–2 Outside Othello's lodging at the Citadel, Aemilia agrees to arrange a meeting for Cassio with her mistress, Desdemona. Meanwhile Othello, with Iago and others, leaves to walk on the battlements.

III.3 In the Citadel's garden, Desdemona assures Cassio that she will urge Othello to make him his Lieutenant again. Seeing Othello and Iago returning, Cassio leaves. Desdemona urges her husband to grant Cassio an interview. Othello agrees. Desdemona and Aemilia leave.

Iago suggests to Othello that Cassio and Desdemona are having an affair. Before departing, he suggests that Othello watch how pressingly Desdemona pleads on Cassio's behalf.

Desdemona and Aemilia return. Noticing Othello's changed disposition, Desdemona asks her husband what troubles him. Othello tells her he has a pain in his forehead. She tries to wrap her handkerchief around his brow, but it falls off. Othello tells her to leave the handkerchief and they exit.

Aemilia picks up the handkerchief which is embroidered with strawberries. It was Othello's first keepsake to Desdemona. Iago now returns and Aemilia gives him the handkerchief before leaving; he had previously asked her to steal it.

Iago plans to leave the handkerchief in Cassio's house, hoping thus to confirm Othello's suspicions of Desdemona's unfaithfulness. Othello enters, now tormented with jealousy, and demands that Iago provide him with proof of Desdemona's adultery. Iago tells him that he has seen Cassio using Desdemona's embroidered handkerchief. Othello asks him to kill Cassio and makes Iago his Lieutenant.

III.4 Elsewhere in the Citadel, Desdemona sends the clown to summon Cassio to come to speak with Othello. She asks Aemilia where her handkerchief might be.

Othello enters and asks to see the handkerchief, stressing its magical properties and importance. Desdemona replies that she does not have it on her person. Othello leaves in anger.

Cassio arrives with Iago, and again asks for Desdemona's help. She replies that she is not at present in favour with her husband. Iago leaves to find the cause of Othello's anger, and Desdemona and Aemilia follow.

Bianca, Cassio's courtesan, enters. Cassio asks her to copy the design on a handkerchief (Desdemona's) he has found in his bedroom.

IV.1 Elsewhere in the Citadel, Iago excites Othello's jealousy to such a pitch that the Moor falls into a trance. Cassio enters and Iago asks him to withdraw until Othello is recovered. When Othello comes to, Iago tells him to withdraw so that he can hear Cassio boasting of his affair with Desdemona.

When Cassio re-enters, Iago leads him on to laugh about Bianca's love for him. Othello believes he is laughing about Desdemona's love for him. Bianca enters, returning the handkerchief to Cassio, as she believes it was given to him by another lover. She leaves, soon followed by Cassio who hopes to pacify her. Othello takes the presence of the handkerchief as a proof of Desdemona's infidelity. He decides to kill her.

Lodovico, a kinsman of Brabantio, enters with Desdemona; he is bearing a letter of state from Venice. The letter recalls Othello and states that Cassio is to be left in command. Othello, after welcoming Lodovico, loses his temper with Desdemona and strikes her. He then invites the amazed Lodovico to supper.

IV.2 Inside the Citadel, Aemilia urges Othello to believe in Desdemona's faithfulness. Othello sends Aemilia for his wife. He accuses Desdemona of being a whore and departs.

Aemilia returns and then Iago arrives. Desdemona asks Iago to convince Othello of her faithfulness. Desdemona and Aemilia leave for supper.

Roderigo comes in and complains to Iago that he has treated him unfairly. Iago persuades Roderigo that he must kill Cassio that night to stop Othello leaving, with Desdemona, for Mauritania.

IV.3 The supper over, Othello asks Desdemona to go to her bed and await his arrival. Desdemona and Aemilia discuss Othello's behaviour, and the nature of faithfulness. Aemilia has put Desdemona's wedding sheets on the bed, as her mistress requested. Desdemona sings the Willow song.

V.1 On a street near Bianca's house, shortly after midnight, Roderigo stabs Cassio, and is stabbed by him in return. Lodovico and Gratiano enter, followed by Iago, who kills Roderigo.

V.2 In his bedchamber Othello looks upon the sleeping Desdemona. She wakes and he tells her to pray, then suffocates her.

Aemilia arrives, and Othello tells her what he has done. She calls for help and Montano, Gratiano, Iago and others arrive. Aemilia upbraids Iago, revealing that she gave Desdemona's handkerchief to her husband. Iago kills his wife and then flees.

Lodovico and Montano return, with Cassio, having caught Iago. Iago refuses to speak. Othello commits suicide, and dies kissing Desdemona.

ACKNOWLEDGEMENTS

The editor and publishers wish to thank the following for permission to use copyright material:

Arizona Quarterly for material from Robert B. Heilman, 'Wit and Witchcraft: Thematic Form in *Othello*', *Arizona Quarterly*, (1956);

The British Academy for material from Helen Gardner, 'The Noble Moor', *Proceedings of the British Academy 1955*, Vol. XLI. Copyright © The British Academy;

Shirley Nelson Garner for material from 'Shakespeare's Desdemona', *Shakespeare Studies*, 1976;

Gayle Greene for material from 'This That You Call Love: Sexual and Social Tragedy in *Othello*', *Journal of Women's Studies in Literature* (1979);

The Estate of G. R. Hibbard for material from '*Othello* and the Pattern of Shakespearean Tragedy', *Shakespeare Survey* (1968);

Modern Language Association of America for material from Paul N. Seigel, 'The Damnation of Othello', *PMLA* (1953), pp.1068–78;

Carol T. Neely for material from 'Women and Men in *Othello*: "what should such a fool/Do with so good a woman?" ', *Shakespeare Studies* (1977);

Shakespeare Quarterly for material from Michael Neill, 'Unproper Beds: Race, Adultery, and the Hideous in *Othello*', *Shakespeare Quarterly*, 40, 1 (1989), and Robert H. Heilman, 'Twere Best not Know Myself: Othello, Lear, Macbeth', *Shakespeare Quarterly*, 25, 2 (1964);

Tulane Studies in English for material from Irving Ribner, 'Othello and the Pattern of Shakespearean Tragedy', *TSE: Tulane Studies in English* (1955);

University of Toronto Press, Inc. for material from Winifred M. T. Nowottny, 'Justice and Love in *Othello*', *University of Toronto Quarterly*, July (1952). Copyright © University of Toronto Press, Inc.;

THE EVERYMAN SHAKESPEARE
EDITED BY JOHN F. ANDREWS

The Everyman Shakespeare is the most comprehensive, up-to-date paperback edition of the plays and poems, featuring:

- face-to-face text and notes
- a chronology of Shakespeare's life and times
- a rich selection of critical and theatrical responses to the play over the centuries
- foreword by an actor or director describing the play in performance
- up-to-date commentary on the play